The complex interrelationship between Russia and Ukraine is arguably the most important single factor in determining the future politics of the Eurasian region. In this book Andrew Wilson examines the phenomenon of Ukrainian nationalism and its influence on the politics of independent Ukraine, arguing that historical, ethnic and linguistic factors limit the appeal of narrow ethno-nationalism, even to many ethnic Ukrainians. Nevertheless, ethno-nationalism has a strong emotive appeal to a minority, who may therefore undermine Ukraine's attempts to construct an open civic state. Ukraine is therefore a fascinating test case for alternative nation-building strategies in countries of the former Soviet Union and Eastern Europe.

Ukrainian nationalism in the 1990s

Ukrainian nationalism in the 1990s

A minority faith

Andrew Wilson

Sidney Sussex College, Cambridge

CAMBRIDGE
UNIVERSITY PRESS

Published by the Press Syndicate of the University of Cambridge
The Pitt Building, Trumpington Street, Cambridge CB2 1RP
40 West 20th Street, New York, NY 10011-4211, USA
10 Stamford Road, Oakleigh, Melbourne 3166, Australia

© Cambridge University Press 1997

First published 1997

Printed in Great Britain at the University Press, Cambridge

A catalogue record for this book is available from the British Library

Library of Congress cataloguing in publication data applied for

ISBN 0 521 48285 2 hardback
ISBN 0 521 57457 9 paperback

CE

To Helen

Contents

Maps

Tables

Preface

The study of Ukrainian nationalism has often been bedevilled by simplistic assertions. The main nationalist organisation of this century, the Organisation of Ukrainian Nationalists founded in 1929, gained an unsavoury reputation as a pro-Nazi and anti-Semitic authoritarian movement. Observers of contemporary Ukraine have too easily accepted the opposite caricature that all modern-day nationalists are model democrats and civic-minded liberals. This work will argue that Ukrainian nationalism has always been a complex and variegated phenomenon.

Chapter 1 therefore seeks to uncover the roots of this diversity of tradition by providing a general historical background, focusing on the pronounced differences between regions and ethno-linguistic groups bequeathed to modern Ukraine by patterns of past development and on the unique interrelationship between Ukraine and Russia. Chapter 2 looks more specifically at the history of the modern national movement and its leaders, organisations and ideas. Unlike other national revival movements in Estonia, Poland and elsewhere, the Ukrainians failed to establish a national state amidst the turmoil of 1917–20, and a second, less significant, opportunity was missed in 1941–3. Ukrainian nationalism has therefore been characterised by the need to react to and explain this failure, and by a wide diversity of ideological and political choice, no single tradition having been sanctified by success in winning independence.

Chapter 3 then considers the process of national revival in the late 1980s and early 1990s, the political parties and civic organisations founded in this period, and the politics of the various Ukrainian national Churches. It is argued that, despite the common assertion that all modern Ukrainian nationalists have embraced the liberal and civic doctrines first espoused by the dissidents of the 1960s, the nationalist tradition remains diverse and includes a significant ultra-radical fringe. Chapter 4 proceeds to an examination of the importance of 'national communism', that is of those former communists who defected to the national cause both before and after independence. (Much of the research for this chapter was undertaken in the Central State Archive of Civic Organisations of Ukraine, CSACOU, formerly the archive of the Communist Party in Ukraine. The classification is by department (*fond*), section (*opus*), document (*delo*) and, where necessary, page.) Chapter 5 demonstrates through electoral and other data that Ukrainian nationalism nevertheless remains a minority movement, largely confined to areas of western Ukraine and to the central Ukrainian intelligentsia.

Chapters 6 and 7 examine how nationalists have reacted to this predicament, and look at the nationalist agenda in both the domestic and the foreign policy arenas. Comparisons are made with other nationalist movements, and the contrary prescriptions of the strong anti-nationalist lobby in Ukraine are also briefly described. Finally, chapter 8 attempts to draw conclusions, examining the prospects for creating a broader base of support for nationalism and speculating how Ukrainian nationalists might react if this fails to materialise.

In transliteration I have used the Library of Congress system, but have chosen not to begin words with 'ie' or 'iu', preferring 'ye' or 'yu', which I hope is easier for the average reader to follow (therefore Yurii rather than Iurii, Yavorivs'kyi rather than Iavorivs'kyi). The Ukrainian soft sign and apostrophe have been rendered respectively as single and double quotation marks (except for by now standard English forms such as 'oblast'). Place names in Ukraine have been transliterated from Ukrainian rather than Russian (Odesa rather than Odessa, Chernihiv rather than Chernigov), except where quoting from Russian sources. Older administrative terms, such as the names of tsarist guberniias, have been rendered in their normal Russian form, although some regional names (Volhynia, Bukovyna) have been standardised throughout for ease of understanding. Certain common Anglicisms (Kiev rather than Kyïv, Dnieper rather than Dnipro) have been retained, as there is as yet no consensus on their replacement. When names or terms have been transliterated differently, as for example the name of a Slavic author of a footnoted book or article, they have been left as they were in the original for ease of reference.

I have too many people to thank. Dominique Arel, my supervisor Dominic Lieven, David Saunders, Stephen White and Graham Smith all made invaluable comments on early drafts of various chapters. I would also like to thank Natalka and Yurii Petrus, my regular hosts in Kiev, Valentyn Yakushyk and Vasyl' Marmazov, Heorhii Kas'ianov, Vladimir Voitsekh in Simferopil', Grigorii Nemeriia in Donets'k, Jonathan Aves in London, Ian Agnew and Jenny Wyatt for assistance with maps, and Helen Morris and all Fellows and staff at Sidney Sussex, above all the Master, Gabriel Horn, for his constant kindly encouragement. At Cambridge University Press I would like to extend warm thanks to Michael Holdsworth, John Haslam and Karen Anderson Howes for their assistance and forbearance. I would also like to thank Leverhulme Trust, the British Academy and the British Council for their generous financial assistance. I would also like to mention all those family and friends who have kept me going over the years. As always, however, final and most important thanks are due to my wife Helen for her love and support.

Abbreviations

CNDF	Congress of National-Democratic Forces
CP(b)U	Communist Party (Bolshevik) of Ukraine
CPU	Communist Party in Ukraine
CPWU	Communist Party of Western Ukraine
CSACOU	Central State Archive of Civic Organisations of Ukraine
DB	Democratic Bloc
DMD	Democratic Movement of the Donbas
DPU	Democratic Party of Ukraine
DSU	Organisation for Statehood and Independence of Ukraine
IBR	Interregional Block for Reforms
KUN	Congress of Ukrainian Nationalists
OUN	Organisation of Ukrainian Nationalists
OUN-b	Organisation of Ukrainian Nationalists-Banderites
OUN-m	Organisation of Ukrainian Nationalists-Mel'nykites
OUN-r	Organisation of Ukrainian Nationalists-revolutionary
OUN-s	Organisation of Ukrainian Nationalists-solidarity
OUN-z	Organisation of Ukrainian Nationalists-abroad
OUN in U	Organisation of Ukrainian Nationalists in Ukraine
PDRU	Party of Democratic Revival of Ukraine
RMC	Republican Movement of the Crimea
ROC	Russian Orthodox Church
RUP	Revolutionary Ukrainian Party
SNPU	Social-National Party of Ukraine
SPU	Socialist Party of Ukraine
UAOC	Ukrainian Autocephalous Orthodox Church
UCDP	Ukrainian Christian Democratic Party
UCRP	Ukrainian Conservative Republican Party
UDRP	Ukrainian Democratic-Radical Party
UHG	Ukrainian Helsinki Group (Ukrainian Group for the Promotion of the Implementation of the Helsinki Accords)

UHU	Ukrainian Helsinki Union
UHVR	Ukrainian Supreme Liberation Council
UIA	Ukrainian Inter-party Assembly
ULS	Taras Shevchenko Ukrainian Language Society
UNA	Ukrainian National Assembly
UNCP	Ukrainian National-Conservative Party
UNDO	Ukrainian Popular-Democratic Union
UNR	Ukrainian People's Republic
UNSO	Ukrainian Self-Defence Force
UOC (KP)	Ukrainian Orthodox Church (Kievan Patriarchy)
UOC (MP)	Ukrainian Orthodox Church (Moscow Patriarchy)
UOU	Union of Officers of Ukraine
UPA	Ukrainian Insurgent Army
UPDP	Ukrainian Peasant-Democratic Party
UPP	Ukrainian People's Party
UPSF	Ukrainian Party of Socialist-Federalists
UPSR	Ukrainian Party of Socialist-Revolutionaries
URP	Ukrainian Republican Party
USDWP	Ukrainian Social Democratic Workers' Party
UUIM	Ukrainian Union of Industrialists and Managers
UVO	Ukrainian Military Organisation
UWPU	Ukrainian Workers' and Peasants' Union
VAPLITE	Free Academy of Proletarian Literature
VNRU	All-Ukrainian Popular Movement of Ukraine, known as All-Ukrainian Rukh
VOST	All-Ukrainian Organisation of Workers' Solidarity
WUU	Writers' Union of Ukraine
ZUNR	West Ukrainian People's Republic

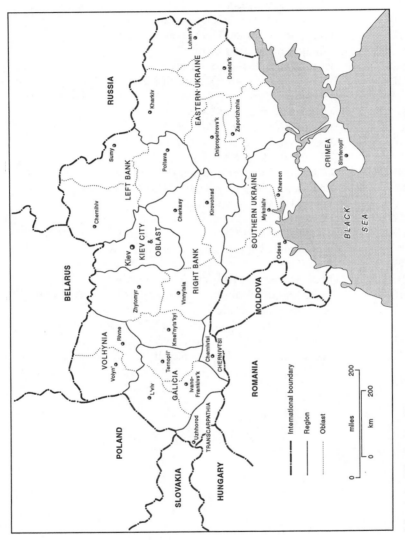

Map 1.1 Ukraine and its regions.

1 Ukraine: historical roots of diversity

Modern Ukraine is a deeply divided society with a pronounced pattern of regional diversity. In the modern era, an independent Ukrainian polity has existed only briefly in the late seventeenth century and in 1917–20, but in neither period was it a secure entity, with firm control over all the territory in present-day Ukraine. Ethnically Ukrainian lands have therefore tended to be subsumed in empires and/or dispersed amongst several states, with at least four separate 'partitions' occurring after 1240, in 1667, in 1772–95 and in 1920–1. The post-1991 borders of the independent Ukrainian state, inherited from the Ukrainian SSR as defined by Stalin's wartime conquests, correspond more closely to Ukrainian ethno-linguistic territory than at any time in the modern era, but the fit is still not exact, and different paths of historical development have left profound differences between Ukraine's regions.[1] Moreover, Ukraine's national history has been marked by a complex and intimate interrelationship with Russia, derived not only from the presence of 11.4 million ethnic Russians on Ukrainian territory, but also from Ukraine's own ambiguous historical and intellectual traditions. In Ukrainian nationalist mythology Ukraine and Russia are diametrical opposites and their cultures and histories essentially antagonistic, but large numbers of Ukrainians continue to believe that the two peoples can coexist in the same cultural continuum, creating a division between nationalist and anti-nationalist Ukrainians that is arguably as important as that between ethnic Ukrainians and ethnic Russians.

The key argument of this work is therefore that inherited regional, historical, ethnic, linguistic and religious differences severely limit the potential appeal of modern Ukrainian ethno-nationalism[2] and create the preconditions for a sharp polarisation in Ukrainian society. Unlike other post-communist states such as Poland or Lithuania, modern Ukraine faces two 'simultaneous tasks: building a Ukrainian state and forming a Ukrainian nation'.[3] More so than with many other states, therefore, the politics of modern Ukraine cannot be understood in isolation from its complex history, which it is the task of this opening chapter to try to explain.

Kievan Rus'

What is now Ukrainian territory has been home to a variety of both nomadic and settled peoples, including the Trypillians (3500–2700 BC), Cimmerians (1150–750 BC), Scythians (750–250 BC) and Greeks (from the eighth century BC), but the origins of the modern Ukrainian ethnie lie in the various Slavic tribes which migrated to the region from the fifth century AD onward, establishing political unity under Viking (Varangian) influence in the ninth century.[4] According to the 'Normanist' theory, the Varangians were responsible for the foundation and development of the Kievan state, but this view is rejected by both Russian and Ukrainian historians as demeaning the local Slavs and their capacity to form a settled civilisation,[5] the Ukrainian view being that 'the leading role in establishing the old Rus' state was played by the Polianian principality with its centre in Kiev'.[6] Most probably, however, the Varangian and Slav influences intermingled, and 'the rise of Kiev [was] not the exclusive achievement of one ethnic group or another, but the result of a complex Slavic/Scandinavian interrelationship'.[7] The Varangians provided a leadership elite, but the influence of the local Slav culture resulted in the formation of a kingdom unlike any other in the Viking sphere of influence.

The kingdom established by the local Riurikid dynasty became known as Kievan Rus', after Prince Oleh established its capital at Kiev, probably in 882.[8] Under its two greatest rulers, Volodymyr the Great (980–1015) and Yaroslav the Wise (1036–54), Rus' was both an integral part of Europe and a centre of religious civilisation, which flourished through its control of the main trade routes from Scandinavia to Constantinople. At its height Rus' spread from the Carpathian mountains in the south-west to Novgorod in the north, encompassing most of modern Ukraine, Belarus and north-western Russia. However, despite modern nationalists' claims to the contrary,[9] there is little evidence of settlement in the southern steppe region, which was controlled first by various nomadic tribes and then by the Crimean Tatars and Ottoman Turks. Moreover, Rus' remained a highly decentralised patrimonial empire. The collective consciousness of its inhabitants, such as it was, was tribal, dynastic and religious rather than ethnic, despite attempts by contemporary Ukrainian or Russian nationalist historians to backdate Ukrainian or Russian national consciousness to this period.

Christianity came to Rus' with the baptism of Volodymyr and his subjects in 988 AD.[10] The Metropolitanate of Kiev, Halych (Galicia) and all Rus' was under the authority of Constantinople, but used Church Slavonic as its liturgical language, which was subject to the gradual penetration of local dialects. After the great schism of 1054, the Kievan Church remained under Constantinople, but sought to maintain links with the Catholic West. The sack of Constantinople by the Crusaders in 1204 increased Kiev's autonomy within the Eastern Church, but the simultaneous drop in trade along the river Dnieper shifted Rus' lands from the centre to the periphery of Europe. Kiev's position as the gateway to the open steppe now became a liability, as it lacked natural barriers against foreign invasion.[11] Moreover, after the death of Yaroslav, Rus' was weakened internally by tribal conflict and the complicated accession system (*lestnichnoe voskhozhdenie*, or 'ascendance by steps') used instead of primogeniture, which virtually guaranteed a permanent contest for succession (thereby establishing a local tradition of internal feuding). After the sack of Kiev by the Mongols in 1240 (repeated in 1416 and 1482), the first 'Partition of Ukraine' began, and Rus' disintegrated into several rival princedoms.

The period after the collapse of Rus' has been the subject of long-running historiographical controversy between Ukrainians and Russians.[12] There is no doubt that Kievan Rus' was the cradle for all three modern East Slavic peoples (Ukrainians, Russians and Belarusians), but there is much dispute as to the exact lines of lineage. Tsarist and Soviet historiography always insisted that first Muscovy and then Russia were the only true successors to Rus'. Originally their argument rested on dynastic right and ecclesiastical authority (Nikolai Karamzin's *translatio imperii* theory), but nineteenth-century Russian historians such as Mikhail Pogodin added a populist ethnic element by asserting that most of the population of Rus' was forced to migrate north after 1240 to what is now Russia.[13] Soviet historians, on the other hand, preferred to argue that all three peoples were descended from a single 'old Rus' nation' (*drevnii russkii narod*). In all three versions, however, the political, religious and cultural traditions of Rus' were deemed to have transferred direct from Kiev to Muscovy, and Ukrainians and Belarusians were therefore denied any historical basis to their claim to be separate nations.

According to Ukrainian historians, however, a separate Ukrainian ethnie has existed in stable continuity in the lands around Kiev since before the time of the Polianians, whereas modern-day Russians are descended from more northerly tribes such as the Slovianians and Viatichians who played only a marginal role in the Kievan state (see also chapter 6).[14] The Ukrainians rather than the Russians are therefore the closest descendants of the inhabitants of Rus'. Moreover, the kingdom of Galicia-Volhynia, which survived on the territory of what is now western Ukraine until the fourteenth century, was a more legitimate dynastic successor to Rus' than Muscovy, which in any case only rose to prominence after its defeat of the Mongols in 1380.

The lines of ecclesiastical succession are also disputed. After the sack of Kiev, Metropolitan Maximos (1283–1305) transferred his residence to Novgorod, and his successor Petro (1308–26) moved on to Moscow. Muscovy unilaterally formed its own metropolitanate in 1448, which from the time of Feodosii onward claimed jurisdiction over 'Moscow and all Rus'', although its authority was not recognised by Constantinople until 1589. However, a rival Rus' Metropolitanate of Halych flourished in Galicia from 1302 to 1406, and Polish and Lithuanian kings who objected to Moscow's interference frequently appointed their own metropolitans. Therefore, although southern Rus' lacked a permanent and stable hierarchy until the seventeenth century, the tug of identity between Moscow and Kiev arguably began as early as the thirteenth century.[15]

Polish–Lithuanian rule and Orthodox revival

Nevertheless, by the fourteenth century the lands of southern Rus' were partitioned between several states.[16] Transcarpathia was occupied by the Hungarian king Stefan I in the eleventh century, Galicia was seized (or inherited, according to many Poles) by the Polish king Kazimierz III in 1340–9, and Volhynia and Kiev fell under Lithuanian rule after 1362. However, Lithuanian rule at least was relatively lax. The Old Rus' nobility retained many of their privileges and the Orthodox were left largely undisturbed in their beliefs.[17] Moreover, Lithuanian rule formalised the separation between the Kievan territories and the northern principalities of Novgorod and Muscovy, especially after the latter fell temporarily under the control of the Golden Horde.

However, the status quo was disrupted by two events: the Union of Lublin in 1569 and the Union of Brest in 1596. The former transferred Kiev and surrounding territories to direct Polish control, replacing relatively liberal Lithuanian rule with a centralising Polish state under strong Jesuit influence (although at the same time it reunited Galicia and Kiev under the same administration and separated both from Belarusian lands to the north).[18] The latter led to the formation of the Uniate Church, a would-be ecumenical union of the Orthodox and Catholic Churches, with an Orthodox rite and Slavonic liturgy but under papal authority.[19]

The Orthodox of southern Rus' reacted to the formation of the new

Church in one of three ways, leaving a legacy of religious discord which has persisted to this day. Many were attracted by Moscow's claim to represent the old united Church of Rus' and sought its protection, such as Metropolitan Borets'kyi (1620–31). On the other hand, many Orthodox bishops and magnates, particularly in more westerly regions, saw the Uniate Church as a genuine compromise, and without a patriarchate in Kiev to resist the Counter-Reformation from the west, decided that it provided the best means of preserving some of the traditions of Volodymyr's Church and avoiding outright Catholicisation and/or Polonisation.[20] Moreover, the Union of Brest offered them equal status with Catholic nobility and clergy. However, further to the east, in areas less subject to Polish influence, the Uniates were seen as apostates and traitors to the Orthodox faith and its associated cultural identity. The affront to the faithful led to pitched battles between Orthodox and Uniates and helped spark the great Orthodox revival of the seventeenth century.

In 1574 Cyrillic printing began in L'viv under the sponsorship of Prince Ostroz'kyi, and in 1580–1 the first Slavonic bible was published in Ostrih. The Mohyla Academy, founded in Kiev in 1632, became one of the leading centres of learning in the Orthodox world and sponsored a new literary, artistic and architectural style, Cossack or Ukrainian Baroque.[21] Fortunately for the Orthodox, the Polish state was increasingly preoccupied with its Russian war and weakened by internal rivalries. The Uniate threat therefore diminished and Patriarch Theophanes of Jerusalem was persuaded to consecrate a new Orthodox hierarchy in Kiev in 1620, which was reluctantly recognised by the Polish Diet in 1632. By the Treaty of Zboriv in 1649, Poland promised to respect Orthodox rights and surrendered much Uniate property to the Orthodox.

Moreover, the Kiev Church under Metropolitans Mohyla (1632–47) and Kosov (1647–57) was now developing in a different direction to the Church in Moscow. Kiev embraced several crucial aspects of post-reformation Western European traditions, such as a modernised liturgy, an expanded role for the laity in Church affairs and experimentation with the use of the local vernacular. Moscow, on the other hand, continued to cling to the original faith of Constantinople (from which Constantinople itself was now supposedly apostate). In fact it would be Kievan priests who would export the new practices northward, helping to provoke the *raskol* ('schism') under Patriarch Nikon. 'By the second half of the seventeenth century' therefore, it is possible to conclude that 'a religious culture that can be called Ukrainian rather than Ruthenian [or Rus'] Orthodox had emerged',[22] although political events were to cut the revival short.

The Cossacks and Bohdan Khmel'nyts'kyi's rebellion

The other key factor in the Orthodox revival was the rise of the Cossack movement. Small groups of Cossacks had lived on the Polish–Lithuanian Commonwealth's steppe borders for a century or more,[23] but large-scale Cossack settlement, centred on the Zaporozhian islands south of the rapids in the river Dnieper, was a result of the Union of Lublin. After 1569 Polish migration to the lands of Old Rus' and the more widespread imposition of serfdom led to the eastward flight of many Orthodox peasants seeking their freedom in the borderlands to the south and east (the sparsely populated steppe, known as the *dike pole* or 'wild' or 'open field', was under constant Tatar and Ottoman pressure but was agriculturally rich).[24] The self-governing Cossacks, who elected their own leaders, or hetmans, therefore found a niche as both free farmers and border patrolmen, adding a new and vital element to the developing sense of Ukrainian national identity.[25]

The Cossacks also saw themselves as the defenders of the Orthodox faith, both against Islam in the south and Catholicism and/or Uniatism in the west. Their frequent rebellions, most notably under Hetman Petro Sahaidachnyi (1614–22), therefore served the interests of the Orthodox Church and nobility in their campaign to defend the 'traditional rights' of Old Rus'. In 1648 a full-scale uprising took place, led by a disaffected noble, Bohdan Khmel'nyts'kyi, who succeeded in establishing an embryonic Cossack–Orthodox polity on both the Left and Right Banks of the Dnieper, thus restoring a form of self-government to Kiev for the first time since the thirteenth century. However, the difficulty of fighting simultaneously on three fronts against the Poles, Russians and Tatars led him to seek an alliance with Moscow, formalised by the Treaty of Pereiaslav in 1654. Nevertheless, warfare between the Russians, Cossacks and Poles dragged on, with the Cossacks increasingly confined to the Left Bank, until the Treaty of Andrusovo in 1667 once again divided southern Rus'. Kiev and the Left Bank went to Russia and the Right Bank to Poland (Russia had already occupied the northern territories of Starodub and Chernihiv in 1522).

The exact meaning of the Pereiaslav Treaty is the subject of much controversy.[26] Russian historiography, proceeding from the notion that Muscovy was the only true heir of Kievan Rus', has traditionally interpreted it as the beginning of, in Catherine II's phrase, the 'ingathering' of former Rus' territory, and either the restoration of control over Russia's patrimonial lands or the reunion of a single ethnic nation unnaturally divided.[27] Moreover, many of the southern Orthodox, such as the authors of the 1674 *Synopsis*, accepted the idea of *Slavia*

Orthodoxa and supported the idea of union.[28] Indeed, it has been argued that they rather than the Russians were the main originators of the idea of East Slavic unity.[29] Whatever the case, Ukrainian historians have always argued that Pereiaslav was an agreement between equal sovereign states, which bound Russia to respect Cossack rights as much as it obligated the Cossacks to accept the suzerainty of the tsar. Moreover, Khmel'nyts'kyi's territories on the Left Bank and Zaporizhzhia (the 'Hetmanate') were granted considerable autonomy, and the area of Cossack settlement continued to expand, resulting for the first time in large-scale penetration into what is now eastern and southern Ukraine, especially in the Slobids'ka Ukraine region around Kharkiv and in New Serbia, now Kirovohrad,[30] although Cossack communities further afield left few significant administrative or organisational traces.[31]

Furthermore, in the late seventeenth and early eighteenth centuries, Kiev continued to flourish as a cultural and religious centre, arguably contributing more to Russian development than vice versa.[32] In 1658, one year after Khmel'nyts'kyi's death, his successors contemplated replacing Pereiaslav with the abortive Hadiach Treaty with the Poles, under which the Hetmanate would have become a third, autonomous 'pillar' of the Commonwealth alongside Poland and Lithuania. Moreover, during the Great Northern War, a full-scale Cossack rebellion under Hetman Mazepa in alliance with Charles XII of Sweden that sought to break the link with Russia was only defeated by Peter I's decisive victory at the battle of Poltava in 1709.[33]

However, Khmel'nyts'kyi's death led to widespread internal feuding (a period known as 'the Ruin'), making it difficult for the Cossacks to develop alternative alliances. Moreover, Russia offered assimilation rather than exclusion, and the attractions of imperial service gradually won over most of the military and secular elite.[34] In 1685–6 the Kievan Metropolitanate was placed under the authority of Moscow, and the fledgling national Church rapidly declined. In the second half of the eighteenth century the Hetmanate came to be seen as an unnecessary obstacle in the way of Russia's drive to the south, and its administrative autonomy was progressively diminished, vanishing altogether by 1783 (the Cossacks' headquarters, the Sich fortress on the Dnieper, was destroyed in 1775).[35] The region of Cossack settlement was dissolved into 'New Russia' (*Novorossiia*)[36] after Russia conquered the northern Black Sea littoral from the Ottoman Turks in 1752–91 and ended three centuries of Tatar rule in Crimea in 1783.

Nevertheless, the Hetmanate survived long enough to establish a strong proto-Ukrainian, or 'Little Russian' identity (*maloros*), with important, if ambiguous results for the modern Ukrainian national character.[37] The Little Russians accepted that they were now part of a dynastic union, but retained a strong sense of local patriotism, arguing that they remained a separate people in service of the tsar. (It is only in the modern period that 'Little Russian' has become a pejorative term, used either by Russians to belittle Ukrainian identity or by nationalist Ukrainians to criticise their fellow countrymen for a lack of national ardour; see also chapter 6.)[38]

The west: the Right Bank, Galicia and Volhynia

After 1667 the Right Bank of the Dnieper, along with Galicia and Volhynia, was once again under Polish control. Nevertheless, elements of a distinct proto-Ukrainian (now commonly called Ruthenian) consciousness survived, although for different reasons than on the Left Bank. Whereas the Orthodox Cossacks of the Left Bank had seen the Uniate Church as the main threat to their religious and ethnic identity, in the west it ironically became the best means of preserving a distinct local culture from Polonising and Catholicising pressures, especially after a stable Uniate hierarchy was established at the Zamość Synod in 1720. Moreover, the ecumenical aims of the Uniates and their continued claim to represent the legacy of Volodymyr's Church kept alive the idea of unity between all Ruthenians, whatever their faith. Moreover, Poland was increasingly weak and politically unstable and was unable to put serious effort into its Polonising project. In the late eighteenth century this weakness became terminal, and Ukrainian lands west of the Dnieper were once again subdivided as the Polish state disappeared in the Partitions.

The Right Bank and Volhynia were seized by Russia in 1793–5. As both were sensitive border regions, the tsarist authorities abolished all remnants of administrative autonomy and local particularism even more quickly than on the Left Bank, especially after the Polish (not Ukrainian) rebellions in 1831 and 1863. In 1835 the system of Magdeburg Law which granted cities self-government was withdrawn, and in 1839 the local Uniate Church was eradicated in favour of Orthodoxy. Thereafter, although Right Bank Ukrainians still had language, social differentiation and a fading sense of historical separateness to mark them off from Poles, Jews and Russians, they no longer had institutions or elites.[39]

The Habsburgs gained the old Rus' territories of Galicia from the second Partition of Poland in 1772 and northern Bukovyna[40] from the Ottomans in 1774 (in addition to Transcarpathia, under Hungarian rule since the eleventh century). In contrast to the situation on the Right Bank, Joseph II granted the local Uniates equality with the Roman

Catholics in 1774, thereby saving the Uniates from the Polish embrace and preserving the main Ruthenian national institution. The Metropolitanate of Halych (Galicia) was restored in 1808, and the Uniate clergy were given a prominent role in local education (in the Ruthenian vernacular), which proved especially important after the introduction of state elementary education in 1777. Uniate control of local seminaries and the often hereditary position of the married clergy resulted in the creation of a local Ruthenian elite to provide the leadership for the national cause that was largely absent in the territories under tsarist control.[41] On the other hand, the consolidation of the Uniate Church in Galicia created a powerful psychological and cultural barrier between the Galicians and their Orthodox brethren in the Russian Empire that has persisted to this day.

The lands of southern Rus' were now divided for the third time, and the Ukrainian national revival of the nineteenth century would therefore take place on several alternative stages.

The nineteenth-century Ukrainian revival

In the early nineteenth century it seemed that Old Rus', Cossack, Little Russian or Ruthenian identity and culture were things of the past. The very proliferation of names seemed to invalidate the idea that Ukrainians formed a unified ethnic group, despite the political boundaries that separated them. Even the term 'Ukrainian' was itself a product of the national revival, and only gained widespread popularity in the later nineteenth century as an alternative to the Russians' linguistic monopoly on the claim of descent from Kievan Rus', and to the Little Russian idea that local and pan-Russian identities were perfectly compatible (the term 'Ukrainian' is therefore used in disussion of this and subsequent periods, as it gained widespread acceptance in this era, but without implying that all 'Ukrainians' had suddenly become one people). However, as in many other parts of Eastern Europe, the percolation of fashionable national-populist ideas sparked a Ukrainian national revival that gathered considerable strength from the middle of the century onward, although by 1914 it was still not as strong as kindred movements in the Czech lands, Finland or Estonia.

The leaders and the politics of the national movement are discussed in more detail in chapter 2. In outline, the movement was strongest in Galicia, where the Uniate Church underpinned a sense of separate identity, political conditions were freer, serfdom was abolished a generation earlier than in Russia (in 1848) and the Habsburgs supported the generally loyal Ruthenians as a counter-weight to the rebellious

Poles; although even in Galicia a rival Russophile movement flourished until at least the 1880s.[42] The Ukrainian movement was also strong in Bukovyna, although progress amongst the heterogeneous local population of Ukrainians, Romanians, Germans and Jews was slower.[43] Neighbouring Transcarpathia also experienced a national revival after 1848, but four rival tendencies competed for the loyalties of the local population, with the Ukrainophiles and Russophiles facing competition from equally powerful Magyarophile and Rusynophile movements.[44] The latter, inspired by the writer Oleksandr Dukhnovych, claimed that the local population were ethnically distinct Rusyns, citing the area's geographical remoteness, separate history and administration, local dialect and separate branch of the Uniate Church (the Transcarpathian Uniate Church was established in 1649 rather than 1596 and a Transcarpathian eparchy was established at Mukachevo in 1772 under the direct authority of the pope).[45]

Conditions in the Russian Empire were less conducive. Social elites on the Right Bank were either Russian, Polish or Jewish, and the old Cossack nobility on the Left Bank was a fading force, increasingly integrated in Russian society.[46] With the development of standard literary Russian in the early nineteenth century, Ukrainian increasingly came to be associated with peasant parochialism and Russian with universalism and access to high culture. Most local elites therefore assimilated to the latter (such as the writer Gogol, who wrote about Ukrainian themes in Russian). Ukrainian society became almost entirely peasant, rural, parochial and illiterate.[47] Moreover, although the great wave of industrialisation that began in the late nineteenth century affected Ukraine profoundly by drawing non-Ukrainian (primarily Russian) immigrants into the expanding cities, it largely passed ethnic Ukrainians by. Most Ukrainians remained on the land, where the harsh redemption terms imposed after the 1861 emancipation served only to worsen their material conditions. Rural overpopulation intensified and millions were forced to emigrate eastward in the quarter century before 1914, creating the large Ukrainian diaspora in Siberia and Kazakhstan.[48] The Stolypin reforms of the 1900s generated some social differentiation, but individual farming was already more common in the Ukrainian guberniias (where the commune did exist, it tended not to be repartitional).[49] On the other hand, the overlapping social and ethnic barriers between the Orthodox peasantry and their Russian or Polish overlords helped to maintain an sense of ethnic otherness, if only in a purely negative sense.[50] Ukrainian peasants understood themselves to be different from 'the lords' (pany) or from Jewish middlemen, but as yet had little or no sense of any broader identity.

Furthermore, the new territories of southern and eastern Ukraine were not fertile ground for the national movement. The northern Black Sea littoral became a trading hinterland for the new imperial economy, and was transformed by the influx of a multi-ethnic settler population, including Greeks, Germans, Serbs, Bulgarians and Gagauz (Christian Turks) alongside Ukrainians and Russians. Odesa in particular became famous as a cosmopolitan city with a large Jewish population.[51] On the other hand, eastern Ukraine, especially the Donbas region, became a leading centre for the mining and metallurgical industries, the vast majority of whose workers were either ethnic Russian or Russian-speaking.[52]

The Ukrainian movement was also handicapped by political repression, especially the severe limits placed on the public use of the Ukrainian language in two decrees of 1863 and 1876. The 1876 Ems Ukaz was partially overturned in the wake of the 1905 revolution, but the imperial authorities continued to make practical use of the language difficult,[53] and frequently proscribed Ukrainian organisations if their popularity threatened to grow. Little progress could therefore be made even in 1906–14, and the Ukrainian national movement remained tentative and cautious in its approach. In the Russian Empire it was the events of 1917–20 that gave real stimulus to the Ukrainian national movement, rather than vice versa.

1917–1920

In the wake of the February revolution, at least four simultaneous movements swept through Ukraine.[54] Would-be nationalist and socialist revolutions had to compete with a peasant uprising, while in southern Ukraine a strong anarchist movement under Nestor Makhno sought to avoid entanglement with all other forces.[55] Ukrainian nationalists formed three short-lived governments in the period: the Ukrainian People's Republic (November 1917 to April 1918),[56] the Hetmanate (April to December 1918)[57] and the Directorate (December 1918 to December 1919),[58] but Ukrainian rule was always precarious and frequently interrupted by the Red or White Armies. The use of the term 'Ukrainian Revolution' to describe the period is therefore somewhat misleading, as it implies that the attempt to create a national state was the one and only drama unfolding on Ukrainian territory.

The Ukrainian intelligentsia responded rapidly to events in St Petersburg, and in March 1917 established a Central Rada (Council) in Kiev under the historian Mykhailo Hrushevs'kyi, which initially supported the Provisional Government and confined its demands to

Ukrainian autonomy within a democratised Russia. Over the summer of 1917, however, the Rada's confidence grew as other Ukrainian organisations pledged their support, including the Ukrainian National Congress held in April and two assemblies of Ukrainian soldiers and peasants in May and June, and it began to claim for itself the right to speak for the Ukrainian nation. After the failure of the June offensive against the Germans left the Provisional Government looking decidedly weak, the Rada issued a 'First Universal' declaring Ukraine's right to self-government and creating a General Secretariat to serve as an executive authority in Ukraine, led by Volodymyr Vynnychenko. In July the Provisional Government was forced to recognise the Secretariat's authority, but only in the five central Ukrainian guberniias of Chernihiv, Volhynia, Podillia, Kiev and Poltava. The limitation was significant. The Rada never had much support in either the Donbas or southern Ukraine (the Bolsheviks even established a short-lived rival Donets'k–Kryvyi Rih Republic in the region in 1918).[59]

The Bolshevik seizure of power in October prompted the Rada to issue its Third Universal in November, which claimed supreme authority over all nine guberniias where ethnic Ukrainians constituted a majority,[60] and transformed the Rada into the Ukrainian People's Republic (in Ukrainian, UNR). Final independence came with the Fourth Universal, issued in January 1918, which broke all ties with Bolshevik Russia and proclaimed Ukraine an independent state. The UNR, however, was subject to the same trends toward internal dissent and external anarchy that had undermined the authority of the Provisional Government in St Petersburg. Growing feuds between Social Democrats and Socialist Revolutionaries plagued the Rada's leadership and delayed action on the vital question of land reform. Elections to an all-Ukrainian Constituent Assembly in January 1918 were incomplete, and the body never assembled (see chapter 2). Moreover, the UNR's idealistic leaders paid too little attention to the task of building up proper armed forces.[61] Therefore when Bolshevik troops invaded in February 1918 the UNR was forced to decamp to the west, and was only able to return as a result of the German occupation of Kiev in March. The Brest–Litovsk Treaty signed in February recognised Ukrainian independence within the territory claimed by the Third Universal, plus territories in Chełm (Kholm) and southern Grodno,[62] but left Ukraine a protectorate of the Central Powers.

German patience with the left-leaning UNR lasted a mere nine weeks and in April they encouraged a coup that established a 'Hetmanate' government under a leading conservative landowner, Pavlo Skoropads'kyi, who claimed descent from an eighteenth-century Cossack leader.[63] Skoropads'kyi's eight-month regime was a curious mixture. On the one hand, he sought to Ukrainianise education, establishing 150 new Ukrainian gymnasia and a Ukrainian Academy of Sciences, and organising the printing of more than a million new Ukrainian-language textbooks. Skoropads'kyi also went beyond the terms of the Brest–Litovsk treaty to claim all ethnically Ukrainian territory (that is southern Minsk and Homel in what is now Belarus, the Don Cossack lands as far as Rostov, and the southern portions of Kursk and Voronezh guberniias in what is now Russia).[64] On the other hand, under Skoropads'kyi, Kiev became a haven for Whites and Russian conservatives (as depicted in Bulgakov's novel *The White Guard*), and his support for the gentry in their struggle with the peasantry forced him to rely on the Germans as the only force capable of applying order.[65]

Skoropads'kyi was therefore increasingly seen as both unpatriotic and reactionary, which allowed the left-wing parties of the UNR to regroup as the Ukrainian National State Union and the nationalist Social Democrat Symon Petliura to organise disaffected peasants into something resembling a military force. Skoropads'kyi made one final attempt to stay in power in November by forming a cabinet of monarchists and announcing an Act of Federation with Russia, but Germany's defeat on the western front sealed his fate, and he was forced to flee before Petliura's advancing armies in December 1918. Petliura and Vynny-chenko announced the reformation of the UNR as the 'Directorate', which in January 1919 merged with the West Ukrainian People's Republic (in Ukrainian ZUNR), formed by the Galician Ukrainians in the wake of the collapse of the Habsburg Empire in November 1918.[66] However, cooperation between the Directorate and the ZUNR was always difficult (the ZUNR was dominated by national-conservative parties, the Directorate by leftists), and Petliura's followers were ill-disciplined and too often sidetracked into destructive pogroms against local Jews.[67] Once both the Central Powers and the Entente had withdrawn from the scene, the Ukrainians' fate depended on the outcome of a five-cornered military struggle among the two Ukrainian republics, the new Central European states and the Whites and Bolsheviks. In the west the ZUNR succumbed to the much larger Polish army in July 1919.[68] A short-lived attempt by a Ukrainian *viche* (people's assembly) to join northern Bukovyna to the UNR was crushed by Romanian forces in November 1918,[69] and its Transcarpathian equivalent was overwhelmed by its numerous rivals and the arrival of Czechoslovak troops in April 1919.[70] The Directorate was no match for the Bolsheviks once progress in the broader civil war allowed them to turn their undivided attention to Ukraine.

Despite a final epilogue in 1920 when Petliura briefly retook Kiev in an alliance of convenience with Polish forces, the Bolsheviks' Ukrainian Soviet Socialist Republic was firmly established (albeit at the third attempt) by late 1920, although it took several more years to eliminate all pockets of nationalist resistance, especially in the still anarchic countryside.[71] Ukrainian lands were therefore partitioned once again. In December 1922 the Ukrainian SSR formally became part of the USSR, while western Ukrainian lands were divided in three. Galicia and most of Volhynia returned to Poland, Transcarpathia became part of the new Czechoslovak state and Bukovyna went to Romania.

Various explanations have been advanced for the Ukrainians' failure to establish an independent nation-state in 1917–20.[72] Some point to external circumstances. Imperial collapse offered the Ukrainians a window of opportunity, which imperial recovery and consolidation (in the absence of any effective third-party intervention) then closed.[73] Others have focused on internal causes, primarily low levels of national consciousness, the Ukrainians' weak position in the crucial urban centres, the lack of elite leadership[74] and divisions amongst the heads of the UNR (see chapter 2). Without much influence in the cities or in eastern and southern Ukraine as a whole, where many Ukrainians supported the Bolsheviks, it was crucial that the nationalists maintained support in the central Ukrainian countryside, but by backsliding on the crucial question of land reform they failed to do so. In the 1920s the next generation of Ukrainian nationalists chose to blame the socialist or liberal idealism of the leaders of the UNR and their consequent lack of military preparedness, while the Ukrainian conservative philosopher V"iacheslav Ly-pyns'kyi identified their key weakness as the failure to win over elements from the old imperial elite to the national cause (see chapter 2).

The number of possible explanations is significant in itself. Any one of the above factors would have proved a severe handicap; in conjunction they simply overwhelmed the Ukrainians' efforts. Therefore, unlike many similar movements elsewhere in Central and Eastern Europe, the Ukrainian national revival was not fully consummated in 1917–20, although the initial successes of the UNR forced the Bolsheviks to concede the creation of the Ukrainian SSR. Moreover, the division of Ukrainian lands was reconfirmed. Diversity and discontinuity would continue to be key features in the development of the national movement.

Western Ukraine between the wars

All four regions of western Ukraine escaped Soviet rule until World War II. On the one hand, Ukrainian national consciousness and civil society therefore had another two decades to mature in the west. On the other hand, the separate development of the four regions means that substantial internal differences exist within western Ukraine, in addition to those between western Ukraine as a whole and the rest of Ukraine.[75]

The postwar settlement left 4.4 million Ukrainians, now deprived of their Habsburg protectors, as distinctly reluctant citizens of the new Polish state.[76] Poland reneged on the promises it made in 1923 to grant Galicia a measure of autonomy and to allow the use of Ukrainian in public administration and state education. A 1924 law banned the use of Ukrainian in state offices, Polish education minister Stanisław Grabski turned previously Ukrainian schools into bilingual institutions in which Polish predominated, Ukrainian organisations were harassed and some 100,000 to 300,000 Poles were encouraged to settle in Galicia and Volhynia.[77] However, the Poles were unable to snuff out the strong Ukrainian civil society that had developed under the Habsburgs and the ZUNR, and the Uniate Church remained the focal point of loyalty for Galician Ukrainians. If anything, persecution only contributed to the rise of radical Ukrainian nationalism and an anti-Polish terrorist movement (see chapter 2). Moreover, despite the best efforts of Henryk Józewski, the Polish governor from 1928–38, to isolate Volhynia from the Galician virus, the traditional links between the two regions were revived and the Ukrainian movement in Volhynia was able to regain much of the ground it had lost under Russian rule from 1795 to 1917.

Transcarpathia remained a rural backwater, but the Hungarian influence was now much diminished and the Ukrainian movement grew slowly in strength. Hitler's dismemberment of Czechoslovakia led to the formation of an autonomous Carpatho-Ukrainian government under the Uniate priest Avhustyn Voloshyn in October 1938, which survived for five months before being crushed by Hungarian invasion in March 1939 (Voloshyn made a symbolic declaration of independence before fleeing).[78] In interwar Romania, on the other hand, the Bukovynan Ukrainians lost the relative freedom they had enjoyed under Habsburg rule and regressed politically. Martial law prevailed until 1928 and was restored in 1937, and a Romanianisation drive after 1924 closed all Ukrainian schools.

Soviet Ukraine

Ironically, the focus of Ukrainian national life shifted briefly to Soviet Ukraine in the 1920s. Although the Bolshevik armies that defeated the UNR had contained a strong native Ukrainian element,[79] Lenin was well aware of the shallowness of Communist Party support in Ukraine. Only 23 per cent of CP(b)U[80] members were Ukrainian in 1922, and many of these were defectors from the leftist parties of the UNR (see chapter 2). Therefore a policy of *korenizatsiia* ('putting down roots') was announced at the Twelfth All-Union Party Congress in Moscow in 1923, and Ukrainian 'national communists' such as Oleksandr Shums'kyi and Mykola Skrypnyk (see chapter 4) were given licence to pursue a programme of Ukrainianisation, starting with the government apparatus and moving on to the Communist Party itself in 1927. Ukrainian-language education was rapidly expanded (by 1932, 89 per cent of all children in Ukraine, regardless of ethnic origin, were studying at Ukrainian-language schools),[81] and Ukraine enjoyed a multifaceted intellectual and cultural revival.

Ukrainianisation also reached into the religious sphere with the campaign to restore the ecclesiastical independence lost in 1686 through the creation of a Ukrainian Autocephalous (that is independent) Orthodox Church, or UAOC.[82] Despite an autocephalisation decree passed by the Directorate in January 1919, successive Ukrainian governments in 1917–20 were too weak to impose full-scale Ukrainianisation, which was supported by the Ukrainian intelligentsia but opposed by virtually the entire Orthodox hierarchy in Ukraine. Ironically, however, although many Bolsheviks opposed the UAOC on the grounds of general atheism or because they feared that it would become a hotbed of Ukrainian nationalism, other communists saw it as a useful weapon in the more important task of weakening the parent Russian Orthodox Church (ROC). The UAOC was therefore able to convene an all-Ukrainian Sobor in 1921 that repudiated the 1686 'Union', and by 1924 it had almost 1,200 parishes and an estimated three to six million believers in the Ukrainian SSR.[83]

However, the national communist tide was beginning to ebb by the late 1920s. It proved much more difficult to enforce Ukrainianisation in Russian-speaking areas of eastern and southern Ukraine and in the trade unions than in the upper reaches of the party, and conservatives in both Moscow and Ukraine began to fear that the policy was unwittingly fostering the growth of nationalism. The Stalinist reaction which engulfed Ukraine in the early 1930s therefore brought the policy to an abrupt end.[84] The leading advocates of Ukrainianisation, both in the party and in society at large, were repeatedly purged (Skrypnyk committed suicide in 1933) and replaced by loyal Stalinists satraps like Pavel Postyshev. The pre-revolutionary Ukrainian intelligentsia suffered particularly heavily, effectively breaking any remaining link with the political generation that had provided Ukrainian leadership in

1917–20.[85] The UAOC was suppressed and its leaders arrested and killed, although it survived in the Ukrainian diaspora.[86]

Furthermore, the basic political premise of Ukrainian populism, that the nationally conscious intelligentsia would 'awaken' the dormant peasantry (as seemed to be happening in the 1920s), was undermined by collectivisation and the Great Famine of 1932–3, especially as richer and better-educated peasants suffered disproportionately. Somewhere between five and seven million peasants perished and the spirit of those who survived was broken.[87] The countryside became a land of dead souls. Millions left for the cities and any potential that rural areas once had for political mobilisation disappeared.

World War II and after: national consolidation?

Amidst the immense human and social toll of World War II (an estimated 4.6 million perished on top of those who died in 1932–3 and 2.3 million so-called *Ostarbeiter* were deported to Germany),[88] a second attempt was made to establish national independence. The defeat of the national communists in Soviet Ukraine, however, meant that this time it began in western Ukraine and was led by the radical nationalists who had risen to prominence since the mid-1920s.[89] Internal and external circumstances were even less favourable than in 1917–20: the Soviet state did not collapse; the German occupiers would not allow the formation of alternative state structures; the Western powers were unable or unwilling to intervene; and Ukrainian society was too traumatised to respond to nationalist exhortation. Nevertheless, nationalist guerrilla warfare continued until the mid-1950s (see chapter 2).

On the other hand, Stalin succeeded where Ukrainian nationalists had failed in 1917–20, and annexed (most) western Ukrainian lands to the Ukrainian SSR, at first temporarily in 1939–41, and then definitively in 1945. As a result of the Nazi–Soviet pact, Galicia and Volhynia were seized in 1939, followed by northern Bukovyna and southern Bessarabia in 1940. The incorporation of Transcarpathia was ratified by the Soviet–Czechoslovak treaty of 1945, and Khrushchev completed the process by transferring Crimea to the Ukrainian SSR in 1954 to mark the 300th anniversary of the Pereiaslav Treaty. Paradoxically, therefore, the Ukrainians achieved a kind of ersatz statehood through external agency, without having progressed significantly beyond the level of national consolidation that had proved insufficient to win independence in 1917–20. However, the creation and expansion of the Ukrainian SSR was in itself a fact of enormous potential significance for Ukrainian national consciousness.

First, the absorption of western Ukraine proved to be a double-edged sword.[90] Perhaps Stalin intended to deal a final blow to the stronghold of Ukrainian nationalism by dealing directly with the problem himself. Certainly Soviet rule in the region, both in 1939–41 and in the decade after the war, was exceptionally harsh.[91] Hundreds of thousands of people were killed or deported and all civic institutions were suppressed, including the Uniate Church, which was forcibly dissolved into the Russian Orthodox Church at the so-called 'L'viv Sobor' in 1946 (the Transcarpathian Uniate Church was dissolved in 1949).[92] In subsequent years the Soviet authorities maintained a tight grip on the region, but were unable to destroy the nationalist virus completely. In fact, with the traditional Polish and Jewish enemies removed by wartime deaths and postwar deportations, Soviet repression only served to bring the anti-Russian side of west Ukrainian nationalism increasingly to the fore. Moreover, the rest of Ukraine was now more open to the circulation of nationalist ideas emanating from Galicia, although Soviet Ukraine was of course not an open society and the psychological gulf between the west and the east and south remained formidable.

Second, it has been argued that a combination of institutional and social change under Soviet rule has ironically served to stimulate national consolidation,[93] and that this serves to explain the otherwise surprising achievement of Ukrainian independence in 1991.[94] The establishment of the Ukrainian SSR created the first bounded territorial entity of the modern era with which Ukrainians could identify as their national homeland (tsarist guberniias reflected administrative convenience rather than ethnic boundaries). Moreover, although the Soviet system may have been federal in form more than in content, Ukraine was furnished with a whole accoutrement of national leaders, political institutions, state symbols, an Academy of Sciences and so on. These served both as foci for popular identification and as incubators for a new national 'comprador' elite. Stalin's manoeuvrings to ensure that Ukraine became a founder member of the UN and kindred organisations also had the unintended side effect of providing important symbolic gains to underpin national sentiment.[95]

Third, Ukrainianisation supposedly was achieved as much by the physical movement of Ukrainian peasants to the cities as by government edict or symbolic and institutional change. Although the first few years of Soviet rule produced little change (NEP ushered in a short-term period of relative prosperity for the Ukrainian peasantry, most of whom therefore stayed on the land), after 1928–9 Stalin's breakneck industrialisation drive and soaring economic growth enticed millions of Ukrainian peasants into urban areas. Furthermore, upward social mobility gradually created ethnic Ukrainian majorities in all leading sectors of society and stimulated the rise of a new Soviet Ukrainian intelligentsia.

However, patterns of social change were in reality more complicated. The old Ukrainian intelligentsia effectively perished in the purges, and the new 'intelligentsia' was often little more than 'a conglomerate of state functionaries', 'barely connected with former cultural traditions which they were educated to abhor, and considerably reduced [in] qualifications and educational standards'.[96] Although the number of 'specialists with secondary or higher education' by 1990 reached some seven million (30 per cent of the workforce), the majority of whom were Ukrainian, this was an 'ethnicised' rather than a 'Ukrainianised' intelligentsia, Ukrainian in name only, a déclassé 'sub-intelligentsia', with no social role other than the service of the state.[97] Moreover, before 1945 the intelligentsia found it difficult to develop a critical mass without reinforcements from western Ukraine. Therefore, although the national revivals of the 1960s and 1980s were undoubtedly led by the intelligentsia, it was far from being a hegemonic social force (see chapter 2).

Furthermore, the fact that the national movement had made so little progress in the countryside before 1917, which was in any case then subject to the horrors of the 1930s, made it difficult for the migrating peasantry to play the role of kulturträger and Ukrainianise the cities. Nor could the new urban generations be expected to develop under the influence of the new Ukrainian intelligentsia as the latter was in effect in simultaneous evolution. Many migrating peasants therefore undoubtedly identified with the institutions and symbols of the Soviet state,[98] and/or managed to combine different loyalties and identities, as in previous eras.

Finally and most importantly, the dynamics of urbanisation and industrialisation varied profoundly from one region to another. Western Ukraine, despite its rich multi-ethnic past, became even more Ukrainian after 1945 (see table 1.2).[99] World War II, the Holocaust and enforced population exchanges in the late 1940s led to the death, departure or expulsion of the vast majority of Ukrainian Jews as well as Poles from Galicia and Volhynia, and Romanians and Germans from Bukovyna.[100] In 1989 therefore, ethnic Ukrainians accounted for an overwhelming 93 per cent of the population in Galicia and 94 per cent in Volhynia.[101] The majority population in Transcarpathia was redesignated as Ukrainian (78 per cent of the total in 1989), although many locals still thought of themselves as Rusyns or possessed only a pre-national consciousness (see chapter 6). Stalin created the artificial modern oblast of Chernivtsi by adding the traditionally Moldovan Bessarabian counties of Hertsa

and Khotyn to northern Bukovyna, but by 1989 a Ukrainian majority
outnumbered the Romanians/Moldovans by 71 per cent to 20 per
cent.[102] In none of the four regions did the one-off influx of Russian
administrators to replace those purged in the immediate postwar period
develop into any pattern of long-term in-migration. Therefore, with the
possible exception of Transcarpathia, migrants to the cities were
entering a basically Ukrainian cultural environment, and the consequent
tendency to acculturate to Ukrainian has resulted in a decline in
Russian-language use since the 1960s.[103]

Kiev has also changed profoundly from the city that was a stronghold
of the Russian intelligentsia before 1917. Less than 23 per cent of the
population of Kiev was Ukrainian in 1897, but the city had a 60 per cent
Ukrainian majority by 1959, rising to 72 per cent by 1989.[104] Kiev,
however, was something of a special case, given the concentration of
government offices, mass media and cultural intelligentsia in the city
after the administration of the Ukrainian SSR was transferred from
Kharkiv to Kiev in 1934. In the rest of central Ukraine, although similar
numerical Ukrainian majorities built up in cities such as Cherkasy and
Poltava, only a handful of university towns had anything approaching
the cultural weight of the capital. 'Ukrainianisation' was therefore more
nominal than real.

'Ukrainianisation' had the least impact in the east and south, where
urban areas were already predominantly Russian in language and culture,
the 1920s Ukrainianisation campaign notwithstanding. Unlike the situation in the nineteenth century, most migrants to urban areas were now
ethnic Ukrainians, but the city tended to acculturate the peasant rather
than the other way around,[105] especially as many Ukrainian peasants were
possessed of only a parochial sense of identity when they left the land.[106]
According to the 1989 Soviet census Donets'k oblast was 51 per cent
ethnic Ukrainian, but only 31 per cent stated that Ukrainian was their
'mother tongue' (ridna mova in Ukrainian, rodnoi yazyk in Russian). In
Donets'k city an overwhelming 82 per cent of the population stated that
their native tongue was Russian. In Kharkiv city the number of Russian
speakers was 70 per cent, in Odesa city 73 per cent, in Simferopil' 90 per
cent.[107] Crimea is the least Ukrainian of all. Even after the mass return of
Crimean Tatars in the early 1990s, the peninsula was still 62 per cent
ethnic Russian and over 80 per cent Russian-speaking.[108] Therefore,
unlike other 'multilingual areas of the world, such as the Czech lands of
the Austro-Hungarian Empire, the Baltic areas of the Russian Empire,
and postwar Quebec, [where] urbanisation has meant the conquering of
the main urban areas by the "indigenous" majority which had heretofore
been confined to the countryside . . . the Ukrainians were not successful

in linguistically "conquering" these urban enclaves' in eastern and southern Ukraine.[109]

Cultural institutions reflected this regional pattern. In education for example from the end of the brief Ukrainianisation experiment in the 1920s until the 1950s Ukrainians and Russians largely studied at their own schools according to local patterns of predominance (in other words rural western and central Ukrainian schools remained largely Ukrainian, while schools in urban eastern and southern Ukraine taught in Russian).[110] However, after Khrushchev's education reforms in 1958–9 gave parents a loaded free choice for the language of their children's study, the number of pupils in Ukrainian schools began rapidly to decline, falling to a mere 47.5 per cent of all children by 1989.[111] Most of these were in rural areas or in western Ukraine; Ukrainian-language schools almost completely disappeared from the cities of the east and south, and even in urban central Ukraine their number was declining. The tools of cultural reproduction, Ukrainian-language publishing, press, television and radio, also declined in relative importance and regional scope.[112]

Two languages, three cultures

Social change since the turn of the century has been profound. The multi-ethnic social patchwork depicted by the 1897 tsarist census has largely been replaced by a society that is both bi-ethnic and bilingual, but which on the other hand is not strictly bipolar because the ethnic and linguistic divides between the Ukrainian and Russian spheres do not coincide.

Ukraine's large Polish, Jewish and German minorities first declined in importance and then almost totally disappeared after World War II (see table 1.1). On the other hand the ethnic Russian minority has grown steadily to reach 11.4 million by 1989, or 22 per cent of the total population, while ethnic Ukrainians have advanced both in terms of percentage of the population and overall levels of social mobilisation (see pp. 18–19 above). However, as stressed throughout this chapter, centuries of Russian influence mean that 'multiple loyalties' are still common. Two languages and cultures, Ukrainian and Russian, compete for popular loyalty across ethnic boundaries, although the unequal nature of the struggle means that there are many more Russophone Ukrainians than Ukrainophone Russians. According to official Soviet census figures, between 1970 and 1989 alone the number of Ukrainians with a working knowledge of Russian increased from 44 per cent to 72 per cent. From 1959 to 1989 the number of Ukrainians speaking

Table 1.1 *The ethnic make-up of Ukrainian lands, 1897–1989 (percentages)*

	1897	1932	1959	1989
Ukrainians	69.9	75.4	76.8	72.7
Russians	9.2	8.1	16.9	22.1
Jews	9.2	6.5	2.0	0.9
Poles	6.8	5.0	0.9	0.4
Germans	2.1	1.5	0.1	0.1
Other	2.8	3.5	3.4	3.8

'Ukrainian lands' means all territories that were eventually incorporated in the Ukrainian SSR by 1954.

Sources: For 1897: Robert Paul Magocsi, *Ukraine: A Historical Atlas* (Toronto: University of Toronto Press, 1985), p. 17; different figures are given by Yevhen Isyp, 'Dynamika etnichnoho skladu naselennia Ukraïny (za danymy perepysiv naselennia 1897–1989 rr.)', in V. B. Yevtukh *et al.* (eds.), *Etnopolitychna sytuatsiia v Ukraïni* (Kiev: Intel, 1993), pp. 22–35, tables 1 and 3, at pp. 23 and 25: namely Ukrainians 72.6 per cent, Russians 8.3 per cent, Jews 9.0 per cent, Poles 4.3 per cent, Germans 2.1 per cent, others 3.8 per cent. For 1932 and 1959: Volodymyr Kubijovyc, 'Ethnic Composition of the Population', in Kubijovyc (ed.), *Ukraine: A Concise Encyclopaedia* (Toronto: University of Toronto Press, 1963), pp. 208–51. For 1989: F. D. Zastavnyi, *Heohrafiia Ukraïny* (L'viv: Svit, 1994), p. 411.

Russian as their mother tongue rose from 2 million to 4.6 million, while the proportion of the republic's population citing Ukrainian as their mother tongue fell from 73 per cent to under 65 per cent.[113]

However, if anything these figures are an *underestimate*. Ukrainian nationalists have traditionally drawn on Soviet census data to bemoan the decline of Ukrainian language and culture, but have themselves been led by the very same data to misunderstand the true dynamics of ethnolinguistic relations in Ukraine and to underestimate the importance of divisions within their own ethnic group.[114] Soviet passport and census practice tended to freeze ethnicity over time by encouraging children to be identified according to their father's ethnic background, and by using the ambiguous concept of 'mother tongue', which tended to mean the language parents were remembered to have spoken rather than language of everyday use. Millions of ethnic Ukrainians have only a nominal command of their 'mother tongue', and/or speak varieties of the Ukrainian/Russian mixture known as *surzhyk*. More recent surveys, focusing instead on language of convenience or competence, have indicated that Ukrainophone Ukrainians make up only 40 per cent of the adult population, whereas 33–4 per cent are Russophone Ukrainians and 20–1 per cent Russophone Russians.[115]

Although *ethnically* predominant (73–22 per cent), the core Ukrainian group is therefore in a *linguistic* minority (43–57 per cent). On the other

Table 1.2 *Regional distribution of ethnic and ethno-linguistic groups in Ukraine in the early 1990s*

Region	Ethnic balance (Ukrainian–Russian)	Linguistic balance (Ukrainophone–Russophone)
Galicia	93.0–5.3	95.0–5.0
Volhynia	93.9–4.5	82.1–17.9
Transcarpathia[a]	78.4–4.0	73.6–26.4
Chernivtsi	70.8–6.7	72.2–27.8
Right Bank	88.8–7.6	73.5–26.5
Kiev	79.7–15.6	45.8–54.2
Left Bank	88.2–10.1	56.8–43.2
East	59.3–36.1	13.4–86.6
South	65.0–23.6	13.9–86.1
Crimea[b]	25.8–67.0	–
Total:	72.7–22.1	43.4–56.6[c]

Notes: [a] The figures for Transcarpathia did not allow for self-identification as Rusyns.
[b] Some 260,000 Crimean Tatars had returned to the peninsula by October 1993, lowering the Ukrainian percentage of the local population to 24 per cent and the Russian figure to 62 per cent. The figures for linguistic balance in Crimea are subsumed in the total for the south, but are between 4 per cent and 5 per cent Ukrainophone and around 82 per cent Russophone.
[c] Figures include Ukrainophone and Russophone 'others'.
Sources: Ethnic balance: author's calculations from 1989 Soviet census data in Zastavnyi, *Heohrafiia Ukraïny*, pp. 413–17. Linguistic balance: calculations from a series of surveys undertaken by Valerii Khmel'ko of the Kiev Mohyla Academy from 1991 to 1994. The total sample size was 18,000 throughout the whole of Ukraine. See also n. 115.

hand, none of the three main ethno-linguistic categories can be considered a real social 'group', with a clear identity and fixed boundaries.[116] Russophone Ukrainians (the 'Little Russians') in particular are likely to be subject to a variety of crosscutting Ukrainian, Russian, Soviet and localist influences. Chapter 3 demonstrates that they have remained a relatively amorphous group, difficult to mobilise politically, but chapter 5 shows that their lack of positive enthusiasm for the nationalist movement has been a vital factor in limiting its influence. Nevertheless it is still possible to write of the three as distinct entities. Although they blur into one another at the edges, they are sufficiently distinct at the extremes.

Table 1.2 shows how the ethnic and linguistic balance between Ukrainians (Ukrainophones) and Russians (Russophones) in the various regions of Ukraine is closely related to patterns of historical development.[117] The proportion of ethnic Ukrainians falls markedly in the east and south, but it is linguistic patterns which demonstrate regional difference best. Ukrainophones are concentrated in the west, but in central Ukraine a considerable historical divide can be observed between the Left and Right Banks of the Dnieper. In both regions ethnic Ukrainians predominate to the same extent, but Russophones are much more numerous on the Left (eastern) Bank. Eastern and southern Ukraine on the other hand, in urban areas at least, are almost monolingually Russian. Significantly the south, although it has a higher percentage of ethnic Ukrainians than the east, has almost the same number of Russophones, largely because of the weakness of the Ukrainian cultural tradition in the region.

Perestroika and independence

Events since Gorbachev's accession to power are described in more detail in subsequent chapters.[118] In outline, little changed in Ukraine until September 1989, when the resignation of Ukraine's veteran Communist Party leader Volodymyr Shcherbyts'kyi coincided with the first congress of the opposition movement Rukh. The latter was only able to win 24 per cent of the seats in the spring 1990 Ukrainian elections (the Communist 'group of 239' had 53 per cent), but the rapidly declining power of the Soviet centre, combined with the pressures of the new electoral politics and the empowerment of local republican institutions, began to open up divisions within the Ukrainian Communist Party, whose 'national communist' wing increasingly sided with the opposition. Cooperation between the two groups led first to the declaration of Ukrainian sovereignty in July 1990, and then to Ukraine sidestepping Gorbachev's proposal to restructure the USSR with a new Union Treaty. When Gorbachev organised a referendum in March 1991 on the preservation of the USSR, Leonid Kravchuk, chairman of Parliament and leader of the national communists, countered with a second question on the defence of Ukrainian sovereignty, which won 80 per cent support as against 70.5 per cent locally for Gorbachev's question, allowing Ukraine to remain a reluctant partner in the treaty process.

Ukraine, however, played no part in the defeat of the August 1991 coup attempt in Moscow. The Ukrainian Parliament passed an act of independence on 24 August and the Communist Party was banned on 30 August, but Ukraine had gained independence with surprising ease and as a result of events elsewhere.[119] There were no real fireworks, no national martyrs, and no real liberation mythology to sustain Ukrainian independence in more difficult times (chapter 2 argues that Ukraine has liberation myths, but they date from 1917–20 or the 1940s, and are divisive). Unlike the Vietcong or the FLN in Algeria, the Ukrainians did not win independence as the result of a long and arduous struggle that created disciplined institutions and parties that could have strengthened the post-independence polity, but as the result of an alliance of convenience between nationalists and national communists. This alliance proved sufficient in the exceptional circumstances of 1991, but was unable to transcend long-term historical difficulties.

The act of 24 August was confirmed by a referendum on 1 December 1991 with 90 per cent of the vote, and on the same day Kravchuk became the first elected president of independent Ukraine. However, divisions that were submerged in late 1991 soon resurfaced. Regional and left-wing groups (including a revived Communist Party after October 1993) campaigned against Kravchuk's increasingly nationalist tendencies and defeated the remnants of Rukh in the spring 1994 parliamentary elections. Kravchuk in turn lost the presidential election the following summer to a strong anti-nationalist campaign by his prime minister from 1992 to 1993, Leonid Kuchma.

Conclusion

The legacy of the past has not served the Ukrainian nationalist movement well. If nations are 'imagined communities' constructed out of a plausible pre-modern past,[120] the modern Ukrainian state has a relative paucity of material with which to work. The various regions that make up modern Ukraine have moved in and out of Ukrainian history at different times, but have never really interacted together as an ensemble. Instead, as is often the case with borderlands in Eastern Europe, local sub-histories have intertwined with those of neighbouring states and regions.[121] There are therefore serious difficulties in imagining Ukrainian history either as a temporal or a geographical continuum.

This historical legacy, as also expressed in the ethnic, linguistic and religious differences between the regions, seriously limits the natural support base for the nationalist cause, as analysed in more detail in chapter 5. On the other hand, national consolidation is always a continuing process and it remains possible that contingent factors, such as an escalation of conflict with Russia or total economic and social collapse, could spark an increase in support for the nationalists. Before examining such possibilities, this analysis will turn to the history of the Ukrainian national movement over the last century and a half.

2   Ukrainian nationalism in the modern era

Ideological and organisational roots

Modern Ukrainian nationalism has its roots in the national revival of the nineteenth century. The revival, however, was slower and less all-encompassing than many similar movements elsewhere in Eastern Europe, such as those of the Czechs or Finns. In the Russian Empire the first organised group appeared in the 1840s, but proper political parties did not emerge until the 1900s. Even then their influence was limited. The Ukrainian movement made little impact in the multi-ethnic cities, where it had many rivals. On the Right Bank Polish nationalism was a more significant force until after the failure of the 1831 and 1863 rebellions,[1] and 'socialism and class-generated appeals still carried more clout than militant Ukrainian nationalism in Kiev in 1914'.[2] Moreover, a strong Great Russian nationalist movement also operated on Ukrainian territory, to which many members of the influential Russian intelligentsia in Kiev lent their support. In Habsburg Galicia, the Ukrainians had to compete with the Poles and were internally divided. Therefore, although a significant movement was created from unpromising beginnings in the early nineteenth century, support for the Ukrainian cause should not be exaggerated.

According to Miroslav Hroch's popular threefold periodisation, national movements in Eastern Europe typically developed in three phases.[3] The first phase ('scholarly interest') involved a handful of local intelligentsia engaged in antiquarian research to validate a sense of national separateness; the second ('patriotic agitation') represented the politicisation of the intelligentsia and the forming of the first nationalist organisations; and the third ('the rise of a mass national movement') the attempt by the intelligentsia to raise the national consciousness of the popular (usually peasant) masses and establish a truly national movement.

Hroch's periodisation can be used to provide useful benchmarks to assess the progress of the Ukrainian national movement, but it will not be assumed that there is any necessary, still less teleological, development from one stage to another. Moreover, Hroch's schema says little about the political dimension, which was particularly important in the Ukrainian case. Given the differing conditions pertaining in Ukrainian lands in the Russian and Austro-Hungarian Empires, the fortunes of the Ukrainian national movement tended to rise and fall with patterns of political relaxation and repression. Nor should it necessarily be assumed that the growth of Ukrainian national consciousness was an irreversible or one-way phenomenon.[4] In both Russian and Habsburg Ukraine, Ukrainophilism had to compete with rival 'Little Russian' or straightforwardly Russophile movements. Even in western Ukraine the supremacy of the Ukrainophile orientation was settled only late in the nineteenth century. Internal diversity and disagreement as much as the division of Ukrainian lands was therefore a key reason why Ukrainians failed to establish an independent nation-state in 1917–20.

With such qualifications in mind, however, in the Russian Empire the first, 'aristocratic', heritage-gathering phase can be roughly dated to the 1780s to 1840s, and the populist, organisational phase to the 1840s to 1880s. In the two decades before 1914, especially during and immediately after the 1905 revolution, there were some signs that the final phase of popular mobilisation was beginning, but true mass politics only arrived in 1917,[5] and even then the embryonic national movement struggled to get off the ground.[6] In Galicia and Bukovyna, on the other hand, the more favourable conditions of Habsburg rule helped to facilitate more rapid progress. The establishment of the constitutional Dual Monarchy in the 1860s (after brief experimentation during the revolutionary year of 1848) produced a much earlier transition to the mobilisation stage, and by the 1900s the rudiments of an entire Ukrainian civil society were in place. Moreover, Galician nationalists had transcended their parochial origins to conceive of themselves in all-Ukrainian terms as both a 'cultural arsenal' and a 'Ukrainian Piedmont' – the true keepers of the national faith and the potential 'awakeners' of the rest of Ukraine.[7] West Ukrainian independence in 1918–19 and the subsequent war with the Poles merely capped these developments.

The Russian Empire

In tsarist Ukraine the antiquarian stage was mainly the work of two groups, both seeking to maintain the Little Russian identity that had developed in the eighteenth century.[8] The first consisted of the rapidly diminishing band of Cossack nobles (*starshyna*) in the former Hetmanate, committed to upholding the rights they considered to have been enshrined in the 1654 Pereiaslav Treaty. The second group were the Kharkiv Romantics (Kharkiv university was established in 1805),[9] followers of the eighteenth-century Ukrainian individualist philosopher Hryhorii Skovoroda (1722–94),[10] who sought to systematise local folklore and maintain the image of the Cossacks as noble Christian free men. Ironically, both groups enjoyed semi-official sponsorship as the Russian authorities were keen to promote antiquarian research that would help refute revanchist Polish claims to 'Little Russia'. Typical examples of their labours were *An Attempt at a Collection of Little Russian Songs* published in 1819 by Prince Mykola Tserteliev, and the *History of Little Russia* by Dmytro Bantysh-Kamens'kyi in 1822. The main work of the period, however, was the *Istoriia Rusov*, circulated anonymously throughout the early years of the century and published in 1846, which again lauded the Cossacks, but more controversially idealised Khmel'-nyts'kyi and his successors Mazepa and Pavlo Polubotok for their opposition to the tsars.

Such works provided the cultural foundations for the first organised Ukrainian group of the century, the secret Brotherhood of Sts Cyril and Methodius, which united a handful of local radicals for two years until its suppression in 1847.[11] The Brotherhood's main figure was the historian Mykola Kostomarov (1817–85),[12] but it was also strongly influenced by the poet Taras Shevchenko (1814–61)[13] and the writer Panteleimon Kulish (1819–97),[14] although neither was a formal member. Like the Kharkiv Romantics, the members of the Brotherhood relied on a idealised image of the Cossacks to underpin their sense of a separate local Ukrainian identity, but they were also strong pan-Slavists (several of their number had taken part in the liberal Decembrist movement of the 1820s). Their political programme envisaged Ukraine's future as part of a broad federation of Christian Slavs that would replace the continental empires (although one of the Brotherhood's members, Georgii Andruz'kyi, devised an alternative plan for a Slavic federation that would exclude Russia).

Indeed, the main argument of Kostomarov's most famous work, *Dve russkie narodnosti* ('The Two Peoples of Rus'') published in 1861, was a development of the Little Russian argument that the Ukrainians and Russians had distinct histories and cultures, but were nevertheless two different branches of the same people.[15] Kostomarov reached back beyond the Cossack period to argue that their fates had diverged after the collapse of Kievan Rus', creating two different political traditions, with the democratic individualism of the Ukrainians in sharp contrast to aristocratic Poland and the patrimonial principles of the Muscovite state, which Kostomarov saw as deriving from the separate Mongol influence. Nevertheless, he maintained that the Ukrainians' quarrel was with Russian absolutism rather than with the Russian people per se, and his political programme amounted to little more than the demand for local self-government.

Shevchenko, however, was a natural radical. As with other stateless East European peoples who lacked political institutions and powerful national elites it was not surprising that the main symbolic building-blocks of Ukrainian national revival should be provided by the image and metaphor of a poet rather than by political figures.[16] Like Lonnröt for the Finns and Mickiewicz for the Poles, Shevchenko's work established a whole new national mythology of heroic struggle and ignoble betrayal, and his decision to write in Ukrainian validated the argument that Ukrainian could function as a self-sustaining and independent culture. His 'poetry became in effect a literary and intellectual declaration of Ukrainian independence'.[17] Moreover, although Soviet historians attempted to paint him as mainly a prophet of social revolution, Shevchenko's frequent references to Russia's tradi-tional oppression of Ukraine would in the long term undercut the philosophical bases of Little Russianism and create the possibility of a more radical ethno-nationalist alternative, although for the moment Kostomarov was the more influential of the two.[18]

Although Shevchenko and the leading members of the Brotherhood were arrested in 1847 (significantly Shevchenko received the harshest punishment, ten years' military service in Kazakhstan), they laid the foundations for the distinctly Ukrainian brand of the all-Russian populist movement that began to emerge as political conditions in the empire were liberalised, first in 1860–3 and then again in the early 1870s. The Ukrainian populists (*khlopomany*) formed small *hromady* ('society') groups, often based in St Petersburg, and journals such as *Osnova* (1861– 2) and the *Kievskii telegraf* (1859–76), which at this stage combined all-Russian and local influences and confined themselves to a largely cultural agenda.[19] The Ukrainian populists, although still usually scions of the gentry, took less and less interest in their Pereiaslav 'rights' (Kulish being a notable exception) and followed Shevchenko's advice to focus on the peasantry as the unconscious repository of national identity (Shevchenko himself was a self-taught redeemed serf).[20] By distilling local dialect, myth and legend the populists provided two key building-blocks for the potential future development of Ukrainian national consciousness.

First, they completed the work begun by Shevchenko and Kulish of systematising the *prostaia mova* (basic speech) of the south-eastern Ukrainian dialect into literary form, creating 'a linguistic development that gave birth to a political movement' once they attempted to spread the new language amongst the peasant masses.[21] Second, historians such as Volodymyr Antonovych (1834–1908)[22] and his disciple Mykhailo Hrushevs'kyi (1866–1934)[23] attempted to go beyond Kostomarov's vision of the past and restore Ukrainians' sense of self by creating a whole new mythology of national descent, as historians such as Palacký had done for the Czechs and Iorga for the Romanians. Hrushevs'kyi in particular argued that the Ukrainians had always been an ethnically distinct people, and attempted to dispel Little Russian stereotypes by arguing that the Ukrainians represented an older and superior culture to that of Russia (Kievan Rus' and the Cossacks). For Hrushevs'kyi, the Treaty of Pereiaslav in 1654, far from being a 'reunion', represented the artificial attempt to foreclose this long pre-history of separate development (see also chapter 6).

The most important political thinker of the age was the humanist and liberal socialist Mykhailo Drahomanov (1841–95),[24] who, under the influence of Proudhon, envisaged the Russian and other European empires becoming a federative 'free union' of scores of self-governing statelets, each with a socialisation of property balanced by respect for civil rights and a rule of law. Like Kostomarov, Drahomanov stressed the different cultural and political traditions of Ukraine and Russia, but rejected any attempts to divide the two peoples on absolutist or ethnicist grounds. As a positivist, secular, non-Marxist socialist he was as opposed to revolutionary socialism and radical nationalism as he was to tsarism.

Moderate though their political programme undoubtedly was, Drahomanov, Antonovych and the *hromady* were too much for the authorities, who were understandably nervous at the prospect of the populist intelligentsia working amongst the peasantry so soon after the emancipation of 1861.[25] The populists' growing contacts across the border with their Galician counterparts (see pp. 34–8 below) were also seen as potentially subversive. Popular publication in Ukrainian was therefore banned in two decrees of 1863 (the Valuiev circular) and 1876 (the Ems Ukaz), which made it extremely difficult to circulate Ukrainophile ideas beyond a narrow circle of the intelligentsia. The more conservative climate at the end of Alexander II's reign and under Alexander III forced many Ukrainian activists into exile in Geneva or Galicia, including Drahomanov. Hrushevs'kyi took up an appointment in L'viv. Although the *hromady* attempted to continue their work, they had to make every effort to appear loyalist and politically innocuous, and the national movement went into virtual hibernation. Many younger and more radical elements therefore turned to socialism and/ or all-Russian politics instead.

Political parties in tsarist Ukraine

Political revival came in the 1890s, when the social tensions produced by industrialisation and the gradual emergence of a Ukrainian working class, coupled with economic crisis in the countryside and the growing influence of the new Galician parties (see pp. 36–7 below), prompted the populists to renew the attempt to organise themselves politically.[26] The first step was taken in 1897, when Antonovych and others established the semi-secret All-Ukrainian Non-Party Organisation, which had some twenty-two branches and 438 members.[27] As political tensions increased in the build-up to the 1905 revolution, the organisation came out into the open, formalising its existence first as the Ukrainian Democratic Party in 1904, and then, minus a few older members, as the Ukrainian Democratic-Radical Party (UDRP) during the 1905 revolution. The UDRP could not be described as a nationalist party, however. The vast majority of Ukrainian populists still adhered to Drahomanov's federal project, and, particularly in the more easterly guberniias, tended to cooperate with the Kadets.[28]

Nevertheless, the October Manifesto and the relatively democratic elections to the first two Dumas provided the Ukrainians with their first real, if short-lived, public tribune. The populists dominated the Ukrainian groups of forty-four deputies in the first Duma and forty-seven in the second (102 deputies were elected from the nine ethnically Ukrainian guberniias),[29] and attempted to copy their Galician neighbours by beginning the construction of the rudiments of a Ukrainian civil society.[30] Between 1906 and 1908 a series of Prosvita ('Enlightenment' or reading societies) sprang up throughout Ukraine, in imitation of those already established in Galicia (see p. 36 below), although many were subsequently closed after a Senate decree declared them subversive in 1908.[31] Fourteen branches were established by 1908, but only seven remained in 1911. The largest branch, the Kiev organisation with 600 active members, was closed in 1910.[32] The restrictions on publication in Ukrainian were only partially rescinded, and although Ukrainophiles began to produce a variety of papers and journals, most collapsed after one or two issues. Only *Hromads'ka dumka* ('Social Thought') and *Rada* ('Council') survived for a significant period.

Once reaction set in 1907 the UDRP, like the *hromady* in the 1870s, realised that it would have to lower its political profile in order to survive. In 1908 it disbanded itself and became the non-party Society of Ukrainian Progressives. The new electoral law of 1907 deprived the Ukrainians of effective representation in the third and subsequent

Dumas, although a handful of deputies continued to press Ukrainian causes in alliance with radical Kadets. Disappointed by the dashing of their hopes, the Ukrainian intelligentsia shared in the general swing to political quietism and conservatism, symbolised by the *Vekhi* essays published in 1909. Moreover, despite their short-lived success in 1905–6, the populists had many rivals. Jewish, Polish, Bolshevik and monarchist groups were all active in Ukraine,[33] and even amongst their own Ukrainian constituency the populists faced a growing challenge from Ukrainian socialists and the fledgling national-separatist movement.

The forerunner of Ukraine's several indigenous socialist groups was the Revolutionary Ukrainian Party (RUP) established by Kharkiv students in 1900,[34] although small groups had appeared as early as 1893–4.[35] From its inception the RUP was debilitated by internal argument over the relative importance of national and social issues. One wing emphasised international class solidarity and sought to cooperate with all-Russian political organisations; the other stressed Ukrainian autonomy, both organisationally and as a political aim, and was therefore attracted to Austro-Marxism or Menshevism rather than Bolshevism. Unfortunately for the latter group, Drahomanov's exile in 1876 had cut short the attempt to build a specifically Ukrainian brand of socialism, and in his absence Marxist and internationalist ideas had grown in influence. Moreover, although the rapid growth of the working class in the prewar years was slowly leading to the emergence of an ethnic Ukrainian proletariat, the vast majority of workers in Ukraine were still Russian or Jewish, so that would-be Ukrainian socialists had no real constituency.[36] Although in the intellectual climate of the times many populists also called themselves socialists, the failure to develop a strong indigenous socialist movement would have serious consequences in 1917–20, when support for Bolshevism came to be equated with opposition to Ukrainian independence.

The socialist majority in the RUP produced two successor political parties. The first was the Ukrainian Social Democratic Union, or Spilka ('Union'), which enjoyed brief popularity during the 1905 revolution, winning fourteen seats in the 1907 elections[37] before rapidly disappearing from the stage. The Spilka supported Ukrainian autonomy, but was in effect a local faction of the all-Russian Mensheviks (all of its propaganda was in Russian).[38] The second group, the Ukrainian Social Democratic Workers' Party (USDWP), also founded in 1905, consisted largely of leftist Ukrainian intellectuals, and proved to be longer lasting.[39] Unlike the Spilka, the USDWP would not accept the tutelage of the Russian Social Democrats, and made greater efforts to combine the principles of socialism and nationalism. Two of its leaders,

Volodymyr Vynnychenko and Symon Petliura, would emerge as key figures in the revolutionary governments of 1917–20.

Although the vast majority of Ukrainian populists and socialists remained committed to the idea of a federal union with a democratised Russia, a genuine, if tiny, Ukrainian separatist movement also emerged in the years after 1900.[40] The first stirrings of separatist sentiment were amongst the Brotherhood of Taras, formed by a handful of student radicals at a meeting at Shevchenko's grave in Kaniv in 1891, which maintained a shadowy existence for two years before being repressed in 1893. Several of its members were instrumental in forming the RUP, and in 1902 broke away to form the Ukrainian People's Party (UPP), the first truly nationalist political group in tsarist Ukraine.

The UPP's main ideologue was Mykola Mikhnovs'kyi, regarded by many as the father of modern Ukrainian ethno-nationalism,[41] although he derived some of his ideas from Franciszek Duchiński (Dukhins'kyi) (1816–93), ironically a Right Bank Pole. Duchiński rejected the idea that the inhabitants of Rus' had migrated northward after the sack of Kiev in 1240, and argued that the Russians were not proper Slavs at all, but 'Turanians', the bastard stock of Finno-Ugric and Mongol blood, as evidenced by their patrimonial communism and autocratic traditions. The Ukrainians and Poles, on the other hand, were the last bastions of 'Aryan' Europe, who should stand shoulder to shoulder against the Russian threat, although this latter point was anathema to most Ukrainians.[42] In the original RUP programme *Samostiina Ukraïna* ('Independent Ukraine') Mikhnovs'kyi bowdlerised Shevchenko's anti-Russian imagery and Hrushevs'kyi's new ethno-history, and called for the creation of 'an independent and unified Ukrainian state from the Sian to the Don' (i.e. from Galicia to the foothills of the Caucasus). He condemned the parochialism of the populists who 'didn't even want to call themselves Ukrainians', and declared that 'he who is not for us, is against us. Ukraine for the Ukrainians. So long as one enemy or stranger remains on our territory, we have no right to lay down our arms.'[43]

However, although Mikhnovs'kyi's xenophobic nationalism provided the first real alternative to the federalist populism of Kostomarov and Drahomanov, his ideas did not gain widespread popularity until the 1920s. During the 1905 revolution UPP radicals flirted with terrorism, calling themselves the 'Ukrainian National Defence Force',[44] but after 1907 the party largely disappeared from sight. A brief coda to their activity was provided in 1914 when radical émigrés formed the Union for the Liberation of Ukraine in Galicia under the sponsorship of the Central Powers. The union proposed that an independent Ukraine would become a Habsburg protectorate after the defeat of Russia,[45] but had little impact outside the Habsburg territories, where it had some success in radicalising Ukrainian prisoners of war.

Overall, the Ukrainian national movement could only make a limited impact before 1914, and its influence waned in the reaction after 1907. Moreover, the movement's regional and social base remained highly restricted. Ukrainian parties and activists had almost no impact at all in key regions such as Odesa and the Donbas.[46] The Ukrainian movement relied for support on the tiny Ukrainian intelligentsia, but at the turn of the century the intelligentsia as a whole represented only 0.5 per cent of the local population, and only 32 per cent of these were ethnic Ukrainians.[47] The populists' focus on the peasantry, and the argument that other Ukrainian elites were lost to the national cause became something of a self-fulfilling prophecy. The populists failed to develop adequate links with the nascent Ukrainian bourgeoisie and working class that began to appear with the onset of industrialisation in the 1880s.[48] Other groups, such as the priesthood, that played an important role in Galicia and in the Baltic national revivals, were largely quiescent in tsarist Ukraine. Nearly half of all priests were Russian, all were Orthodox after 1839, and most were impoverished, dependent on their parishioners and in no position to challenge the authority of their hierarchs. Moreover, the 1876 Ems Ukaz made it difficult for urban Ukrainian intellectuals to expand their contacts with the rural intelligentsia, or 'third element' (primary-school teachers, heads of cooperatives, zemstvo officials). Therefore the activists of the national movement were too often outsiders who found it difficult to proselytise in the villages, rather than locals to whom peasants would have paid greater respect.[49]

In 1914 therefore the embryonic Ukrainian national movement remained hamstrung by its 'isolation from the broad mass of the peasantry, its lack of a clear socio-economic programme, organisational amorphousness, and lack of preparedness (or lack of desire) for intensive political activity'. The peasantry, who represented 93 per cent of the population, remained an 'ethnographic mass' for whom the economic (i.e. land) question was all-important.[50]

Western Ukraine to 1914

Early stages

In Habsburg eastern Galicia, as indicated in chapter 1, Ukrainian national consciousness was more pronounced, and by 1914 the national movement had progressed much further than its counterpart in the Russian Empire. However, the Galician Ukrainian movement was not a mere 'Austrian invention'. The original heritage-gatherers in Galicia, the 'Rusyn triad' of writers based in L'viv (Lemberg), Markiian Shashkevych, Ivan Vahylevych and Yakov Holovats'kyi, took their inspiration from the Kharkiv Romantics and relied heavily on central Ukrainian myths and symbols (the Cossack era in particular) for their 1837 work *Rusalka Dnistrovaia* ('The nymph of the Dniester').[51] On the other hand, the Ukrainians (then called Ruthenians) undoubtedly benefited from the support of the Habsburg authorities as they tried to counterbalance what they considered to be the more serious Polish threat.

However, the 'springtime of nations' in 1848 came too early for the Ruthenians, although they were able to form a Supreme Ruthenian Council which won 25 of Galicia's 100 seats in the short-lived revolutionary parliament. The post-revolutionary reaction inevitably led to a decline in the Ruthenians' fortunes, but they had now acquired a taste for political organisation, which was given further stimulus by the democratic reforms of the 1860s and by the 1867 settlement, which devolved local administration to the Poles and threatened to reverse the gains the Ruthenians had made. As in the Russian Empire, however, nationalism had to compete with other political philosophies, even for the favours of the more nationally conscious. More conservative groups, influential amongst the local Uniate hierarchy, supported the St George Circle, which sought to uphold the traditions of the Rus' Church and opposed the use of the vernacular, and the Russophile Rus'ka Rada, which espoused pan-Slavic ideals and sought the protection of the tsars. Indeed, for much of the 1860s and 1870s it seemed that the Russophile movement might emerge the stronger, given the attraction of Russian power at its zenith.

On the other hand, the populists (*narodovtsi*) took their inspiration from Shevchenko and popularised the idea that the Ruthenians were really 'Ukrainians', kith and kin of their brethren across the border. After the 1860s the two regions could communicate with each other in the new standard literary language (which came from Russian Ukraine), and the repressive measures of 1863 and 1876 forced many leading Ukrainians west to settle in Galicia (where they disabused many locals of their romantic image of life under Russia). The Ukrainophiles' literary language was much closer to Galician dialects than standard Russian (which the purist 'new wave' of Russophiles insisted on using after 1900), and their populist socialism and support for agrarian cooperatives gave them the edge over the conservative Russophiles. Moreover, increasingly open Russian support for the Russophiles led Vienna to take repressive measures against them, including a major treason trial in 1882, after which the Russophiles were a declining force.[52]

The second half of the century also saw a rapid growth in Ukrainian civil society. The Ukrainian movement already had a strong base in the Uniate Church, which in 1848 embraced nearly 1,600 parishes with a total of 2.15 million faithful,[53] and under Andrei Sheptyts'kyi, who served as metropolitan from 1901 to 1944, became more unambiguously Ukrainophile as the influence of the conservatives declined.[54] The Ukrainophiles also promoted popular literacy through the Prosvita society established in 1868 (a task vastly simplified by the spread of universal primary education in the Habsburg Empire after 1867), and the Shevchenko Society set up in 1873.[55] By 1914 Prosvita, with its network of 2,944 Ukrainian reading rooms, had over 197,000 members.[56] Scout and sporting groups for the young, Sokil and Sich, were established after the Czech example in 1894, and by 1914 had 33,000 members.[57] Agricultural cooperatives and a land bank also flourished, adding the hope of material improvement to peasants' motives for joining the Ukrainophile movement.[58]

This rapid growth of Ukrainian civil society was reflected in the increasing confidence of the new generation of young radicals who emerged in the late 1880s and 1890s and styled themselves 'Young Ukraine'. The radical spurt was also encouraged by the decline of the Russophiles, the failure of the Poles to deliver on the promise of a 'new era' of major concessions to the Ukrainians in Galicia in the early 1890s, and by the upsurge of Ukrainian political activity in Russia. V"iacheslav Budzynovs'kyi ('The Cultural Poverty of Austrian Ruthenia', 1891) and Yulian Bachyns'kyi (*Ukraïna irredenta*, 1895) argued that Ukrainians on both sides of the border should join forces against the Russians and/or Poles, and openly embraced the idea of a united and independent Ukrainian state.[59] Moreover, unlike Mikhnovs'kyi and the student activists in the RUP, they were not marginal figures isolated from the older generation. By the 1900s older Ukrainophiles, such as the writer Ivan Franko (1856–1916), were prepared to admit that their labours since the middle of the century had basically been successful and it was time to move on to more openly political activity. Franko's essay 'Beyond the Limits of the Possible' published in 1900 symbolised this change, and finally moved the idea of Ukrainian statehood into the Galician political mainstream.[60]

Political parties

Political parties appeared earlier in Galicia than in tsarist Ukraine, and Galician Ukrainians grew used to open political activity in the two decades before 1914, especially after Austria introduced direct, universal suffrage in 1907.[61] Moreover, the Galician parties were much more radical than their counterparts in the Russian Empire, which remained wedded to the federalist idea. The 'Young Ukrainians' helped to set up two parties: the Ukrainian Radical Party in 1890, which was anti-clerical and agrarian-socialist, but nevertheless nationalist; and the Marxist Ukrainian Social-Democratic Party in 1899. The main Galician organisation however was the National-Democratic Party founded in 1899, a broad-church alliance supported by Hrushevs'kyi, Prosvita and the Uniate Church.[62]

The National Democrats dominated Ukrainian representation in both the Viennese Chamber of Deputies and the Galician Diet. In the former the Ukrainians progressed from a mere three seats in 1879 to 27 out of 516 in the 1907 elections. In the latter the number of Ukrainian seats rose from eleven in 1888 to thirty-two in 1913 (out of 150).[63] Only the outbreak of war in 1914 prevented the implementation of a deal brokered by the Habsburgs that would have institutionalised power-sharing in the Galician Diet (although the Poles would still have been in a majority), as well as meeting the Ukrainians' long-standing demand for the creation of a Ukrainian university in L'viv.

Bukovyna and Transcarpathia

In the two other Habsburg Ukrainian lands, however, progress was slower. In Bukovyna, as in Galicia, political conditions were relatively free and interchange between the two regions was considerable. However, the local Ukrainian movement had to compete with its Romanian equivalent, and Romanian influence on the local Orthodox Church meant that it was unable to play the same role as the Uniate Church in Galicia (the fact that most local Ukrainians were Orthodox also made a full meeting of minds with the Galicians difficult). Nevertheless, a Ruthenian Society (Rus'ke tovarystvo) was established in 1869, as were local branches of Prosvita and the Galician parties. The latter sent five deputies to the Vienna parliament, and occupied seventeen out of sixty-three places in the local Diet after a system of national curiae was introduced in 1911.[64]

Transcarpathia, on the other hand, remained something of a political backwater. The local Hungarian regime was decidedly less liberal than the Austrians in Galicia, especially after 1867, and the system of estate curiae was maintained on Hungarian territory until 1918, denying the local Slavs the chance of effective political representation. The struggle between the local Russophile, Rusynophile and Ukrainophile move-

ments therefore remained latent and unresolved, and continued up to
1914 and beyond.

1917–1920

With the outbreak of war in 1914, the Ukrainians of Galicia were able to
make enthusiastic common cause with the war aims of the Central
Powers, and formed a Supreme (later General) Ukrainian Council to
promote the goal of a united, independent Ukrainian state under
Habsburg protection. On the other hand, the first action of the tsarist
authorities in 1914 was to arrest leading Ukrainian activists. Ironically,
however, it was the less well-prepared Ukrainians of the Russian Empire
who gained the chance to try and form a Ukrainian nation-state in 1917.
The Galicians were not able to enter the fray until the Habsburg Empire
collapsed in turn in autumn 1918, by which time the succession of weak
governments in Kiev were being overwhelmed by the social maelstrom
unleashed by the revolution and the collapse of central authority (see
chapter 1).

In 1917–20 the main actors on the Russian side of the border were the
populists and socialists. Radical nationalists such as Mikhnovs'kyi had
little influence, and the Union for the Liberation of Ukraine only
operated in territories controlled by the Central Powers.[65] Before
October 1917 nearly all Ukrainians in the Russian Empire remained
committed to the federal idea.[66] Nevertheless, populist leaders such as
Hrushevs'kyi were quickly radicalised by events to adopt positions they
had previously considered 'beyond the limits of the possible', much as
other European 'founding fathers' such as Tomas Masaryk did not really
contemplate national independence until the latter stages of the war.

Three main Ukrainian parties emerged in 1917. Ukrainian liberals
linked to the all-Russian Kadets founded the Ukrainian Party of
Socialist-Federalists (UPSF), but the main party of the populist
intelligentsia was the Ukrainian Party of Socialist-Revolutionaries
(UPSR), in effect a reincarnation of the Ukrainian Democratic-Radical
Party of 1905–7, which was still committed to the nineteenth-century
dream of 'awakening' the peasantry. For a time this seemed possible. At
its peak in 1917 the UPSR claimed at least 75,000 members;[67] it was the
largest party in the Central Rada and its activists controlled the
Selians'ka spilka ('Peasant Union'),[68] helping the party to win a clean
sweep in the Ukrainian countryside in the all-Russian Constituent
Assembly elections in 1917 (see table 2.1).

The UPSR's main rival was the revived Ukrainian Social Democratic
Workers' Party (USDWP). The USDWP's influence was due more to

the then predominance of socialist ideals rather than to genuine mass support (the party only elected two deputies to the Constituent Assembly),[69] but the Ukrainian socialists helped to pull the populists to the left, making it difficult for them to consummate their alliance with the peasantry, and leaving them unsure of how to deal with the challenge of the Bolsheviks.[70]

The initial successes of the Ukrainian movement, however, were quite impressive. As an embryonic civil society once again began to develop, key groups such as the soldiers' and peasants' councils decided to back the Ukrainian parties and their political programme. Even at the First Congress of Soviets of Ukraine in December 1917 Ukrainian activists received more support than the Bolsheviks.[71] The Ukrainian parties also attempted to win over Ukraine's many national minorities. From July 1917, 202 of the Central Rada's 822 seats were set aside for non-Ukrainians,[72] and in January 1918 the UNR passed a Law on National-Personal Autonomy that was a model of Austro-Marxist principles of non-territorial national accommodation (although the civil war prevented its implementation).[73]

Most importantly, the Ukrainian parties won a majority in the all-Russian Constituent Assembly elections in November 1917, as shown in table 2.1. (A similar pattern was evident in the incomplete and ultimately meaningless Ukrainian Constituent Assembly elections held in January 1918. Voting was only possible in 171 out of 301 constituencies in areas not controlled by the Bolsheviks, but Ukrainian parties won an estimated 70 per cent of the vote.)[74]

As was to be expected, the vote for the Ukrainian parties was strong in the countryside but weak in the cities and in the new lands of the east and south. A strong showing in mainly rural central Ukraine (the guberniias of Kiev, Poltava, Podillia and Volhynia) was offset by a lower vote in Kharkiv, Yekaterinoslav and Kherson, as shown in table 2.2 (the figures for Taurida, that is Crimea and its environs, are not available). The Ukrainian parties also polled relatively poorly in Chernihiv, which, unlike the rest of the Left Bank, came under Russian rule in 1522 rather than 1654.

As a point of comparison, all of the major all-Russian parties were active in Ukraine at this time, and usually had more support than the Ukrainian parties in the crucial urban centres. In Kiev the Ukrainian parties received only 21 per cent of the vote in the summer 1917 city Duma elections, and 26 per cent in the Constituent Assembly vote. In Odesa the Ukrainian parties received a derisory 4 per cent.[75] Of the all-Russian parties, 50,000 of the Mensheviks' national strength of 200,000 was concentrated in Ukraine (30,000 in the Donbas alone), as were nine of sixty-four of the

Table 2.1 *Votes cast in eight Ukrainian guberniias at the 1917 Constituent Assembly elections*

	Number of votes	Percentage of total
Ukrainian parties	5,557,560	67.8[a]
Bolsheviks	859,330	10.0
Mensheviks	108,933	1.3
SRs	304,328	3.7
Kadets	247,500	3.0
Jewish and minority parties	441,104	5.3
Other	512,408	6.1
Total	8,201,063	

Note: [a] Includes joint lists of the Ukrainian and Russian SRs. Figures are incomplete, and therefore do not add up to 100 per cent. Army votes are excluded. Around 60 per cent of the total vote went to the UPSR: Jurij Borys, 'Political Parties in the Ukraine', in Taras Hunchak (ed.), *The Ukraine, 1917–1921: A Study in Revolution* (Cambridge, Mass.: Harvard Ukrainian Research Institute, 1977), p. 137.
Sources: Jurij Borys, *The Sovietisation of Ukraine, 1917–1923* (Edmonton, Ont.: CIUS, 1980, rev. edn), p. 170; and Steven L. Guthier, 'The Popular Basis of Ukrainian Nationalism in 1917', *Slavic Review*, vol. 38, no. 1 (March 1979), pp. 30–47, at pp. 36–7.

Table 2.2 *The vote for Ukrainian parties by guberniia in November 1917 (percentages)*

Poltava	80.5
Podillia	79
Kiev	77
Kharkiv	72.8[a]
Volhynia	71
Kherson	53[a]
Chernihiv	49.7
Yekaterinoslav	46.6

Note: [a] The figures for Kharkiv and Kherson are exaggerated by the inclusion of joint lists with the all-Russian SRs.
Source: Guthier, 'Popular Basis of Ukrainian Nationalism in 1917', pp. 37–9.

Kadets' guberniia organisations and one-sixth of the Trudovyky's strength. The SRs claimed a Ukrainian membership of 300,000,[76] while Bolshevik strength in Ukraine fluctuated widely between 4,000 and 60,000.[77] The Jewish Bund and Polish Socialist Party were also influential in Ukraine. Under the Hetmanate Kiev was home to a broad range of anti-Bolsheviks, including Whites, chauvinists and even liberals, while southern Ukraine was the preserve of the Whites (including Denikin's forces in 1919), and Makhno's anarchists.

Although the one obvious lesson of the elections was that the Ukrainian movement's support lay almost entirely amongst the peasantry, Ukrainian leaders failed to meet the peasants' key social demand, namely expropriation of the land, and the support won in 1917 quickly evaporated in 1918–19. The land law passed by the UNR in January 1918 completely misjudged the mood of the peasantry by attempting to socialise the land rather than hand it over to individual peasant ownership.[78] The Hetmanate (and the German occupiers) backed the large landowners in the defence of their estates, and the Directorate was preoccupied with military survival. The peasantry therefore looked to their own salvation and each individual village either made tactical alliances with whichever political and/or military force happened to come along, or tried to keep itself to itself.[79] Even if 'the ethnic and socio-economic grievances of the Ukrainian peasant proved mutually reinforcing and provided the foundation for a political movement which combined nationalism with a populist social programme',[80] that opportunity had been missed by the end of 1918 and leaders and masses drifted apart.[81]

After the defeat of the Directorate in 1920, many Ukrainian activists fled abroad or lapsed into political quietism. However, both the UPSR and Social Democrats split in 1919–20, with their more left-wing members forming separate parties, the Borotbisti and Ukapisti, which were eventually absorbed by the Communist Party. Their leaders then played a key role in the national communist movement of the 1920s before falling victim to the purges of the 1930s (see chapter 4). On the whole, however, the nationalist movement was now confined to western Ukraine and to émigré circles, where a bitter debate emerged over the causes of the failure of the Ukrainian experiment and Ukrainian nationalism proper began to take shape.

Dmytro Dontsov

The main protagonists in this debate were Dmytro Dontsov (1883–1973) and V"iacheslav Lypyns'kyi (1882–1931), the two most influential Ukrainian nationalist thinkers of the twentieth century, whose intellectual confrontation was symptomatic of the broader clash between militant and democratic nationalism that has continued to be a feature of Ukrainian politics to this day.

Dontsov, like Mussolini, had originally been a socialist but joined the Union for the Liberation of Ukraine in 1914 and moved quickly to the right.[82] Dontsov also took much of his political philosophy from Italian fascism, but developed his own uniquely Ukrainian brand of extremist nationalism, which he dubbed 'forceful', 'action' or (after Maurras) 'integral' nationalism (*chynnyi natsionalizm*),[83] borrowing eclectically from the likes of Nietzsche, Fichte, Pareto and Sorel. As with Mikhnovs'kyi, Dontsov's starting point was a violent critique of the alleged provincialism, inferiority complex and Little Russian mentality of the Ukrainian intelligentsia, Drahomanov in particular, whose failure to liberate themselves from Russian culture and the illusory hope of cooperation with non-existent Russian 'democrats' left Ukraine adrift and leaderless in 1917–20. A failure of will was therefore the main reason why Ukraine had not seized its chance of statehood (important elements of this critique were shared by the Soviet Ukrainian writer Mykola Khvyl'ovyi; see chapter 4).

Instead of liberal populism and the romanticisation of the peasantry, Dontsov therefore advocated the 'initiative of the minority', composed of 'new men' (an idea taken from Nietzsche), inspired by emotive forces of the will (Schopenhauer) and embodying a true and pure 'national idea', a clear and simple programme around which the popular masses could consolidate. Dontsov understood this 'national idea' not as the product of rational thought or the agglomeration of social interests, but (from Hegel) as an abstraction to which all other values should be subordinated (his favourite slogan was 'The Nation Above All!'). Dontsov also tended to anthropomorphise the nation by talking of its 'will to power' and the natural struggle of nation against nation in a Social Darwinist world.

Dontsov's vision of the Ukrainian nation, like Mikhnovs'kyi's, was essentially ethnicist. A pure and inspiring 'national idea' could only exist as the representation of the spirit of a homogeneous ethnic nation, free from all internal 'impurity' and disunity (Dontsov here borrowed from the populist myth of a homogeneous Ukrainian peasantry). Ukraine therefore had to be purged of all Jewish, Polish and above all Russian influence.[84] Moreover, the homogeneous ethnic nation would in Dontsov's vision be run as a corporate state, with the nationalist political party providing its 'ruling caste'. This would be the Organisation of Ukrainian Nationalists (see pp. 47–8 below).

V"iacheslav Lypyns'kyi

Dontsov's ethnicist authoritarianism, although increasingly in tune with the climate of the times, did not go unchallenged. V"iacheslav Lypyns'kyi had also been a leading figure in one of the minor parties under the UNR (the landowners' Ukrainian Democratic-Agrarian Party), but his analysis of the events of 1917–20 was in complete contrast to that of

Dontsov.[85] Lypyns'kyi also attacked the populist intelligentsia, but for their idealised view of the peasantry. Contrary to the populist vision of a 'bright peasant paradise, a free community without peasants or lords, of private homesteads wreathed in flowers',[86] the peasantry was not a cohesive social force but an impoverished mass, more interested in anarchy and land seizure than in building the strong political institutions and stable civil society that were the two necessary foundations of a Ukrainian nation-state. Like Stolypin before the war, Lypyns'kyi's political prescription was to copy what he saw as the virtues of English society, where the wider spread of land ownership supposedly gave the majority a material stake in society and helped to maintain social cohesion and a rule of law through the creation of a class of prosperous yeoman farmers (kulaks, or in Ukrainian *kurkuli* or *khliboroby*). Moreover, Lypyns'kyi thought that Ukraine, with its 'European' tradition of individual farming rather than the peasant commune (*obshchina*), was better placed to make the transition to such a society than Russia.

Lypyns'kyi therefore stood against the climate of the times by arguing that greater social differentiation would underpin rather than undermine social stability. The society the populists had sought to create was dangerously unstable, with an angry and anarchic peasant mass no longer balanced by political elites and institutions. Because Ukrainian society was 'incomplete', it was too weak to achieve independence as a result of its own premature efforts. The rapid descent into disorder in 1917–20 could therefore only have been prevented by compromise with nationally conscious elements in the old elite. Furthermore (and here Lypyns'kyi followed Dontsov), only an elite or aristocracy would have the moral authority to lead the mass of society in any repeat of the state-building experiment of 1917–20. This explains his otherwise bizarre support for the introduction of a hereditary hetmanate in a nation with no real monarchical tradition. Lypyns'kyi argued that a hetman would provide a focus for unity amongst an otherwise divided nation, while the hereditary element would prevent the damaging succession struggles that had undermined Ukrainian society throughout history, such as after the deaths of Yaroslav and Khmel'nyts'kyi, and after the downfall of Skoropads'kyi in 1918. Lastly, territorial rather than ethnic patriotism was the best means of integrating all social groups into a single stable society. Excluding other classes or ethnic groups from the Ukrainian state-building project had been a key source of weakness in 1917–20. The slogan 'Ukraine for the Ukrainians!' only 'perpetuated the nation's incompleteness, and hence its perennial statelessness'.[87]

Lypyns'kyi's ideas were certainly ahead of the time. His continued support for the exiled Skoropads'kyi government in the 1920s was certainly a minority cause. However, his main ideas (social differentiation and wider property ownership, compromise with the old ruling elite and territorial patriotism) would, like Dontsov's, again be influential in the 1990s.

Western Ukraine: democratic or 'integral' nationalism?

Galicia and Volhynia

In sharp contrast to Russian Ukraine where the popular support won by the nationalists in 1917 quickly dissipated, the national movement in Galicia emerged from the years of war and revolution as strong as ever. The Russophiles were fatally discredited by their collaboration with tsarist governor Bobrinskii during the brief Russian occupation of Galicia in 1914–15, and during its brief existence in 1918–19 the West Ukrainian People's Republic (ZUNR) maintained relatively stable government and held on to popular support (partial elections in November 1918 showed relatively high support for the National Democrats).[88] The lost war of 1919 between the ZUNR and the Poles only served to further solidify Ukrainian national sentiment.

Support for liberal nationalism, however, was now less secure. At first Ukrainians maintained a united front behind the former leaders of the ZUNR. Their call to boycott the 1922 Polish elections reduced local turnout to 38 per cent (mostly local Poles, Jews and others).[89] Only the collaborationist Ukrainian Agricultural Party participated, winning five seats. Their leader Sydir Tverdokhlib was promptly assassinated.[90] However, after the international recognition of Polish administration over east Galicia in 1923 the Ukrainians were faced with difficult choices, and the national movement split into three.

The majority sullenly recognised Polish rule as an established fact and participated in Polish political life with the aim of maximising Ukrainian autonomy. The main vehicle for this sentiment remained the establishment National Democrats, who in 1925 became the Ukrainian Popular-Democratic Union (in Ukrainian, UNDO) as a result of unification with several smaller parties.[91] As in its previous incarnation before 1914, UNDO was supported by the bulk of Ukrainian civil society, including Prosvita, the cooperative movement, the main Ukrainian paper *Dilo* ('Affairs') and, in practice, the Uniate Church.[92] The high point of the moderates' success was the 1928 elections, when UNDO won twenty-five seats in the Polish Sejm out of a Ukrainian total of forty-six, and nine of eleven in the Senate (there were 444 seats in the Sejm and 111 in the Senate). UNDO won 48 per cent (594,000) of the total Ukrainian vote of 1,225,000.[93]

In the 1930 elections fraud and growing Polish repression during the 'pacification' campaign reduced Ukrainian representation to twenty-eight seats (plus five in the Senate),[94] but in 1935 UNDO leader Vasyl' Mudryi negotiated the so-called 'normalisation' agreement with the Poles, according to which the Ukrainians were guaranteed nineteen seats in the Sejm and six in the Senate (as also in the 1938 elections).[95] Mudryi also became deputy speaker of the Sejm. However, Poland was moving rapidly to the right in the wake of Marshal Piłsudski's death in 1935, and no more substantial concessions were forthcoming. UNDO's 'collaborationist' policies were consequently steadily losing popularity on the eve of war in 1939, although arguably only the outbreak of war destroyed the party as a viable political force.[96]

The second tendency amongst Galician Ukrainians was pro-Soviet or pro-Russian. First of all this meant the diminishing ranks of the Russophiles, but they could only muster 95,000 votes at the 1928 elections.[97] More importantly, the establishment of the Ukrainian SSR and the undoubted appeal of communism to many poor Ukrainian peasants resulted in the creation in 1923 of the underground Communist Party of Western Ukraine (CPWU) and its front organisation Sel'rob, which sought to unite all Ukrainian lands within the USSR.[98] At the height of the left-wing parties' influence in 1928 they won 242,000 votes, or 20 per cent of the Ukrainian total. (Pro-Soviet sympathies were also widespread in UNDO. The initial successes of Ukrainianisation even persuaded Yevhen Petrushevych, former president of the ZUNR, to join the Sovietophiles.) However, the end of Ukrainianisation in 1929, the onset of collectivisation and the Great Famine of 1932–3 destroyed the appeal of the Soviet option. The CPWU pursued too independent a line and was too critical of policy in Soviet Ukraine, where it was a strong supporter of Ukrainianisation, and Stalin forcibly dissolved it in 1938.

More important in the longer term was the increasing popularity of a third, ultra-nationalist current, and its call for an independent Ukraine free of both Polish and Soviet influence. On the whole radical nationalism was a product of the specific circumstances of the 1920s, but it also drew on some of the ideas first outlined by Mikhnovs'kyi in 1900.[99] Like Sinn Fein in Ireland or Herri Batasuna in the Basque country, the far right condemned 'collaborationist' politics and combined open political activity with terrorism, finding a ready constituency of support amongst former combatants from 1914–20, radical youth and workers and peasants impoverished by the Great Depression (something of a paramilitary tradition had already developed amongst the 'Sich Riflemen' who fought under the Habsburgs in 1914–18). Moreover, the heavy-handed tactics of the Polish authorities and the seeming failure of UNDO's tactics drove many natural moderates into the arms of the far right (UNDO's right wing split from the party in 1933).[100] Incited by publicists like Dontsov, increasing numbers of western Ukrainians tended to feel that there was little point in participating in a parliamentary democracy in which they were a permanent minority treated with contempt by their Polish overlords. Internationally, the appeal of the (diminishing number of) western democracies was in decline, and the Ukrainians tended to look instead to Germany because of a shared desire to revise the Versailles settlement (see the following section, on the Organisation of Ukrainian Nationalists).

Bukovyna and Transcarpathia

Similar tensions existed in both Bukovyna and Transcarpathia, although as before 1914 political conditions were less favourable for the Ukrainians. In Romanian Bukovyna a Ukrainian National Party was established in 1927 under Volodymyr Zalozets'kyi, but it was forced to cooperate with all-Romanian parties because of the requirement that political parties win at least 2 per cent of the national vote to secure representation in the Romanian parliament. With the traditional connection with Galicia broken, the Ukrainian movement declined in power and authority, and growing frustration at Ukrainian powerlessness led to a rise in support for the far right in the 1930s.[101]

Transcarpathia was denied the self-government it was promised in 1918 and deliberately underrepresented in national elections, but, whereas in Bukovyna Ukrainian civil society largely regressed in the interwar period, under the relatively liberal Czechoslovak regime the Transcarpathian Ukrainians were able to regain some lost ground. Ukrainian nationalists such as the Uniate priest Avhustyn Voloshyn expanded the Prosvita and Plast network, which soon surpassed the rival Rusynophile network, the Dukhnovych Society;[102] and Voloshyn's Christian People's Party (later the Ukrainian National Union), like UNDO basically a Uniate Catholic and conservative party, was the dominant force behind the creation of the short-lived Carpatho-Ukrainian government in 1938–9. In the February 1939 elections to the Carpatho-Ukrainian Sejm, the Ukrainian National Union won 86 per cent of the vote (on a high turnout of 93 per cent).[103]

The Organisation of Ukrainian Nationalists (OUN)

Ultra-nationalist groups first began to appear in Galicia and émigré circles in the early 1920s, including the paramilitary Ukrainian Military Organisation (UVO) set up in 1920 (which narrowly failed to assassinate Piłsudski on his first official visit to L'viv in 1921), and student groups such as the Union of Ukrainian Nationalist Youth, established by radicals from Prosvita and Sokil in 1926.[104] In 1929 the previously disparate forces of the right united to form the Organisation of Ukrainian Nationalists (OUN) at a conference in Vienna.

The OUN's mentor was Dontsov, although he himself was never formally a member of the party, which 'placed little emphasis on systematic ideology'.[105] His heady mixture of simplistic ethno-politics, lack of tolerance toward political opponents and messianic programme of national salvation through uncompromising struggle offered tempting solutions in a climate of defeat and disillusion. The OUN therefore revived Mikhnovs'kyi's slogan of 'Ukraine for the Ukrainians!', and declared that a future independent 'Ukrainian state would be a national dictatorship [*natsiokratiia*]', defined as 'the power of the nation in the state'. Under the OUN's proposed new order rival political parties would be banned, and the OUN and its leader (*vozhd'*) would function 'as the foundation of state power and the leading force in national leadership and the organisation of social life'.[106]

The OUN's paramilitary wing copied and extended the UVO's terror tactics, both against Polish rule in Galicia (their most famous victim was the Polish interior minister Bronisław Pieracki in 1934) and against moderates in their own community. The OUN was therefore regularly condemned by the leaders of UNDO and by Metropolitan Sheptyts'kyi, but periods of particularly harsh Polish repression, such as the 'pacification' campaign of 1930–1 or the late 1930s, helped to maintain the flow of recruits. After Pieracki's assassination the Poles established a concentration camp for Ukrainian radicals at Bereza Kartuska, which, like Long Kesh in Northern Ireland or the Soviet camps of the 1960s and 1970s, merely served to radicalise its inmates and incubate a new generation of nationalist leaders.

After the Nazi rise to power in Germany in 1933, the OUN became increasingly subject to German influence, both in terms of ideology and organisational support (contacts had already been established between the UVO and the German General Staff in the 1920s, which helped the former set up bases in Czechoslovakia, Lithuania and Danzig (now Gdańsk) to run operations in western Ukraine). The Nazis' external pressure on the Polish state and increasing Ukrainian disillusion with the moderate tactics of UNDO encouraged the OUN to operate with greater boldness. At this crucial juncture, however, the organisation split.

In 1938 its charismatic leader Yevhen Konovalets' was shot dead by a Soviet agent in Rotterdam, and the OUN proved unable to agree on a successor. Younger and more radical members, particularly in Polish Ukraine, many of whom were former prisoners released from Polish prisons after 1939, supported Stepan Bandera and called themselves the OUN-b,[107] while the elder, more moderate generation, stronger in émigré circles, was led by Andrii Mel'nyk (OUN-m). Of the two, the OUN-b was closer to Dontsov's ideal-type party, more radical in its ideology and its commitment to violent direct action, even running its own internal security service (*sluzhba bezpeky*) under Mykola Arsenych. The succession struggle left the OUN ill-prepared for the events of 1938–41, when it was unable either to save the Carpatho-Ukrainian mini-state from Hungarian invasion or to organise mass resistance to the Soviet occupation of Galicia,[108] despite rapid and widespread popular disillusion with communist rule. On the other hand, the OUN's underground structure allowed it to survive while legal parties such as UNDO all but disappeared.

Wartime nationalism

The OUN's great opportunity came with the German invasion of the USSR in 1941. OUN units crossed the border with the Wehrmacht, along with the special Nachtigall and Roland divisions, composed largely of OUN-b activists under German tutelage. The OUN has therefore been tainted ever since by accusations of collaboration with the Germans, especially as thousands of mainly west Ukrainians also served in the regular army and worked as Ostpolizei or as simple bureaucrats under the occupation (not all of course were members of the OUN).[109] One estimate puts the total number of Ukrainians in all such units as high as 250,000.[110]

As argued above, many nationalists were indeed sympathetic to Nazi Germany, and the OUN had a long history of contact with the Abwehr (German military intelligence). On the other hand it has been claimed that the Ukrainian units were more or less autonomous, fighting under a German flag of convenience as a short cut toward establishing a national army, and that disillusion with the Germans set in rapidly after 1941 (see pp. 49–51 below).[111] However, the last point is difficult to square with the fact that another semi-autonomous German-backed Ukrainian division, the SS-Galicia, was formed in the latter stages of the war, only to be almost completely wiped out by the Soviets at the Battle of Brody in 1944.[112] Nevertheless, on balance the nationalist attitude toward the German authorities seems to have been more instrumental than ideological; nationalists collaborated in so far as they thought such collaboration would further the nationalist cause.

Controversy also surrounds the extent of nationalist anti-Semitism and participation in the wartime Holocaust. Anti-Jewish sentiment was certainly a long-standing feature of Ukrainian nationalism, nurtured by the Church and by the Jews' awkward social position as trading middlemen at the sharp end in the conflict between what Ukrainian peasants saw as the 'natural' economy and its nascent capitalist rival.[113] Violent pogroms had been a regular feature of Ukrainian life since at least the time of Khmel'nyts'kyi.[114] The OUN's Cracow congress in April 1941 stated that 'the Jews in the USSR are the most loyal prop of the ruling Bolshevik regime and the avant-garde of Muscovite imperialism in Ukraine', and declared its intention to 'vanquish' them from Ukraine.[115] Many Ukrainians participated in the L'viv pogroms of July 1941, worked as concentration camp guards and assisted in the murder and deportation of Jews during the final phases of the Holocaust in 1942–4. On the other hand many Ukrainians, notably Metropolitan Sheptyts'kyi, defended and sheltered their Jewish neighbours.[116] Quantifying the relative balance is probably impossible, and no doubt many Ukrainian actions were inspired by German provocations or by perceptions of Jewish collaboration with the Soviet occupying forces in 1939–41. Nevertheless, it cannot be denied that many nationalists cooperated with the Nazis and played a role in the Holocaust, and after the war Soviet propaganda made great play of both facts.

However, the establishment of a Ukrainian state had no part in German war aims (despite Alfred Rosenberg's advice to Hitler), and when Bandera and Yaroslav Stets'ko had the temerity to issue a symbolic declaration of Ukrainian independence in L'viv in June 1941 they were promptly arrested. Thereafter the Germans and the nationalists regarded each other with increasing suspicion, and the OUN largely struck out on its own. In 1941–3 both wings of the OUN sent groups of their supporters (*pokhidni hrupy*) across the prewar border into Soviet Ukraine proper to try and spread the nationalist message, although few managed to cross the Dnieper into Left Bank or south-east Ukraine.[117] Moreover, the OUN activists tended to be young and idealistic and paid little attention to bread-and-butter issues. The new Soviet working class was already becoming used to some degree of job and welfare security and was largely impervious to the OUN's right-wing message, while the countryside was still cowed by the experiences of the early 1930s. Those who did rally to the nationalist cause were therefore nearly all intelligentsia 'drawn from the academic or literary profession'.[118] In the main central Ukrainian cities Prosvita groups were reestablished, and Ukrainian newspapers published, such as *Ukraïns'ke slovo* ('Ukrainian Word') in Kiev.[119] Some towns even set up short-lived Ukrainian administrations under German tutelage, although many were undermined by internal squabbling or suppressed by the Germans for presuming too much independence. In Kharkiv the nationalist House of Popular Culture 'came close to developing into an unofficial government'.[120] In Kiev a Ukrainian National Council was set up with OUN-m backing in October 1941 in the hope that it could later be converted into a de facto Ukrainian administration, but the limits of German tolerance were demonstrated in 1942 when Volodymyr Bahazii, the city's mayor, was summarily executed.[121] In contrast to 1918, the Germans now preferred to govern directly rather than through Ukrainian proxies.

The Ukrainian Autocephalous Orthodox Church (UAOC) was revived at a Sobor in Volhynia in August 1941, but (as in the 1920s and 1990s) soon split into two factions led by Archbishop Polykarp who wanted a truly independent Church and the more Russophile Alexius. The UAOC found it difficult to proselytise in the east, and internal divisions left it incapable of responding to Metropolitan Sheptyts'kyi's historic overtures in 1942 to establish a single national Church through the merger of the Uniates and UAOC. The vast majority of UAOC priests fled west before the advancing Soviet army in 1943–4.[122]

As the *pokhidni hrupy* reported back the difficulty of generating support outside western and parts of central Ukraine both wings of the OUN (like the Vlasovites) realised they would have to deemphasise authoritarian nationalism if they were to broaden their appeal (one group, led by Ivan Mitrynga, even favoured adopting a form of watered-down socialism as the movement's ideology).[123] Bandera's supporters remained relatively radical, but Bandera himself was in prison, and the OUN-b's military wing was now under the more moderate leadership of Mykola Lebid' and Roman Shukhevych. The moderates prevailed at a special OUN-b congress in August 1943, at which Dontsovite and neo-fascist ideas were largely displaced by democratic rhetoric and a commitment to maintain key aspects of the Soviet multi-ethnic welfare state, including 'the equality of all citizens of Ukraine, regardless of their nationality', 'the full right of national minorities to cultivate their own national culture', the right to 'a just wage and a share for workers in the profits of industry', 'compulsory secondary education', 'security in old age' and even 'freedom of the press, speech, thought, conviction, faith and world-view'.[124] The OUN-b also declared itself in equal opposition to 'Russian communo-Bolshevism and German national-socialism', and began to finalise plans for full-scale armed struggle against both.[125]

The OUN's switch in tactics also led in July 1944 to the creation of an underground coalition, the Ukrainian Supreme Liberation Council (in Ukrainian UHVR), with the remnants of other parties such as the UNDO. The only qualification for membership in the UHVR was support for Ukrainian independence, and its programme provided further evidence of the moderation of the national movement since 1943, calling for 'freedom of thought, world-view and belief, a just social order free of class exploitation and oppression, a genuine rule of law and citizenship rights for all national minorities'.[126]

As the military situation turned against the Germans, and Soviet troops threatened to return, the OUN encouraged the various Ukrainian irregular armed groups to merge together as the Ukrainian Insurgent Army (known by its Ukrainian acronym, UPA).[127] From the beginning OUN influence in the UPA was considerable, but the latter was a military rather than a political organisation; 'the UPA came into being rather spontaneously . . . and its rapid growth forced the OUN leadership to impose an organizational framework on this movement'.[128] The extent of west Ukrainian hostility toward the Soviets meant that at its peak in late 1944 the UPA had an estimated 90,000 to 100,000 men under arms. Moreover, in their first year or two of fighting, UPA units roamed throughout western Ukraine before being pushed back into the Carpathian foothills and the marshes and forests of Volhynia.[129]

Although the UPA also engaged the retreating Germans and the Poles, its timescale of operations (serious fighting continued until the late 1940s and the last units were only rounded up in 1954–5) meant that most of its actions were against Soviet forces.[130] Not surprisingly, therefore, Soviet history has always painted the UPA in the blackest possible terms. For many ethnic Russians and eastern Ukrainians (two million Ukrainians fought on the Soviet side),[131] fighting the Red Army was bad enough in itself, but the UPA was also accused of organising a reign of terror against fellow Ukrainians who cooperated with the Soviets or joined collective farms. However, many alleged atrocities were undoubtedly propaganda, and it was mainly the *consequences* of UPA actions, i.e. the increasingly unfavourable balance between victories and reprisals, that caused enthusiasm for the fight gradually to decline in west Ukraine. Nevertheless the UPA remains one of the most divisive historical symbols in Ukraine. If the concentration of UPA support in west Ukraine was originally due to historical regional differences, the subsequent celebration of their exploits in the west and demonisation in the east has only served to widen the divide (see also chapter 6).

After the final round-up of the last members of the OUN and UPA in the mid-1950s, the OUN began an exile existence, although small successor groups continued to appear in Galicia for twenty years or more (see pp. 55–6 below). Like many émigré organisations, however, the OUN was weakened by internal arguments, Soviet infiltration, and the constant raking of the embers of wartime differences. By the late 1950s the émigré OUN had split into three factions. Those who remained loyal to Dontsovite authoritarianism, including Bandera himself and a substantial body of UPA veterans, radicalised by their long and arduous struggle, renamed themselves the OUN-r (for 'revolutionary'). If anything, Bandera's group now regressed politically to an idealised version of integral nationalism, now that wartime compromises were no longer necessary (Bandera was assassinated by a Soviet agent in Munich in 1959). The Mel'nykites on the other hand stayed loyal to the 1943 programme, and renamed themselves the OUN-s (for 'solidarity'). Two further splits in 1949 and 1954–5 resulted in the formation of the broadly social democratic but short-lived OUN-z (for *zakordonnyi*, or abroad).[132] Both the Banderites and Mel'nykites were able to survive with the support of the large Ukrainian communities in North America and elsewhere, and began to revive their activity in Ukraine in 1989–90 (see chapter 3).

Although the OUN at its most radical gained an unsavoury reputation for authoritarianism, collaboration with the Nazis and anti-Semitism, the OUN tradition was relatively diverse and politically flexible. Ukrainian nationalists in the 1930s and 1940s were therefore not all followers of Dontsov, although postwar Soviet propaganda managed to convince many Ukrainians that this was the case. Ironically, it is the latter, largely mythologised, tradition that many Ukrainian radicals would seek to revive in the 1990s.

The 1960s: a civic revolution?

Although the defeat of the OUN-UPA seemed to have confined organised Ukrainian nationalism to the diaspora, arrests of 'bourgeois nationalists' continued to run at a surprisingly high level. According to KGB records, 183 'nationalist and anti-Soviet' groups involving 1,879 individuals were broken up in Ukraine in 1954–9, and 46 groups (245 individuals) in the period 1958–62.[133] Nearly all of these arrests were in Galicia. However, despite the continuing appeal of radical nationalism in western Ukraine, it was becoming increasingly clear to most Ukrainians that the OUN's traditional methods of violent underground struggle were now obsolete. The national dissent of the 1960s and 1970s would therefore take a different form.

The Ukrainian Workers' and Peasants' Union (UWPU)

The first group to go beyond the traditions of the OUN was the Ukrainian Workers' and Peasants' Union (UWPU), active in Galicia from 1958 to 1961 under the leadership of a dissident jurist Levko Luk"ianenko.[134] Like the OUN, the basic aim of Luk"ianenko's group was Ukrainian independence, but it based this demand on Article 17 of the then constitution of the USSR, which formally guaranteed all Soviet republics the right of secession. Moreover, the UWPU proposed that secession would only be possible after a referendum and specifically renounced the use of force.[135] Although Luk"ianenko later characterised the differences between the UWPU and OUN as 'ones of means rather than ends',[136] the UWPU also soft-pedalled on the OUN's original anti-communism, calling for 'an independent Ukraine with a highly developed socialist political system'. Luk"ianenko insisted that the UWPU base its ideology on 'Leninist' principles.[137] The UWPU's membership was also more typical of the 1960s than the 1940s, as it was essentially 'an intelligentsia group: three lawyers, an agronomist, a militiaman, party workers. Until then the national liberation movement [i.e. the OUN] had a military character and was made up of simple peasants.'[138]

The UWPU therefore represented a crucial transition stage in the Ukrainian national movement as it accommodated itself to the new realities of Soviet rule. However, as with the nineteenth-century *hromady*, their relative moderation failed to impress the authorities. The UWPU's leading members were all arrested in 1961. Luk"ianenko was initially sentenced to death, but this was later commuted to fifteen years in the camps.

The shistdesiatnyky

The UWPU was a portent of the much more significant *shistdesiatnyky* ('generation of the 1960s') movement.[139] In sharp contrast to the OUN, the new wave of dissidents that emerged in the early 1960s was led by members of the new Soviet Ukrainian intelligentsia, such as the writers Vasyl' Symonenko and Ivan Dziuba, the poet Ivan Drach and the journalist V"iacheslav Chornovil, whose generational and ideological roots lay in the Khrushchev thaw and the all-Soviet dissident movement rather than the wartime struggles of the UPA. On the whole therefore the *shistdesiatnyky* movement ebbed and flowed with patterns of repression and relaxation in the USSR as a whole rather than to a specifically Ukrainian rhythm.

Like their predecessors in the 1860s or 1920s, the *shistdesiatnyky* initially confined themselves to 'the linguistic-cultural sphere', and in public at least 'limited their demands to national enlightenment' (*prosvitianstvo*),[140] although some were contemplating open political activity as early as 1963, and the writers Yevhen Proniuk and Ivan Svitlychnyi discussed forming an underground movement in 1966.[141] A series of small discussion circles were organised, including the Club of Creative Youth in Kiev from 1960 to 1964 and Prolisok ('clearing'), its equivalent in L'viv, but nothing amounting to an established political organisation.[142] Nevertheless, protest often became semi-public, as at the 1963 Kiev conference on the Ukrainian language or the twice-delayed congress of the Writers' Union of Ukraine in 1966.[143]

Drach and others spearheaded a Ukrainian literary and poetic revival and campaigned against the growing 'Russification' of Ukrainian schools and culture in the wake of Khrushchev's education reforms of 1958–9. Attempts were also made to rehabilitate national myths and symbols and individuals such as Skrypnyk and Hrushevs'kyi. Like other dissidents elsewhere in the USSR at this time, however, the leitmotiv of the *shistdesiatnyky* was individual rights and a rule of law. The ethnic nationalism of Mikhnovs'kyi and Dontsov was explicitly rejected, and the Ukrainians strove to build a common front with Russian and other 'all-Union' dissidents. Moreover, like Luk"ianenko's UWPU, the *shistdesiatnyky* consciously sought to protect themselves by working within the Soviet Constitution, hoping the authorities could be shamed into living up to their own legal standards.

The authorities, however, conspicuously failed to do so. A first wave of arrests coincided with the fall of Khrushchev and the Daniel' and Siniavskii trial in Moscow in 1965–6. Those who protested, most notably Chornovil, were themselves imprisoned in 1966–7.[144] A second, much larger wave of arrests in 1972 coincided with the downfall of the Ukrainian party leader Petro Shelest, with Dziuba being forced into a humiliating public recantation in 1973 (see below).[145] A third round of repression in the late 1970s finally silenced public dissent. If anything, however, repression only served to radicalise opposition. Many *shistdesiatnyky* became in effect 'professional revolutionaries' in permanent opposition to the system.[146]

The most important text of the era was Ivan Dziuba's *Internationalism or Russification?* published in samizdat in 1966. Dziuba concentrated on a long historiographical critique of traditional 'Russian expansionism', 'Russian great-power chauvinism' and policies of 'coercive Russification', but remained within the bounds of orthodoxy by calling for a return to 'Leninist nationalities policy' (that is removing the 'distortions' of the Stalinist era and returning to the Ukrainianisation policies of the 1920s).[147] Similarly, the other main publication of the era, the samizdat journal *Ukraïns'kyi visnyk* (Ukrainian Herald), six issues of which appeared under Chornovil's editorship in 1970–2,[148] reported human rights violations without editorial comment in a dry legalistic style reminiscent of the 'Chronicle of Current Events' in Russia. However, after Chornovil's arrest in 1972 issue no. 7–8, edited by Stepan Khmara, adopted a much more radical tone, echoing the political language of the 1940s by referring to the 1972 arrests as a 'pogrom' and characterising Moscow's policies as 'ethnocide', providing a foretaste of future arguments between the two men.[149]

Radical nationalists and other dissidents

Nor was Khmara the only radical amongst the *shistdesiatnyky*. In the mid-1960s a would-be manifesto for the Ukrainian dissidents, written by Yevhen Proniuk and circulated in samizdat ('The Condition and Tasks of the Ukrainian Liberation Movement'), stressed the importance of maintaining the traditions of the OUN-UPA in the face of 'Russian great-power chauvinism', and advocated a 'democratic-revolutionary path' of struggle combining 'legal and illegal' activity.[150] The most prominent opponent of the *shistdesiatnyky*, however, was the author Valentyn Moroz. His violent criticism of Dziuba's 'recantation' as symptomatic of the feeble-mindedness of the Ukrainian intelligentsia recalled Dontsov's attacks on intellectual 'provincialism' in the 1920s.[151] As an alternative, Moroz invoked the cult of the noble and heroic individual, inspired by *oderzhymist'* ('noble frenzy') to resist the might of the Soviet state – again, a not particularly coded reference to Dontsov. Moroz was forced into exile in 1979, but returned to L'viv to preach Dontsovite nationalism in the early 1990s.

Therefore, although several authors have claimed that the 1960s marked a decisive break with the mid-century traditions of Ukrainian nationalism,[152] the transition was far from complete and Ukrainian nationalism remained a complex and variegated phenomenon.[153] Groups operating in the tradition of the OUN continued to appear, such as the 51-man Ukrainian National Committee arrested in L'viv in December 1961 (twenty of whom were eventually imprisoned).[154] The largest and longest-lasting was the Ukrainian National Front, many of whose members were UPA veterans. Most of its leaders were arrested in 1967, but it reemerged in 1975–9.[155] Moreover, such groups were not just a holdover from the 1950s. The Ukrainian Patriotic Movement that surfaced in 1980 reverted to terminology much stronger than anything used by the *shistdesiatnyky*, referring to the Ukrainian SSR as an 'occupying regime', practising a policy of 'national genocide' against Ukraine.[156] Several dissidents did little to hide their anti-Semitism.[157]

Others combined campaigning for the revival of national language and culture with continued loyalty to socialism. Yurii Badz'o, for example, one of the more prominent *shistdesiatnyky* (he was expelled from the Kiev Institute of Literature in 1964), described himself as a 'Eurocommunist', although his main dissident publication, the 1,400-page *Pravo zhyty* ('The Right to Live') written in the late 1970s, concentrated almost exclusively on issues of linguistic and educational Russification.[158] Other left-leaning dissidents included Leonid Pliushch, a leading figure in the Ukrainian Helsinki Group (see pp. 57–8 below), and, transiently, Danylo Shumuk.[159]

Religious dissent was also a feature of the late Soviet era, although it was largely confined to Galicia. As in Poland and Lithuania, (Uniate) Catholic dissent was given an enormous boost by the election of John Paul II as pope in 1979. In 1982 an Initiative Committee for the Defence of the Rights of Believers of the Church emerged under the leadership of Yosyp Terelia, which from 1984 onward published a samizdat bulletin, 'The Chronicle of the Catholic Church in Ukraine'.[160] After Terelia was expelled to Canada in 1987, the group was led by Ivan Hel', who adopted a more explicitly political agenda, condemning Moscow's policy of 'ethnocide' against Ukraine.[161]

Lastly, not all dissidents were nationalists. In 1978 two Donbas miners, Aleksei Nikitin and Vladimir Klebanov, attempted to form a 'Free Trade Union Association of the Soviet Working People', and were promptly arrested for their pains.[162] Klebanov would reemerge in 1989 as a violent opponent of Ukrainian nationalism.

The camps

A final factor limiting the supposed turn away from radical nationalism in the 1960s was the hibernation of traditional nationalism in the Soviet prison camps in Mordovia and elsewhere. According to Luk"ianenko, nearly half the camps' inmates in the early 1960s were Ukrainian,[163] and most of these were OUN-UPA veterans, who formed a radical Galician clique. They cooperated easily with other non-Russian prisoners, but not with 'chauvinist' Russians or even prisoners from central and eastern Ukraine, who were less fervent in their commitment to the national idea and had not taken up arms in the 1940s.[164] As Luk"ianenko admitted, intellectual life in the camps was then somewhat sterile, amounting to little more than idle 'fantasies about a future struggle for Ukraine's freedom'.[165]

The mass arrests of 1965–6 and 1972–3 brought a new generation of prisoners into the camps and helped to establish links between the *shistdesiatnyky* and their more radical predecessors.[166] Although the Banderites were moderated by the *shistdesiatnyky*, they in turn were radicalised by the Banderites (and by incarceration itself). The new prisoners refused to cooperate with the camp authorities, organised frequent hunger strikes for political status and continued to smuggle out samizdat.[167] An appeal signed by eighteen prisoners who styled themselves the Ukrainian National Liberation Movement in 1979 referred to the 'genocide of Russian colonists' against Ukraine.[168] As with Bereza Kartuska in the 1930s, the Soviet camps helped to incubate a new generation of political leaders who would provide more radical alternative leadership to the establishment intelligentsia when political conditions were liberalised in the late 1980s. If anything, former political prisoners were granted a privileged position because of the moral authority acquired as a result of their suffering, often causing considerable resentment amongst the younger generation of activists who cut their teeth in student politics in the 1980s.[169]

The Ukrainian Helsinki Group

The only organised group of the period was the Ukrainian Group for the Promotion of the Implementation of the Helsinki Accords, or Ukrainian Helsinki Group (UHG), formed in November 1976 and in existence until 1981 (although it never formally disbanded). Like the other Helsinki Groups elsewhere in the USSR, the UHG was not an overtly nationalist group, even though leading figures such as Luk"ianenko (who had resumed political activity immediately after his release in 1976) and the UHG's first leader Mykola Rudenko were professed nationalists.[170] According to Luk"ianenko, 'in the first year of its existence, the group gave 70 per cent of its time to the defence of individual rights, and only 30 per cent to the defence of national rights'.[171]

The UHG's main demand in its founding Declaration was that the Helsinki Accords should 'become the basis of relations between the individual and the state'. Its only mention of specifically national issues was that 'Ukraine, as a sovereign European state and member of the UN, should be represented by its own delegation at all international conferences at which the implementation of the Helsinki Accords will be discussed' (although the 1978 UHG document 'Our Tasks' specifically declared that the group saw itself as the direct successor of earlier nationalist groups).[172] In fact, the UHG would be strongly criticised by later generations of radical nationalists for concentrating 'more on defending the rights of Soviet individuals than on defending the rights of the Ukrainian people'.[173]

The UHG had at most thirty-seven declared members (plus an outer circle of sympathisers of unknown numbers), and its ranks were soon decimated by arrest. Twenty-three were imprisoned and six forced to emigrate to the West.[174] Four members (Oleksa Tykhyi, Vasyl' Stus, Valerii Marchenko and Yurii Lytvyn) died in the camps, and were later to be mythologised by reburial in Kiev in November 1989.[175] Luk"ia-nenko later claimed that, given the high risks associated with dissent at the time, 'we did not attempt to expand our circle of association and did not demonstrate the associations we had so as not to bring misfortune on innocent people'.[176] The UHG's narrow circle was drawn mainly from the central Ukrainian cultural intelligentsia. They were 'predominantly the literati': 52 per cent of its members came from the arts and humanities, 22 per cent from the scientific intelligentsia (the reverse of the proportions in the Moscow group, indicating the centrality of cultural concerns) and 15 per cent from other professions.[177] A broader study of 942 Ukrainian dissidents active in 1960–72 draws similar conclusions: 89 per cent of this group were urban dwellers, 86 per cent were 'white-collar staff' and a large majority (63 per cent) came from either Kiev or L'viv.[178]

Although the *shistdesiatnyky* and the UHG had some success in spreading national dissent from Galicia to central Ukraine, it is impossible to estimate the breadth of their support amongst the wider public. Anecdotal evidence suggests that the authorities were quite successful at isolating the dissidents, whilst the silent majority enjoyed slow but steady material improvements. Nevertheless, the prior experience of the 1960s and 1970s made it easier to relaunch an opposition movement in the late 1980s, and also provided a powerful mythology on which the nationalists of the modern era were to draw heavily.

Conclusion

Three times in the last 150 years, Ukrainian national revivals have unfolded in a common pattern. The populists of the late nineteenth century and *shistdesiatnyky* of the 1960s all initially confined themselves to a cultural agenda before eventual radicalisation, as did the national communists in the 1920s (see chapter 4). This was not mere dissimulation. Given Ukraine's huge Russophone population and profound and persistent regional differences the national movement was often torn between a Little Russian mentality seeking autonomy from, but federal links with, Russia, and demands for outright independence. On the other hand, this lack of resolution tended to produce a hyperbolic extreme nationalism amongst the more radical and impatient minority (Mikhnovs'kyi in 1900, Dontsov in the 1920s, Moroz in the 1970s), often directed as much against moderate Ukrainians as against Russian rule. The same pattern was to recur in the Gorbachev period, albeit greatly accelerated.

Despite this common pattern, however, the sharp discontinuities in the history of the Ukrainian national movement have meant that no single intellectual tradition has ever become dominant. Moreover, it would be fallacious to assume that phenomena that bear the same name at different times of appearance are nevertheless essentially similar. Diversity of choice and tradition have always been key features of the Ukrainian national movement. Chapter 3 now turns to an examination of the development of Ukrainian nationalism after Gorbachev's accession to power in 1985, and the rapid return to diversity.

3   Channels of nationalist discourse: political parties, civil society and religion

This chapter seeks to describe the main nationalist political parties, social organisations and pressure groups that appeared as political conditions were liberalised in Ukraine during the late 1980s and early 1990s. The politics of the various national Churches in Ukraine are also described. In practice of course nationalist discourse has not been narrowly confined to such groups alone, and individual parties or groups may well prove ephemeral, but the analysis of the general contours of their development will help illustrate the framework within which nationalist politics has evolved.

Prelude, 1987–1990

The period of the late 1980s had much in common with the quarter-century before 1917. In both eras the Ukrainian national movement was divided between supporters of independence and advocates of some kind of federal solution with Russia, with the former initially in a minority until the collapse of the imperial centre brought about rapid radicalisation. Moreover, in both cases an extreme right-wing fringe emerged, characterised by its hyperbolic reaction against what it saw as the spineless caution of the moderate majority. The key difference of course was that the earlier revival had been incomplete and unsuccessful. This time independence was secured.

As elsewhere in the USSR,[1] the early stages of the perestroika period in Ukraine (1987–9) were characterised by the emergence of a large number of small 'informal' or non-party organisations, although a perhaps over-generous report to the Central Committee of the CPU in July 1987 estimated the numbers active in such circles at 20,000.[2] The hard core of this group were the former political prisoners released in 1987–8, as at this stage the establishment intelligentsia remained largely quiescent.[3] Therefore the new 'informal' groups initially returned to the dissident agenda of the 1960s and 1970s. For most, as argued in chapter

2, this meant some form of 'civic nationalism', but as in the previous period a more radical, even ethnicist, alternative also revived.

The 'informal' groups, like the nineteenth-century *hromady*, were allowed to function as safe havens for the opposition-minded so long as their members followed self-limiting precepts confining them to 'apolitical' areas. However, these 'discussion groups' nurtured an explicitly political agenda in private and served to widen the base of dissent gradually by providing the breeding ground for a new generation of political activists. Such groups included the Ukrainian Culturological Club set up in Kiev in August 1987,[4] the Tovarystvo leva ('The Lion Society', named after the city's symbol) established in L'viv in October 1987,[5] and the Ukrainian Association of Independent Creative Intelligentsia, also formed in October 1987.[6] A student *hromada* group appeared at Kiev university in the spring of 1988,[7] and the Committee in Defence of the Ukrainian Catholic Church reemerged in Galicia in early 1988, again under Ivan Hel'.[8]

However, the main 'informal' group was the revived Ukrainian Helsinki Group, renamed the Ukrainian Helsinki Union (UHU) in spring 1988.[9] The UHU described itself as 'a federative union of self-governing human rights groups and organisations', but V"iacheslav Chornovil later admitted that 'we considered the name "Helsinki" from the very start to be temporary, a clearly tactical measure'. 'In practice', he continued, 'the authorities understood our true nature well and began to call us an organised political alternative to the CPSU.'[10] Moreover, the UHU was already something of a broad church for various different strands of Ukrainian nationalism, as was revealed by the Declaration of Principles it issued in July 1988. Individual members were allowed to campaign for Ukrainian independence, but the declaration confined itself to a call for the USSR to become 'a confederation of independent states', and/or 'federal ties between the republics' to be established so long as they fell short of 'unifying and regulating the organisation of economic, political and cultural life in each republic' – indicating both a terminological confusion typical of the times and the degree of the UHU's dissimulation.[11] The UHU's tactics were quite deliberate. Levko Luk"ianenko, the UHU's leader, wanted the Union to 'accelerate the renewal of national consciousness', but at the same time argued that it should 'never run too far ahead' of public opinion. 'If the UHU had gone to the people with its plans for independence in 1988', he later admitted, 'it would have remained a tiny groupuscle.'[12] The UHU only began to campaign openly for independence after the first congress of the Popular Movement of Ukraine in September 1989 provided it with a degree of cover (see pp. 65–6 below).[13]

Nevertheless, unlike the UHG in the 1970s which had seen its role as the defence of both national and individual rights, the UHU defined 'the principal aim of its activity' more boldly as 'the defence of national rights, first and foremost the right of a nation to self-determination'.[14] According to one UHU activist, 'the Union was always a party which stood both for the liberation of Ukraine and against the totalitarian system – but if we speak frankly, the latter always came second'.[15] Moreover, ideologically the UHU reflected the ambiguous nature of the supposed civic revolution of the 1960s. On the one hand, the Declaration promised that 'the reestablishment of Ukrainian statehood ... would be the principal lasting guarantee of the ... economic, social, cultural, civic and political rights of the Ukrainian people as well as those national minorities living on the territory of Ukraine'. On the other hand, it attacked 'the artificial intermixing of the population of the Union' [i.e. the USSR] and derided the concept of 'Soviet Man'. The UHU's proposed future criteria for Ukrainian citizenship were particularly strict, and similar to those being developed by radical Estonian and Latvian nationalists.[16] The Declaration of Principles suggested that 'anyone can be a citizen of Ukraine with compulsory and adequate knowledge of the state language of the republic [which would of course be Ukrainian], or who lived on this or on other Ukrainian territory before its inclusion into the USSR'.[17] Nevertheless, many of the more radical nationalists in the UHU soon grew impatient with its carefully weighted compromises and left to form a series of ultra-nationalist groups in 1988–9 (see pp. 71–2 below).

Cultural fronts

In 1988–9 the 'informal' groups were gradually able to expand their contacts with the establishment intelligentsia. As the possibility began to loom of an alliance between the two groups, the CPU decided to try to coopt and control more moderate elements in the opposition by accepting the formation of cultural 'front' organisations. All were initially under the CPU's tutelage, but the authorities' control over their activities steadily weakened, and they became channels for the penetration of nationalist values into the official sphere rather than the other way around.

The first such 'front' was the Zelenyi svit ('Green World') ecological association, set up under the auspices of the CPU-controlled Ukrainian Peace Committee in December 1987, but soon slipping out of its control under the leadership of two writers Serhii Plachynda and Yurii Shcherbak.[18] By the time of Zelenyi svit's first national conference in

October 1989 the association had grown rapidly, mainly because the 1986 Chornobyl' disaster had sparked off a mass movement of ecological protest that the authorities could not contain, but also because Zelenyi svit functioned as a flag of convenience for a wide range of activists.[19] As elsewhere in the USSR, Zelenyi svit's members were increasingly able to raise overtly political issues under the cover of ecological protest, normally by using 'ecological genocide' as a metaphor for all other forms of national, cultural and linguistic repression. A case in point was a 10,000-strong demonstration in Kiev on 13 November 1988 ostensibly concerning ecological issues, which was hijacked by radicals demanding the creation of a popular front.[20] (Although both Zelenyi svit and the parallel Green Party of Ukraine have continued to operate in the early 1990s, their influence has sharply declined as the growth of political pluralism has led many activists to find more natural homes elsewhere, and the salience of ecological issues has declined as problems of economic stagflation have worsened.)

The second main 'front' organisation in this period was the Taras Shevchenko Ukrainian Language Society (ULS), allowed to hold its first congress more or less with official blessing in February 1989. The ULS grew out of the unofficial Ridna mova ('Native Language') society that emerged in Galicia in 1988,[21] but the inaugural congress was also supported by the Institutes of Philology and Literature.[22] The first head of the ULS was therefore the poet Dmytro Pavlychko, at the time still an establishment Communist Party member capable of commanding the confidence of the authorities. However, most of the society's rank-and-file membership, estimated at 70,000 in mid-1989,[23] saw the ULS as a reincarnation of the nineteenth-century group Prosvita, and their campaign to establish Ukrainian as the official state language soon slipped the bonds of state control. Ukraine was forced to copy the other Soviet republics and adopt a law proclaiming Ukrainian the official state language in October 1989.[24]

Finally there was the Ukrainian branch of the all-Union Memorial society, set up in March 1989 in order to promote the restoration of 'national memory' by uncovering the 'blank spots' in Ukrainian history. It gained begrudging official support from the Ukrainian Cultural Fund, but its main sponsors were the Kiev cultural intelligentsia, namely the theatrical, cinematographers' and architects' unions (the head of the first, Les' Taniuk, became Memorial's chairman).[25] Despite the authorities' oversight, Memorial's work was inescapably political in so far as its members concentrated on the rehabilitation of specifically national myths and symbols and the commemoration of national heroes or tragedies, such as the highly sensitive topics of the 1932–3 famine and the purges of the 1930s (the importance of the new nationalist historiography is discussed in more detail in chapter 6).

Rukh

Origins as a catch-all movement

The 'informal' phase of the nascent Ukrainian national movement ended with the first congress of the all-Ukrainian Movement for Perestroika, or Rukh ('movement' in Ukrainian) in September 1989 – the Ukrainian equivalent of Sajudis in Lithuania or the Civic Forum in Czechoslovakia.

The first attempt to form such a 'Popular Front' was made by the UHU and other 'informal' organisations in the summer of 1988, after the failure of the Nineteenth CPSU Party Conference in Moscow to condemn the Baltic Popular Fronts emboldened Ukrainian radicals and encouraged them to believe that a similar organisation could be formed in Ukraine. In June and July 1988 a series of public demonstrations in L'viv numbering some 1,000 to 10,000 people demanded the formation of a 'Democratic Front in Support of Perestroika'.[26] A parallel demonstration in Kiev in June calling for the creation of a 'Popular Union in Support of Perestroika' attracted some 500 people, and initiative groups also appeared in Vinnytsia, Khmel'nyts'kyi and elsewhere.[27]

The attempt proved premature, however. In contrast to the Baltic states or Transcaucasia, national communists who might have made common cause with the opposition were still thin on the ground. A handful of individuals, such as Bohdan Kotyk, head of the L'viv city CPU, and Ivan Salii, CPU first secretary in Podil', Kiev, were reportedly sympathetic to the campaign, but they were unable to act independently of their political masters in Kiev or Moscow.[28] Moreover, the nationalist opposition was still perceived as too radical by the majority of the population (and certainly by the authorities). Despite formulating their demands in terms of a loyal petition to Gorbachev, the demonstrators were soon dispersed by the militia.

Although it was advisable to claim to act in the name of Gorbachev's perestroika, in Ukraine this in itself was not enough. The UHU therefore stepped into the background,[29] and allowed semi-official bodies, most importantly the Kiev branch of the Writers' Union of Ukraine, to take the lead, as the authorities would find it much harder to suppress their activity.[30] In October and November 1988 initiative groups appeared in the Writers' Union (headed by Ivan Drach), the Institute of Literature

(Mykola Zhulyns'kyi and Vitalii Donchyk) and the Institute of Philosophy (Myroslav Popovych).[31] The Communist Party was in two minds about how to react. Its first instinct may have been to attempt to strangle Rukh at birth. However, Shcherbyts'kyi, already contemplating resignation as his health faded, was in no real state to lead the attack.[32] It was left to the ideology secretary Leonid Kravchuk to issue a warning at the January 1989 plenum of the Writers' Union against party members joining the initiative group. Some, such as the writer Borys Oliinyk, were duly dissuaded.[33] However at the same time Kravchuk reported back from the plenum that something had to be done to release the pressure building up from below, and that it would be preferable if any Popular Front were formed on the party's own terms. The publication of Rukh's draft programme was therefore delayed until February 1989 while the party attempted to make its impact felt.[34]

The version finally published in the main intelligentsia paper *Literaturna Ukraïna* conformed to most of the CPU's demands.[35] Rukh explicitly recognised both the CPU's constitutional leading role and the socialist character of Ukrainian society. Rukh would not seek to usurp the role of the party, but would act as a 'unifying link between the programme of perestroika proposed by the Party, and the initiative of the broad mass of the people'. In the crucial area of the national question, the programme confined itself to some safe remarks concerning the desirability of republican sovereignty, and concentrated instead on general issues of 'humanity, peace and progress', a rule of law and individual rights. At a subsequent roundtable meeting with CPU leaders in March 1989 Rukh's leaders came under immense pressure to confine themselves to a basically cultural programme, but Ivan Drach pointedly refused, citing Gorbachev's words of encouragement during his February visit to Kiev.[36]

Rukh's cautious approach was not due only to the heavy hand of the CPU. Rukh's founders were also aware of the need to create as broad-based a coalition as possible to counterbalance the influence of party conservatives. Ukrainian nationalists were always likely to provide the bedrock of the movement's membership, but Rukh also hoped to attract into its ranks CPU moderates, 'general democrats' (that is liberals and centrists) and if possible Russian-speaking Ukrainians or Russian radicals from eastern and southern Ukraine.[37] This bridge-building strategy had its roots in the ideological and generational changes of the 1960s, but it was also dictated by an anti-nationalist onslaught in the CPU-controlled mass media, which Rukh's then leadership feared would isolate Rukh from public opinion in the east and south.[38] This approach held steady until Rukh's first all-Ukrainian congress in

September 1989, by which time the movement had 280,000 members. A disproportionately high 29 per cent of these were from Galicia, but 19 per cent were from eastern and southern Ukraine, a much higher percentage than in subsequent years.[39]

The September congress formalised Rukh's existence as a 'general democratic' movement, which remained formally under the tutelage of the CPU.[40] Although Mykhailo Horyn' and Luk"ianenko from the UHU spoke in favour of independence, they remained in the minority. The programme adopted at the congress stated that Rukh 'conducts its activity according to the principles of humanism, democracy, glasnost, pluralism, social justice and *internationalism*, proceeding from the interests of all citizens of the republic, regardless of nationality'. Moreover, it declared that 'while advocating respect for national dignity and rejecting national nihilism, Rukh considers the propaganda of racial and national exclusivity and chauvinistic and nationalistic views to be incompatible with its principles'.[41] No mention was made of Ukrainian independence, although the sections on the economy and culture strongly emphasised the importance of creating true republican sovereignty.

The dominant moderate tone, however, concealed long-term divisions. For leading centrists such as Myroslav Popovych, Rukh's first public spokesman, the moderate line was necessary in itself.[42] Others, in particular Ivan Drach, Rukh's newly elected leader, had only deemphasised the national question because of massive pressure from the CPU. Moreover, Drach and the core of Rukh's leadership from the Writers' Union of Ukraine (WUU) saw themselves as tribunes for the Ukrainian language and culture, and tended to assume that a programme of national 'rebirth' would appeal as strongly to 'Russified' Ukrainians as to Ukrainophones. Once the hegemony of the CPU began to decline, the nationalists came increasingly to the fore.[43] Moreover, the radicals were more in tune with Rukh's rank and file. A poll of delegates to the congress showed that 73 per cent thought that Rukh's first priority should be to 'support the development of Ukrainian culture and language'. Only 46 per cent placed the 'solving of pressing economic problems' in first place. A simultaneous poll of the general population, however, showed a reverse order of priorities, with the highest number (44 per cent) mentioning economic problems and only 12 per cent language and culture.[44]

After the first congress events progressed rapidly. The promise of republican elections in March 1990, the final departure of Shcherbyts'kyi, the rapid move to political pluralism in the rest of the USSR and the collapse of communism in East-Central Europe dramatically transformed Rukh's vision of the politically possible and allowed the nationalists to seize control. Unity was maintained during the campaign for the March 1990 Ukrainian elections, allowing Rukh's front organisation the 'Democratic Bloc' to win 24 per cent of the seats, which, despite irregularities, was probably a fair reflection of Rukh's strength at the time (see chapter 5). However, after the elections, growing differences between nationalists and centrists could no longer be contained and, like Solidarity in Poland or Civic Forum in Czechoslovakia before it, Rukh fell victim to the political pluralism it had so forcibly advocated.[45]

Rukh becomes a nationalist front

Rukh underwent rapid radicalisation in 1990, particularly at the local level in Kiev and in western Ukraine.[46] Drach began to talk openly of his desire for full independence, and steered Rukh toward outright opposition to Gorbachev's new idea of a renegotiated Union Treaty between Moscow and the republics.[47] In eastern and southern Ukraine, on the other hand, local branches went into decline, many having in effect been created from above by the local CPU. In Kharkiv and in Donets'k Rukh split in two, largely along linguistic lines.[48] Further splits followed after the proposal to turn Rukh into a formal political party was rejected in March 1990.[49] Moderates feared that the nationalists would inevitably dominate such a party, but ironically the same effect was achieved by the general process of party formation (see pp. 68–75 below). Liberals and left-centrists tended to leave the movement altogether, whereas the new nationalist parties began a dual existence, half inside, half in parallel to Rukh.

October 1990 marked a decisive turning-point for the national movement. On the one hand, Rukh's second congress formalised its transformation from a catch-all movement into a nationalist front.[50] On the other hand, student hunger strikes and mass demonstrations brought thousands onto the streets of Kiev, but their relative failure and the subsequent growing popular apathy demonstrated that the nationalists did not have the powers of political mobilisation the authorities had feared they had had in January 1990.[51] The social profile of the congress delegates (now representing a total of 630,000 members) reflected the changed situation. The percentage of ethnic Ukrainians was up from 89 per cent to 95 per cent, and the proportion from the nationalist strongholds of Galicia and Kiev rose from 47 per cent to 57 per cent.[52] Only 1.5 per cent of delegates still belonged to the CPU or Komsomol, compared to 23 per cent in 1989, whereas almost half belonged to the new nationalist parties and the Ukrainian Language Society. Most delegates were male, middle-aged members of the Ukrainophone intelligentsia.[53]

Ivan Drach's keynote speech demanded 'the full sovereignty of the Ukrainian people, and a completely independent Ukrainian state', and called on the Ukrainian people to prepare for civil disobedience and 'extra-parliamentary action', as Gorbachev's and the CPSU's turn to the right since the summer of 1990 had created the real possibility of a 'Peking variant' in Ukraine (i.e. the use of force as in Tiananmen Square).[54] Mykhailo Horyn' also declared that 'parliamentary methods for achieving democratic laws are not enough'.[55] The words 'for perestroika' were dropped from the movement's title, and the congress declared that 'Rukh has naturally transformed itself from a movement for perestroika into a movement for the state independence of Ukraine, and become a real force in opposition to the CPSU and the totalitarian state-party system.'[56] The main aim of Rukh was now explicitly 'attaining Ukrainian sovereignty in accordance with the principles of the Declaration of Ukrainian State Sovereignty on 16 July 1990', and the full 'state independence of Ukraine'.[57] Furthermore, membership in Rukh was now banned to those who belonged to organisations whose 'leading organs were located outside the Ukrainian SSR' (obviously such a move was directed against the CPSU, but it left the door open for possible future reconciliation with a truly independent CPU). On the other hand, provision was made for collective representation of all the new non-communist parties on a new Political Council. Formally, the offer remained stillborn as centrist groups were no longer interested.[58] Informally, Rukh's leadership was dominated by the two main national-democratic parties, the Democrats and Republicans.

Political parties

The CPU succeeded in delaying the formal formation of political parties until after the republican elections in March 1990, but could no longer hold back the tide after article 6 of the USSR Constitution granting the Communist Party a monopoly on public political activity was abolished in February (a similar clause was excised from the Constitution of the Ukrainian SSR in October). Over a dozen new parties appeared in 1990–1.[59]

Left and centre

The left of the political spectrum was still occupied by the CPU, but the party helped to sponsor a series of movements to entice leftists away from Rukh, including the Fatherland Forum, the Union of Workers of Ukraine for Socialist Perestroika (a would-be all-Ukrainian 'Interfront') and a smaller equivalent in eastern Ukraine, the Donbas 'Intermovement'.[60] At this stage, however, they did not become as immediately successful as their counterparts in the Baltic republics. A report to the Ukrainian Politburo estimated that 8 per cent of workers were under the influence of the nationalists, 20 per cent supported the liberal-democrats and 20 per cent, mainly in the 'large industrial centres of the east', backed the anti-nationalist left, but 'more than 50 per cent' of workers remained resolutely apolitical.[61]

On the other hand, the liberals and centrists who had played a prominent part in Rukh in 1989 were now increasingly critical of Rukh's 'anti-democratic ideology and national ultra-radicalism',[62] and either drifted out of politics or found a home in the new centre and centre-left parties. The most important was the Party of Democratic Revival of Ukraine (PDRU), an alliance of Ukrainian liberals and Russophone intellectuals, who declared themselves 'the successors of Drahomanov',[63] and who in January 1991 organised a 'Democratic Congress' in Kharkiv with like-minded groups from Ukraine and other Soviet republics to promote the idea of a loose 'Confederation of Independent States' or 'European–Asian Commonwealth' as an alternative to both the USSR and Rukh's absolutist position on independence.[64]

The Ukrainian Republican Party

The first and also the best-organised nationalist party was the direct successor to the UHU, which renamed itself the Ukrainian Republican Party (URP) at a congress in April 1990.[65] Levko Luk"ianenko led the party until 1992, when he was succeeded by Mykhailo Horyn'. Both men were former political prisoners, as were a majority of the party's leadership, and their long years of clandestine struggle predisposed them toward creating a tightly disciplined, even conspiratorial, party, designed to act as a nationalist vanguard.[66] (At the party's founding congress V"iacheslav Chornovil accused his former colleagues of 'creating a deeply centralised organisation of the Bolshevik–Fascist type', and disassociated himself from the new party.)[67] Indeed, on two occasions in 1990–1, following the arrest of the party's deputy leader Stepan Khmara on trumped-up charges of assault in November 1990 and during the August 1991 coup, the party seriously contemplated returning to an underground existence.[68]

The URP, like the UHU before it, pursued Trotskyist 'entryist' tactics, seeking to 'displace the liberalism of certain informal organisations, and give them a [more] radical direction'.[69] These tactics succeeded in pulling Rukh and other organisations to the right (seven Rukh secretaries were URP members, as were 13 per cent of delegates at the 1990 Rukh congress),[70] but provoked widespread resentment and helped to split Rukh in 1992 (see pp. 75–6 below).[71] Moreover, although the party was the direct successor to the Ukrainian Helsinki Group, its commitment to civic nationalism and working within the institutions of the Ukrainian SSR was less than total. The party always had a strong radical wing, which urged the leadership to embrace Dontsovite nationalism and concentrate on extra-parliamentary politics.[72] The leadership's commitment to 'democratic nationalism' prevailed at a theoretical conference called to debate the party's ideology in February 1991 and at the party's second congress in June 1991,[73] but the party always had an ambiguous attitude toward what even Luk"ianenko characterised as 'an occupying administration'.[74]

However, the URP's perception of its place in Ukrainian politics changed utterly after the declaration of Ukrainian independence in August 1991. Most of the party's leading radicals, including deputy leader Stepan Khmara, were purged at the third party congress in May 1992, and the URP sought to redefine itself as a party of state nationalism and 'respectable conservatism', dedicated to playing an active role in the process of building a new Ukrainian nation-state.[75] The party embraced Lypyns'kyi as its ideological mentor and stressed the importance of building strong political institutions and coopting existing elites to underpin Ukraine's fragile statehood.[76] If anything, the party now swung to the opposite extreme of providing relatively uncritical support for the Ukrainian authorities, especially Leonid Kravchuk's presidential apparat and the security and defence ministries. On the other hand, the party's long history and semi-conspiratorial past provided it with the organisational strength to survive when many other parties fell by the wayside, and the party remained the main rival to Rukh as the dominant national-democratic organisation. The URP had 13,000 members in 1994 and twelve deputies in the new Ukrainian Parliament, the same number as the UHU originally elected in 1990.[77]

The Democratic Party of Ukraine (DPU)

The second main nationalist party to emerge in 1990 was the Democratic Party of Ukraine (DPU). While the URP leadership was dominated by former political prisoners and its rank and file by workers and radical teachers,[78] the DPU was above all the party of the *shistdesiatnyky* and the establishment Ukrainian intelligentsia.[79] One of the party's leaders, the poet Dmytro Pavlychko, went so far as to describe the DPU as 'the brain of our nation' in June 1991.[80]

In 1990 the DPU seemed well placed to become the leading party on the Ukrainian right. The party's draft manifesto, published in March 1990, was signed by a virtual who's who of the Ukrainian intelligentsia, and sought to maximise the party's appeal as a 'general democratic party', committed to a civic state and a social democratic economy.[81] The party's leaders repeatedly condemned 'nationalism based on the Nietzscheanism of Dontsov', and claimed to be a centrist party that 'understands by Ukrainian patriotism not only patriotism for Ukrainians, but also for Ukrainian citizens of any other nationality'.[82] Yurii Badz'o, the veteran dissident who led the party from 1990 to 1992, defined the party's 'vocation as performing the role of a political centre, balancing the turbulent political primitives to the right and left'.[83] However, the party always leaned to the right. Proposals in 1990–1 to unite with the centrist Party of Democratic Revival were rejected because the latter contained too many 'people of a cosmopolitan direction, indifferent or even hostile [chuzhy] to the idea of Ukrainian national revival'.[84] The DPU's position on key issues such as Ukrainianisation, opposition to federalism and in latter years opposition to the CIS was little different to the URP.[85]

By 1992 therefore the DPU could be attacked by liberals for becoming 'a mono-national party', which had moved too far to the right.[86] Structurally, however, the DPU was a shambles, and its near-disappearance by 1994 was symptomatic of the general organisational weakness of the Ukrainian intelligentsia in particular and Ukrainian nationalism in general. Despite being led by well-known figures such as Ivan Drach, Dmytro Pavlychko, Yurii Badz'o and Volodymyr Yavorivs'kyi, the DPU was never equal to the sum of its parts. It was therefore increasingly forced to take second place to the better-organised URP. After the DPU's second congress in December 1992 the issue of union between the two parties was endlessly discussed, but shelved at the third party congress two years later, with the debate only serving further to encourage the DPU's political passivity.[87] The DPU never had more than 3,000 members and in the 1994 elections collapsed to a rump of three deputies (twenty-three deputies claimed allegiance to the party in the 1990 Parliament, but all were originally elected as independents).

The revival of traditional ultra-nationalism

Although the national movement in the late 1980s was dominated by national-democrats such as Drach and Chornovil who had been prominent *shistdesiatnyky*, the ambiguous nature of the supposed ideological revolution of the 1960s was reflected in the reemergence of Dontsovite nationalism as early as 1988–9. Even the relatively radical Ukrainian Helsinki Union was unable to maintain unity amongst the right, and a series of defections from its ranks led to the formation of no fewer than five radical splinter groups by mid-1990 (the Ukrainian Christian-Democratic Front, Ukrainian National Party, Ukrainian People's Democratic Party, Ukrainian Peasant-Democratic Party and the Organisation for Statehood and Independence of Ukraine, or DSU). All were largely confined to Galicia, although some also had a handful of supporters in Kiev.[88]

The main point of disagreement between the national-democrats and ultra-nationalists before 1991 was the latter's desire to copy the tactics of radical Estonian and Georgian nationalists and treat all Soviet institutions as part of an 'occupying regime', and refuse to 'collaborate' either with Moscow or with 'imperial' institutions in Kiev. Negotiations with Russians were deemed a waste of time because in Stepan Bandera's words, 'there can be no common language with Muscovites [*Moskaly*]', whilst participation in Soviet-organised elections was immoral as 'one generation in a state of subjugation [cannot] pledge the destiny of the coming generation'.[89] The ultra-nationalists tended to see the minutiae of the new democratic politics as a distraction from the basic issue, arguing that 'the cardinal question of today is not the conflict between democracy and communism, but the struggle between nations – the struggle of the Russians for domination, and of the non-Russians for liberation'.[90]

At a special congress in June–July 1990 most of the ultra-nationalist parties united to form the Ukrainian Inter-party Assembly (UIA), which then began a petition campaign, modelled on the Congress of Estonia movement, to restore the pre-Soviet government of 1917–20.[91] Once 50 per cent of the population had signed, the UIA planned to convene a national assembly that would proclaim the revival of the Ukrainian People's Republic and seek to usurp power from the Ukrainian SSR (see also chapter 6). The UIA claimed to have collected 2.8 million signatures by April 1991, but this could not be verified, although one respected source accepted a figure of 729,000 signatures by September 1990. However, more than half of these (450,000) were from L'viv oblast alone, and the total number of signatures collected represented only 1.4 per cent of the Ukrainian population, compared to the 93 per cent of Estonia's 'eligible citizens' (some 850,000) who signed in support of the Congress of Estonia movement.[92] The UIA's campaign was nevertheless significant as the national-democratic mainstream now had to worry for the first time about significant competition from the right, especially as many members of Rukh and the URP were sympathetic to the petition campaign.[93] The UIA therefore helped both to stretch the nationalist political spectrum and to shift its centre of political gravity to the right (Rukh was pulled to the right by the URP, which was pulled to the right by the UIA). As is often the case in nationalist movements, despite their liberal intentions moderate parties were compelled to compete with radicals for the favour of the core national group, rather than risk appealing across group boundaries and being outbid to the right.[94] Therefore from now on the national-democrats would be forced to pay less attention to wooing eastern and southern Ukraine.

Moreover, the UIA itself moved further to the right as it fell under the control of radical student activists from the Ukrainian Nationalist Union who forced out more moderate parties.[95] By 1991 the UIA, now led by Yurii Shukhevych, long-term political prisoner and son of the UPA's wartime military commander, was seeking to model itself on an idealised version of an original and 'pure' Dontsovite OUN, and posed as the potential leader of a Ukrainian 'new order', capable of 'standing against social chaos' and 'building a great nation, which will not adapt to circumstance, but will dictate its own terms to the world'.[96] One of the UIA's leaders, quoting Nietzsche's Zarathustra, declared that 'I call you not to peace but to war. The war started by our ancestors [for freedom from Russia] has not finished even today. It will continue using every possible method and form, as long as one of us remains alive.'[97]

Other ultra-radical groups kept their distance from the UIA, but shared many of the same ideological precepts. Significantly, however, would-be clerical and rural nationalist parties were both failures, illustrating the problems in building or reviving civil society, even in western Ukraine. The Ukrainian Christian Democratic Front (actually a mono-confessional ginger group of Uniate activists) became a party (UCDP) in April 1990, but suffered a series of damaging splits in 1992, and was eclipsed by its offshoot, the more moderate and ecumenical Christian Democratic Party of Ukraine.[98] Although Christian agrarian populist parties were common throughout East-Central Europe between the wars (UNDO in Galicia, the Ukrainian National Union in Transcarpathia) and several were revived after 1989 (the Hungarian Smallholders' Party, the Bulgarian Agrarian National Union), bitter inter-confessional struggle in western Ukraine after 1990 made the formation of an overtly clerical party impossible (see pp. 86–8 below).

The difficulty of nationalist mobilisation in the countryside outside western Ukraine was also illustrated by the complete lack of success of a second group, the Ukrainian Peasant-Democratic Party (UPDP) established in June 1990.[99] Despite initial support from prominent national-democrats such as Ihor Yukhnovs'kyi, the party stagnated at a membership of a mere 4,000 and became something of a one-man show for the idiosyncratic writer Serhii Plachynda.[100] As argued in chapters 1 and 2, outside western Ukraine, rural nationalism had little chance to develop before the imposition of Soviet rule (and the calamity of the Great Famine). Moreover, even the party's own leaders characterised their target constituency as in effect an 'internal colony' of the Soviet system, an ageing cohort of rural labourers, totally dependent on collective farm chairmen for their livelihood, welfare benefits and even, because all farm machinery was owned by the collective farms, the very ability to till the land.[101] Although 32 per cent of the Ukrainian population remained on the land in late 1994, only 2 per cent of the land was in private hands.[102] The only significant political force in the Ukrainian countryside (outside Galicia) was therefore the Agrarian Union (Selians'ka spilka), formed by collective farm chairmen and heads of agro-industry on the basis of rural Communist Party organisations in September 1990,[103] which became the Agrarian Party of Ukraine in January 1992 (see chapter 4). In the 1994 parliamentary elections the Peasant-Democratic Party received a derisory 5,928 votes compared to the Agrarian Party's 795,642 (the latter elected eighteen deputies in the spring, and a total of forty-eight eventually joined its parliamentary faction).

A third independent fringe group was the Organisation for Statehood and Independence of Ukraine (DSU), which also consciously modelled itself on Bandera's OUN (several of its founder members had also belonged to the Ukrainian National Front in the 1960s), and regarded even the émigré OUN-r as apostates to the true faith. Although always a fringe group, which split in 1993, the party thrived on the notoriety of its increasingly rabid attacks on national-democrats, and its Russophobia and anti-Semitism. The party argued that 'the main reason for Ukraine's [current] mess is the absence of Ukrainian leadership, Ukrainian in origin and in spirit', in which respect the 'Judeophile dissidents' were just as bad as former party apparatchiks.[104] The DSU's notoriety was not matched by political influence, however, although it was notable for being often the first group to raise previously taboo subjects, condemning 'the spread of non-Ukrainian stock on Cossack land', and calling for the 'ethnic cleansing' of Ukraine's national minorities and the 'creation of an atmosphere of social discomfort for Russians' to encourage their rapid departure from Ukraine.[105]

Despite party divisions, certain key themes united most members of the ultra-nationalist right. One was the romanticisation of the past history of the nationalist movement. Far right publications were soon awash with reprints of Dontsov's works and material eulogising the OUN and UPA (a tendency that soon spread to the national-democratic press).[106] Second was the boycott of the 'occupation' institutions of the Ukrainian SSR and contempt for its 'democratic' procedures. Third was the revival of Mikhnovs'kyi's twin slogans: 'Ukraine for the Ukrainians',[107] and a 'Ukrainian Independent United State!', where 'united' (*soborna*) meant a Greater Ukraine in its maximum ethnographic boundaries, stretching 'from the Sian to the Caucasus under the black and red flag' (the colours of the OUN).[108] Not surprisingly, therefore, the ultra-nationalists undermined the best efforts of the national-democrats to appear as born-again liberals, especially as they were happy to cooperate with the far right when convenient, and the anti-nationalist press began to fill up with material crudely lumping together the extremist fringe and the moderate mainstream.[109]

After independence: political realignment

The growing tendency toward political pluralism and internal disagreement within the nationalist movement was placed into sharper focus by the unexpectedly sudden achievement of independence in August 1991 and by the elections to the Ukrainian presidency that autumn. For most nationalists, independence changed everything. The far right was forced to reconsider its boycott tactics, although their candidate Yurii Shukhevych was unable to obtain the necessary 100,000 signatures to place his name on the ballot. The national democrats, on the other hand, were split over whether to oppose the national communist chairman of Parliament, Leonid Kravchuk, whom many regarded as having delivered independence (see chapter 4).[110] V"iacheslav Chornovil ran a strongly anti-communist campaign, but was challenged by Levko Luk"ianenko and Ihor Yukhnovs'kyi, who emphasised the need to deepen cooperation with the likes of Kravchuk in order to secure national independence.

Not surprisingly the result was a fractious campaign and a divided opposition vote (see chapter 5). Moreover, Kravchuk's overwhelming victory with 61.6 per cent of the vote and the simultaneous 90.3 per cent vote for independence on 1 December 1991 brought divisions to a head. Rukh's more nationalist faction regarded Kravchuk's victory as an endorsement of their programme and called for the movement to 'go over to constructive work, and assist the state-building activity of the president, supreme council and government',[111] and condemned Chornovil's continuing anti-communist crusade.[112] A formal schism was narrowly averted at the third Rukh congress in spring 1992,[113] but in August the right wing of Rukh split away to form the Congress of

National-Democratic Forces (CNDF), leaving Chornovil to take control of a rump Rukh at the movement's fourth congress in December (when Rukh finally turned itself into a political party).[114] A short-lived attempt in January and February 1993 to reunite all nationalist forces in an 'Anti-Communist Anti-Imperial Front' soon disappeared without trace.[115]

Chornovil's Rukh claimed a re-registered membership of 50,400, plus two million 'supporters' (who were required to do no more than sign a statement of sympathy with Rukh's aims and values) and 100,000 collective associate members belonging to groups such as the Union of Ukrainian Women, Memorial and the Association of Farmers.[116] The CNDF on the other hand was dominated by the URP (the DPU and other satellite parties also joined, but were a declining force; member parties had a combined membership of little over 20,000, but 13,000 of this was the URP).[117] Although the difference between Rukh and the CNDF was partly about tactics and personalities, it also reflected ideological strains in the national-democratic camp, with the CNDF further to the right.[118] Rukh remained closer to the liberal nationalism of the 1960s and continued to emphasise anti-communism, to the extent of calling for the Communist Party to face a Ukrainian 'Nuremberg-2'.[119] The CNDF remained within the same political tradition, but the most distinctive points in its programme referred to 'the national character of Ukrainian statehood' and 'the strengthening of the Ukrainian nation on her ethnic territory'.[120] Furthermore, the CNDF accepted Lypyns'kyi's argument that governing elites had to be won over to the national cause and gave relatively uncritical support to 'national communists' such as Leonid Kravchuk during his tenure as president, cooperating closely with the presidential apparat through the medium of Bohdan Ternopils'kyi, a leading member of both bodies.[121] On the other hand, both groups crept further to the right in 1992–5, reaching common ground on most foreign and defence policy issues, on Ukrainianisation and opposition to a federal Ukraine (see chapters 6 and 7). Rukh therefore suffered further splits in 1993–4, with the defection of many leading liberals, disillusioned with the lack of effective economic reform under Kravchuk and the rise of the far right (see pp. 77–80 below). They formed the New Wave group in L'viv,[122] which successfully elected four deputies in the spring 1994 elections, and in the new Parliament organised the centrist Reforms faction (see chapter 5).

Russophone Ukrainians and liberal centrists were also forced to rethink their political strategy after independence. The main centrist group, the PDRU, was increasingly split between rightists such as

Oleksandr Yemets', who wanted to build bridges with the national-democrats, and Russophiles, led by the deputy speaker of Parliament Vladimir Griniov (Volodymyr Hryn'ov), who circulated a manifesto entitled 'On the Dangers of the Politics of Isolationism' at the party's third congress in Luhans'k in May 1992.[123] The same uncertainties plagued the New Ukraine movement, a 'union of politicians and industrialists' set up by the PDRU and other centrist parties in January 1992.[124] Moreover, Ukrainian independence made cooperation with their natural allies, Russian liberals, difficult. The key problem for New Ukraine, however, was that its target constituency, Russophone Ukrainians and moderate Russians in the east and south, remained amorphous and difficult to mobilise politically. Under Soviet rule Russophone Ukrainians had never needed to give precise definition to their collective identity, which, in combination with a free-rider problem caused by sheer weight of numbers, created powerful barriers to successful collective action.

Despite initially attracting fifty-eight deputies to its banner in early 1992, New Ukraine never developed into a mass movement and was moribund by 1993.[125] Similar difficulties beset New Ukraine's successor, the Interregional Block for Reforms (IBR) formed in January 1994.[126] Although Russophone voters were instrumental in winning the 1994 election for Leonid Kuchma, Russophone elites found it difficult to translate that general support into creating a powerful political organisation.

After independence: the new right

The Ukrainian National Assembly-Ukrainian Self-Defence Force (UNA-UNSO)

After 1991 the old OUN strategy of refusing to recognise the legitimacy of the Ukrainian SSR was redundant, as the latter had metamorphosed into an independent Ukrainian state. The most interesting example of attempted adaptation was provided by the leading ultra-nationalist organisation, the Ukrainian Inter-party Assembly, which changed its name to the Ukrainian National Assembly (UNA) at a special congress in September 1991, and began to distance itself from 'romantic nationalism' and the arcane disputes of the 1940s.[127] The UNA's goal remained a Dontsovite *natsiokratiia* or authoritarian nation-state, but they were happy to elicit support across ethnic and linguistic barriers. According to the UNA leadership, 'what is important today is not whether people speak pure Ukrainian or with some accent or mixture of

Russian [*surzhyk*] but how people think, what ideas they believe in'.[128] The number of 'pure' Ukrainians was too small, and a political programme designed for them alone was likely to find support only in Galicia. Given the lack of national consciousness amongst the majority of the population, hostility toward the Galician 'Piedmont' and the absence of other suitable instruments, only the state could serve as 'an instrument for forming the nation'.[129] The final part of the UNA's intellectual gymnastics was the replacement of the simplistic slogan 'Away from Moscow!' with the idea that Ukraine should seek to become a regional superpower by seizing back from Russia the leadership of all *Slavia Orthodoxa* that it supposedly enjoyed at the time of Kievan Rus' (see chapter 7). How the Galician Uniates fitted into this world-view was not explained.

The UNA were also skilful populists. The party's election slogan in 1994 was 'our people are used to living in a great state. We will make Ukraine a great state again, so that people don't have to change their habits.'[130] The UNA therefore mined a rich vein of nostalgia for past 'strength, order and prosperity', and combined it with a nationalist programme for a Nietzschean 'revaluation of values', the establishment of a national corporate state to provide law and order, a protectionist route to national economic recovery and a strong hand against internal 'fifth columnists'.[131] To help begin the task, the UNA founded its own paramilitary wing, the Ukrainian Self-Defence Force (in Ukrainian, UNSO), modelled on similar militias active in Ukraine in 1917–21 and 1941–4,[132] which quickly gained notoriety for its participation in the Dniester and Abkhazian conflicts and for violent confrontation with Russian and Crimean organisations at home, as well as a degree of popularity by claiming, like the IRA, to act as the defender of the common man against 'Mafiosi'.[133] Despite the passing of a law in November 1993 imposing stiff sentences for the organisers of illegal paramilitary units, the UNSO carried on its activities. The UNSO claimed to have 5,000 under arms, and the UNA a membership of 14,000. Three leaders of the party were elected as deputies in the 1994 elections.[134]

Congress of Ukrainian Nationalists (KUN)

If the UNA were ideologically innovative, the Congress of Ukrainian Nationalists, established by the émigré OUN-r after its belated return to active Ukrainian politics in 1992, deliberately harked back to the 1940s. So long as the Communist Party continued to dominate public political life in Ukraine the various branches of the OUN in the diaspora (see chapter 2) were reluctant to return to open political activity, although arguably this hesitation cost them a year or two's crucial momentum compared to similar organisations such as the Armenian Dashnaks who established themselves as the main opposition force in the 1990 Armenian elections. In 1989–91 the Ukrainian émigrés' activity remained indirect. They financed extensive reprints of the works of Dontsov and other mid-century nationalists, and attempted to work through front organisations. The Banderite OUN-r chose other would-be ultra-radical parties, such as the Ukrainian National Party, the DSU and UIA, but the latter either proved to be ephemeral and/or marginal groups, or were unwilling to act as the OUN-r's puppets.[135] The more moderate and national-democratic OUN-s (the successor to the Mel'ny-kites) on the other hand backed first the Ukrainian Helsinki Union and then the Ukrainian Republican Party.

After independence, however, the OUN-r changed tactics and set up the Congress of Ukrainian Nationalists (KUN) at two congresses in October 1992 and July 1993 (the OUN-s also held a public congress near Kiev in May 1993, but its impact was much less than that of the better organised and richer OUN-r).[136] The original aim of KUN was to use the OUN's historical prestige and financial clout to unite all far right groups under one roof, possibly later linking up with Rukh to form one catch-all national party. Additionally, for some of the OUN-r's older members, still used to the years of clandestine struggle, it was also a more attractive substitute to the OUN's direct reentry into Ukrainian politics. KUN therefore initially attempted to present a modernised and respectable face and the party programme made all the right references to democratic values and a civic state.[137]

However, KUN's émigré leaders retained the habits of conspiratorial discipline they had formed in the diaspora, while their domestic recruits (primitive nationalists such as Serhii Zhyzhko, who had been thrown out of both the URP and DSU) ironically wanted to recreate an idealised version of Bandera's OUN.[138] KUN therefore soon reverted to type and veered off to the right.[139] Nevertheless, KUN enjoyed the prestige of direct association with the wartime underground and considerable financial backing from the diaspora, and became a powerful force in Galicia in 1993–4. It was easily able to see off the challenge from a rival home-grown would-be successor to the OUN, named 'OUN in Ukraine', formed in L'viv in January 1993 to campaign for all three factions of the OUN to unite and return to Ukraine.[140] KUN elected eight members as deputies in the 1994 elections, and 'supported' the election of a further eight. The KUN group adopted the informal name '30 June' after the date of the symbolic OUN declaration of Ukrainian independence in L'viv in 1941. The organisation claimed 15,600 members in spring 1995.[141]

Smaller groups

Other ultra-nationalist groups worthy of mention include, first, the Ukrainian Conservative Republican Party (UCRP), led by the veteran dissident Stepan Khmara after his expulsion from the Ukrainian Republican Party in 1992.[142] Despite the party's small size (Khmara claimed a membership of 3,500), Khmara kept it going by his high-profile populism, outspoken Russophobia and advocacy of a nuclear Ukraine.[143] Khmara was also parliamentary spokesman for the Union of Officers of Ukraine (see pp. 81–2 below). Khmara and a colleague, Roman Kuper, were elected deputies in 1994 (Khmara having defeated the URP leader Mykhailo Horyn' in a working-class district in L'viv), but after Kuper's untimely death the party was once again little more than a personal vehicle for Khmara.

The UNSO were not the only paramilitary organisation in Ukraine. The even more radical Social-National Party of Ukraine (SNPU) first appeared in L'viv in 1991 amongst radical students who provided 'escorts' at nationalist rallies, and rose to prominence in summer 1992 as the shock troops for the 'Nationalist Block' (a local alliance of ultra-nationalist groups led by Valentyn Moroz, Ivan Dziuba's critic in the 1970s), which unsuccessfully attempted a violent takeover of the local branch of Rukh in October.[144] Like the UNSO, the SNPU's black-shirted followers have gained easy publicity for their torch-lit processions and violent attacks on political rivals, but the SNPU, which like the DSU only admits ethnic Ukrainians, is more traditionally Dontsovite in its reliance on Russophobia and anti-Semitism. The party's key programmatic slogan calls for the militarisation of Ukrainian life through the transformation of Galicia into the 'Prussia' rather than the 'Piedmont' of Ukraine.[145] The SNPU's twenty-two candidates in the 1994 elections won 49,000 votes, and seven members of the party were local deputies in 1995 in L'viv oblast.

The L'viv Nationalist Block also had links with the All-Ukrainian Popular Movement of Ukraine (in Ukrainian, VNRU), established at a congress in Kharkiv in February 1993 after yet another split at the fourth Rukh congress the preceding December.[146] The 'All-Ukrainian' Rukh was organised by members of the Congress of National-Democratic Forces, Mykola Porovs'kyi and Larysa Skoryk, who hoped to confuse the electorate and draw support away from Rukh proper.

Nationalist civil society

As well as political parties, the foundations of a nationalist civil society also appeared in the late 1980s and early 1990s. Many new social groups were of course not nationalist. They are not considered here. Nor is it argued that nationalist civil organisations and pressure groups amounted to a fully fledged network of powerful non-state institutions (the demise of the communist state does not necessarily lead to a corresponding flowering of civil society).[147] Nevertheless, many have exercised a powerful influence on the new Ukrainian state.

Prosvita

Reference has already been made to the Ukrainian Language Society, founded under official sponsorship in 1989 on the understanding that it confine itself to a largely cultural agenda. As with Rukh, however, the Communist Party's declining powers allowed the society to slip the bonds of official control and move quickly to the right. In October 1991 it renamed itself Prosvita in imitation of its nineteenth- and early twentieth-century predecessor (see chapter 2).[148]

The name change symbolised a broadening of functions from the dissemination of Ukrainian-language media to a new emphasis on political lobbying and promoting the Ukrainianisation of public life. The 1989 Ukrainian Languages Law stated that Ukrainian, as the new state language, should become the language of bureaucratic and pedagogic communication, but envisaged an extremely slow timetable of five to ten years to achieve this (see chapter 6). Prosvita therefore became the leading advocate of the law's more vigorous implementation, especially after a split in 1992 left the organisation under the control of a more radical faction led by people's deputy Pavlo Movchan.[149] Prosvita's other leading figure, Anatolii Pohribnyi, was appointed deputy education minister in 1992 and became something of a bête noire in eastern and southern Ukraine, where attacks on his 'Galicianisation' policy led to his downfall in 1994 (see chapter 6). Prosvita was the largest non-party nationalist organisation in Ukraine, with 105,000 registered individual members on 1 January 1993.[150]

Defence

The Union of Officers of Ukraine (UOU) was established at two congresses in July and November 1991.[151] After its original aim, the establishment of independent Ukrainian armed forces, was achieved in

December 1991, the union has sought to promote the Ukrainianisation of the armed forces and a strongly nationalist line in defence and foreign policy (see chapter 7). In 1992–4 the UOU came under the increasing influence of the far right, and began to demand a veto over appointments and dismissals in the armed forces, a 'quota' for UOU members at the highest level and the replacement of the 'corrupt and the compromised' with 'nationally conscious officers'.[152] An attempt by the radical faction, backed by the UNA-UNSO, to take over the union was only narrowly defeated at the fourth UOU congress in April 1993.[153]

The UOU sees itself as the patriotic core of the new Ukrainian armed forces, and many of its leading members assumed key positions in the ministry of defence, particularly in the so-called Social-Psychological Service until its influence was reined in late in 1993. Nevertheless, the UOU has continued to court controversy by its high political profile. Forty of its members ran in the spring 1994 parliamentary elections and five were elected, along with two independents closely linked to the UOU, Volodymyr Muliava, head of the Social-Psychological Service from 1992 to 1993 and Borys Kozhyn, former head of the Ukrainian navy. Claims for the union's membership have varied between 25,000 and 70,000.[154]

Other organisations in the defence field include the Committee of Soldiers' Mothers of Ukraine (which played a key role in frustrating the draft for the Soviet Army in 1990–1), and the Union of Officers of the Ukrainian Diaspora (Za povernennia na bat'kivshchynu), set up in Kiev in July 1992 under the sponsorship of the UNA-UNSO to campaign for ethnic Ukrainians serving elsewhere in the former USSR to be allowed to return and replace non-Ukrainians in the armed forces.[155]

Trade unions

The first cracks in Ukraine's monolithic communist-era unions began to appear in 1989, when the miners' strikes of that year left behind a network of informal workers' committees in the Donbas. Thereafter many leading nationalists sought to copy the example of Jacek Kuroń's Workers' Defence Committee in Poland and construct an alliance between intellectuals and workers by coopting or influencing such committees. However, as in 1917–20 or 1941–4, Ukrainian nationalists found it difficult to garner working-class support outside western Ukraine (which is disproportionately rural in any case). No Ukrainian equivalent of Solidarity was ever established.

In L'viv a relatively successful independent strike committee was formed by Stepan Khmara of the UHU as early as the autumn of

1988,[156] but the attempt in June 1991 by Khmara and other leading nationalists such as Larysa Skoryk and Anatolii Lupynis of the UIA to help create a national equivalent, the All-Ukrainian Organisation of Workers' Solidarity (VOST), was largely a failure.[157] VOST's specifically political agenda alienated most workers, especially after it fell increasingly under the influence of the ultra-radical Inter-Party Assembly. VOST never attracted more than 100,000 to 200,000 members, despite original claims of between one and three million supporters.

The vast majority of workers remained in the old official trade unions (some twenty million),[158] or joined the new independent trade unions. By the end of 1993 the latter had some 110,000 members in the railways, ports and airlines, but remained resolutely apolitical, despite overtures from Rukh.[159] The independent miners' unions in the Donbas, on the other hand, were strongly anti-nationalist.[160] Nationalists and trade unionists could still make common cause on occasion, as in September 1993 when a coordinated campaign of protest was instrumental in forcing the Ukrainian Parliament to concede pre-term presidential and parliamentary elections, but on the whole the two had little contact. Indeed, after independence, many nationalists began to denounce as 'destructive' the kind of strike action they had supported back in 1990–1.[161]

Industry

For similar reasons it is impossible to describe any of Ukraine's industrial groups as nationalist per se. All are sectional lobbies first and foremost. Nevertheless some have adopted contextually nationalist positions.

The parent industrial body in Ukraine is the Ukrainian Union of Industrialists and Managers (UUIM), formed in late 1991 under the patronage of then deputy premier Vasyl' Yevtukhov, and taken over by former prime minister Leonid Kuchma in December 1993.[162] The UUIM was analogous to, and had close links with, the heavy industry lobby formed by Arkadii Volskii in Russia in the early 1990s, and therefore represented those state managers who favoured the maintenance or restoration of close links with Russia. Indeed in eastern and southern Ukraine, an offshoot of the UUIM, the Interregional Association of Industrialists formed in November 1992, has openly lobbied for some form of economic union between Ukraine and Russia.[163]

Two other industrial lobbies could be described as functionally nationalist, however. One, the Union of Independent Industrialists, established in February 1993 and led by Oleksandr Yemel'ianov,

President Kravchuk's adviser on economics, tended to support national-protectionist policies. The other was the National Association of Businessmen of Ukraine, set up in March 1993, which favoured the creation of a national market economy oriented more toward European markets and was close to liberal national-democrats such as Volodymyr Lanovyi.[164]

Youth

Youth, and in particular student, politics in Ukraine is as fractious as its adult counterpart.[165] A variety of nationalist youth organisations emerged in the early 1990s, but none had more than a few thousand members (except in L'viv, where the Komsomol simply renamed itself the Democratic Union of L'viv Youth). After the initial euphoria of 1989–91, Ukrainian youth tended to become either apolitical or ultra-radical,[166] but in Galicia at least high levels of ideological commitment compensated for lack of numbers.

As with adult politics, the first step in the late 1980s was to revive supposedly apolitical organisations, such as the Sich and Plast scout and sporting groups (although, like their nineteenth-century predecessors, they functioned in practice as covers for explicitly nationalist activity).[167] The first openly nationalist group was the Union of Independent Ukrainian Youth, established by younger members of the Helsinki Union in May 1990. However, like Rukh, it soon split along ideological lines, although youthful impatience meant that the process took only a few months. The radicals formed the Dontsovite Ukrainian Nationalist Union, where the future leaders of the UNA-UNSO learned their political trade. The rival Union of Ukrainian Youth on the other hand was broadly national-democratic, as was the Kiev-based Union of Ukrainian Students, which organised the October 1990 student hunger strikes.[168] Both were close to the URP.

Predictably, the radicals tended to embrace simplistic slogans and violently attacked every compromise made by the national-democrats.[169] Noisy public demonstrations and unrestrained Russophobia won them easy publicity. Moreover, ultra-nationalist parties such as the Ukrainian National Assembly consciously sought to attract radical youth, who formed the mainstay of paramilitary groups like the UNSO and Social-National Party. On the other hand, the existence of a moderate strain amongst Ukrainian youth should not be overlooked. In L'viv student activists who styled themselves the 'Third Republic' were instrumental in helping to found the liberal nationalist New Wave movement in late 1993.[170]

Diaspora

In the early 1990s Ukrainian nationalists began attempting to forge links with Ukrainians in both the eastern and western diaspora (6.8 million Ukrainians lived in other Soviet republics according to the 1989 Soviet census, and approximately 3 million lived elsewhere in the world).[171] Small Ukrainian organisations began to appear in Poland, Slovakia, Latvia, Belarus, Moldova, the Kuban' and elsewhere even before 1991,[172] but real, if limited, progress was only made after Ukrainian independence. In January 1992 the authorities in Kiev sponsored a Congress of Ukrainians of the Former USSR, followed by an All-World Forum of Ukrainians in August of the same year. As a result of the latter, Ivan Drach was appointed to head a Ukrainian All-World Coordinating Council, which held its first congress in January 1993.[173] Official encouragement has also prompted the Ukraïna society, originally established in 1960 as the Society for Cultural Relations with Ukrainians Abroad as a means of depoliticising relations with the American and European diaspora, to remodel itself as a more nationally conscious organisation and to turn its attention eastward as well as westward.

Partly as a result of prompting from Kiev, around fifty Ukrainian groups united in Moscow in October 1993 to form the Federation of Ukrainians in Russia.[174] The Federation then played a key role in setting up the Congress of National [i.e. ethnic minority] Associations of Russia in April 1994, which sided with Yegor Gaidar's United Democrat coalition in the December 1995 Russian elections. However, both groups have found the authorities in Moscow relatively impervious to their lobbying efforts, and overall levels of mobilisation amongst the diaspora have proved disappointing (see chapter 7).

Miscellaneous

Other nationalist organisations include the Union of Ukrainian Women, officially registered in February 1992 and led by the poet Atena Pashko (V"iacheslav Chornovil's wife), which is a collective associate member of Rukh.[175] The organisation Helsinki-90 took over the Ukrainian Helsinki Union's functions as a civil rights watchdog after the latter transformed itself into the Republican Party in 1990, while the All-Ukrainian Society of the Repressed acts as a pressure group to defend the rights of former political prisoners.[176] The All-Ukrainian Brotherhood of Veterans of the OUN-UPA, established in L'viv in April 1991, has worked to rehabilitate the 'national heroes' of the 1940s and early 1950s, both in terms of historiography and material restitution (pension rights, etc.).[177] A small

Association of Ukrainian Farmers was formed in 1991 to press for land privatisation and the revival of the Ukrainian village.[178]

Religion

Until the early 1990s, Ukraine lacked a true national Church. All parishes in Ukraine remained under the jurisdiction of the Russian Orthodox Church (ROC); the Ukrainian Autocephalous Orthodox Church (UAOC) existed only in exile after 1944, although after its forcible dissolution in 1946–9 the Uniate Church retained both an underground network and the loyalty of many nominally 'Orthodox' priests.[179] Although the fate of the Uniates received more publicity, the suppression of the UAOC was arguably equally important as it left the majority of Ukrainians once again under the common roof of *Slavia Orthodoxa*, depriving them of a crucial cultural marker with which to distinguish themselves from other East Slavs.

The Uniates

Both Churches were quick to take the opportunity to reestablish themselves as the political climate was liberalised in the late 1980s. The Uniates were the first to revive.[180] The Initiative Committee for the Defence of the Rights and Believers of the Church, in operation in Galicia since 1982 (see chapter 2), organised a series of mass demonstrations in support of the Church in 1988–9, culminating in a mass rally of some 150,000 in L'viv in September 1989, which resulted in relegalisation if not reestablishment after Gorbachev's historic Vatican meeting with Pope John Paul II in December 1989. The Soviet authorities continued to obstruct the Uniates, fighting every attempt to reclaim Church property from the ROC and promoting the UAOC as a local rival to the Uniates in western Ukraine (whilst simultaneously hindering the UAOC's return elsewhere).[181] Only after the nationalist victory in the local elections held in Galicia in March 1990 did the Uniate revival really begin to gather pace (an estimated 2,800 parishes had returned to the Uniate fold by January 1993; see table 3.1).

The Uniates continued to face other problems, however.[182] The conflict with the UAOC in Galicia has continued despite Uniate expectations that all their pre-1946 patrimony would be restored once the Soviet state collapsed (see p. 88 below). In Transcarpathia the local Uniate hierarchy in Mukachevo, led by Bishop Ivan Semedii, has refused to submit to the authority of the restored archeparchy in L'viv, and has been accused by nationalists of abetting Rusyn 'separatism'.

The Uniates have found it extremely difficult to expand their support outside western Ukraine. In January 1991 1,895 out of 2,031 registered Uniate parishes were in Galicia (93.3 per cent), 129 (6.4 per cent) in Transcarpathia and a mere 7 (0.3 per cent) elsewhere.[183] The same pattern was evident in January 1993 (see table 3.2), with 2,566 out of 2,807 parishes in Galicia (91.4 per cent), 209 in Transcarpathia (7.4 per cent) and only 32 (1.1 per cent) further afield. Despite a long-running campaign by Kiev's 30,000 Uniates, the authorities repeatedly delayed permission for them to build a church in the capital.[184]

The Vatican has also been less helpful than might be imagined. It has never formally responded to the request by the May 1992 Uniate synod to confirm the L'viv authorities' control over the three eparchies of L'viv, Uzhhorod and Permyshyl (now Przemyśl in eastern Poland), and to allow it to establish eparchies in the rest of Ukraine. The Vatican's support for the use of Latin rite is somewhat insensitive even in Galicia, and makes it more difficult for the Uniates to spread their appeal to Volhynia and Right Bank Ukraine where the Church was only suppressed in 1839. Moreover, it appeared that the Church might have to wait until the 400th anniversary of the Union of Brest in 1996 for a restoration of its patriarchal status. Uniates have come to suspect that the Vatican is more interested in the broader goal of ecumenical accommodation with Moscow than with encouraging a Uniate revival. Lastly, the Uniates have been plagued by doctrinal and political disputes between three factions: the 500 clergy who operated underground before 1990, the 400 who converted from the ROC after 1990, and the approximately 40 clergy and lay administrators imported from the diaspora.[185] The first two groups tend to be highly traditionalist and nationalistic and are used to stressing the Latin rituals that distinguish Uniatism from Orthodoxy, whereas the diaspora clergy tend to be 'Easternisers' who wish to restore the proselytising and theological traditions of 1596.

The return of the UAOC

The UAOC hierarchy, led by the veteran Patriarch Mstyslav, also returned to Ukraine in 1990, after a long campaign by Kiev-based dissidents in 1988–90 to rehabilitate the Church.[186] In May 1990 an all-Ukrainian Sobor elected Mstyslav as patriarch in his absence, and he returned to Ukraine in person for his formal installation in Kiev's St Sophia's Cathedral in November 1990 (the UAOC was officially registered in October). As in the 1920s and 1941–4, however, the UAOC's main supporters were members of the central Ukrainian urban intelligentsia, who supported the Church because they were already nationalist, rather than vice versa. The UAOC was therefore not yet much of a factor in promoting the spread of Ukrainian national consciousness.

Nevertheless, the modern UAOC has two advantages it did not enjoy in its previous incarnations. First, it has retained considerable strength in western Ukraine, not only because of the manipulative tactics of the authorities, but also because of parishioners' inertia and the UAOC's claim to be the only 'truly independent' Ukrainian Church (the Uniates being supposedly creatures of Rome). In January 1991, 97 per cent (1,088) of the UAOC's 1,122 parishes were still in Galicia (78 per cent in 1993).[187] Second, the UAOC's situation was transformed after 1991 by the achievement of Ukrainian independence. Leading nationalists and state officials, including President Kravchuk and Arsen Zinchenko, a nationalist deputy and chairman of the Ukrainian Council for Religious Affairs, began to encourage a merger between the UAOC and the existing Orthodox hierarchy in Ukraine (despite a cosmetic name change in 1990 when it became the Ukrainian Orthodox Church under Metropolitan Filaret, the UOC was still an organic part of the old Russian Orthodox Church).[188]

However, the would-be united Church soon faced problems from both parties to the merger. As in the two earlier periods, a substantial proportion of the existing Orthodox hierarchy and flock in Ukraine refused to cooperate with the venture and remained loyal to Moscow. In May 1992 a majority of bishops attempted to head off plans for a merger with the UAOC and voted to replace Filaret with Metropolitan Volodymyr of Rostov and Novocherkassk at a council in Kharkiv.[189] Moreover, many of the Orthodox faithful, even ethnic Ukrainians (particularly in the countryside), valued the Church for the stability of its ritual, and had become used to the Russian liturgy and the idea of Moscow as the centre of *Slavia Orthodoxa*. On the other hand, many in the UAOC (and elsewhere) saw Filaret as an opportunist with a long history of collaboration with the communist authorities,[190] and particularly in Galicia and in the diaspora the clergy risked losing their nationalist flock to the Uniates if they were seen to compromise with him.

The Orthodox split

The unity Sobor held in Kiev in June 1992 was therefore only partially successful.[191] Filaret's followers in the UOC agreed to merge with the UAOC under the banner of the Ukrainian Orthodox Church (Kievan

Patriarchy), or UOC (KP). Mstyslav was elected head of the new Church and Filaret became his deputy. The Ukrainian authorities moved quickly to register the UOC (KP) as the official successor to both the UAOC and UOC, and declared that only the decisions of the new Church had canonical effect.[192] By January 1993 the UOC (KP) claimed control over nearly 2,000 parishes (see table 3.1), almost twice the number loyal to the UAOC two years earlier, rising to 2,500 by September 1994.[193]

However, the new Church was soon assailed from both sides. The UAOC die-hards seized on an alleged death-bed condemnation of the merger by Mstyslav in December 1992 and refused to participate in the new Church. After his death in Canada in June 1993, they unilaterally elected their own successor, Archbishop Dmitrii of Pereiaslav and Sicheslav (Dnipropetrovs'k), and began a campaign to reestablish the UAOC as an independent organisation.[194] The UOC (KP) held its synod in October 1993, with the support of the Ukrainian state and most nationalist groups in Kiev. Vasyl' Romaniuk (Volodymyr), a veteran of the 1970s Helsinki Group who spent seventeen years in Soviet camps, was elected as patriarch over the head of Filaret and the synod voted to change his official title to Patriarch of Kiev and all Rus'-Ukraine, laying claim thereby to the legacy of the tenth-century Church.[195] However, the UOC (KP) failed to grow as expected and after Kravchuk's defeat in the 1994 presidential election, it lost official backing from the state (see chapter 6). Volodymyr's untimely death in June 1995 allowed the controversial Filaret to take over as patriarch the following October.

Those Orthodox who remained loyal to Moscow christened themselves the Ukrainian Orthodox Church (Moscow Patriarchy), or UOC (MP), under Metropolitan Volodymyr (Sabodan). The UOC (MP) retained the support of the 'Kharkiv Group' of bishops (twenty-nine bishops as opposed to the Kievan Patriarchy's eighteen) and controlled key institutions such as the Pechers'k monastery in Kiev. Furthermore, five senior hierarchs led by Metropolitan Antonyi defected from the Kievan to the Moscow Patriarchy in January 1994, citing hostility to Filaret and his continued abuse of power.[196] At the grass-roots level the Moscow Patriarchy remained the largest of the three Orthodox Churches, with a total of 5,449 parishes in January 1993, concentrated in eastern and southern Ukraine and the central Ukrainian countryside. Table 3.1 summarises the number of parishes in Ukraine as of January 1993.

Table 3.2 shows how these parishes were spread across the various regions of Ukraine. The Uniate Church remained concentrated in

Table 3.1 *Number of parishes in Ukraine, 1 January 1993*

UOC (MP)	5,449
UOC (KP)[a]	1,904
Uniates	2,807
Protestant and evangelical	3,070
Roman Catholic	517
Jewish	52
Muslim[b]	42
Other	196
Total	14,037

Notes: [a] The UOC (KP) rather implausibly claimed 2,500 priests and 15 million faithful after its Sobor in October 1993; the UAOC (Independent) claimed 1,500 parishes, and 300 priests after its Sobor the previous September; and the UOC (MP) was reported as having 6,200 parishes and 'over 6 million faithful' in December 1993: *Ukrainian Weekly*, 31 October, 19 September and 26 December 1993. Bohdan Bociurkiw, 'Politics and Religion in Ukraine: The Orthodox and the Greek Catholics', in Michael Bordeaux (ed.), *The Politics of Religion in Russia and the New States of Eurasia* (Armonk, N.Y.: M. E. Sharpe, 1995), pp. 131–62, at p. 147 cites a lower figure of 672 parishes who by 'not amending their statutes' to join the UOC (KP) had presumably remained with the UAOC (Independent).
[b] Three-quarters of all Muslim parishes were Crimean Tatar.
Source: F. D. Zastavnyi, *Heohrafiia Ukraïny* (L'viv: Svit, 1994), pp. 450–9. Cf. Serhii Zdioruk, 'Tserkovna polityka i heokonfesiini interesy Ukraïny', *Viche*, August 1993, pp. 93–4.

Galicia and Transcarpathia, but had to share the former with the UOC (KP). The UOC (KP) had by 1993 established a presence in the central Ukrainian cities, but its disappointing performance overall left the UOC (MP) with the broadest geographical spread of support.

The number of parishes, however, is an inexact indicator of the number of faithful, particularly as levels of atheism and religious indifference are much higher in eastern and southern Ukraine. Sociological surveys can, however, reveal nominal religious allegiance if not actual practice. One such poll taken in 1993 indicated much higher levels of support for the UOC (KP).[197] Nearly two-thirds of those asked (64 per cent) identified themselves as Orthodox, with 48 per cent supporting the UOC (KP), and 16 per cent either the UOC (MP) or ROC. Another source, whose findings are shown in table 3.3, gave a better indication of patterns of regional support, but its small total sample size justifies a degree of caution.

By the mid-1990s therefore Ukraine effectively had three Orthodox Churches, the UOC (KP), the UOC (MP) and the UAOC (Independent), none of which was officially recognised by Istanbul. This split both reflects and further contributes to national disunity, and is a key

Table 3.2 *Number of parishes by region for the three main Ukrainian Churches, 1 January 1993*

Region	UOC (MP)	UOC (KP)	Uniates
Galicia	168	1,492	2,566
Volhynia	899	120	3
Transcarpathia	459	–	209
Chernivtsi	335	68	9
Right Bank	1,682	61	5
Kiev	263	87	3
Left Bank	520	24	2
East	598	14	5
South	442	37	2
Crimea	83	1	3
Total	5,449	1,904	2,807

Source: Author's calculations from Zastavnyi, *Heohrafiia Ukraïny*, pp. 450–9. There were no separate figures for the UAOC (Independent).

Table 3.3 *Number of adherents by region for the main Ukrainian Churches (percentages), December 1994*

Region	UOC (MP)/ROC	UOC (KP)	Uniates	UAOC (Independent)
West	7.5	34.9	40.9	6.9
Right Bank/Kiev	14.8	61.5	1.5	3.1
Left Bank[a]	17.1	54.5	–	3.4
East[a]	54.1	29.5	0.8	4.3
South[a]	50.7	30.1	–	1.6
Total	23.1	41.2	16.4	4.3

Note: [a] Regions here were defined somewhat differently from the schema used in this work. 'West' and 'Right Bank' were the same, but 'Left Bank' was defined as Chernihiv, Sumy, Poltava and Dnipropetrovs'k; 'East' comprised Kharkiv, Donets'k and Luhans'k; 'South' Zaporizhzhia, Kherson, Mykolaïv, Odesa and Crimea.
Source: Information provided by Valerii Khmel'ko at the Kiev Mohyla Academy. The total survey size was 2,123, but 1,235 were not religious, indicated no allegiance to any particular Church or declined to reply. A total of 8.8 per cent indicated other Churches (including 0.8 per cent Islamic, 0.5 per cent Jewish, 1.1 per cent Protestant and 1.7 per cent Roman Catholic); therefore the figures do not total 100 per cent.

reason why the Ukrainian national movement was much weaker than in mono-confessional states such as Catholic Poland or Lithuania. As in the 1920s, the drive to autocephaly was a consequence rather than a cause of growing national consciousness, and Ukraine was unable to create a truly national Church to help underpin fragile national unity.

The UOC (KP) remained weak, and the Uniates confined to the west (moreover many Ukrainians were turning to the Roman Catholic and the new evangelical Churches).

Conclusion

Nationalist political parties and social organisations in Ukraine remain weak and fractious,[198] and inter-confessional divisions strong. The weakness of political parties and civil society is a common factor in virtually all post-communist states,[199] but in Ukraine is also a reflection of the specific historical legacy described in chapters 1 and 2. On the other hand, the relative intensity of ethno-national sentiment amongst the nationally conscious Ukrainian minority has at least facilitated political mobilisation in comparison to Russophone Ukrainians, who remain as yet an amorphous group without a strong tradition of political leadership.

Most Ukrainian nationalists are perfectly well aware of the problems caused by these inherited historical limitations. Developments among the 'opposition' are only one-half of the story, however, and chapter 4 will now turn to an analysis of the phenomenon of Ukrainian national communism and its importance as a second strand of the national movement.

4 National communism

In twentieth-century Ukraine, organised political nationalism has often been unable to play a role in domestic politics. It has, however, also appeared in ersatz or sublimated form as 'national communism'. The term was first coined to describe the initiators of the Ukrainianisation policy of the 1920s, men such as Mykola Skrypnyk and Oleksandr Shums'kyi who were both committed communists and nationally conscious Ukrainians. It then resurfaced in the 1960s to denote republican leaders in Ukraine and elsewhere such as Petro Shelest, who combined continued loyalty to the USSR with an attempt to defend certain republican interests. However, by the time the term became popular for a third time in the late 1980s and early 1990s it had become purely adjectival. Men such as Leonid Kravchuk may have been card-carrying members of the Communist Party, but their ideological commitment to communism had largely dissipated. Moreover, the political context allowed, even encouraged, them to become nationalist in substance rather than merely national in style, and to become the first of the three groups to place Ukrainian interests over those of the USSR as a whole.

Therefore, although this chapter will use the term 'national communism' as a common denominator to provide a useful thread of continuity stretching back to the 1920s, it is recognised that, as with nationalism itself, it has meant different things at different times. The analysis will concentrate on the third group, who provided vital reinforcements to the national movement at a crucial juncture in 1990–1, allowing the 'Ukrainian state to stand on two legs' rather than one,[1] and were arguably decisive in securing independence. As Lypyns'kyi recognised in the 1920s, the historical weaknesses of the Ukrainian national movement made it necessary for nationalists to seek a historic compromise with the former ruling elite, but in comparison with other former communist states such as Lithuania it was never likely that the latter would convert to national communism wholesale. The same historical factors that circumscribed the power of the national movement also divided the Communist Party in Ukraine.

The roots of national communism

The 1920s

The first factor paving the way for the national communist revival of the late 1980s was the example set by the 1920s. Like Latvia, but unlike Belarus, Ukraine had a strong native national communist tradition on which to draw, despite its virtual extermination in the early 1930s.[2] In fact many Ukrainians would claim that they invented the phenomenon long before the likes of Tito or Dubček. First of all this reflected the fact that national and social goals were often bound together in the national movement before 1917 (see chapter 2). Many leaders of the Ukrainian People's Republic in 1917–20 were professed socialists,[3] and others were influenced by the left-leaning intellectual climate of the time. Moreover, although Ukrainian leftists were unable to build a mass native working-class movement, the formation of the Borotbisti and Ukapisti parties in 1918–19 and their subsequent defection to the Bolshevik cause helped to strengthen the constituency in favour of Ukrainianisation in the 1920s.[4]

The Ukrainian Communist Party in fact began its existence as a formally independent group for a few brief months between the Tahanrih party council in April 1918 and the first congress of the CP(b)U in Moscow in July.[5] In 1919–20 the so-called 'federalist opposition' in the CP(b)U, led by Yurii Lapchyns'kyi, argued that social revolution was impossible without national liberation and campaigned both for equality between the Ukrainian and Russian Communist Parties and an equal federation between their respective states. The first national communist 'manifesto', the essay *Do khvyli* ('On the current situation') written by Serhii Mazlakh and Vasyl' Shakhrai in 1919, went further and argued that Russia and Ukraine should have entirely separate parties, whose only formal contact would be through the Communist International.[6] All three men were expelled or resigned from the party and the issue of party and/or state independence was off the agenda after 1922, but they helped to persuade Lenin and others of the need to maintain a separate Ukrainian SSR and laid the groundwork for the launch of the Ukrainianisation campaign in 1923 (see chapter 1).

Nevertheless, the men who ran the Ukrainianisation campaign could not be described as nationalists. Rather, Skrypnyk and Shums'kyi subscribed to the Austro-Marxist belief that communist goals were only achievable within a national context, and argued that communist ideology could only be expected to have an impact on the indigenous population if it came to them in their own language.[7] Furthermore, the

Communist Party in Ukraine was deeply split. The national communists were never in a secure majority, and their apparent supremacy in 1923–9 was more a reflection of the balance of power in Moscow than of their own internal strength.[8] Urban and ethnic Russian elements, particularly in the Donbas (the 'Yekaterinoslav faction'), remained deeply suspicious of the Ukrainianisation campaign, and in the Republican Party Skrypnyk's supporters in Kiev and Kharkiv were opposed by the faction led by Dmytro Lebid', which remained violently anti-nationalist, even anti-Ukrainian. (Lebid' supported the 'two cultures' theory, according to which 'urbanised' Russian culture was inherently superior to its 'rural' Ukrainian equivalent. In 1920 his patron Zinoviev had 'proposed to limit the use of Ukrainian to village inhabitants alone'.)[9] From its very inception therefore the CP(b)U was something of a two-headed beast, and a strong anti-nationalist but native communist tradition has persisted to this day.

Nevertheless the national communists were influenced by the intellectual climate of Soviet Ukraine in the 1920s, which, while dominated by utopian Bolshevism, also contained important echoes of nationalist debates in western Ukraine. Returnees such as Mykhailo Hrushevs'kyi helped revive the ideas of the pre-revolutionary era;[10] the economist Mykhailo Volobuiev argued that Ukraine was as much an exploited economic colony under Soviet rule as it had been under the tsars.[11] However in the long term the most significant figure of the period was the writer Mykola Khvyl'ovyi, leader of the VAPLITE (the Free Academy of Proletarian Literature) literary circle briefly in existence from 1925 to 1928. Khvyl'ovyi believed in world revolution rather than national isolationism, but his analysis of the events of 1917–20 and his attempt to provide a philosophical basis for the Ukrainianisation campaign touched many of the same themes as the work of Dmytro Dontsov (see chapter 2).[12]

The elitist (vanguard) theories propagated by Dontsov were also popular with Leninist idealists and the intellectual avant-garde throughout the USSR in the 1920s, but Khvyl'ovyi's disdain for 'cultural epigonism' was above all national in inspiration, spilling over into a violent attack on the pre-revolutionary Ukrainian intelligentsia for their political timidity, provincialism and the 'Gogol syndrome' of cultural and intellectual dependence on Russia. For Khvyl'ovyi, the intelligentsia's populist tendency to synthesise Ukrainian peasant culture and reflect it back on itself only served to perpetuate national underdevelopment and prevent the necessary modernisation of Ukrainian arts, culture and society (similar points were made by the dramatist Mykola Kulish).[13] The populists, in other words, had put the cart before the horse in 1917–20. A Ukrainian state could not be wished into being without the prior establishment of a Ukrainian nation, which in turn required the creation of a truly independent Ukrainian culture (by an elite). Khvyl'ovyi therefore coined the slogan 'Away from Moscow!', and urged the embrace of 'psychological Europe' instead.[14]

The desire to embrace European culture was derived from the by now long-standing nationalist emphasis on Ukraine's 'European' tradition, but it also reflected the idea that Ukraine's 'backwardness' had cost it the chance of independence in 1917–20. Like nationalists in many other developing countries, Soviet Ukrainian intellectuals sought to graft on aspects of the West to kick-start their growth as a nation,[15] and transcend the limits placed on the growth of national consciousness by the long-standing link with Russia. However, the implications of this approach were more radical than they seemed. Not only did it imply the self-isolation of Ukraine from Russian cultural influence, but it also suggested that the new Ukrainian intelligentsia would seek to usurp the role of the Soviet state as a modernising agent. Moreover, Khvyl'ovyi's argument that cultural self-sufficiency would lead to political independence was just what Moscow feared would be the consequence of the Ukrainianisation campaign. Not surprisingly therefore Khvyl'ovyi and his circle fell out of favour as the tide turned against the national communists after 1928–9. Most were purged at the same time as their political patrons, and Khvyl'ovyi himself committed suicide in 1933. Nevertheless, Khvyl'ovyi and his circle left a long-term legacy of vital importance by creating a theoretical basis for intellectual crossover between nationalism and national communism.

Federal structures

It has also been argued that the national communist temptation reflected the manner in which the Soviet polity was constructed back in the 1920s, and was 'an inevitable consequence of the contradiction between a centralised Communist Party and an Austro-Marxist state [sic]'.[16] Despite the totalitarian ambitions of the Soviet state, it proved impossible to concentrate all decision-making, information control and economic powers at the centre. Therefore during periods when the Soviet state felt compelled to decentralise (the 1920s, late 1950s and late 1980s), the formally federal structures of the state enabled local power-brokers to 'pursue their own interests, accumulate resources and mobilise constituencies'. The result would inevitably be a 'descent into the national communist and contextually nationalist maelstrom',[17] which could only be countered by an aggressive reassertion of central power. National communism is therefore seen not as a product of secretly harboured beliefs or ethnic loyalties coming out in the open, but as the result of contradictions inherent in the imperial-federal system which encouraged even orthodox local leaders to become nationalists *malgré eux*, 'contextual nationalists' whose actions were de facto nationalist in effect if not in design.[18]

According to this model, there was nothing necessarily special about Ukraine. All the republics were affected by the same cyclical pattern, as demonstrated by the simultaneous enactment of republican language laws in 1989 and declarations of republican sovereignty in 1990. Leonid Kravchuk was therefore simply the Ukrainian equivalent of Algirdas Brazauskas in Lithuania or Geidar Aliev in Azerbaijan. The pattern of decentralisation and recentralisation was however broken by Gorbachev's reforms in the late 1980s, which went far enough to ensure that the centre's attempt to seize back the reins in August 1991 was a failure. National independence resulted.

Social change

A third factor was social change. Supposedly the same processes of industrialisation and urbanisation that helped to transform Ukrainian society as a whole in the Soviet period (see chapter 1) also reshaped the Communist Party and therefore all significant elites in Ukraine. A disproportionately urban and Russian (and Jewish) party in the early 1920s, by the 1980s it more closely resembled the actual ethnic and social make-up of Ukrainian society. Whereas Ukrainians comprised only 23 per cent of the membership of the Communist Party in Ukraine in 1920, by 1990 that figure had risen to 67 per cent.[19] Furthermore, after Stalin's death, the leadership of the party was restored to ethnic Ukrainians: Oleksii Kyrychenko (1953–7), Mykola Pidhornyi (better known by the Russian version of his name, Podgornii; 1957–63), Petro Shelest (1963–72) and Volodymyr Shcherbyts'kyi (1972–89).[20] Arguably, this helped to predispose the party toward a more nationalist line once it was granted increasing political freedom in the late 1980s, the federal structures of the local party-state having been 'Ukrainianised' from within (the Ukrainian party had its own Politburo and Central Committee). Ukrainian nationalists have tended to rely on a cruder form of this theory, arguing that national communists are simply ethnic Ukrainians returning to the fold, as love for their native land is part of their 'genetic understanding'.[21]

None of these three elements were decisive in themselves. The historical factors that limited the appeal of nationalism within Ukrainian society as a whole also operated within the Communist Party, where potential national communists always coexisted with orthodox internationalists. Other things being equal, a larger percentage of ethnic Ukrainians obviously made the CPU more 'Ukrainian', but, as with the new Ukrainian intelligentsia (see chapter 1), this often amounted to little more than nominal 'ethnicisation'. Similarly, the national communist precedents of the 1920s would have meant little without the changes of the late 1980s and early 1990s, when political conjuncture and personality were also important, in particular the role played by Leonid Kravchuk. Moreover, the 1920s also left a legacy of factional and ideological divisions which resurfaced when true politics returned to the CPU in 1989–90.

Petro Shelest: closet national communist?

The second wave of Ukrainian national communism came in the 1960s. In the 1990s both nationalists and national communists attempted to paint as their patron and predecessor Petro Shelest, first secretary of the CPU from 1963 to 1972, a quintessential national communist who supposedly oversaw a 'second Ukrainianisation' during his period in office.[22] The fact that modern-day politicians feel the need of past precedents to justify their behaviour is interesting in itself, but there is little evidence for such retrospective myth-making. In truth Shelest did little more than ruffle a few feathers by speaking up for Ukrainian interests within an all-Union context. His rise and fall had as much to do with all-Union politics and his association with Khrushchev and Podgornii as with events in Ukraine, and Shelest never went out on a limb in defence of his republic like Janis Kalberzins in Latvia in 1959 or Vasilii Mzhavanadze in Georgia.

There was no officially sponsored 'second Ukrainianisation' because the Ukrainian party had no such power of independent initiative. For example, the proposal by education minister Yurii Dadenkov in 1965 to revive the Ukrainianisation of higher education was vetoed by Moscow. The pace of 'Russification' of the schools and media was arrested somewhat, but this was mainly the result of a temporary slackening of pressure from above, and Ukrainian officials had no power to reverse the process. Shelest was admittedly more tolerant of the *shistdesiatnyky* than Shcherbyts'kyi (see chapter 2), but this was also a reflection of changes in the political climate in the USSR between the early 1960s and early 1970s. Claims that Shelest's circle encouraged Ivan Dziuba to write *Internationalism or Russification?* in 1966 have never been substantiated. The best that could be said is that the book 'provided them with weighty arguments in bureaucratic disputes with the centre'.[23] Shelest did nothing to stop the 1965–6 trials, nor did he defend his friend the writer Oles' Honchar from accusations of nationalism after the publication of his controversial novel *Sobor* ('Cathedral') in 1968.[24]

Nor was economic nationalism any more acceptable. During Shelest's tenure Ukrainian officials became increasingly critical of the distorted development of the Ukrainian economy, underinvestment and over-reliance on heavy industry (he was later accused of 'national-autarkic deviationism'), but again this was largely a reaction against decisions made in Moscow to shift investment away from Ukrainian coal and metallurgy toward Siberian oil and gas.[25] Shelest remained a committed communist and loyal member of the Moscow Politburo, as perhaps best demonstrated by his call for quick and resolute action against the Prague Spring in 1968.[26]

Volodymyr Shcherbyts'kyi: loyal internationalist

On the other hand, it cannot be denied that Shcherbyts'kyi represented a considerable change of mood, and that, in alliance with other arch-conservatives such as ideology secretary Valentyn Malanchuk (replaced in 1979 by Yurii Yel'chenko) and local KGB chief Vitalii Fedorchuk, he kept a tight lid on Ukraine until September 1989.[27] Moreover, during Shcherbyts'kyi's rule the decline of Ukrainian schools and culture greatly accelerated, threatening even the limited gains of the 1920s.[28] Ukraine was therefore ill prepared for the opportunities that began to open up in the wake of Mikhail Gorbachev's reforms, and few would have predicted in the mid-1980s that Ukraine would soon be the site of a nationalist revival.[29] Shcherbyts'kyi, however, was not just a tool of Moscow. In exaggerated form, he represented the other side of the coin from Shelest, the internationalist and centralist tradition in Ukrainian communism.

Until Shcherbyts'kyi's final departure in September 1989, resolute opposition to nationalism remained the dominant mood within the Communist Party in Ukraine. As late as 1988–9 the Ukrainian Politburo continued to organise the harassment of 'extremists', 'parasites' and 'hostile elements', and to oppose 'attempts by anti-socialist elements to create political structures in opposition to the CPSU'.[30] The militia was instructed to act more resolutely against what was dismissed as 'rally democracy' (*mitingovaia demokratkiia*), and to break up unsanctioned gatherings.[31] During Gorbachev's visit to Kiev in February 1989, Shcherbyts'kyi surprised his guest by arguing that the Communist Party's main task remained not the leadership of reform, but 'the struggle with groups of political demagogues [i.e. Rukh and the Helsinki Union], who frequently come out with nationalist positions', declaring that 'we must unmask them and not allow these microbes to propagate'.[32] Even 'informal' organisations like the Ukrainian Language Society or Zelenyi svit (see chapter 3) were not to be trusted, as 'cultural problems often become the object of political speculation'.[33] Moreover, Shcherbyts'kyi continued to argue that foreign agents and the 'bourgeois nationalist' diaspora were the main source of politically inspired assistance for the 'informals'.[34] Therefore he had no time for negotiating with the fledgling opposition.[35] Instead, those branches of the party (Shcherbyts'kyi named L'viv, Kiev and Kharkiv) which had 'passed under the influence of extremists' should be brought to heel, by expulsions if necessary.[36]

Furthermore, Shcherbyts'kyi's approach to the broader national question remained resolutely Brezhnevite. Although he paid lip-service to the need to promote Ukrainian cultural and linguistic revival, he preferred to emphasise the importance of 'the harmonious and natural development of national-Russian dual-language politics' and the continued use of Russian as the 'language of international intercourse' in Ukraine. 'Free choice' of language, he argued, must take precedence over 'administrative' or 'forceful' attempts to promote the revival of Ukrainian. Party meetings took place in Russian. Moreover, Shcherbyts'kyi remained totally opposed to the rehabilitation of 'Petliurite' and 'Banderite' national symbols, and even to a reconsideration of the role of relative moderates such as Hrushevs'kyi. 'We must never allow ourselves to bow low before former Banderites', he argued, or allow them 'to shriek and wave their flags'.[37] Although the preparation of a new official programme of historical research began in January 1989, it was only after Shcherbyts'kyi's resignation that it was able to widen its remit to examine key 'blank spots' in Ukrainian history such as the Great Famine.[38]

Volodymyr Ivashko: a transitional figure

Shcherbyts'kyi's final departure in September 1989 and his replacement by Volodymyr Ivashko therefore marked a decisive change within the party.[39] Although some commentators greeted the change with scepticism,[40] by the end of Ivashko's nine months in office the rules of the political game in Ukraine had been profoundly transformed. Initially this was mainly because Ivashko was attempting to make up for lost time and align the CPU with the policies of Gorbachev, his patron and mentor, but it also reflected the beginnings of an opening toward the nationalist opposition in Ukraine (this was arguably the basic contradiction in Gorbachev's policies: the pressure on more conservative republics to adopt a more reformist line also pushed them in the direction of their own nationalist constituencies).[41] On the other hand, the CPU's strong native anti-nationalist tradition remained strong, and by 1990 the party was therefore profoundly split. Unlike the Communist Party in Lithuania or Georgia, the CPU was unable or unwilling to convert to the national cause wholesale.

As early as October 1989, Ivashko had (in private as well as in public) adopted several key nationalist concepts, including the importance of creating 'a legal mechanism to defend the interests of the republic', 'strengthening her economic sovereignty', the introduction of citizenship of the Ukrainian SSR as 'an inalienable attribute of statehood and sovereignty', the right of the republic to 'enter into relations with foreign states, to make agreements with them and exchange diplomatic and consular representation', and the importance of 'including Ukraine in the general European process'.[42] He began to criticise slow progress in reversing the postwar decline in Ukrainian schooling and the public use of Ukrainian, although he accepted in 1990 that 'it was too early to talk of fundamental changes in the language situation in the republic'; and he sped up attempts to rehabilitate Stalinist victims and revive national historiography.[43] In marked contrast to Shcherbyts'kyi, Ivashko declared that Ukrainians 'should strengthen our relations with our fellow countrymen beyond the borders of the republic', where necessary 'on the state level'.[44] He also resisted calls to revive Shcherbyts'kyi's methods and unleash the militia and mass media against the opposition. 'The political approach' was more appropriate, he argued.[45]

At two key party plena before the republican elections in February and March 1990, the CPU adopted surprisingly radical resolutions on the economic and political sovereignty of Ukraine.[46] Leonid Kravchuk later claimed that these documents, which predated the Ukrainian Parliament's July 1990 declaration of sovereignty by five months, laid the basis for the whole sovereignty drive of 1990–1, for which the CPU therefore deserved as much credit as Rukh.[47] The changed political climate could be judged by Ivashko's keynote statement at the Twenty-Eighth Ukrainian Party Congress in June 1990:

the basis of our whole policy is strengthening the state sovereignty of the Ukrainian SSR. We understand the state sovereignty of Ukraine [it is perhaps significant that Ivashko interchanged the two proper names for the republic] as the full power of its people on their own territory; the supremacy, completeness and indivisibility of its power; the right independently to decide questions of political, economic and cultural life in the republic and to determine the form and structure of the organs of state power and governance; the priority of republican laws; the [ability to] annul those Union laws which go beyond the competence of the Union; the inviolability of the territory of the republic; and the establishment of Ukraine as a real subject of international relations.[48]

Ivashko also insisted that any new Union Treaty could only be based on what Ukraine was prepared 'voluntarily to cede to the centre'. Ukraine would happily join a 'free union of sovereign socialist states', but this would have to be on the basis of the recognition of Ukrainian sovereignty.[49]

The rapid transformation of the CPU's public posture after the departure of Shcherbyts'kyi was of course not just Ivashko's doing. The party was forced to adapt by the sheer pace of change over the winter of 1989–90 in the USSR and by the collapse of communist regimes throughout East-Central Europe. Moreover, despite Kravchuk's claims, the CPU's embrace of republican sovereignty in February 1990 was obviously dictated by the need to compete electorally with Rukh. In the run-up to the March elections the CPU could only guess at the breadth and depth of Rukh's support, and many feared that the results would be worse than they actually were.[50] Furthermore, Rukh's leaders were careful to encourage Ivashko to move in their direction. They accepted Lypyns'kyi's analysis of the mistakes made in 1917–20 (see chapter 2), and adopted a conscious strategy of winning over local satraps to create 'a new unified Ukrainian ruling elite, composed of . . . the separatist part of the old ruling elite [i.e. national communists] . . . and those new, dynamic leaders who emerged from the popular masses [themselves]'.[51] Yurii Badz'o described the national-democrats' strategy more simply as 'searching for a split between [orthodox and national] communists and widening it'.[52]

Nevertheless, the swing to national communism in 1989–90 should not be exaggerated. Ivashko could hardly adopt the nationalist agenda wholesale, and any leader of the CPU would have seemed radical in contrast with Shcherbyts'kyi. The CPU remained a constituent part of the CPSU. Conservatives argued that 'we must not follow the example of the Lithuanian Communist Party, in other words departure from the CPSU. On the contrary we must confirm our support for unity within the ranks of the CPSU.'[53] Ivashko may have become party leader, but there were few 'Ivashkoites'. Moreover, many in the party were profoundly disturbed by changes at the all-Union level, and after spring 1990 tended to back the conservatives in Moscow against Gorbachev. According to Kravchuk, most of the party leadership were 'shocked' and disoriented by the changes brought about by perestroika. 'Hurenko

[Ivashko's conservative rival] and other members of the [Ukrainian] Politburo thought that Gorbachev had ruined the party. They were deeply disappointed with his behaviour.'[54]

Many of the changes made by the party were therefore grudging and reactive, and there was little evidence of any grass-roots pressure for change.[55] Even in Galicia many communists were in two minds about embracing the national cause. As the local party was under mortal threat, some were more sensitive to the need to accommodate nationalist sentiment, while others, fearing for their political lives, called instead for 'more resolute' struggle against 'national-extremism'.[56] Members of the Kiev intelligentsia made important and telling arguments in favour of a more independent line, but many left the party in frustration in 1990.[57] Most of the CPU rank and file elsewhere remained highly orthodox and stressed the importance of remaining immune to 'the moral-psychological pressure of separatist forces'.[58] Moreover, sovereignty was as far as many communists would go. Once more radical national communists began to flirt with the idea of independence, the party would be profoundly split.

Renovators defeated

Although the CPU was edging toward the nationalist opposition, certain issues therefore remained taboo. Ivashko drew the line against proposals for economic 'separatism' or 'autarky', and criticised 'the illusion that economic independence can become a panacea for all our misfortunes'.[59] Moreover, the unity of the USSR and the Soviet armed forces remained absolutes (only a 'united army' was capable of defending the 'Soviet order'). As Kravchuk later remarked, the majority of the CPU leadership 'were prepared to discuss the form the Union might take, but no further. The Union had to stay!'[60] Furthermore, Ivashko was resolutely opposed to the key national communist demand, the creation of a truly independent Communist Party of Ukraine, arguing that it would 'federalise' the CPSU and 'divide communists on national grounds'.[61]

The campaign to create an independent CPU raged throughout 1990 and 1991, both in private and in public.[62] Supporters argued that Ukraine needed 'an independent party of the Ukrainian people and the Ukrainian state', that would no longer be subject to the dictates of Moscow,[63] but Ivashko insisted it had to remain clear 'that we are not leaving the CPSU', and that Ukraine should 'not set a bad example to other republican Communist Parties'. Other party leaders expressed their sympathy for 'the anxiety of many communists that adopting our own statute would push us in the direction of isolationism and separatism'.[64] The issue was therefore glossed over at the twenty-eighth congress of the CPU in June 1990. The delegation from L'viv proposed that the party should adopt an independent programme and statute, and even change its name, but only 314 delegates out of 1,700 voted to put such issues to a party referendum.[65] Instead the Ukrainian party decided to delay discussion until a special second stage of the congress in December 1990 so that it could wait and see what was decided at the Twenty-Eighth CPSU Party Congress in Moscow.[66]

By then, however, conservative communists were making a comeback throughout the USSR, and the issue was shelved.[67] The CPU was content to describe itself as 'an independent party sharing the programmatic principles and strategic aims of the CPSU', 'a voluntary union of like-minded communists, which acts as part of the united CPSU on the basis of self-rule in accordance with the constitution of the USSR and the constitution and laws of the Ukrainian SSR'.[68] Despite appeals by Oleksandr Moroz, the leader of the communist majority in Parliament, and others to 'distance themselves from the centre' [i.e. Moscow] in order to regain the political initiative and help 'neutralise attacks' on the party from the nationalist right,[69] the party leadership attached little importance to the issue in 1991. In the last year of its existence the CPU was therefore in a sort of limbo, still part of the CPSU, but claiming the right to act autonomously. Many communists were understandably confused, uncertain whether 'we are the CPSU or CPU'. One delegate to the twenty-eighth congress asked rhetorically whether it was a normal 'congress, the founding congress [of a new party], or a conference of Russian communists?'[70]

It was only in the aftermath of the August 1991 coup that the decision was finally made (at the final party plenum on 26 August) to break with the CPSU and establish the CPU as a truly 'independent political organisation'.[71] Even then conservatives had grave doubts and originally proposed to put the issue to a special party congress or party referendum,[72] although Moroz had already threatened in Parliament 'to take responsibility on [him]self for the organisation of a Ukrainian Communist Party' if others failed to do so.[73] By then of course it was too late. The Presidium of the Ukrainian Parliament declared the dissolution of the party on 30 August.

The party leadership also showed little tolerance for a second renovation movement, the Ukrainian branch of the all-Soviet Democratic Platform movement, which briefly flourished in early 1990 in an attempt to promote internal democracy within the CPSU as a whole (the Ukrainian branch was largely made of members of the liberal intelligentsia who still tended to think in all-Soviet terms).[74] Despite a public facade of tolerance at the twenty-eighth Ukrainian party congress, including the granting of 'minority rights' to any group of more than 200 delegates (out of approximately 1,700), Ivashko and his colleagues were secretly resolved to refuse all demands for internal democratisation.[75] Only forty-nine delegates signed the Democratic Platform's appeal,[76] and the Ukrainian group broke with the party after the congress, as with the all-Union parent group after the twenty-eighth congress of the CPSU. Twenty-eight Ukrainian deputies went with it, and the platform later became the Party of Democratic Revival of Ukraine (see chapter 3).[77]

The strength of CPU conservatives could also be explained by the party's changing membership base, creating an ageing party that was rapidly haemorrhaging members and supporters from both the intelligentsia and the working class (most of the early departures in 1989–90 were from the intelligentsia, whereas 51 per cent of those who left in 1991 were workers). Only 6,200 left in 1989, but 250,000 resigned in 1990 and 191,000 in the first five months of 1991. Of the somewhere between 2.5 and 3 million who remained, many were only nominal members, neglecting to pay their dues and taking no part in party activities. The party was therefore increasingly reliant on career apparatchiks and aged and conservative veterans. Only 3 per cent of the delegates to the June 1990 congress had joined the party in the last five years.[78]

The rise of Leonid Kravchuk and his supporters

Significantly therefore the main stronghold of the national communists in 1990–1 was not the Ukrainian Politburo and Central Committee, but Parliament, where the key role was played by the future president Leonid Kravchuk.[79] Retrospective myth-making, such as his own assertion that as early as '1987 I came to the conclusion to demand more independence for our state',[80] has made analysis of Kravchuk's behaviour difficult. Moreover, his motives for embracing the national cause are obscure. Some have pointed to personal factors such as naked ambition, his west Ukrainian origins (Kravchuk was born in Volhynia in 1934 when it was a part of Poland), or the contacts that he developed with the Kiev intelligentsia during his twenty years' work in the ideology department of the CPU. However, it is indisputable that Kravchuk played his part with aplomb. The dynamics of Soviet dissolution might well have eventually produced a similar figure if Kravchuk had not been around, but his personal impact was immense, ensuring that full-blown national communism appeared earlier than would otherwise have been the case.

Even under Shcherbyts'kyi, Kravchuk demonstrated a certain political independence by taking advantage of the first secretary's failing health to act as midwife to the birth of Rukh (see chapter 3). After Shcherbyts'kyi's resignation Kravchuk eased aside the arch-conservative Yurii Yel'chenko to take charge of an expanded portfolio of responsibilities including culture, ideology and links with 'creative unions and independent [samodiial'ni] organisations'[81] – arguably as important a change as the handover from Shcherbyts'kyi to Ivashko. From this strategic fiefdom, Kravchuk was now well placed to build up support amongst the nationalist opposition. In early 1990 he sponsored a programme to promote national cultural revival, and called for the development of a new and more positive attitude to the Ukrainian diaspora.[82] Kravchuk has also claimed that he 'was the author' of the key CPU declarations on economic and political sovereignty for the republic in February and March 1990.[83]

As yet Kravchuk had few supporters and could make little impact on all-Soviet politics, but Ivashko's sudden departure to Moscow in July 1990 to become Gorbachev's deputy (second secretary) in the CPSU allowed him to make unexpectedly sudden progress through the ranks.[84] The lack of an agreed successor meant that Ivashko's functions were divided, and the traditional stranglehold of east Ukrainians on the party was unexpectedly broken. Stanislav Hurenko, a traditional conservative, was elected to lead the CPU, but the post of chairman of Parliament went to Kravchuk (a vote ironically boycotted by the nationalist opposition).[85] Personal and political divisions between reformers and conservatives now increasingly coincided with an institutional divide. As throughout the USSR, the new dynamics of electoral competition were forcing republican parliaments to pay more attention to building up support amongst local constituencies, almost regardless of their political complexion.[86] On the other hand CPU party institutions, the Ukrainian Politburo and Central Committee, remained more closely tied to all-Union structures. Kravchuk later complained that 'although I was a member of the [Ukrainian] Politburo, they didn't believe in me ... [nor] whenever it came to the crunch, did I had any support in the [Ukrainian] Central Committee'.[87] He was therefore forced to concentrate on Parliament.

Moreover, the balance of forces within the Ukrainian Parliament encouraged the growth of the national communist faction and increased incentives to cooperate with the nationalist opposition. Orthodox communists were frequently absent from proceedings.[88] Communist

Party sources admitted that 'of the 190 deputies who regularly work in the committees of the Supreme Council almost 80 are members of the opposition'.[89] The Ukrainian Politburo continually bemoaned its loss of control over communist deputies and the inactivity or absence of orthodox communists, and criticised Kravchuk's failure to use his position in Parliament to put the nationalist opposition in its place.[90] Furthermore, Kravchuk chaired the crucial parliamentary Presidium, which prepared the parliamentary programme and, given the structure of Ukrainian political institutions (sovereign soviets and no executive president until June 1991), increasingly promoted itself as an ersatz collective Ukrainian presidency, allowing it to take charge of all-important negotiations with Moscow.[91] Moreover, only six out of twenty-five members of the Presidium could be considered hard-line communists, whereas nine (counting two sympathisers) belonged to the opposition, thanks to Ivashko's earlier decision to allocate them more than their due share, and around eight were national communist supporters of Kravchuk.[92]

Moreover, the logic of local electoral accountability increasingly tended to transcend other potential divides in Parliament. Other things being equal, it might have been expected that the communist majority in Parliament would have splintered along ethnic, linguistic and regional lines, with ethnic Russians, Russophones and/or deputies from the east and south the most reluctant converts to the national cause. However, support for Kravchuk grew across the board in the Ukrainian Parliament from late 1990 onward.[93] Underlying divisions were suppressed by the speed of the USSR's collapse. Economic disorder, the decline of the CPSU and all-Union ministries as career institutions and mechanisms of control, plus the discrediting of party conservatives by the January 1991 killings in the Baltic republics, all combined to disorient Moscow's natural supporters in Parliament. Moreover, the decline of Communist Party authority increased the relative weight of the nationalist parties as alternative poles of attraction, especially as centrist, regional or new left-wing groups were struggling to get off the ground (see chapter 3). Orthodox communists were therefore increasingly bewildered by the party's failure to wield an influence proportionate to its theoretical strength. After all, with somewhere under three million members, it was by far the largest political organisation in Ukraine.[94] Anti-nationalist forces should have been much stronger, but were weakened by contingent factors in late 1990 and 1991.

By October 1990 the party was beginning to split. Hurenko complained in private that Kravchuk 'belonged only nominally to the party' and was too fond of consorting with nationalists such as Yukhnovs'kyi and Mykhailo Horyn'.[95] Kravchuk on the other hand urged the party to help Ukrainians become 'masters of their own land, their own fate' and 'follow the path toward making Ukraine a true state that independently makes its own decisions'. Moreover he attacked Hurenko and his circle for excessive concern with Moscow politics (Hurenko had close links with the conservative opposition to Gorbachev) and for backsliding on the February 1990 programme and Parliament's July declaration of sovereignty, asking 'why, when the attempt is made to pass other laws based on the declaration of sovereignty, are we always opposed?'[96]

Alongside growing personal and institutional estrangement, the divergence between national and orthodox communists was also apparent in symbolic discourse. Whereas Hurenko and his allies continued to attack 'Galician messianism' and 'separatism',[97] Kravchuk and Ivan Pliushch, then deputy chairman of Parliament,[98] were beginning to coopt the semiotic language of the nationalist opposition, or at least several of its safer and less divisive themes. Kravchuk spoke warmly of Hrushevs'kyi and Drahomanov and declared that he felt a close affinity with Vynnychenko, although he steered clear of more controversial figures, preferring the safer waters of Cossack mythology to commenting on the historical record of the OUN-UPA.[99] Moreover, Kravchuk accepted the nationalist dictum that Ukraine was making its 'third attempt' to win independence (after Khmel'nyts'kyi and the Ukrainian People's Republic),[100] and coopted the 1990–1 celebrations to commemorate Ukraine's Cossack heritage that had originally been planned by Rukh.[101]

The split between the two camps became public and irreversible between January and March 1991, after Kravchuk and Hurenko took opposing positions over the killings in Lithuania, the proposed Union Treaty and Gorbachev's plan to hold a referendum on preserving the USSR.[102] Orthodox communists continued to argue that 'the key, central question today is the preservation of the USSR'. Moreover, they argued that it should remain a federation rather than a confederation, and on the constitutional basis of Gorbachev's proposed Union Treaty rather than Ukraine's declaration of sovereignty. Hurenko's preferred formula was for 'a sovereign, socialist Ukraine in a renewed Union'.[103] Conservatives also argued that the proposed new Ukrainian constitution should place supreme executive authority in the president of the USSR and should recognise that Ukraine was a multi-ethnic and multilingual republic, where sovereign authority resided with all of its citizens rather than ethnic Ukrainians alone.[104]

Kravchuk in contrast defined the main political problem not as Ukrainian nationalism, but central intransigence. Although there were 'manifestations of separatism, it is impossible not to see that the centre [Moscow] too often forgets about the sovereignty of the republics, and is even of the opinion that they don't exist'.[105] Kravchuk argued that there was little point 'remaining in the old Union [so long as it] means remaining in something undefined. The central government and central leadership is simply not capable today of a political approach [that would] strengthen our statehood. It has no other means [of keeping the republics in the Union] than, forgive me, repressive [ones].'[106] Moreover, the new Ukrainian constitution had to be seen as a weapon in the struggle with Moscow. Its guiding principles should be the absolute value of Ukrainian sovereignty and the minimum transfer of powers to the centre. Kravchuk and his supporters also favoured vesting power in a Ukrainian presidency to counterbalance Gorbachev's belated and ineffectual attempts to recentralise power in Moscow.[107]

By mid-1991 Kravchuk's tactics were paying off. Orthodox communists in the CPU had weight of numbers, but were hopelessly disoriented and unable to respond to the drift of power away from Communist Party institutions to the Ukrainian Parliament. The conservative reaction in Moscow that culminated in the abortive action against Lithuania had faded away, and Kravchuk skilfully sidestepped Gorbachev's referendum plan. The CPU Central Committee rejected Kravchuk's proposal to postpone the poll,[108] but despite its clear instructions to take a pro-Union line, communist deputies in Parliament split and allowed Kravchuk to manoeuvre his second question onto the ballot[109] ('Do you agree that Ukraine should be part of a Union of Soviet Sovereign States on the basis of the Declaration of State Sovereignty of Ukraine?'). Thereafter Kravchuk was able to campaign against too centralised a treaty on the basis that his question received 80.2 per cent support against Gorbachev's 70.5 per cent (see chapter 5).[110] Furthermore, Kravchuk's success was cementing his growing alliance with the national democrat opposition. Only the far right now argued that he was not to be trusted.[111]

Kravchuk's position was further strengthened by two additional factors. First, although the CPU Central Committee continued to liaise with its Moscow counterpart, public negotiations on the Union Treaty were his responsibility as chairman of Parliament. Second, although debate on the new Ukrainian constitution was largely stalled, his supporters succeeded in passing a 'Law on the Presidency of the Ukrainian SSR' in July 1991, creating a position tailor-made for Kravchuk with sweeping powers 'to suspend the action of decisions of the executive power of the USSR on the territory of the Ukrainian SSR if they contradict the constitution and the laws of the Ukrainian SSR'.[112]

After his return from the Novo-Ogar'ovo meeting with Gorbachev and other republican leaders in June 1991, Kravchuk was able to ignore the protests of the Central Committee and most local party leaders and steered a proposal through Parliament to delay all discussion of the Union Treaty until September 1991.[113] The national communists were therefore riding high on the eve of the attempted coup in Moscow in August 1991.

After independence: national communism triumphant?

Although Kravchuk himself prevaricated during the early stages of the coup,[114] its failure brought about a victory for the national communists more decisive than any they could have hoped to arrange themselves. The steady movement of support in their direction became a stampede, especially after the citadels of orthodox communism, the Ukrainian Politburo and Central Committee, were dismantled. However, the post-coup reaction masked the extent to which underlying divisions and old-style communism survived amongst the old ruling elite.

This was not immediately apparent. The pressures of the autumn 1991 election campaign and Kravchuk's continued fondness for compromise and tactical adjustment masked the extent of the change,[115] but it was soon obvious that he had moved sharply to the right, seemingly taking most of the former elite along with him. In late 1991, although Kravchuk had already coopted most of the nationalist agenda, he did so on his own terms and still kept his distance from its more radical propositions. Kravchuk repeatedly warned against 'dividing people into better or worse according to national attributes', and insisted that an independent Ukraine could only be built as a state of all its peoples. In particular he stressed that 'Ukrainians and Russians have lived together for centuries, have shared grief and joy in equal proportions and have spilt blood together for this land. As president I envisage Ukraine as a state of Ukrainians, Russians and all the nationalities who inhabit it. It simply cannot be any other way.'[116] Kravchuk also emphasised the importance of making 'a clear distinction between national and nationalist'. Those 'deputies from western oblasts who stubbornly promote the idea of creating a national state', he argued, should be aware of 'the problem that in many regions "national" is perceived as nationalist'.[117]

However, by mid-1992 Kravchuk's tone was already beginning to alter. In the past, he argued, 'we have only looked at the negative features in nationalism, rather than [seeing it as] some sort of creative force. A national-liberation movement, if we do not attempt to blacken it, can be a creative force in building the state.'[118] The nationalist agenda which Kravchuk now embraced in full is analysed in more detail in chapters 6 and 7, but a few examples will serve to indicate the extent to which national communism and nationalism were now increasingly indistinguishable.

In his attitude to Ukrainian history, Kravchuk dropped the careful, selective approach he had followed in 1989–91 and endorsed the nationalist view of the past as an endless series of misfortunes at Russia's hands. At the congress of Ukrainians in the former USSR in January 1992, he bemoaned 'the history of our people, who have endured centuries of tragic trials and decades of outright ethnocide. The evil will of tyrants, the cruel perfidy of our enemies, the fatal and sometimes criminal mistakes of our own statesmen have turned Ukrainians into orphans in our own home.'[119] Even if he did not mention Russia by name as the culprit, the implication was clear. Constant references to Russian 'chauvinists', Russian 'territorial pretensions' and 'crude interference in our affairs', and statements such as 'Russians are psychologically used to thinking of everything else as a part of Russia' did little to help encourage ethnic Russians or Russophone Ukrainians to think of the Ukrainian state as their natural home.[120] Nor did Kravchuk's categorical statement that 'the Ukrainian people in their culture, form of life and outlook on life differ from the Russians'.[121]

Furthermore, the attempt to move 'away from Moscow' meant that Kravchuk and Pliushch consistently refused to contemplate closer integration within the CIS, arguing that it was unlikely 'to exist for long'. According to Kravchuk, 'the Commonwealth is not a state formation and cannot be a subject of international law. Only the states which make up the Commonwealth can be such subjects', and only they are the 'legal successors to the USSR'.[122] Although he resisted nationalist demands to leave the CIS altogether and insisted that Ukrainian foreign policy remained 'multilateral', the preference of Kravchuk and foreign minister Anatolii Zlenko for a basically Eurocentric foreign policy in place of an 'orientation toward Russia alone' became increasingly clear in 1992–4.[123]

As president of a newly independent state, Kravchuk was particularly keen to cloak himself in the symbolic trappings of office. In 1991 on the eve of the coup, Kravchuk was still insisting that 'national symbols should satisfy everyone – those who live in the east and those who live in the west, as well as those in the north and south',[124] but after independence he accepted the nationalist flag, hymn and state emblem, although they remained anathema to many in the east and south (see chapter 6). Indeed, unlike the post-Soviet leadership in neighbouring

Belarus, he associated himself enthusiastically with their public use and with 'nation-building' myth and ceremony, such as the fiftieth anniversary commemoration of the Great Famine in September 1993,[125] and the public rite and ritual of the Kievan Patriarchate of the Ukrainian Orthodox Church. At the special all-Ukrainian religious forum called to consolidate support for independence in November 1991, Kravchuk had insisted that 'all religions, Churches and organisations of believers are equal. Calls to create a single national Church originate with nationalist romantics' and failed to take account of the multi-confessional realities of Ukrainian society.[126] Now he gave preferential support to the UOC (KP) instead of the much larger Moscow Patriarchate (see chapters 2 and 6).

Kravchuk rejected any policy of forcible Ukrainianisation, but accepted the historical premises of its advocates, namely that 'Ukrainian culture, language, national self-consciousness and historical memory have been subject to so much damage for so long, that we must apply enormous force in order to revive them.'[127] Kravchuk showed little sympathy for the demand for 'two state languages, [which was] just an illusion'. On the contrary, he complained that it was 'painful and offensive when a Ukrainian does not wish to speak his native language, and in official declarations registers himself and his children amongst the legion of the Russified. And we are not talking only about Ukrainians! Every moral adult, regardless of their nationality, is obliged to know the language of the people on whose territory he lives.' Otherwise, it was simply 'disrespect, disrespect to that people, its culture and tradition ... without a language there can be no people'.[128] Similarly, by standing firm on the principle that 'Ukraine is not a federal republic' and by caricaturing demands for autonomy in Crimea and elsewhere as 'imperialist, chauvinist politics, and the long-term, planned and coordinated action of certain political circles in Russia',[129] Kravchuk and his colleagues were sending out political messages that undermined the credibility of their commitment to a multi-ethnic civic state.

In economic policy, sensitivity to the possibility that market reforms might spark unrest in heavily industrial and Russophone areas of eastern Ukraine was a key reason why Kravchuk avoided their implementation and toyed instead with the chimerical myth of a Ukrainian 'third way'. On the other hand, his consistent opposition to economic reintegration within the CIS worried many in the east and south, as did Ukraine's first post-independence 'programme' of economic reform put forward by Kravchuk's main economic adviser Oleksandr Yemel'ianov in March 1992.[130] Yemel'ianov's simplistic slogans, blaming Russia for all of

Ukraine's economic difficulties and arguing that Ukraine should be quarantined from further deleterious influence, were neither realistic nor likely to appeal to Russophone Ukrainians.

By the time of the presidential election in 1994, therefore, Kravchuk was widely seen as a partisan of the nationalising state.[131] According to his opponents, 'having been elected by the voters simply in order to ensure that the Rukh candidates did not win, the president is in practice carrying out Rukh's anti-socialist and national chauvinist policies'.[132] In fairness to Kravchuk, this was a caricature which ignored his continued preparedness for concession and compromise, but in such matters perception is all-important, and Kravchuk's policies and pronouncements gave anti-nationalist leaders plenty of scope to construct him in such an image.

On the other hand, Kravchuk did not necessarily carry all his former colleagues with him. It has been argued that the transition from national communism to the nationalising state is a systematic feature of all post-Soviet states. Under the USSR,

ethnocultural nations were given their own political territories, but not the power to rule them. With the collapse of the Soviet Union, the sense of ethno-national entitlement [for titular nationality elites] and ownership of national territory persists, but is now joined to substantial powers of rule. Successor state elites can use these new powers to 'nationalize' their states, to make them more fully the polities of and for the ethnocultural nations whose name they bear.[133]

Nevertheless, the Ukrainian case is sui generis. There is no natural 'ethnocultural' unity in Ukraine. Divisions within the titular nationality as well as between ethnic groups meant that Ukrainian elites were never likely to convert to the national cause overnight and en masse. Despite the unanimity with which independence was embraced in the autumn of 1991, by no means all the Ukrainian ruling elite were 'national communists', either before or after. Ukrainian commentators like to refer to the so-called 'party of power', a catch-all term for the former elite, implying that it has maintained a degree of unity and common purpose after independence, despite a lack of formal party organisation,[134] but it would be more accurate to say that elites were as divided as society as a whole.

Ukrainian national communism was therefore unable to institutionalise itself. Kravchuk and Pliushch developed their own political factions, but neither made any serious attempt to form a political party until they were out of office.[135] Only in January 1995 did Kravchuk finally place the long-standing cooperation between nationalists and national communists on a formal footing by creating the non-party but firmly nationalist organisation Porozuminnia ('accord' or 'understanding') with leading members of the CNDF and others.[136] By then, however, he was out of office, having lost the 1994 presidential election to a strong left-wing revival and fierce anti-nationalist campaign (see chapter 5).

After independence: the persistence of anti-nationalism

The progeny of the Communist Party was therefore not only on the right. Russophone centrists formed first the New Ukraine organisation and then the Interregional Block for Reforms (see chapter 3). Former communists were also instrumental in establishing left-centre parties, such as the Labour Party and the Civic Congress of Ukraine, both of which were based in Donets'k.[137]

Ukraine also has three strong left-wing parties. In contrast to the hardliners who remained in a deep state of shock after the dissolution of the CPU, former communist moderates who were reconciled to Ukrainian independence were able to form a Socialist Party of Ukraine (SPU) as early as October 1991.[138] With 60,000 members and the support of between thirty and forty deputies, the socialists could claim to be the largest party in Ukraine between 1991 and 1993, although their ranks were artificially swollen by nostalgics for whom it was the closest thing to the CPU proper.[139] In January 1992 the socialists were joined by the Agrarian Party of Ukraine,[140] which, like its counterpart in Russia, was based on the communist-era Agrarian Union and claimed a massive 1.6 million members in the Ukrainian countryside. Seventy-six deputies joined the Agrarian parliamentary faction in 1992.[141]

Most importantly, however, the old CPU never fully disappeared. An informal committee led by former CPU secretary Yevhenii Marmazov, supported by a hard core of around sixty deputies in Parliament, was formed after August 1991 'to defend the interests of the party and its supporters' and to work to overturn the ban on the CPU;[142] it brought its revival campaign out into the open in June 1992.[143] Despite bitter nationalist protests, the CPU was reborn at a two-stage congress in March and June 1993, surpassing the SPU to become once again the largest political party in Ukraine after it was officially registered the following October (although like the original CPU in the last years of its life, it was disproportionately a party of aged veterans).[144]

The new CPU avoided declaring itself the formal reincarnation of the Communist Party of old, describing the 1993 congress as the First (Twenty-Ninth), but unlike other successor communist parties in Eastern Europe it remained largely unreformed. It called for the recreation of a 'Union of Communist Parties/CPSU', and declared itself to be a 'vanguard party' in total opposition to 'bankrupt bourgeois-nationalist ideas'.[145] The party's nostalgia for the Soviet era was uncompromising. The CPU 'stood against the Belovezhkaia agreement and the criminal destruction of our single unified state, the USSR, and in favour of the restoration on a new basis of a Union of fraternal, equal peoples, as a voluntary coming together of sovereign socialist states';[146] and argued that all the problems of the old USSR 'could have been successfully dealt with within the limits of socialist society, without the destruction of the united Union state, social shock and the impoverishment of the people'.[147] The CPU was therefore one of the most conservative successor communist parties in the former USSR, somewhat to the left even of Gennadii Ziuganov's Communist Party of Russia.

The three left-wing parties emerged from the spring 1994 parliamentary elections with the largest number of seats (44 per cent of the total), and Kravchuk lost the presidential election the following summer to his former prime minister Leonid Kuchma, whose campaign skilfully combined an appeal both to the left and to Russophone Ukrainians. Although in part this reflected the swing back to the left common to all reforming Eastern and Central European economies (not that reforms were yet much in evidence in Ukraine), it would be more accurate to say that the two results simply restored the balance of forces between nationalists, national communists and leftist internationalists first revealed in 1989–91 (see chapter 5). As a national communist Kravchuk was able to win 45 per cent of the vote in the 1994 presidential election, whereas a straightforward nationalist could only have expected the 25 per cent to 30 per cent won by nationalists in previous elections. Nevertheless, his defeat demonstrated that, however useful the addition of national communist elites and resources to the national cause, they were not yet in themselves sufficient to create a natural majority for ethnic Ukrainians in their own state.

Conclusion

The first stirrings of Ukrainian national communism in the Gorbachev era were in 1989–90, a good two years before independence was declared in August 1991. Although this was somewhat later than in the Baltic republics or Transcaucasia, the 'nationalisation' of the CPU was already well advanced before it became a stampede after August 1991. Nevertheless, this was only ever a partial process. The conservative wing of the party remained highly orthodox and the CPU was never fully 'Ukrainianised' in the manner of the Communist Party in Lithuania or

Armenia. The national communist camp led by Leonid Kravchuk was of enormous assistance to the former nationalist opposition in the crucial period between 1990 and 1994, but anti-nationalism and 'internationalist' communism remained a powerful political force that revived strongly from 1993 onward. Consequently, Ukraine was never able to become a paradigmatic 'nationalising state'. Chapter 5 now turns to an analysis of the factors that limited support for both nationalism and national communism in the early 1990s.

5 A minority faith: the limits to nationalist support

It has been argued throughout this work that support for Ukrainian nationalism has historically been confined largely to western and central Ukraine, albeit with important variations within both regions. This chapter gathers the evidence to demonstrate that this continued to be the case in the early 1990s. In central Ukraine, however, the rural and small-town base of the national movement in 1917 has been turned on its head, and it is now the larger cities, Kiev in particular, that provide the bedrock of nationalist support.

The 1989 all-Union elections

The first serious test of Ukrainian public opinion in the modern era was the all-Union elections of March 1989. Although revolutionary for the time, they were far from being fully democratic. The Communist Party, the Komsomol and related organisations had reserved seats, the mass media remained a one-party preserve, and awkward candidates were filtered out by a selection process largely controlled by local Communist Party committees.[1] Moreover, the two-tier Parliament ensured that many deputies with a popular mandate did not make it to the second (working) chamber, the Supreme Soviet of the USSR.

Nevertheless, turnout in Ukraine was a traditionally high 93.4 per cent.[2] The overwhelming majority (88 per cent) of those elected still belonged to the CPSU/CPU. Moreover, nearly half (124 out of 262, or 47 per cent) were stalwarts of the party, ministerial, collective farm or industrial apparat.[3] Non-communist organisations were not allowed to put up their own candidates, although the main opposition group, the Ukrainian Helsinki Union (UHU), in practice supported sympathetic individuals, especially in Galicia (the UHU had originally decided to boycott the elections, but reversed itself under pressure both from the union's eastern branches where the boycott call was having little effect and from those in the west who felt confident that some seats in Galicia could be won).[4] In L'viv for example the UHU supported Rostyslav

Bratun, who was eventually elected with 60 per cent of the vote, whereas in the three okrugs where the UHU called for a boycott (nos. 488 and 492, plus the L'viv national-territorial okrug), no candidate was elected on the first round, with between 60 per cent and 94 per cent of the vote cast against the official candidates – a reasonable result in the conditions of the time.[5]

Some notable party figures were defeated, mostly in western Ukraine and the central Ukrainian cities. In L'viv first secretary Yakiv Pohrebniak won a miserable 12 per cent of the vote, Kiev's party secretary Kostiantyn Masyk lost by 569,738 votes to 963,994, and mayor Valentyn Zhurs'kyi received a 'no' vote of 143,869. Three other first secretaries were defeated in Transcarpathia, Chernihiv and Luhans'k (a somewhat lower rate of attrition than in the USSR as a whole, where a total of forty local party leaders were defeated). Between 45 and 50 of the 262 deputies elected in Ukraine (17–19 per cent) were sympathetic to the opposition.[6] Most were *shistdesiatnyky* such as the writers Oles' Honchar, Volodymyr Yavorivs'kyi and Yurii Shcherbak, the leader of Zelenyi svit, elected in Kiev or the west. In Moscow they formed a Republican Club faction, which, like the Ukrainian populists in the early Dumas, cooperated with Russian liberals, with Andrei Sakharov's Interregional Group playing the role of the Kadets.

The March 1990 Ukrainian elections

The elections held in the Ukrainian SSR a year later were substantially freer and fairer.[7] Proposals for a two-tier legislature and for a quarter of the seats to be reserved for the CPU and kindred organisations were dropped over the winter of 1989–90,[8] and multi-candidate contests were allowed in every constituency (the voting system was majoritarian in the manner of the French Fifth Republic: candidates required an absolute majority to be elected on the first ballot; otherwise a run-off was to be held between the two best placed candidates two weeks later). Nevertheless, many members of the opposition still complained that the process was unfair. Leonid Kravchuk was unable to keep the promise he had made at the first Rukh congress in September 1989 and official registration of the main opposition group was delayed until February 1990,[9] by which time it was too late for it to participate directly in the elections. Similar treatment was handed out to other groups with potentially high levels of public support, such as Zelenyi svit.[10] The mass media again lined up behind the CPU, and opposition voices were confined to samizdat and the two main reformist papers: *Literaturna Ukraïna*, the intelligentsia's house journal, and *Vechirnii Kyïv*, Kiev's evening daily. Over 800 complaints of malpractice were eventually received by the Central Electoral Commission.[11]

Some results were indeed suspicious. No opposition candidates were elected in remote Chernivtsi, but 49 per cent voted for nationalist candidates in the December 1991 elections. Voting patterns in rural constituencies were often suspiciously uniform.[12] However, this largely reflected the continuing social and economic power of (ex-)communist elites in the countryside, rather than direct corruption or coercion, which could hardly be expected to act as a constant variable in every constituency. On the whole the opposition did about as well as it could have expected. The real factor limiting the appeal of nationalism was the historical and ethno-regional legacy described in chapter 1, as demonstrated by the fact that subsequent elections in 1991–4 produced similar results.

Although Rukh was not formally able to participate, it was the leading force behind the creation of the opposition umbrella group, the Democratic Bloc (DB) in November 1989, along with Zelenyi svit, the UHU, Memorial and the Ukrainian Language Society.[13] The DB's programme, however, was a detailed critique of the communist system rather than a common manifesto and contained few positive proposals.[14] Moreover, DB candidates, even those from the supposedly more organised UHU, were allowed to run on their own individual programmes,[15] despite attempts by V"iacheslav Chornovil and others to organise a more professional and disciplined campaign.[16] No central line emerged on the all-important national question, as Rukh/the DB was still poised between its first and second congresses and between commitment to a federalised USSR and an independent Ukraine. Stepan Khmara called for Ukrainian independence in his personal manifesto, while Levko Luk"ianenko did not.[17] Some DB candidates even ran against one another, such as in the Pechers'k region of Kiev, where Rukh's original spokesman Myroslav Popovych was opposed by Oles' Serhiienko of the UHU, resulting in the loss of the seat to the Communist Party.

On the other hand, the CPU's programme moved some way toward the opposition by promising to defend republican rights and calling for 'the affirmation of sovereign Ukrainian statehood' (see chapter 4).[18] However, this was qualified by the statement that 'the CPU, in the light of historical experience, does not consider that all [problems] can be solved on the basis of the state sovereignty of Ukraine' and aims for 'a new Union ... of equal, sovereign, socialist states, united on the basis of common values and interests'. Moreover, the CPU also restated its commitment 'to defend the ideas of the October revolution and of socialism', and stressed that the party continued 'to organise itself on the principle of democratic centralism'.[19] The communist campaign concentrated more on socio-economic issues than on national, cultural and linguistic rights, as polls showed that the electorate was mainly concerned with the former.[20]

Turnout in the two-stage elections was again high, with 85 per cent voting in the first round, and 79 per cent in those constituencies which required a run-off two weeks later.[21] Originally, 108 of those elected (24 per cent) belonged to the DB, while 385 (86 per cent) were members of the CPU/CPSU (in comparison the opposition won between 65 per cent and 74 per cent of the seats in the Baltic republics and over 40 per cent in Russia, but only 8 per cent in Belarus).[22] The overlap in Ukraine is explained by the fact that many members of the DB still carried party cards, but a series of resignations and the defection of the Democratic Platform from the CPU to the opposition soon clarified the DB/CPU split. By July 1990 the DB had christened itself the Narodna rada (People's Council) and expanded to 122 members, or 27 per cent of the total (see table 5.1). The shrunken CPU majority on the other hand came to be known as the 'Group of 239' (53 per cent), after the number of deputies who supported Leonid Kravchuk in the controversial vote for parliamentary chairman in July 1990.[23] The remaining deputies were nominally independent. One comprehensive survey of voting behaviour in 1990–1 showed that these groups remained quite stable; 129 deputies (29 per cent) were regular supporters of nationalist positions, 244 (54 per cent) could be classed as conservative communists, and 77 (17 per cent) were centrists.[24]

Table 5.1 shows the regional distribution of DB strength in April, and that of the Narodna rada in July. Map 5.1 shows the former only, as this is a truer measure of nationalist support. Even though the DB was arguably boosted by generalised anti-communist sentiment, regional patterns strongly reflected the historical legacy outlined in chapters 1 and 2. The DB swept the elections in Galicia, which was fast returning to the role of a 'Ukrainian Piedmont' that it had played earlier in the century,[25] and polled well in Volhynia, but elsewhere in the west its performance was disappointing. Two apparent supporters in Transcarpathia soon defected, and surprisingly the DB failed to pick up a single seat in Chernivtsi/Bukovyna (see table 5.1). The DB did moderately well in large towns in central Ukraine, and its support in Kiev city was second only to that in Galicia (seventeen of twenty-one seats in Kiev city went to the opposition and two of seventeen in the surrounding oblast), but it had no success at all in the countryside. In eastern Ukraine the hard core of Narodna rada supporters were in fact members of the

Table 5.1 *Seats won by the Democratic Bloc in the spring 1990 elections (and seats held by the Narodna rada in July)*

	Seats won		Total	Percentage of total seats won	
Region	April	July	seats	April	July
Galicia	42	43	46	91.3	93.5
Volhynia	9	11	19	47.4	57.9
Transcarpathia	3	1	11	27.3	9.1
Chernivtsi	0	0	8	0.0	0.0
Right Bank	9	12	69	13.0	17.4
Kiev	19	19	38	50.0	50.0
Left Bank	6	6	42	14.3	14.3
East	17	28	150	11.3	18.7
South	2	1	44	4.5	2.3
Crimea	1	1	22	4.5	4.5
Total	108	122	449[a]	24.1	27.2

Note: [a] One seat vacant, not included in this total.
Sources: Narodni deputaty Ukraïny – predstavnyky Demokratychnoho bloku, list supplied by the Rukh secretariat; Dominique Arel, 'The Parliamentary Blocs in the Ukrainian Supreme Soviet: Who and What Do They Represent?', *Journal of Soviet Nationalities*, vol. 1, no. 4 (Winter 1990–1), pp. 108–54, at pp. 113–14; *Literaturna Ukraïna*, 14 and 28 June 1990.

Democratic Platform, who were far from being nationalists. In the other cities of the east the absence of a tradition of working-class Ukrainian nationalism (see chapter 2) meant that the DB won very little support. Where the Communist Party was unpopular, as in urban regions of Russia, voters turned to independents, thirty-six of whom were elected in eastern Ukraine (of 150 seats). In southern Ukraine, the region's tenuous historical connections with the heartlands of long-term Ukrainian settlement made nationalist mobilisation next to impossible. The great majority of deputies were therefore CPU stalwarts (fifty-two out of sixty-six). Only in Odesa was big city anti-communism a factor, but again voters opted for independents rather than nationalists (six deputies out of twenty-three). Two deputies who initially declared their allegiance to the DB defected by the summer.[26]

Despite adopting a formal statute,[27] the Narodna rada did not constitute an opposition faction as such. It often held common sittings, but the decisions of such meetings were only recommendatory. Due to the rather anarchic and decentralised DB election campaign most Narodna rada deputies felt that they owed their election to their own individual efforts, rather than to collective party discipline. Moreover, the DB's supporters soon subdivided into three more or less formalised sub-groups, which were themselves ill disciplined and fractious.[28]

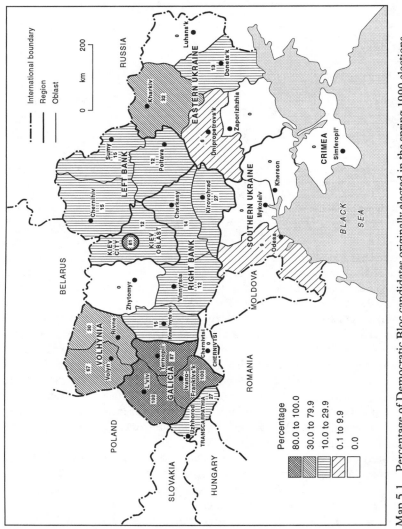

Map 5.1   Percentage of Democratic Bloc candidates originally elected in the spring 1990 elections.
Source *Narodni deputaty Ukraïny – predstavnyky Demokratychnoho bloku*, list supplied by the Rukh secretariat.

Twelve deputies were originally members of the UHU, which in April 1990 became the Ukrainian Republican Party. Eleven of these were elected in Galicia, and seven were former political prisoners, with almost 100 years of sentence between them.[29] Along with some radical independents the UHU formed the 22-strong Nezalezhnist' (Independence) faction, whose platform called for Ukrainian independence 'on the basis of the Helsinki final act' and 'the organisation of the [Ukrainian] state, socio-political, economic and cultural life in accordance with the national spirit and traditions of our people'.[30]

Twenty-three deputies eventually joined the Democratic Party (sixteen were from Galicia and three from Volhynia).[31] The party claimed a further sixteen 'sympathisers', but in contrast to the UHU always had great difficulties in organising even its own deputies as a faction. As the party's first leader Yurii Badz'o complained, 'our deputies are not people who were elected *from* political parties on a multi-party basis, but deputies who *became* members of parties, *after* the elections. They don't necessarily work in the party's structures.'[32] Moreover, Badz'o himself was not a deputy; the leader of the DPU's faction, Dmytro Pavlychko, was usually too busy chairing the foreign affairs committee; and his deputy Stepan Volkovets'kyi was unable to organise any effective whip system.

The third group was the Party of Democratic Revival of Ukraine (see chapter 3), roughly speaking the non-nationalist wing of the anti-communist opposition. Significantly, half of its thirty-six deputies (twenty members and sixteen 'sympathisers') were from eastern Ukraine, including six from Kharkiv oblast.[33] In Parliament its deputies tended to support de-communisation measures and proposals for economic reform, but consistently opposed narrowly nationalist initiatives.[34]

Most of the other members of the Narodna rada were formally non-party, but were closer to the nationalist URP and DPU than the PDRU. The Narodna rada elected the academic Ihor Yukhnovs'kyi as its leader, but formalised its internal divisions by burdening him with three deputies: Levko Luk"ianenko for the UHU, Dmytro Pavlychko for the Democratic Party and Oleksandr Yemets' for the PDRU. Moreover, the Narodna rada's fragile unity did not survive independence. In spring 1992 the PDRU formally left its ranks and joined up with smaller centrist parties, liberal independents and former communists to form the 58-strong New Ukraine faction.[35] After the disputes at the third Rukh congress in spring 1992 the nationalist camp divided into the more radical Congress of National-Democratic Forces faction, dominated by the URP and DPU, which had forty-one supporters,[36] and Chornovil's liberal nationalist Rukh, which had fifty.[37]

The Narodna rada and its successor groups were always a minority. Arguably the nationalists performed better than their numbers might have suggested in 1990–1 due to greater ideological and physical commitment, the intellectual and political tide flowing in their favour, and the institutional logic promoting the severance of ties between Parliament and Communist Party (see chapter 4). However, even the dissolution of the Communist Party in August 1991 failed to lead to a nationalist takeover of Parliament. Most former communists remained resolutely non-party. Many national communists voted with the former opposition, but did not form their own faction. The conservative majority, although leaderless, remained intact.

Local elections

The local elections in spring 1990 showed a similar pattern to the republican elections. Nationalists took control of the three oblast councils in Galicia (with between 60 and 80 per cent of the seats) and performed strongly in Volhynia and Kiev (40 per cent), but made little progress elsewhere. Kharkiv, where two-thirds of those elected were from the Democratic Bloc, was the only exception to the opposition's poor performance in the east and south.[38] On the other hand, fifteen out of twenty-five oblast councils were headed by local CPU first secretaries, as were 459 out of 696 town councils, and 52 per cent of local deputies (some 307,000 at all levels) were members of the CPU.[39] Consequently, although an Association of Democratic Councils and Democratic Blocs was formed in July 1990, local soviets were increasingly seen as left-wing or conservative bastions, and in the constitutional debate after 1990 most nationalists were strongly in favour of their abolition (see chapter 6).

The author's only detailed figures for nationalist support are for the UHU, which elected 427 deputies to local councils (although many soon followed a relatively independent path).[40] The vast majority (362, or 85 per cent) were elected in Galicia (see table 5.2). The UHU's largest body of deputies was elected in L'viv, although it was in opposition to Chornovil, who was leader of the oblast council from 1990 to 1992. It had twenty-three deputies on the oblast council (out of 200), between twenty and twenty-two on the town council (out of 150), and 210 in the oblast as a whole.[41] The UHU, later boosted by defections, helped form the Democratic Platform faction in Transcarpathia,[42] and it exercised considerable influence on the Ternopil' and Ivano-Frankivs'k councils. However, the UHU had few deputies outside the west (except for Kiev city) and its deputies were rarely capable of disciplined action as a faction.[43]

Table 5.2 *Local UHU (URP) deputies elected in spring 1990*

Region	Total	Percentage of total
Galicia	362	84.8
Volhynia	5	1.2
Transcarpathia	1	0.2
Chernivtsi	4	0.9
Right Bank	9	2.1
Kiev	21	4.9
Left Bank	7	1.6
East	9	2.1
South	8	1.9
Crimea	1	0.2
Total	427	

Source: URP secretariat document, as of 12 May 1991. In Galicia the URP had 210 deputies in L'viv, 81 in Ivano-Frankivs'k, and 71 in Ternopil'. Cf. the estimate of 305 deputies at all levels made by V. Lytvyn (Litvin), 'Ukrainskaia respublikanskaia partiia', *Politika i vremia*, no. 7 (May), 1991, p. 78.

The DPU claimed to have more deputies at all levels than all other parties, including the URP, especially in Galicia.[44] However, estimates of 500 deputies or more could not be substantiated because of poor communication with local party cells.[45] However, the DPU's Stepan Volkovets'kyi was head of Ivano-Frankivs'k oblast council, and many DPU stalwarts were appointed as provincial prefects after March 1992, such as Professor Roman Hrom"iak in Ternopil' and Vitalii Donchyk (deputy prefect) in Kiev.

The March 1991 referendum

The next test of Ukrainian public opinion came in the March 1991 referendum called by Gorbachev on the future of the USSR.[46] Nationalists were predictably opposed to Gorbachev's question ('Do you consider it necessary to preserve the USSR as a renewed federation of equal sovereign republics, in which human rights and the freedoms of all nationalities will be fully guaranteed?'), but were placed in a dilemma after Kravchuk accepted Luk"ianenko's proposal to place a second question on the ballot ('Do you agree that Ukraine should be part of a Union of Soviet Sovereign States on the basis of the Declaration of State Sovereignty of Ukraine?'), and the three Galician councils decided to hold their own vote on outright independence.

The ultra-nationalists (UIA, DSU, UNP) called for a boycott of the main vote as the act of an occupying power.[47] Significantly, many mainstream national-democrats sympathised with the ultra-nationalists as Kravchuk's second question stopped well short of endorsing Ukrainian independence. Nevertheless moderates argued that its defeat would undermine republican sovereignty and the increasing cooperation between nationalists and national communists.[48] At a special session of Rukh's Coordinating Council in February the call for a boycott was defeated, but only by 117 votes to 84, and Rukh decided to campaign against Gorbachev's question but in favour of Kravchuk's,[49] as did the DPU.[50] The URP, on the other hand, eventually decided to call not for a boycott, but for a 'no' to both all-Ukrainian ballots, and a 'yes' to the Galician question.[51]

The Communist Party was also divided. Conservatives urged voters to support Gorbachev's original proposal, whereas Kravchuk's national communists of course promoted their own alternative question. However both sides were astute enough to avoid committing themselves to advising a 'no' vote to their rivals' preferred question, although both pretended to ignore the Galician poll. Centrist parties such as the PDRU advised a 'no' to the first question and a 'yes' to the second.[52]

On 17 March, 70.5 per cent of Ukrainian voters supported Gorbachev's question, but 80.2 per cent backed Kravchuk's alternative (turnout was 83 per cent). In the three Galician oblasts 88 per cent voted in favour of independence. As the two main questions were similar in meaning and subject to a variety of interpretations and the Galician ballot purely local, map 5.2 estimates the level of nationalist support by taking the vote against the Gorbachev question as an unambiguously nationalist statement. The results confirmed the regional pattern established in March 1990 and showed that overall nationalist support had barely advanced, from between 24 and 27 per cent to 29.5 per cent.

Independence referendum, December 1991

By the time of the next test of public opinion on 1 December 1991 the political situation had changed utterly. The declaration of independence and the formal dissolution of the CPU meant that there was no substantial challenge to the new nationalist/national communist consensus in favour of national independence, although many nationalists opposed a referendum either because they argued that there was no need to confirm Parliament's decision or because they feared a majority would be difficult to obtain.[53] Even the newly formed Socialist Party fell into line,[54] while hardline communists were disoriented and disorganised. Anti-nationalist regional groups, such as the Democratic Movement of the Donbas and the Republican Movement of the Crimea were

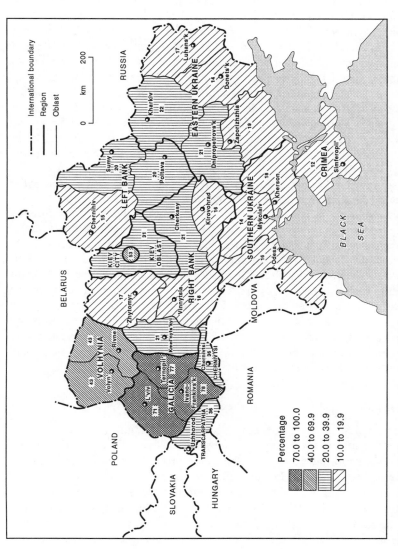

Map 5.2   The nationalist vote in the March 1991 referendum. Source: Oleksii Redchenko, 'Hotuimo sany vlitku', *Narodna hazeta*, no. 12 (April), 1992. The boycott campaign obviously reduced the 'no' vote in the west.

still struggling to get off the ground, and as yet commanded little support.[55] Moreover the Ukrainian mass media converted en masse to the independence cause.[56]

Popular support for independence therefore rose steadily from 63 per cent in September 1991 to 71 per cent in the first week of October and 88 per cent in mid-November,[57] before finally reaching 90.3 per cent in the actual vote on 1 December (turnout was 84 per cent). As shown in map 5.3, in the absence of a real alternative support for independence was both high and relatively uniform throughout Ukraine. However, if allowance is made for lower turnout in eastern and southern Ukraine by calculating the percentage voting 'yes' as a percentage of the total electorate, rather than as a percentage of those who actually voted, it was again clear that backing for the nationalist cause was lower in eastern and southern Ukraine, although unlike previous votes this time there was only a gradation in what were high levels of overall support.

Nevertheless, only 7.6 per cent actually voted against independence (some ballots were unused or spoilt). Such a consensus would have been inconceivable only a few months earlier. In part popular accord simply reflected newfound unity amongst elites and in the mass media, but subsequent surveys indicated the predominance of economic motives in winning many voters' support.[58] Apparent near-unanimity therefore masked the fact that the new Ukrainian state was from the very beginning built on highly conditional foundations. The non-nationalist majority accepted the argument that independence would leave Ukraine better off economically,[59] a notion that was soon proved to be totally without foundation (see chapter 6).

The presidential election of December 1991

Ukraine's first-ever democratic presidential election (already planned before the attempted coup in August) was also held on 1 December 1991. Six candidates were on the ballot. Kravchuk now stood unambiguously for independence, but his official programme, 'A New Ukraine', emphasised its likely economic benefits and traditional socialist themes of work and welfare for all.[60] This strategy ensured that Kravchuk, despite his drift to the right in 1990–1, was able to prevent a challenge from the left and position himself in Ukraine's natural centre of political gravity, leaning to the centre-left and south-east (an important point given Kravchuk's subsequent even sharper lurch to the right). The Socialist Party leader Oleksandr Moroz decided not to stand, and the conservative agriculture minister Oleksandr Tkachenko withdrew in Kravchuk's favour.[61]

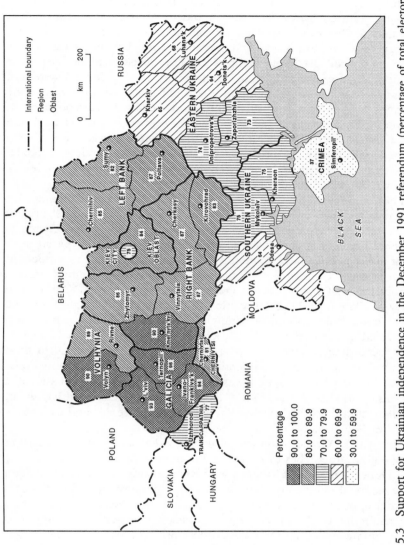

Map 5.3 Support for Ukrainian independence in the December 1991 referendum (percentage of total electorate).
Source: *Uriadovyi kur"ier*, no. 38–9 (December), 1991.

Significantly however, Kravchuk was opposed by Vladimir Griniov (Volodymyr Hryn'ov), deputy chairman of the Ukrainian Parliament, who put himself forward as the candidate of Ukraine's Russophone population. Griniov declared in his programme that centuries of common history between Russia and Ukraine should not be buried under 'the debris of the collapsed Soviet empire', and proposed that Ukraine should adopt Russian as a second state language, introduce a federal system of government and form a 'common economic space' with the rest of the former USSR.[62] Griniov was therefore supported by the Russophone half of the PDRU, various organisations in his home town of Kharkiv, the leftist United Social Democratic Party, the Ukrainian Kadets, and several of the Donbas strike committees. (A second centrist candidate, Leopol'd Taburians'kyi, leader of the tiny People's Party of Ukraine, made only a minimal impact on the campaign.)[63]

The nationalists on the other hand could not reach agreement on whom to support, or even on whether it was worth opposing Kravchuk at all (see also chapter 3). V"iacheslav Chornovil argued that Ukraine's national revolution should be accompanied, as in Russia, by an anti-communist political and economic revolution, and won the support of Rukh's Grand Council as the official Rukh candidate,[64] along with the endorsement of some centrist groups such as the Social Democratic Party of Ukraine and the Association of Democratic Councils.[65] On the other hand, Rukh's Political Council backed Levko Luk"ianenko, who advocated a 'Grand Bargain' between nationalists and national communists, according to which the latter would be left undisturbed in their positions in return for their continued commitment to the national cause. Luk"ianenko's strategy was endorsed by more overtly nationalist organisations such as the URP, DPU, Prosvita, the Union of Ukrainian Students and the All-Ukrainian Society of the Repressed and by leading individuals such as Ivan Drach.[66]

The Rukh Grand Council also endorsed a disastrous decision allowing local branches to campaign for any candidate of their choosing (the Donets'k branch of Rukh ended up supporting Kravchuk).[67] After a third national-democratic candidate, Ihor Yukhnovs'kyi, former leader of the opposition in Parliament, entered the field, it was hardly surprising that the Rukh campaign was racked by disunity and produced much animosity within the nationalist camp.[68] (Three other nationalist candidates had stood in the first phase of the election, Yurii Shukhevych for the Ukrainian National Assembly, Volodymyr Pylypchuk for the Democratic Party and the Green Party's Yurii Shcherbak, but had failed to collect the necessary 100,000 signatures to place their name on the ballot.)[69]

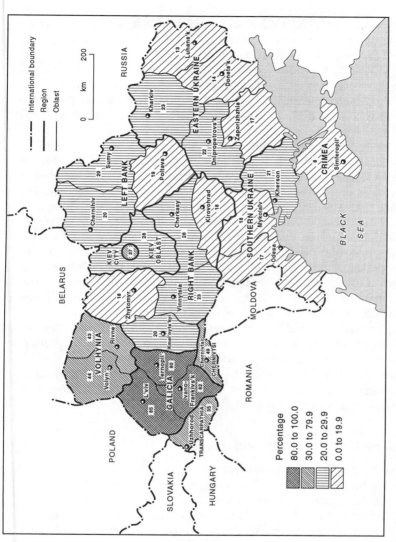

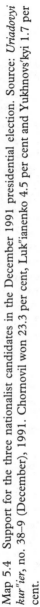

Map 5.4 Support for the three nationalist candidates in the December 1991 presidential election. Source: *Uriadovyi kur"ier*, no. 38–9 (December), 1991. Chornovil won 23.3 per cent, Luk"ianenko 4.5 per cent and Yukhnovs'kyi 1.7 per cent.

As the urbane Yukhnovs'kyi found it difficult to promote his message beyond the ranks of the big city intelligentsia, the Rukh vote was basically divided between Chornovil and Luk"ianenko (with Griniov arguably siphoning off some liberal-minded Russophone voters). The total vote for the Rukh troika is shown in map 5.4.

In total, the Rukh trio received 9,393,654 votes, or 29.5 per cent of the total (turnout was 84.2 per cent), exactly the same as the nationalist vote in the March referendum. Despite the huge vote for independence on the same day, underlying support for the nationalist cause had failed to advance. Moreover, the results once again confirmed the regional pattern of Rukh support established in March 1990 and March 1991. The Rukh trio swept the board in Galicia, and the restoration of nationalist strength in Chernivtsi was confirmed. They performed better than average in Kiev and other central Ukrainian cities (for example 30.7 per cent in Sumy city as against 20.4 per cent for the oblast as a whole),[70] but remained weak in eastern and southern Ukraine, especially in the Donbas and in Crimea. Rukh could make little impact on the countryside outside western Ukraine. Opinion poll evidence showed that support for the Rukh trio, as for independence as a whole, was strongest among ethnic Ukrainians, the intelligentsia, students and Uniate and Autocephalous Orthodox believers, but dropped substantially amongst workers and collective farmers.[71]

The centrist Taburians'kyi received a mere 0.6 per cent, but the maverick Griniov won a creditable 4.2 per cent, performing even better in areas with a large Russophone population such as his native Kharkiv (10.9 per cent) and Donets'k (11.0 per cent). Kravchuk, however, was a clear winner with 61.6 per cent of the total vote and substantial majorities throughout the centre, east and south.[72]

Party membership and organisation

Figures for party membership confirm electoral patterns. Table 5.3 shows that the membership of the main nationalist groups (as of spring 1995) was significantly less than that of the three main left-wing parties.

Support for nationalist groups was also drawn disproportionately from Galicia (which accounts for only 10.3 per cent of Ukraine's population), and Kiev city and oblast (8.8 per cent of the population), as shown in table 5.4.

If anything, the pattern of over-dependence on western Ukraine grew more pronounced as the 1990s advanced. For example, only 29 per cent of Rukh's 280,000 members in September 1989 were from Galicia, but by November 1992 Rukh membership had fallen to 50,000, and

Table 5.3 *Membership of main political parties in Ukraine, spring 1995*

Nationalist		Left	
Rukh	50,000	Communists	140,000
KUN	15,600	Agrarians	72,000
URP	13,000	Socialists	29,000
UNA	10,000		
DPU	4,000	Centre	
UCRP	3,500	IBR	2,000
		PDRU	1,500

Source: Zerkalo nedeli, no. 8, 1995.

Table 5.4 *Membership of key nationalist groups by region (percentages)*

Region	URP	DPU	Rukh	Prosvita
Galicia	55.1	33.6	28.9	52.4
Volhynia	6.2	4.8	12.1	5.7
Transcarpathia	3.9	3.5	1.4	4.1
Chernivtsi	1.8	2.8	2.2	1.8
Right Bank	6.1	16.5	12.8	6.8
Kiev (city and oblast)	10.2	8.3	18.1	6.3
Left Bank	3.8	4.8	6.2	1.9
East	9.3	18.9	12.0	11.8
South	3.1	6.5	6.4	8.9
Crimea	0.5	0.4	0.8	0.3

Sources: URP data are from information from party secretariat, as of June 1991, when the party had a total of 8,881 members, including 116 from the RSFSR excluded from the calculations. DPU data are from the party secretariat, as of the DPU's official registration on 28 June 1991, when the party had 3,015 members. For Rukh, the 1,109 delegates to the first Rukh congress in September 1989 were elected proportionately by the movement's then 280,000 members (George Sajewych and Andrew Sorokowski (eds.), *The Popular Movement of Ukraine for Restructuring – Rukh: Programme and Charter* (Ellicott City, Md.: Smoloskyp, 1989), p. 4); eight delegates from the Baltic republics were excluded from the calculations, and figures do not add to 100 per cent due to rounding. Prosvita information is from the Prosvita secretariat, as of 1 January 1993, when the society had 104,492 individual members. The figures are from different years, but that does not affect the overall point.

between 20,000 and 30,000 of these were from L'viv oblast alone.[73] Moreover, the nationalist parties' supposed all-Ukrainian profile was more apparent than real. Rukh, the URP and DPU claimed to be national parties, but many of their branches in eastern and southern Ukraine only existed on paper and did not even 'act like separate political subjects' at all.[74] According to Yurii Badz'o, 'some of the local leaders of the DPU simply "forget" about the party'.[75]

Both Rukh and the URP were dominated by Galicians to an even greater extent than is suggested by membership figures alone. Galicians frequently travelled elsewhere in Ukraine to take part in public demonstrations, petition campaigns and the like (in 1989–91 the Communist Party was able to attack the idea of Galician 'flying pickets' descending on Kiev or the Donbas to considerable propaganda effect),[76] and the Galician branches of both organisations were often twinned with weaker organisations in eastern and southern Ukraine to provide practical help and assistance (in 1991 the URP helped to organise a series of exchanges of schoolchildren between eastern Ukraine and Galicia to try and help overcome misconceptions concerning 'Galician extremism').[77] Many of the URP's leaders elsewhere in Ukraine were actually born in Galicia.[78]

The membership of ultra-nationalist organisations was even more sharply concentrated in Galicia. Of the main ultra-nationalist groups, only the Ukrainian National Assembly had substantial membership outside western Ukraine (5,000 out of the UNA's claimed membership of 14,000 in February 1993 came from western Ukraine, of which 950 were in L'viv). On the other hand 73 per cent of the Ukrainian Peasant-Democratic Party's membership in January 1991 were from Galicia, and 75 per cent of those who attended the first congress of the DSU were from L'viv oblast alone.[79]

The 1994 parliamentary elections

Despite three years of independence the nationalist cause had made few advances by the time of the next major test of public opinion, the spring 1994 elections to the Ukrainian Parliament. In fact the most striking feature of the 1994 elections was that the overall results barely diverged from the pattern already established in 1989–91.[80]

In late 1991 and early 1992, with the Communist Party banned and conservative and regional elites disoriented, it seemed for a time that the nationalists would be able to exploit the relative political vacuum to impose their agenda. President Kravchuk's open flirtation with Rukh around the time of its third congress in spring 1992 represented the high-water mark of this process.[81] However, from late 1992 onward anti-nationalist forces began to revive (see chapters 3 and 4) and to reanimate the structures and networks of the old left, both inside Parliament and outside, a process capped by the revival and (re)registration of the Communist Party of Ukraine in 1993.

Moreover, as well as opposing economic hardship and (then still largely unimplemented) market reforms, the new left coopted the anti-nationalist themes raised by Vladimir Griniov in his 1991 presidential campaign. The new left attacked the nationalists for failing to recognise that 'in the economic, cultural, religious and ethnographic spheres, Ukraine is like a bouquet of flowers – diverse',[82] and argued that nationalist domination in Kiev under the pressure of 'fascists in the Ukrainian Piedmont'[83] amounted to the rule of a Dontsovite minority and the artificial attempt to 'Galicianise' Ukraine (see chapter 6).[84] The left therefore proposed an alternative agenda of a federalised state, Russian as a second state language and closer links with the CIS.[85]

With a more natural balance of forces restored, the nationalists were once again made to feel the constraints to their influence. Despite the concession of early elections in September 1993, they were unable to obtain an election law to their liking, namely some variant of the mixed majoritarian and party list system used in the Russian elections of December 1993. Instead, the form chosen (no party lists, all seats elected in territorial constituencies on the second ballot system, workplace as well as party nomination of candidates) was designed to discourage party formation and favour the 'non-party' conservatives who still dominated Parliament. Moreover, two tough hurdles were imposed in order for elections to be valid in any given constituency: 50 per cent plus one of the electorate had to vote, and 50 per cent plus one of votes were required for eventual victory, raising fears that even the very process of securing election would be difficult.

So it proved. Only three-quarters of the seats (338 out of 450) were filled at the first attempt. Less than 10 per cent of the 5,835 candidates were formally nominated by political parties, but many more declared an allegiance when registered by the Central Election Commission. Independents won 60.9 per cent of first-round votes, but the three main parties of the left (Communists, Socialists and Agrarians) were clearly ahead. In the first round they won over five million votes or 22 per cent of the total, as opposed to 3.4 million (14 per cent) for the nationalist parties and just over one million votes (4 per cent) for parties of the centre (see table 5.5). In the second round some independents were filtered out, but they still won 55 per cent of the vote. The left vote rose to 29 per cent, while the right and centre parties slipped back to 12 per cent and just under 4 per cent respectively.

As well as losing out to the left, the right was also weakened by fierce intra-nationalist competition, both between the national-democrats and the ultra-nationalists and amongst the individual parties in both camps. In 388 out of 450 constituencies a common candidate on an Ukraïna list was supposedly supported by most mainstream nationalist parties, but the agreement was widely flouted and most of the open contests were in

Table 5.5 *Total vote for main blocs in the spring 1994 elections*

Block	First round Vote	Percentage of total	Second round Vote	Percentage of total
Non-party	14,963,548	60.9	11,609,653	54.6
Left	5,349,711	21.8	6,225,108	29.3
Centre[a]	1,056,985	4.3	835,591	3.9
National-democrat	2,701,042	10.9	2,208,005	10.4
Ultra-nationalist	690,048	2.9	370,546	1.7

Note: [a] Centrist political parties were even weaker than those on the left or right. A higher proportion of centrists therefore stood as independents and the figure in the table must be regarded as an underestimate.
Source: Author's calculations from information provided by parties and by the Slavonic Centre, Kiev.

the crucial (and winnable) region of western Ukraine.[86] Table 5.5 therefore distinguishes between the national-democrats and ultra-nationalists, and the respective fortunes of both groups are shown in more detail in table 5.6.

Table 5.6 shows the support for the various nationalist parties in the first round of the election. Fewer parties made it to the second round. The national-democratic parties held steady with 2,208,005 votes or 10.4 per cent of the total, while the ultra-nationalists slipped back to 370,546 votes (1.7 per cent). The national-democrat vote was divided between Rukh (1,378,043 or 6.5 per cent of all votes cast), the URP (632,428 or 3.0 per cent) and the DPU (197,534 or 0.9 per cent). Most of the ultra-nationalist votes were won by KUN (214,302 or 1.0 per cent), followed by the UNA-UNSO (82,104), UCRP (53,431) and DSU (20,709).

The regional breakdown of the vote was much the same as in 1990 or 1991. Volhynia and Chernivtsi (Bukovyna) were confirmed as catching up with Galicia (although Transcarpathia remained a special case), but the nationalists made no progress whatsoever in central Ukraine and in the east and south they won even fewer seats than in 1990. Moreover, only five out of twenty-three seats in Kiev city produced a result, mainly because of low turnout, leaving nationalist support even more slanted to the west than in 1990. In Galicia (Ivano-Frankivs'k excepted) national-democrats only just outpolled ultra-nationalists (in L'viv national democrats won 24.8 per cent of the vote as against 18.4 per cent for the radicals, in Ternopil' 36.2 per cent against 13.2 per cent), but elsewhere the ultra-nationalists were some way behind. The far right also had pockets of support in Kiev city (3.7 per cent), Khmel'nyts'kyi (4.8 per

Table 5.6 *Support for nationalist parties in the spring 1994 elections*

Party	Number of candidates	First-round vote	Percentage of total vote	Deputies elected after second round
National-democrat				
Rukh	212	1,484,294	6.0	27
URP	137	722,408	2.9	9
DPU	67	310,411	1.3	6[a]
UOU	40	[b]	[b]	5
New Wave	11	177,300	0.7	3
UNCP	6	6,629	<0.1	–
Subtotal	473	2,701,042	10.9	50
Ultra-nationalist				
UCRP	28	98,758	0.4	2
UNA	25	110,399	0.5	3
SNPU	22	49,212	0.2	–
KUN	14	355,857	1.4	8
OUN in U	11	15,529	0.1	–
DSU	11	24,429	0.1	–
UCDP	6	5,928	<0.1	–
UPDP	5	11,836	<0.1	–
VNRU	4	18,100	0.1	–
Subtotal	126	690,048	2.9	13
Total	599	3,391,090	13.8	63

Notes: Ukraïns'ka hazeta, 12–25 May 1994 lists 264 Rukh candidates and 60 from KUN. KUN also 'supported' eight other nationalists who were elected as independents or on the Rukh list: *Shliakh peremohy*, 16 April 1994. See also Yurii Kur"ianovych, 'L'viv"iany yak vyborche syto', *Post-postup*, 15–21 April 1994 on the results in L'viv.
[a] Only three deputies stayed with the DPU.
[b] Detailed figures for the UOU were unavailable.
Sources: Author's calculations from information provided by parties and by the Slavonic Centre, Kiev.

cent), Vinnytsia (2.3 per cent) and Rivne (2 per cent), but everywhere else polled less than 2 per cent. The left-wing parties, on the other hand, were strongest in the east and south, especially in the Donbas and Crimea, and in small town and rural areas. As in 1990, Russophone liberals polled best in east-central regions such as Kharkiv and Dnipropetrovs'k. Map 5.5 shows how the percentage of the popular vote won by nationalist parties varied across the regions.

Tables 5.5 and 5.6 record the vote only for those candidates formally affiliated with nationalist parties. Clearly, however, many nominally 'independent' candidates were also nationalists, especially in the west, just as many others gravitated to the parties of the left or centre.

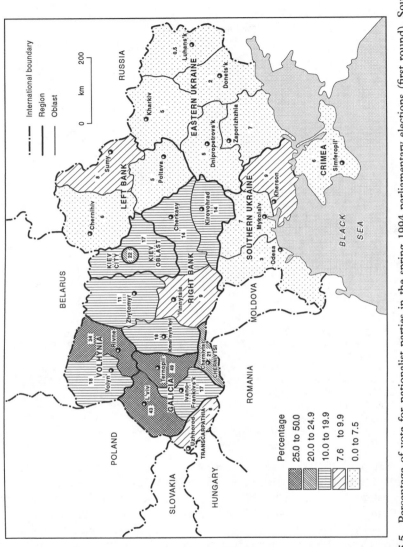

Map 5.5 Percentage of vote for nationalist parties in the spring 1994 parliamentary elections (first round). Source: author's calculations from information supplied by parties and Slavonic Centre, Kiev. A higher percentage of nationalist, but non-party, candidates stood in Ivano-Frankivs'k.

Information about non-party candidates is inherently less precise, but a survey of candidates' platforms in the west Ukrainian press indicates that nearly all nominal independents in fact adopted nationalist positions.[87] In Kiev city nationalist support also ran deeper than was immediately apparent, primarily because the rate of participation was substantially down on 1989–91. Eighteen of twenty-three seats failed to elect candidates in the spring, but unsuccessful nationalist candidates still won 498,000 votes or 59 per cent of the total in the second round, including 48,200 for four candidates from the UNA-UNSO.[88]

Classification of deputies actually elected is easier, because of the smaller numbers involved and the fact that faction formation was more pronounced than in the 1990 Parliament (new parliamentary rules encouraged faction formation by allocating parliamentary time and committee positions in proportion to the strength of the factions, and by allowing deputies to belong to only one group). On the basis of their individual programmes and press reports, an additional nineteen deputies could be classified as definite nationalists, making a total of eighty-two, or 24 per cent (as opposed to 147 on the left, or 43.5 per cent). Although in some areas of nationalist support, notably Kiev, many seats remained empty, the relative proportion of seats won by nationalists was therefore identical to that in 1990, allowing for the fact that the performance of the Democratic Bloc in eastern Ukraine in 1990 had been boosted by the presence of the Democratic Platform of the CPU.[89]

The regional origin of the eighty-two nationalist deputies is shown in table 5.7 and map 5.6, and confirms the regional division of the vote shown in table 5.6. In fact the regional bias of the popular vote was exaggerated by the second-ballot electoral system, which tended to deprive the nationalist minority of any representation in the east and south, whilst similarly shutting out the left in the west.

One final possibility is to look at the factions formed in Parliament after the elections. However several factors make this method inexact. The minimum number of deputies required to form a faction was twenty-five, leaving most of the thirteen ultra-nationalists in the independent camp. Two factions were definitively nationalist – as in 1992–4 the national democrats were split between Rukh (twenty-seven deputies) and the more radical Congress of National-Democratic Forces (twenty-five members of the 'Statehood' faction). However, many liberal nationalists, disillusioned with the lack of real economic reform in the 1990–4 Parliament, left Rukh to team up with centrist liberals as the 'Reforms' faction (twenty-seven deputies). Not all of the members of this faction could therefore be considered nationalists, as was also true of the thirty-eight members of 'Centre', a centrist faction dominated by

Table 5.7 *Regional breakdown of seats won by nationalists in the spring 1994 elections*

Region	Seats won	Total seats	Percentage of total
Galicia	40	40	100
Volhynia	11	14	79
Transcarpathia	1	7	14
Chernivtsi	3	6	50
Right Bank	10	46	22
Kiev	9	17	53
Left Bank	6	31	19
East	1	129	1
South	1	37	3
Crimea	0	11	0
Total	82	338	24

Sources: Official results; *Post-postup*, 15–21 April 1994; International Foundation for Election Systems, *Ukraine's New Parliament* (Kiev: April 1994); information supplied by URP; and the list of deputy factions in *Holos Ukraïny*, 12 July 1994.

national communists (see the following section). On the other hand, the political centre split along regional and ethno-linguistic lines, with Russophones forming their own factions ('Unity' and 'Interregional Block', with twenty-five deputies each). The three left-wing factions had the greatest support, with 145 deputies overall.[90]

Three rounds of repeat elections in July, August and November 1994 resulted in another seventy-one seats being filled, but only four of the new deputies were formally allied to a nationalist group (one supported Rukh and three were members of the URP, including Levko Luk″ianenko and Bohdan Horyn').[91] If anything, therefore, the nationalists' proportional strength in Parliament was reduced. By October 1994 the left factions had gained twenty-seven deputies, the Russophone centrists seventeen and Reforms eight; but Rukh remained on twenty-seven, Statehood only advanced to twenty-eight and the Centre group actually lost one deputy[92] (see table 5.8). A moratorium on further elections was finally agreed in December 1994, with forty-five seats still empty.[93]

The national communists

On the one hand, it could be said that the 1994 elections were the first in which the national communists had stood as a more or less identifiable group. On the other hand, the national communists had no party structure as such and the vast majority stood as independents (see

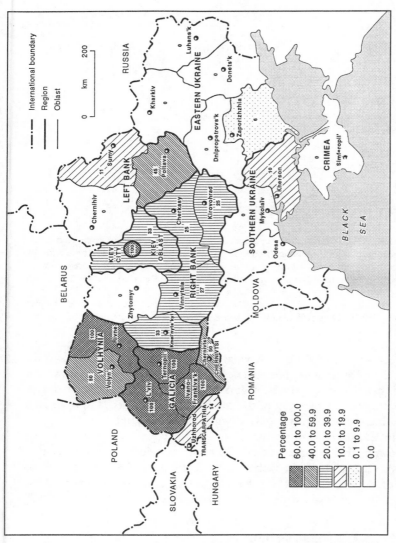
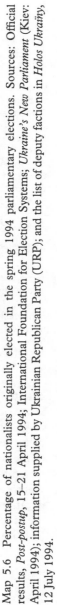

Map 5.6 Percentage of nationalists originally elected in the spring 1994 parliamentary elections. Sources: Official results, *Post-postup*, 15–21 April 1994; International Foundation for Election Systems; *Ukraine's New Parliament* (Kiev: April 1994); information supplied by Ukrainian Republican Party (URP); and the list of deputy factions in *Holos Ukraïny*, 12 July 1994.

Table 5.8 *Factions in Parliament after the 1994 elections*

Group and faction	Deputies July	October
Left		
Communists	84	90
Socialists	25	30
Agrarians	36	52
Russophone Centre		
Interregional Block	25	33
Unity	25	34
Ukrainophone Centre		
Centre	38	37
Reforms	27	35
National-Democrat		
Rukh	27	27
Statehood	25	28
Independents	23	36
Total	335[a]	395[b]

Notes: [a]One deputy died. Two others were under investigation for campaign irregularities.
[b]Seven deputies apparently belonged to more than one faction in contravention of parliamentary regulations. The factional allegiance of those elected in November was unknown.
Sources: Holos Ukraïny, 12 July 1994; *Vseukrainskie vedomosti*, 22 October 1994. See also Artur Bilous, 'Pivtory sotni reformatoriv shche ne riatuiut' ukraïns'ku demokratiiu', *Demoz*, no. 5, 1995.

chapter 4). It is therefore somewhat pointless to try and assess their share of the popular vote. Nevertheless the Centre faction created in the wake of the elections, which originally claimed the support of thirty-eight deputies or 11 per cent of the total, was more or less the remnants of the national communist group. Significantly, its members were nearly all ethnic Ukrainians (thirty-three out of thirty-eight), the majority of whom came from rural central Ukraine or Volhynia (twenty-two deputies). Only eight came from eastern Ukraine and a mere two from the south.[94] Ex-president Kravchuk (see next section) returned to Parliament in a special by-election in September.

The 1994 presidential election

Lastly, and most spectacularly, the presidential election in June and July 1994 demonstrated the near-impossibility of winning Ukrainian elections on a nationalist ticket. The incumbent Leonid Kravchuk attempted to polarise the election around the basic issue of support for Ukrainian independence by painting his main opponent, former prime minister Leonid Kuchma, as the leader of a Russophile fifth column, but still lost decisively by 45 per cent to 52 per cent (on a turnout of 72 per cent in the second round).[95]

The parliamentary elections had convinced the nationalists that one of their own had no chance of victory, and Kuchma's record as prime minister from October 1992 to September 1993, when he had struggled against Kravchuk's opposition to integrate Ukraine more closely into the CIS, sufficed to persuade them that Kravchuk's caricature was accurate.[96] The nationalist parties therefore closed ranks behind Kravchuk as the only man capable of beating Kuchma. Only the maverick Stepan Khmara refused to fall into line.[97] Kuchma, on the other hand, was backed by the left and by Russophone centrists. Neither man campaigned on a clear economic programme (Kuchma's commitment to market reforms was tempered by his need to court the left), but each developed clear and contrary positions on the national question.

Kravchuk campaigned in favour of maintaining a unitary state with an independent foreign policy orientation, opposed closer ties with the CIS and stressed the defence of Ukrainian language and culture. Kuchma, of course, was far from being a separatist. His programme called for a decentralised federal system of government in Ukraine, the adoption of Russian as a second state language and the creation of a 'strategic partnership' between Ukraine and Russia, but promised that this would strengthen rather than undermine Ukrainian independence.[98] As argued in chapter 2, this combination of local patriotism with the recognition of Ukraine's and Russia's common interests is as much a part of the Ukrainian national tradition as the exclusionary nationalism of Mihknovs'kyi or Dontsov. The fact that Kuchma was unfairly characterised as pro-Russian by all too many nationalists says more about their own refusal to countenance the existence of alternative native Ukrainian intellectual and political traditions as it does about Kuchma himself.

The other main candidates were Oleksandr Moroz, leader of the Socialist Party and chairman of Parliament since the spring elections; his predecessor Ivan Pliushch, fighting on a nationalist platform but effectively out of the race once most of the right united behind Kravchuk; Volodymyr Lanovyi, a former economics minister pushing a populist programme of market-based reforms; Valerii Babych, an east Ukrainian businessman; and Petro Talanchuk, minister of education and broadly nationalist. Only Moroz and Lanovyi were a significant factor in the campaign. The 13.1 per cent who voted for Moroz in the first round plumped heavily for Kuchma in the second, while Lanovyi's supporters (9.4 per cent of the first-round vote) gave a slight edge to Kravchuk.[99]

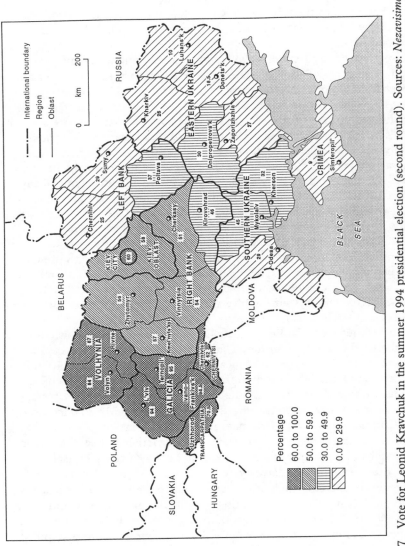

Map 5.7 Vote for Leonid Kravchuk in the summer 1994 presidential election (second round). Sources: *Nezavisimost'*, 13 July 1994; Dominique Arel and Andrew Wilson, 'Ukraine Under Kuchma: Back to "Eurasia"?', *RFE/RL Research Report*, vol. 3, no. 32, 19 August 1994.

Map 5.7 shows the results of the second-round showdown between Kravchuk and Kuchma. Some nationalists, after the shock of defeat had set in, claimed to take comfort from the fact that an unprecedented 45 per cent, or 12.7 million voters, had voted for a clearly nationalist candidate.[100] There is some truth in this claim, but equally striking was the fact that the choice facing voters was characterised in the starkest terms and Kravchuk lost.

Of all the elections in 1990–4, the presidential election of summer 1994 showed the polarisation between Ukraine's historical regions most sharply, with Kravchuk's electoral profile being almost the complete opposite of his winning coalition in 1991. Support for Kuchma dropped to single figures in Galicia, as was also the case for Kravchuk in Crimea. Kravchuk won every oblast in western and central Ukraine west of the Dnieper, bar Kirovohrad; Kuchma swept the Left Bank, east and south.[101] However, Kravchuk's massive lead in western Ukraine was not enough to overcome Kuchma's broader base of support, and Kravchuk lost the election through his relatively poor performance in central Ukraine. The Left Bank, with its closer historical ties to Russia, backed Kuchma by 66 per cent to 31 per cent, while on the Right Bank, Kravchuk only led Kuchma by 55 per cent to 45 per cent. The dichotomy between town and country in central Ukraine also worked against Kravchuk. In urban areas, especially in Kiev, Kravchuk's popularity was offset by low turnout,[102] but he had no offsetting lead in the countryside.[103] Even in his old parliamentary constituency in rural Vinnytsia, Kravchuk won only 37 per cent of the vote.[104]

The presidential election therefore once again demonstrated the asymmetries in Ukrainian voting behaviour. Although the nationalist stronghold in the west is perhaps evenly matched with that of the anti-nationalist left in the Donbas, the latter has broader support throughout eastern and southern Ukraine and in significant parts of central Ukraine, where only the leading urban centres and the intelligentsia can be counted as firm supporters of the nationalist cause. With turnout in Kiev again low, nationalism became even more lopsidedly dependent on the west.

Conclusion

The striking factor about all elections from 1989 to 1994 is both continuity and conformity with the historical patterns described in chapters 1 and 2. Differential levels of support for nationalist politics in Ukraine's historic regions are stark and, for the moment at least, remarkably stable. As expected, the Ukrainian national movement is strongest in Galicia, Volhynia, Chernivtsi and urban central Ukraine, especially Kiev, but extremely weak everywhere else.

On the other hand, socio-economic factors do not seem to have been as influential as historic ones in determining patterns of support for nationalism.[105] It is often argued that support for the anti-nationalist left in east Ukraine, the Donbas in particular, comes primarily from insecure workforces in antiquated heavy industry.[106] This may indeed create overlapping cleavages that make anti-nationalism in regions like the Donbas a particularly powerful force, but the same argument cannot be made in the more rural south, apart from in a few shipbuilding centres. Moreover, eastern Ukraine is not a homogeneous economic entity. Kharkiv and Dnipropetrovs'k, for example, have much better economic prospects than other regions in the east. They may therefore vote for Russophone liberals, but they do not vote for Ukrainian nationalists. Lastly, socio-economic factors alone cannot explain why west Ukrainians, despite their equally distressed economic circumstances, still support nationalist candidates with appalling records of economic management, like Leonid Kravchuk.

Chapters 6 and 7 now turn to an examination of the nationalist agenda in both domestic and foreign policy, and how it has been shaped by Ukrainian nationalists' reactions to their minority status.

6   The nationalist agenda: domestic politics, Ukrainianisation and the state

This chapter seeks to analyse the nationalist agenda in domestic politics, focusing on issues that revolve around the national question, including the degree of ethnic Ukrainian predominance in the new state, the promotion of the Ukrainian language, the structure of the Ukrainian polity and the construction of a national economy.[1] Given the historical and regional limits to nationalist support outlined in previous chapters, the nationalist approach in each area is likely to prove controversial and meet with substantial resistance. Therefore the anti-nationalist agenda is also briefly summarised where appropriate. At the same time, it will be argued that the intensity of nationalist commitment to issues such as Ukrainianisation can best be understood in terms of their frustration at the strength of the anti-nationalist lobby.

'The Ukrainian people' or the 'people of Ukraine'?

The key question to be faced by Ukrainian nationalists in building a new Ukrainian state is whether it should be the state of the 'Ukrainian people' (*ukraïns'kyi narod*), that is of ethnic Ukrainians alone, or of the 'people of Ukraine' (*narod Ukraïny*), in other words of all Ukraine's inhabitants regardless of their ethnic origin.[2] Ukraine is not of course the only Soviet successor state attempting to strike a balance between the rights of the eponymous nationality and those of the population at large, but in Ukraine's case the dilemma is particularly acute. Only Kazakhstan has national minorities comparable in size to Ukraine's 11.4 million Russians and 2.7 million others, but the sheer scale of Ukraine's problem is arguably unique in Europe. Moreover, only Belarus has suffered a greater degree of 'Russification',[3] which nationalists argue should be reversed by positive discrimination in favour of the indigenous population. In Ukraine sensitivity to the issue is such that even simple names can be controversial and indicative of political preference. An organisation or institution that calls itself 'Ukrainian' (such as the Ukrainian Republican Party or the Ukrainian Christian Democratic

Party) is likely to be perceived as narrowly ethnicist, while those that style themselves 'of Ukraine' are probably seeking to emphasise their open, non-ethnic nature (the Christian Democratic Party of Ukraine).

Most Ukrainian nationalists have gone to great pains to stress their adherence to the principles of a liberal and civic state. According to Rukh's centrepiece 1992 programme for example, 'for historical, ethnic, economic, political and social-psychological reasons Ukrainian society is not homogeneous'. Therefore 'Rukh views Ukraine as a multinational state [formed] from the multinational nature of Ukrainian society'.[4] In a similar vein, one of the Republican Party's spokesmen has argued that 'the most effective integrating factor [in building a new Ukrainian state] will be "territorial patriotism", that is a sense of solidarity between all inhabitants of Ukrainian lands regardless of their social status, religious affiliation, ethnic origin or even national-cultural consciousness'.[5]

The basis for this approach was supposedly laid by the ideological metamorphoses of the 1960s, when the civic approach became 'a genuine element of an indigenous national tradition, not a tactical device to dupe Ukraine's Russians into passivity'.[6] According to many commentators, nationalist moderation on this issue has been a key factor in helping independent Ukraine establish itself as a model civic polity, whose liberal citizenship and language laws are in marked contrast to the more restrictive approach of Estonia or Latvia.[7]

Formal public policy on the nationality issue has indeed to date undoubtedly been more liberal than in Estonia or Latvia. Nationalists supported a 'zero-option' citizenship law in October 1991, according to which citizenship was automatically granted to all those resident on Ukrainian territory at the time,[8] after which the issue was largely diffused, although some groups objected to new passport proposals because they no longer classed citizens ethnically.[9] (In the run-up to the 1994 elections the ultra-radical DSU sought unsuccessfully to reopen the question, proposing that only those loyal to the Ukrainian state and language should be allowed a vote; 'foreigners' and 'separatists' should be excluded in order to prevent the new Parliament being dominated by 'aliens who will be elected by other aliens'.)[10] On the other hand, nationalists have objected strongly to Russian demands for the introduction of dual citizenship between the two states.

A declaration on the rights of nationalities was passed with nationalist support in November 1991 and a law on national minorities in June 1992.[11] The former promised that all Ukrainian citizens would be granted 'equal political, economic, social and cultural rights', including the 'right to free contacts with their historical fatherland', and declared that 'the Ukrainian state guarantees its citizens the right to use the

Russian language freely. In regions where several national groups live compactly, then the language which is convenient for the population of the said region as a whole may function side by side with the Ukrainian language.'[12]

This chapter will argue, however, that the true picture is rather more complex. On closer examination the structure of Ukrainian nationalist argument on questions of nationhood, citizenship and ethnic 'rights' is not too dissimilar to that of their supposedly more extreme Baltic counterparts, and conforms to standard patterns observable in many other ethno-nationalist movements. The consequent potential for an anti-nationalist backlash in eastern and southern Ukraine is therefore as real as it is in north-east Estonia or in Moldova east of the Dniester.

Indigenousness and occupation

Ukrainian nationalists and anti-nationalist and Russophone groups in eastern and southern Ukraine have radically different conceptions of what is meant by a civic state. The latter understand by the concept of the 'people of Ukraine' a recognition that modern Ukraine is a multi-ethnic society, and a promise that the Ukrainian polity should be either multi-ethnic or anational in recognition of this fact.[13] In a true multi-ethnic state, 'the development of the national culture, language and traditions of the Ukrainian people' would go hand in hand with that of other peoples, without any group 'interfering with the rights of others',[14] and no individual ethnic group or region (i.e. Galicia) would be allowed to set themselves up as 'the official standard [etalon] for the whole state'.[15] 'Civic patriotism' would be acceptable, but 'ethnic patriotism can [only] lead to inter-ethnic conflict'.[16] Alternatively, an anational Ukrainian polity would enshrine the absolute 'equality of all citizens, regardless of nationality' and the supremacy of individual over group rights, and refrain from 'asserting the priority of one language, nation or culture' over another.[17] 'Without the free individual', it is argued, 'there can be no free state.'[18] Such terminology echoes the anti-nationalist discourse of the late Gorbachev era, when it was felt inappropriate to express minority opposition to titular nationality dominance in the kind of collectivist language that might only reinforce the latter's conceptual framework.

Ukrainian nationalists, however, tend to deny that Ukraine is a multinational state at all. Moreover, their argument draws on three of the same concepts that underlie Baltic and other forms of ethno-nationalism:[19] namely the idea of 'homeland' and the special rights of the indigenous people,[20] the right to cultural self-preservation and (to a much lesser extent) the notion of forcible incorporation into the Soviet state and the consequent illegitimacy of subsequent changes to national demographics or patterns of language use.

The first, the 'claim to indigenousness', is a common feature of many nationalist movements, given their need to create 'an association with a specific homeland ... a historic territory that locates a community in time and space',[21] and to establish a bounded area of proprietal right. According to Ukrainian nationalists, only

states on whose territory different peoples have lived since time immemorial can be considered multinational (such as India or the Russian Federation). On the bulk of its territory Ukraine is mononational, because only one people has lived here since time immemorial – the Ukrainian (in Crimea – Ukrainian and Crimean Tatar). Other peoples arrived later, at different times and for different reasons, having left their ethnic fatherland.[22]

In fact, the Ukrainians have supposedly been a uniquely well-settled people, having 'since the Neolithic age' avoided the resettlement and forced migration that has had such 'fatal consequences' for so many other peoples.[23]

Therefore Russian and other minorities in Ukraine can make no claim for privileged treatment. Only the Crimean Tatars and the tiny Karaïm community (also native to Crimea) deserve special consideration, because they are the only other peoples who have no homeland outside Ukraine. Poles or Romanians in Ukraine, on the other hand, already have a nation-state of their own, where the special rights of a sovereign people can be exercised. Above all, granting ethnic Russians or 'the Russian-speaking population' special rights (and still worse, allowing Russia to oversee the defence of those rights) would, it is argued, create a system of 'apartheid and national segregation',[24] and allow Russia to undermine Ukrainian sovereignty just as Hitler undermined Czechoslovakia in 1938–9. If Ukraine's inhabitants are all equal citizens, then they are also equal subjects, and only the Ukrainian state can be allowed to exercise authority over them.

On the contrary, therefore, it is the Ukrainians who should have special rights as the indigenous people (in Ukrainian *korinnii narod*, or 'rooted people') in their one and only national homeland, which is, moreover, a trust from God which they are morally obliged to retain and to nurture.[25] In the words of one leading nationalist, Mykhailo Horyn', 'we see Ukraine as a national state. This means that [both] its form (language, attributes, structure of power and so on) and content should be Ukrainian. Ukraine is the state of the indigenous Ukrainian nation.'[26] Although Horyn' went on to say that 'Ukraine is at the same time the state of the Ukrainian political nation, that is of all citizens of Ukraine regardless of their nationality', it is clear that on this issue nationalist discourse is at the very least ambiguous. Alongside the liberal nationalism formally proclaimed in party programmes and documents, many nationalists are in practice advocating a form of 'ethnic-led territorialism', involving elements of both civic liberalism and ethnic supremacism.[27] That is, their liberal or 'territorial' approach to questions of citizenship and minority rights is predicated on the assumption that minorities remain minorities, and that the rights of the indigenous nation to cultural and political leadership in its own backyard are not questioned. According to the (admittedly more nationalist) Congress of National-Democratic Forces, for example, the key principle in building a Ukrainian state must be the 'national character of Ukrainian statehood'. This should be combined with the 'broad participation of national minorities' in public life, but without the latter being able to challenge the former.[28]

A second common theme in Ukrainian nationalist discourse is that centuries of Russian and then Soviet domination 'gave such a colossal blow to the national organism' that 'the very existence of our ethnos' was in doubt.[29] If anything, this theme is even stronger in Ukrainian than in Baltic nationalism, as most of Ukraine has been under Russian influence for much longer, and Ukraine failed to obtain the vital breathing space provided by independence in the interwar period. Supposedly, 'in Ukraine there was not just an era of standstill or stagnation, but of continuous ruination and the merciless destruction of all things Ukrainian'.[30] Consequently, Ukrainian nationalists, like nationalists the world over, frequently claim that their own nation's sufferings have been without parallel in history. The Ukrainians are 'a unique people, a people chosen by God even, like the Jews or the Armenians, a suffering people'.[31] The element of hyperbole in myths of national suffering is also typical of nationalist discourse, as in claims that over '12 million' died in the Great Famine, or that 'in the Soviet period alone half of the Ukrainian nation was physically destroyed by Moscow'.[32] Three centuries of Russian rule have supposedly been a demographic catastrophe for Ukraine. In 1654, it is claimed, there were more Ukrainians than Russians, six million as opposed to five, whereas today the population of Russia outnumbers that of Ukraine by almost three to one (147 million to 52 million, and only 37 million of the latter are actually ethnic Ukrainians).[33] The mere need to ensure national survival therefore becomes a premise in itself in the argument that Ukrainian language and culture needs special treatment and positive discrimination (see pp. 153–7 below).

The third concept shared with many Baltic nationalists is the idea of forcible incorporation. Most nationalists believe that the Ukrainian People's Republic (UNR) of 1917–20 was only overthrown because 'Russian chauvinist Bolshevism unleashed a war of conquest against the young Ukrainian state',[34] rather than because of internal weaknesses, and many consequently referred to the Ukrainian SSR before 1991 as 'an occupying administration'.[35] Even relative moderates sympathised with the campaign by the ultra-nationalist Ukrainian Inter-party Assembly to restore the UNR in 1990–1 (see chapter 3), and Leonid Kravchuk was happy to accept a symbolic handover of authority from the would-be president of the UNR in exile (Mykola Plav"iuk) in 1992. Many nationalists have therefore argued that the principle that modern 'Ukraine is the legal successor of the UNR ... should be fixed in the new constitution of Ukraine',[36] and have idealised the 1917–20 period as a legitimate status quo ante, a benchmark against which subsequent changes in language policy or Russian in-migration can be condemned as artificial 'Russification'[37] (anti-nationalist groups can also play the same game, beginning their historical myths at different times and using different conceptions of geographical space; see pp.154–5 below).

In western Ukraine the argument of forcible incorporation also applies to 1939–45, although Ukrainian nationalists cannot denounce the 1939 Nazi–Soviet pact in the same terms as their Baltic counterparts, as it led to the unification of most Ukrainian lands. However, the myth of the liberation struggle of the OUN-UPA against Soviet force of arms retains considerable potency, both as a mobilising symbol in western Ukraine and as a factor dividing public opinion elsewhere (see the section on 'nationalist historiography', pp. 157–61 below).[38]

If it were to be generally accepted, this line of reasoning would have important consequences in delegitimating the whole period of Soviet rule. However, it has much less popular resonance in Ukraine than arguments based on indigenous rights or the need for cultural renewal, as memories of the 1917–20 period are hazy and many Ukrainians fought on the Soviet side both in the Civil War and during World War II. The psychologically important refusal of the Western powers to accept the legality of Soviet occupation of the Baltic states did not apply to Ukraine. The campaign to restore the UNR was therefore a pale shadow of the 1990 Congress of Estonia movement, and Ukrainian nationalism has been comparatively free of the radicalising influence of 'rejectionist' ideology.

Nevertheless, it can be argued that even mainstream Ukrainian national-democrats use many of the same core concepts as their Estonian and Latvian counterparts, in particular the rights of indigenes as against in-migrants, the privileged status of a single national home-land and the need for positive discrimination in favour of a language and culture supposedly on the verge of extinction. On the other hand, most Ukrainian nationalists also express commitment to the idea of a civic state. There is therefore a strong element of contradiction, or dual voice, in nationalist discourse in Ukraine. Nationalists often therefore simply fail to comprehend the complaints made by national minorities in Ukraine, pointing to the formal civic framework of the state, without realising that non-Ukrainians (and many Russophone Ukrainians) are in fact reacting to the strong emphasis on 'indigenous rights' in nationalist discourse. This helps to explain why Ukrainianisation has become a contentious issue since independence, despite the apparent restraint of the Ukrainian authorities in pushing the issue.

Ukrainianisation

Even before independence in 1991 a fierce argument had begun over the extent to which Ukraine should be 'Ukrainianised', in particular the question of how far the Ukrainian language should predominate. For the vast majority of Ukrainian nationalists, linguistic Ukrainianisation is simply the reversal of historical injustice. The domination of the 'Russian language in the eastern and southern oblasts of Ukraine did not happen by itself. The Russification of these regions is the result of the persistent migration and language policies of Russian tsars and Kremlin ideologues. The majority in [these regions] are Ukrainians, who have lost their language and culture as a result of the colonial status of Ukraine.'[39] As Ukrainian is the only true indigenous language in Ukraine (apart from Crimean Tatar), for nationalists Ukrainianisation is more accurately described as 'de-Russification', that is the reversion to a more natural status quo ante.[40] Moreover, as outlined above, it is argued that the sheer extent of 'Russification' threatens the very survival of the Ukrainian language. The Ukrainians have supposedly become a 'popula-tion, not a people', a multilingual 'tower of Babel', who find themselves in the position of the black majority in apartheid South Africa, 'with a [Russian-speaking] minority having usurped power, despising and oppressing the national majority'.[41]

Ukrainian nationalists are also fond of the Herderian argument that a nation's language embodies its own special genius and unique contribu-tion to global civilisation. For example, 'if in the beginning was the Word and the Word was God, then for every people its language is a blessed substance, its own form of self-expression and realisation of its unique mission on the earth'.[42] Moreover, language 'does not arise only for communication ... language is, as it were, a type of collective outlook on the world'. 'Language makes an individual an individual.' An individual who loses his language therefore loses contact with his true self. 'Language is above all psychology, it is related to genetics.'[43] Without it, an individual is adrift in a materialistic world.

The logic of such arguments is that the Ukrainian people have a collective right to the preservation of their own language that should if necessary take precedence over individual preferences on language use, as is implied when today's nationalists quote Mykola Skrypnyk's dictum of the 1920s: 'as the tide of history has moved for 300 years toward Russification, so let it turn back in the opposite direction for thirty years'.[44] In the crucial area of language politics therefore Ukrainian nationalists once again tend to give out mixed signals. Although both the Ukrainian languages law of 1989 and the 1991 declaration on the rights of nationalities guaranteed individuals 'the right to use their native languages freely in all spheres of social life',[45] nationalists consistently argue that the Ukrainian tongue should enjoy special privileges on its 'ancient land'.[46] 'Only the language of this [indigenous] ethnos', it is claimed, 'has the legal right to play the role of a state language.'[47]

Ukrainian nationalists tend to assume that Ukrainianisation will be a relatively simple, even natural, process. On the one hand, Ukraine's ethnic Russian minority, despite its undoubted size, remains a minority and should defer to the rights of the indigenous language and culture. On the other hand, most nationalists have derived from Khvyl'ovyi or Dontsov the view that Russophone Ukrainian culture is essentially artificial. It therefore tends to be assumed that 're-Ukrainianisation' policies will automatically be welcomed by the 'denationalised', those ethnic Ukrainians who have supposedly been severed forcibly from their mother tongue, but who remain in essence Ukrainian. Both assumptions are questionable.

The Russian minority is likely to contest its immigrant status, arguing that, outside western Ukraine, they too are indigenes with a long history of continuous settlement, particularly in the east and south.[48] From their point of view, therefore, 'the contemporary dual-language situation in Ukraine did not arise because of the Russification policies of tsarist bureaucrats, but has deep historical roots'.[49] The use of the Russian language on Ukrainian soil is as natural as the use of Ukrainian. Some would even argue that Ukrainian is in fact less natural, formed mainly as a result of Polish and Turkish imports into Old Rus' dialects, and Ukrainianisation policies are therefore tantamount to the 'Galicianisation' of eastern and southern Ukraine.[50] The status quo or the status quo ante, at least in eastern and southern Ukraine, has always involved the domination of Russian. What nationalists would call the 'Russification' of the east and south after 1945 was in fact merely the reversal of the consequences 'of the artificial Ukrainianisation of the 1920s'.[51]

Moreover, the nationalist assumptions that collective loyalties are always at heart ethnic and irrevocably set at birth, and that Russophone Ukrainians will therefore naturally welcome Ukrainianisation policies are also highly debatable. Many Russophone Ukrainians are not 'Russified' at all, in the sense that they never had much of a previous Ukrainian identity to lose. Moreover, the pattern of incentives to take up Ukrainian for adults living and working in a basically monolingual (i.e. Russian-speaking) environment in urban eastern and southern Ukraine are not favourable. Unless Ukraine's economic performance improves relative to that of Russia, material incentives to use Ukrainian are likely to remain weak (Russian in any case remains disproportionately the language of business).[52] Previous use of Ukrainian would of course make reversion to Ukrainian easier, but Ukrainian was so little used in public discourse after the 1930s that even ethnic Ukrainians are not necessarily fluent. Ethnic Ukrainians will receive symbolic collective benefits from the elevation of the status of the Ukrainian language, but Russophone Ukrainians are highly likely to free ride to such public goods. Russophone Ukrainians are therefore likely to be a swing group, feeling the attractions of both Ukrainian and Russian culture.[53] However, by denigrating Russophone Ukrainians as the 'denationalised', 'Janissaries' or 'Mankurty', who 'have lost all feeling of responsibility for their ethnic homeland' Ukrainian nationalists may be pushing them into the Russian camp.[54] (The Janissaries, soldiers of the Ottoman Empire, were taken from their homes at birth and, according to myth, would return to put their own brethren to the sword. 'Mankurty' is a pejorative term for those who have turned against or forgotten their forefathers.)

Language, bureaucracy and education

The Ukrainian Languages Law passed in October 1989, as with many other similar laws passed in the Soviet republics at this time, established the titular language (Ukrainian) as the state language, required state bureaucrats to use Ukrainian within five years and envisaged a rolling programme for the Ukrainianisation of higher education by the end of the century.[55] A state programme issued in November 1991 and a decree of September 1992 aimed to accelerate this process. Moreover, because Ukrainian is the state language, many nationalists have insisted that all citizens should have the option of using it in their contacts with the state bureaucracy. Bureaucrats must 'work in the Ukrainian language, not just know it in the abstract'.[56]

However, nationalists were soon complaining that progress was painfully slow. Less than half (47.5 per cent) of children in Ukraine studied at Ukrainian-language schools in 1989, but this figure had only risen to 49.3 per cent by early 1993, despite the slogan 'Ukrainian children in Ukrainian schools!'[57] Only 36 per cent of total book circulation was in Ukrainian in late 1993, and only 27 per cent of newspaper circulation in early 1994.[58] A critical mass of teachers and authors still had to be developed, leading to a shortage of trained staff and Ukrainian-language teaching materials that made conversion in the schools and universities difficult. Whether as a cause or a consequence, the market for Ukrainian-language media remained limited. Large numbers of Ukrainians continued to watch Ostankino (Russian television) and listen to Mayak radio rather than their Ukrainian equivalents.[59] Nevertheless, nationalists hope that the use of Ukrainian in entrance examinations for higher education and in courses of study will gradually raise the prestige of the language and encourage a trickledown effect in lower schools as parents come to realise that a knowledge of Ukrainian will be necessary for their children's future progress (reversing the pattern of incentives favouring the learning of Russian after 1958–9).

It appears that there has been considerable change in Kiev, with some universities and many leading government departments going over to Ukrainian. However, there has been great resistance further down the hierarchy and in eastern and southern Ukraine,[60] where it is often claimed that nationalists only support Ukrainianisation policies in order to get themselves better state jobs.[61] Official communications with Kiev supposedly have to be in Ukrainian, but local business is still conducted in Russian. The election of Leonid Kuchma as president in 1994 led to a sharp decline in official enthusiasm for Ukrainianisation policies and de facto acceptance of the dual-language situation. Moreover, the campaign to establish Russian as a de jure second state language also received a shot in the arm, much to the nationalists' chagrin.[62]

More radical nationalists have therefore raised the stakes by blaming the lack of progress on the resistance of 'the Russian national minority, which has been granted rights which no other national minority in the world enjoys', and whose call for 'two [state] languages amounts to the preservation of the Russian language alone' in eastern and southern Ukraine.[63] To overcome this resistance nationalists have called for a programme of 'active discrimination' in favour of Ukrainian-language media, including press, textbooks and television and radio. If necessary, high differential taxes should be placed on Russian-language publications and Russian television and radio broadcasts blocked in order to help stimulate a Ukrainian national revival.[64] Furthermore, many nationalists have argued that the *content* of education should also serve the interests of the Ukrainian state. Anatolii Pohribnyi, deputy education minister from 1992 to 1994, declared that 'education should be directly subordinated to the demands of building an independent Ukrainian state', and was fond of quoting Bismarck's remark that 'if he was given a few thousand good primary school teachers, he would build a new Germany in a few years'.[65] Others have specifically argued that Ukrainian schools should help to cultivate a new national spirit and 'patriotic revival'.[66]

Nationalist historiography

Many new teaching materials have therefore been strongly influenced by nationalist thinking, especially in history and political science.[67] Nationalists have understandably focused on the two subjects as crucial fundaments of the nation as an 'imagined community', and have sought to complete the task begun by Hrushevs'kyi in the nineteenth century of systematising and popularising a distinctly Ukrainian version of the national past.[68] (The Ukrainian Politburo accepted the need for a new programme of national history as early as January 1989; it was approved in July 1990.)[69]

As is often the case with national historiography in emerging nations (and indeed in established nation-states),[70] historical narrative in Ukraine is both an academic exercise and a political phenomenon. The analysis in this section concentrates solely on the latter, that is historiography as a series of symbolic constructs, 'a set of repetitive "mythic" patterns, containing a migration story, a founding myth, a golden age of cultural splendour, a period of inner decay and a promise of regeneration'.[71] Furthermore, the focus is specifically on nationalist historiography and its critique of rival versions of the Ukrainian past, particularly the Little Russian narrative of long-term peaceful coexistence with Russia.[72] The two are often in conflict. In early 1994 controversy erupted over planned changes to history and political science syllabuses, with critics accusing nationalist officials of seeking to replace 'scientific communism with scientific nationalism', and the subsequent furore placed nationalists on the defensive.[73] However, the issue remains a live one. For nationalists the refutation of the Little Russian version of Ukrainian history is an essential means of verifying their sense of identity, separate from that of Russia and the product of a long and glorious past.

The nationalist version of Ukrainian history begins not with a 'migration story', but with the common alternative, namely a demonstration that the Ukrainians have always been an indigenous people, whose long history of continuous settlement establishes their patrimonial claim to the local land.[74] (Moreover, this claim is held to be equally true in all areas of modern Ukraine, supposedly proving that Ukraine's current borders are coterminous with those of historical right; see the section 'A federation in the making?', pp. 163–8 below). Ukrainian historians now argue that national ethnogenesis can be traced back to pre-Christian tribes such as the Scythians, Sarmathians or even the Trypillians,[75] who are held to have been 'the direct predecessors of [the inhabitants of] Kievan Rus'' and therefore the ancestors of modern Ukrainians.[76] It has even been claimed that the Huns were in fact 'the local Slav population from around the river Dnieper' rather than 'newcomers from the east', and that Attila was therefore a Ukrainian.[77]

The establishment of a long and distinguished pre-history allows modern Ukrainians to invert traditional stereotypes and assert that their civilisation has much deeper roots than that of Muscovy or Russia. In the words of the 1991 declaration of independence therefore, the Ukrainians have a 'thousand-year tradition of state-building',[78] dating from the time of Kievan Rus'. Moreover, it is the Kievan period which provides nationalists with three key elements of their 'founding myth'. First, the primary role in both the foundation and governance of Rus' was supposedly played by the local Polianian principality. Rus' was therefore a proto-Ukrainian rather than a proto-Russian state. More northerly tribes such as the Viatichians and Slovianians, the ancestors of modern-day Russians, played only a marginal role in the history of Rus'.[79] Some nationalists have even argued, like Duchiński in the nineteenth century, that the Russians are not really Slavs at all, as 'the foundations of the [later] Muscovite state were [built on] the basis of the non-Slavic population of Suzdal ... Slavic influence from Kiev on Muscovy only appeared after five hundred years of our [Ukrainian] era'.[80]

Second, although Rus' was an Orthodox state, unlike pre-Petrine Russia it was also firmly European. Rus' 'united the mainly eastern Greco-Byzantine religion and cultural tradition with a mainly western social and political structure',[81] and was always open to Latin influence and commercial interchange with the West.[82] Third, embryonic differences between the ethnically distinct Kievan and northern territories were already undermining the unity of Rus' before the sack of Kiev in 1240. Relations were if anything downright hostile. Twice, in 1169 and

1203, the armies of the northern princes sacked Kiev, reflecting and exacerbating this growing divide and setting the pattern for future conflict between Ukrainians and Russians. Internal conflict, not the Tatar invasion, was therefore decisive in causing the decline of Rus'. The significance of the latter was subsequently exaggerated by Russian historians seeking to prove that nothing of significance survived in the southern lands after 1240.[83]

In fact the most important consequence of the Tatar incursion was to widen still further the division between north and south. Slavic colonists in the north, 'finding themselves in a foreign Finno-Ugric environment' and faced by the Mongol threat from the south-east, developed their own 'distinct form of Golden-Horde despotism', first in defence against the Mongols and then under the influence of their occupation.[84] The northern lands drifted away from the traditions of Rus' and Moscow's relation to Kiev became one of 'borrowing, not direct inheritance'.[85] On the other hand, while the Kiev lands experienced the same Mongol threat, 'the primeval force [stykhiia] of the Eurasian nomads acted on the Ukrainian people from outside, it was not "internalised". It did not become a constituent part of the Ukrainian national character', as it did for the Russians.[86] The traditions of Rus' were therefore better preserved in the south, first in the Galician principality and then under the Lithuanian kingdom, where Ukrainian lands supposedly enjoyed almost complete self-rule until 1569.[87] Therefore 'it is impossible to include Kievan Rus' in Russian history as the first step in the development of the Russian state, just as Americans do not look at the history of England as the first step in the history of the United States'.[88]

This version of events establishes two key nationalist *mythomateurs*. First, Ukraine is a European 'frontier civilisation', on 'the boundary of European culture',[89] defending civilisation from barbarism. 'Asiatic' Russia on the other hand always lay firmly on the wrong side of this divide.[90] Second, Ukrainians, rather than Russians, are the true 'elder brothers'. This point is made most clearly by an element of terminological revisionism. It is now argued that the term 'Little Russia', which later became a pejorative term,

came from the name 'Little Rus'' (*Mala Rus'*) and originally had no disdainful meaning at all. On the contrary it referred to a metropole rather than a colony, the Greeks having established the term 'little' to mean the centre and 'great' that which surrounded it. Thus Grecia Minor was the true Greece and Grecia Major the Greek colonies.[91]

In other words Ukraine–Rus' was the original centre of East Slavic civilisation, and 'Great Russia' its offshoot.

Furthermore, it is argued that Ukraine's closer ties to Europe were strengthened by Ukrainian participation in, and Moscow's isolation from, the great European upheavals of the Renaissance, Reformation and Counter-Reformation. The 'Europeanisation' of Russia only began with Peter the Great, when the lateness of the attempt meant that the transformation was only ever skin-deep.[92] In Ukraine, however, the Orthodox revival of the sixteenth and seventeenth centuries produced a second 'Golden Age', culminating in the restoration of a Ukrainian nation-state in 1648. Four key subsidiary arguments underpin this version of events. In the first place, Khmel'nyts'kyi's polity is depicted as a fully fledged state rather than merely the semi-autonomous military encampment of the Cossack army, the Zaporozhian Host. Secondly, his Cossack supporters were ethnic Ukrainians rather than a multinational body of Orthodox free men. Thirdly, the Cossack state was not an entirely new phenomenon but a reincarnation of the traditions of Rus', and therefore a crucial link between medieval and modern Ukraine.[93] Fourthly, for almost a century after 1654 Ukrainian culture remained more advanced than that of Russia, and it was only through Ukrainian influence that Russia was able to half-civilise itself.[94] Art and architecture continued to flourish, as did the political arts.[95]

Incorporation into the Russian Empire, however, brought national decline and 'inner decay'. Ukrainian institutions were abolished, the local social and economic structure subjected to Russian *Gleichshaltung*, and Ukrainian culture impoverished by unnatural severance from its European tradition. As often in nationalist discourse, the period of 'foreign rule' is presented as one of continuous misfortune. The positive aspects of inclusion in the Russian Empire and the USSR are glossed over and Russian–Ukrainian relations stylised as colonial exploitation. Nationalists have claimed for example that since 1654 Russia has committed no fewer than 112 acts 'of planned and purposeful assault on the Ukrainian language and culture',[96] attempted cultural 'linguicide' through Russification[97] and even plotted outright 'genocide'/'ethnocide' during the Great Famine of 1932-3.[98] Ukrainians on the other hand are portrayed as engaged in a ceaseless struggle for national 'regeneration' and eventual liberation, from Mazepa and Pavlo Polubotok, through the Ukrainian People's Republic to the OUN-UPA and the dissidents of the 1960s, thereby refuting the Little Russian stereotype of voluntary incorporation into the Russian cultural space.[99] Independence in 1991 was only the last step in this teleological process.

The manner in which Ukraine reinterprets its national history will have a crucial influence on its evolving national identity. Despite the relatively unpromising historical material described in chapter 1, an emotive and simplistically anti-Russian version of national history is easily constructed and has great mobilising potential amongst the nationalist minority. Moreover it is crucial to nationalists' self-image as normal 'Europeans' in natural antagonism with Russia (see chapter 7). However, all too frequently Ukrainian–Russian relations are depicted by nationalists in Manichaean terms, and the complex interrelationships and ambiguities described in chapters 1 and 2 are excluded, glossed over or denied. Otherwise discrete events such as the Great Famine of 1932–3 are 'ethnicised', and made to play their part in the morality play of Ukrainian–Russian relations. However, it is not only the ethnic Russian minority who are unaccustomed to thinking of relations with Russia in such terms. Many Ukrainians, Russophones in particular, regard the complex interrelationship with Russia as part and parcel of their own sense of self. Too stylised a portrayal of Russia and its place in Ukrainian history can therefore only contribute to the image of Ukraine as a narrowly national state and encourage the alienation of the Russophone majority.

National symbols

A nation's view of its history is also reflected in the national symbols it chooses to use. According to Ukrainian nationalists their national symbols 'arose in the greyness of antiquity to distinguish one race from another'.[100] Their constant presence through otherwise discrete periods of Ukrainian history 'beginning with Kievan Rus' and ending with the present day' supposedly proves that 'the Ukrainian nation was formed completely separately from the Russian and the Belarusian', and vindicates Hrushevs'kyi's view of Ukrainian history as a continuum.[101] It is argued that the trident symbol and blue and yellow colouring for flags and heraldry have been part of Ukrainian history since time immemorial. The former symbolised Ukraine's geostrategic position astride the trade route 'from the Varangians to the Greeks', while blue over yellow (sky over corn) stood for the simple peasant virtues of the Ukrainian people. The contrary theory of many Russian and Soviet historians that a common preference for red colouring was a sign of unity amongst the peoples of Rus' is turned on its head to prove the opposite, as red was supposedly only popular in the north-eastern territories.[102]

For Ukrainian nationalists, therefore, national symbols can help to reconstruct Ukrainians' historical memory, as well as playing their traditional role as focal points for patriotic sentiment. According to Levko Luk"ianenko, national symbols are our 'national riches, dearer than life for any given member of our tribe or citizen of the state'.[103]

However, a substantial proportion of the Ukrainian population still believe the official Soviet version, according to which Ukrainian national symbols more or less appeared ex nihilo in 1917–20, after their invention in Galicia in 1848. Moreover, significant numbers still associate them with the wartime OUN-UPA (although the latter in fact also used red and black). According to one anti-nationalist group in the Donbas, 'our visiting guests from the west [i.e. Galicia] are perfectly entitled to brandish the blue and yellow flag – it's their regional symbol, but it is blasphemy to the inhabitants of the Donbass'.[104]

In the immediate aftermath of independence nationalists successfully pushed for the adoption of the trident and the flag as the official symbols of the new Ukrainian state (along with the national hymn used in 1917–20, 'Ukraine has not yet died'), but only over the opposition of deputies from eastern and southern Ukraine.[105] The Republican Party published a list of those deputies who voted against, denouncing them as 'Russian chauvinists'.[106] Ivan Pliushch hardly reassured objectors with his bland and wishful statement that 'the trident wasn't invented only yesterday and isn't only revered in the west' of Ukraine.[107] The passage of time has stilled some opposition, but left-wing parties have continued to campaign against the flag and the trident.[108]

Significantly nationalists have had much less success with removing the symbols of the Soviet period. Despite a decree of President Kravchuk's in May 1992 requiring the removal of Soviet and/or communist monuments and symbols, it is only really in Galicia and to some extent in Kiev that statues have been pulled down and streets renamed. Elsewhere the legacy of the Ukrainian SSR largely remains.[109] Even the parliament building still has Soviet-era symbols on its facade. Whether this is an appropriate means of avoiding too sharp a break with the past or a mistake likely to fuel a rising sense of nostalgia only time will tell.

Religion: searching for unity

The difficulties faced by Ukrainianisation policy in the religious sphere were described in chapter 3. Nevertheless, nationalists have continued to chase the chimera of a united and truly national Church. In the immediate aftermath of independence, nationalists' first instinct was to promote the Ukrainianisation of the Orthodox Church in central, eastern and southern Ukraine. However, the disappointing results of the unity Sobor in June 1992 and the residual strength of the UOC (MP) forced a tactical rethink. Moreover, after 1994, Kravchuk's policy of more or less overt backing for the UOC (KP) was replaced by the more even-handed approach of his successor Leonid Kuchma,[110] symbolised by the authorities' refusal to allow the burial of Patriarch Volodymyr (Romaniuk) in Kiev's St Sophia cathedral in July 1995, which sparked bloody clashes between the militia and the UNSO.[111]

The dead-end reached by the autocephalisation strategy produced three different types of response.[112] More extreme nationalists have continued to call for stronger state backing for the official Kievan Patriarchy and tougher measures against its Muscovite rival, up to and including the banning of the UOC (MP).[113] The UNSO has provided armed escorts for Filaret and has frequently resorted to violence in the attempt to force parishes still loyal to the UOC (MP) to come over to the Ukrainian Church.[114] Filaret himself, however, continues to be the main obstacle to reconciliation between the Churches, especially after his election as Volodymyr's successor in October 1995, despite erstwhile supporters urging him to step aside. On the other hand, a minority of moderate national-democrats have recognised that the UOC (KP) was too narrow a base on which to build a true national Church and accepted that the UOC (MP) itself may be a more appropriate multi-ethnic and multilingual vehicle, and have sought to encourage it to complete the process of autonomisation begun in 1990.

The other route toward a national Church, as with Metropolitan Sheptyts'kyi's unsuccessful initiative in 1942–3, is through reconciliation and eventual union between the Uniates and the UOC (KP).[115] However, the bitterness of historical divisions between the two Churches means that it would be extremely difficult to consummate such a union. Moreover, the main nationalist organisations can do little more than pay lip-service to the idea, as their own supporters are divided between partisans of both Churches. Furthermore, the pursuit of such a union would confirm long-standing suspicions in Moscow that the Uniate Church is merely a Trojan Horse for the Catholicisation of the east, and for that reason the unity campaign is unlikely to be backed by the Vatican, so long as the latter is more interested in broader questions of ecumenical reconciliation between Catholics and Orthodox. Moreover, it would widen the split between the Kievan and Moscow Patriarchies of the Ukrainian Orthodox Church.

A federation in the making?

Given the deep historical divisions between the Ukrainian regions and the fact that 'Ukraine has no tradition of strong unitary statehood',[116] a federal form of government for the new Ukrainian state might be thought appropriate, providing in particular for a degree of self-government for the Russian (or Russophone) population in the east and south, and Romanians, Hungarians and Rusyns in the west.[117] However, despite a rising chorus of localist demands since 1991, Ukrainian nationalists have refused even to contemplate the idea, standing firm on the principle that 'Ukraine is a unitary national state.'[118] V"iacheslav Chornovil was vilified for flirting with the federal principle in 1990–1, and soon dropped the suggestion.[119] Nationalists even decided to dismantle the 'Galician Assembly' set up after the opposition victory in the three western oblasts in the 1990 local elections to increase their lobbying power in Kiev, because it set a bad example to would-be separatists in the east and south.[120] Moreover, nationalists have called for those 'parties and organisations, who call for the infringement of Ukraine's territorial inviolability, or the transfer of Ukraine to another state' to be banned,[121] and secured an amendment to the criminal code in October 1991 that made 'appeals and other activities aimed at the violation of the territorial integrity of Ukraine' punishable by up to three years' imprisonment.

Nationalists tend to argue that the Ukrainian state is too weak to decentralise power, a concession which would in any case only empower local separatists and/or encourage Russia to interfere in Ukrainian affairs, placing intolerable centrifugal strains upon the state.[122] Moreover, the regional 'problem' is seen as somehow artificial, the result either of third-party machination aimed at 'disrupting the process of Ukrainian national revival, cultivating separatism and fomenting hostility between the population of different regions of the state',[123] or of the insufficient development of national consciousness in the east and south. According to Mykhailo Horyn', for example,

there is a paradoxical situation in Ukraine, when it is not the nation which is building the state, but the state which, having established itself on [Ukrainian] ethnic territory at the same time as the nation's emergence, is now assisting the latter's consolidation. Federalism would only strengthen regional consciousness and obstruct the process of creating a single national organism.[124]

In neither case is there any recognition of the need to accommodate a genuine, indigenous regional pluralism in Ukraine, or any real acceptance that the problem has deep historical roots. For Horyn' the problem lies with ethnic Ukrainians who have lost touch with their traditions rather than Russians or Russophone Ukrainians who remain in touch with theirs.

The intellectual justification for rejecting demands by Russophones, Rusyns and others to self-government on 'Ukrainian land' is basically an extension of the historical claim to indigenousness referred to above.[125]

Ukrainians, it is argued, were the first to settle Transcarpathia, the Donbas and Crimea, just as they were the first to settle any other part of modern Ukraine. Regardless of subsequent administrative or demographic changes therefore, these regions have always been and must always remain Ukrainian. Even when under foreign rule they possessed a natural historical trajectory toward reunification with other Ukrainian lands.[126] Normally the decisive period of Ukrainian settlement is dated to the Kievan era, as for example in Transcarpathia.[127] However in the steppe region, despite some earlier links as far back as the Scythian period, the story tends to begin with the Zaporozhian Cossacks, whose area of settlement is now depicted as extending far beyond the central Ukrainian heartlands to include most of what is now southern and south-eastern Ukraine.[128]

This story is hardest to tell with respect to Crimea, as the peninsula was controlled first by the Crimean Tatars and then by Russia after annexation in 1783. The Ukrainian case is that Crimean Tatar and Crimean Ukrainian histories have always been intertwined. The Kievan state controlled the east of the peninsula before the Tatars' arrival in the thirteenth century, the latter then intermingled and intermarried with local Ukrainians, and the Tatar Khanate developed a close political and military alliance with the Zaporozhians in the two centuries before 1783.[129] Moreover, hundreds of thousands of Ukrainians arrived as slaves during the Tatar era (although how this fits with the idea of friendly relations between Tatars and Ukrainians is not explained). The progressive reduction in Tatar numbers after 1783 and their deportation in 1944 therefore left the Ukrainians as the 'largest national group amongst the indigenous population of Crimea'.[130] Local Russians, on the other hand, are only military occupiers or post-World War II immigrants.[131]

Nevertheless, regional problems have grown considerably since 1991, both in the west and in the east and south.[132] In Transcarpathia the Rusyn movement, thought dead and buried in 1945, has revived. One survey in 1991 reported that only 55 per cent of the 977,000 who were classed as local 'Ukrainians' in the 1989 Soviet census actually thought of themselves as such, whereas 27 per cent considered themselves to be Rusyns or a mixture of Rusyn and some other ethnic group.[133] The Rusyns established their own political party in 1992, the Subcarpathian Republican Party, which has demanded cultural and even political autonomy for the region.[134] However, Ukrainian nationalists continue to insist that the Rusyns are merely exotic Ukrainians, who therefore have no special claim to self-government in the region.[135] In December 1991, 78 per cent of local voters (on an 83 per cent turnout) backed the idea of Transcarpathia becoming a 'special self-governing administrative territory' within Ukraine, but Kiev has stalled on the implementation of this proposal.[136]

As the Ukrainian nationalist movement in Transcarpathia is weak, Kiev has granted the local ex-communist elite considerable economic freedom in order to discourage it from making common cause with the Rusyns. To date this strategy has worked reasonably well, and the region has remained strongly independent not only from Kiev but also from the parties of the left (Transcarpathia has tended to follow its own path electorally; see chapter 5).[137] Kiev has also played divide-and-rule by meeting most of the demands of the estimated 150,000 to 200,000 Hungarians who live in the region. Interstate relations between Hungary and Ukraine have remained friendly, and the local Hungarian Democratic Alliance has therefore tended to concentrate on cultural rather than political demands.[138]

In Chernivtsi, because of the historical links between northern Bukovyna and Galicia, the Ukrainian national movement is much stronger, and the Romanians/Moldovans a more containable minority (the fact that the latter are also mainly a rural population, concentrated in the Hertsa region, makes them more difficult to mobilise politically).[139] Nevertheless, a Christian Democratic Alliance of Romanians in Ukraine has been active since 1991 and organised a Congress of Romanians in Bukovyna in June 1992 (one Romanian deputy, Ivan Popescu, was elected from the region in 1994). As in Transcarpathia, nationalists have condemned such groups as 'separatists' backed by foreign irredentists, and argued that their main newspaper *Plai Romanesc* should be banned.[140] Limited tolerance of Romanian-language schooling and the public display of Romanian national symbols has not extended to accepting demands for political autonomy. In southern Bessarabia, Kiev has to cope with a mosaic of Romanian, Moldovan, Bulgarian and Gagauz groups in addition to the overspill from the conflict in Moldova, but despite a weak Ukrainian presence in the region, there is little evidence of the local minorities joining forces.[141]

However, by far the most serious problems for Ukraine have been among the Russian-speaking population in the arc stretching through southern and eastern Ukraine from Odesa in the south-west to Kharkiv in the north-east. Problems have been especially acute in the Donbas, where a series of powerful lobbies has emerged since late 1992 to campaign for a federal state, local self-government, Russian as a second state language and the strengthening of links between Ukraine and the rest of the CIS.[142] In a local poll conducted simultaneously with the parliamentary elections in March 1994, 80 per cent of Donets'k voters supported the principle of a federalised Ukraine; 87 per cent (90 per cent in Luhans'k) agreed that Russian should be made a second state language in Ukraine and 89 per cent (91 per cent in Luhans'k) that Russian should be the local 'language of education, science and administration' in the Donbas. The proposal that Ukraine should become a full member of the CIS Economic Union and Parliamentary Assembly was supported by 89 per cent (91 per cent in Luhans'k).[143] As shown in chapter 5, the 1994 elections demonstrated that such sentiments were widespread throughout the east and south, although pressure subsided somewhat after the election of Kuchma in summer 1994.

The most serious trouble spot has been Crimea, where more or less every step taken by local politicians since 1991 has been denounced with nationalist fury. A 'Crimean Autonomous SSR' was restored in 1991, and was upgraded to the 'Crimean Republic' in 1992. In January 1994 the avowed separatist Yurii Meshkov was elected Crimean president with 73 per cent of the vote, and his 'Russia bloc' won fifty-four out of ninety-four seats in elections to the local 'parliament' in March.[144] On every occasion nationalists have called for extreme measures, ranging from the dissolution of the Crimean parliament to the imposition of direct presidential rule on the peninsula, the arrest of Crimean leaders and outright military intervention.[145] The UNA-UNSO notoriously declared in 1992 that 'Crimea will either be Ukrainian or depopulated!'[146] Ironically, it was Kuchma rather than Kravchuk who met some of these demands by exploiting political infighting in Simferopil' and Russia's preoccupation with the Chechen war to take greater control over the peninsula in March 1995.[147] However, Kuchma was unable or unwilling to bow to nationalist pressure and deprive local autonomists of key institutional resources by abolishing the Crimean parliament and government. Moreover, Ukraine's main long-term problems in Crimea – tenuous historical links, the overwhelming dominance of the Russophone population (almost 90 per cent of the total) and the weakness of organised Ukrainian nationalism – are unlikely to be solved by short-term political measures alone.

Many analysts would support the nationalist contention that stronger central power rather than a decentralised federation is the best way to deal with ethno-regional (and lingua-regional) differences.[148] On the other hand, nationalists have never really addressed the alternative possibility that a federal state might actually help to reduce tensions between Kiev and the regions. The regions might feel less beholden to the caprice of a nationalising state, and would no longer be able to blame Kiev (or the hidden hand of Galicia) for all their ills. Whatever the case, the political and electoral weight of Ukraine's Russophone regions means that the federal question will remain on the political agenda for the foreseeable future.

Other constitutional issues

Nationalist attitudes to other constitutional questions are not so fixed or predictable. Many nationalists grew used to opposing the political structures of communism as much as its ideology, and the programmes of nationalist parties are full of exemplary references to the importance of a constitutional division of powers, procedural democracy, a rule of law and a multi-party system.[149] In particular nationalists are understandably strongly opposed to the system of local soviets, as this is where their opponents were most firmly entrenched. On the other hand, like nationalists the world over, the Ukrainian right often hankers after a 'strong hand' to provide the nation with leadership and direction in times of crisis.

A minority, particularly on the ultra-nationalist fringe, have expressed openly anti-democratic sentiments. Stepan Khmara, for example, has declared that 'although in general I am a supporter of republicanism, of a parliamentary form for the state, in a transition period a positive role could be played by an authoritarian regime ... in such circumstances we must rely on strong individuals'.[150] Organisations such as the UNA-UNSO have never bothered to hide their contempt for democracy. Even mainstream national-democrats, despite their opposition to 'Communist Party dictatorship' before 1990, developed a marked preference for presidential over parliamentary government as 'a guarantee of stability' and a bulwark against 'anarchic radicalism',[151] although this feeling understandably declined somewhat after Leonid Kuchma took office in 1994.[152] Levko Luk''ianenko, for example, quoted Lypyns'kyi to argue that Ukraine's natural proclivity for democracy had too often been allowed to foster anarchic individualism, and ought therefore to be counterbalanced by strong presidential rule.[153] A tough line against regional 'separatists' would of course require considerable centralisation of power, as would a serious attempt at economic reform (see the section below).

The economy

Before 1991 it was a standard tenet of Ukrainian nationalism that Ukraine was an exploited 'internal colony' of the USSR, just as it had been under the tsars; this argument was first explicitly formulated by the

Soviet Ukrainian economist Volobuiev in the 1920s (see chapter 4). Not only was over 95 per cent of economic activity in Ukraine controlled from Moscow, but Ukraine supposedly also suffered a net outflow of national income due to over-taxation, under-investment and the under-pricing of key Ukrainian products, especially agricultural goods, iron, steel and coal.[154] On a longer historical perspective, many nationalists bemoaned the fact that political union with Russia after 1654 had forced the Ukrainian economy into unnatural economic interchange with 'Asia', and lost it supposedly more natural markets in Central Europe, the Near East and the wider world, especially after the removal of tariff protection in the eighteenth century led to the effective disappearance of an autonomous local economy. Furthermore, the exploitation of raw materials in the Donbas and the development of a maritime trading economy on the northern Black Sea coast were never conducted to Ukraine's benefit.

Therefore in 1989–91 it was an almost universal theme in nationalist propaganda that Ukraine would benefit economically by withdrawing from the USSR.[155] In October 1990, for example, Leonid Kravchuk argued in private that 'every schoolboy knows that independence begins with the economy. If we decide to become truly masters in our own land and enter into direct economic relations with other republics then I am certain that in the nearest future we will be able to look after the people of Ukraine and provide them with a decent standard of living.'[156] Nationalists expected that independence would allow Ukraine to gain control of its export surpluses, escape the fiscal and monetary chaos of the last days of the USSR, and free itself from discriminatory tax and investment policies. Moreover, independence would supposedly release the productive energies of the Ukrainian people, who, unlike work-shy Russians, were before 1917 accustomed to European labour practices, private property (individual or family farming having been the norm before collectivisation) and capitalist interchange.[157] Lastly, free of the 'Eurasian' orientation imposed by Russia, Ukraine would be able to take proper advantage of its geographical location as one of the natural crossroads of world trade.

These themes, endlessly repeated in both nationalist and official media in the autumn 1991 election campaign, helped to secure the 90.3 per cent vote for independence on 1 December, indicating the possibility that instrumental economic nationalism might appeal to a broader spectrum of the population than ethno-nationalism alone. However, Ukraine's actual economic record in the first three years after independence was abysmal, and much worse than in Russia. National product fell by a cumulative 40 per cent and inflation averaged 45 per cent a month.[158] However, nationalists were reluctant to face up to the failure of their predictions. Some continued to blame the legacy of the USSR, which had burdened Ukraine with an excess of energy-guzzling heavy industry, huge environmental costs (the Chornobyl' clean-up in particular) and a chronic lack of self-sufficient industry. Another option was to bemoan the 1991–2 settlement and Russia's seizure of all the USSR's assets (gold, embassies abroad, foreign currency), which deprived Ukraine of any official reserves to service trade or back the introduction of a proper new currency (the fact that the USSR's liabilities were almost certainly much larger than its assets was ignored or portrayed as Russian manipulation of the figures). A third argument was to blame Russia for exporting inflation and general economic chaos to Ukraine after its unilateral price reforms in January 1992 and the huge energy price increases of 1993–4.[159] Energy dependency in particular has become a nationalist obsession, as has the search for alternative sources of supply.[160] The Western powers also came in for their share of criticism for failing to provide prompt aid and assistance. Others clung to new panaceas, in particular the much-discussed but repeatedly postponed introduction of a proper national currency, the talismanic *hrivna* (the name of the currency used by Ukrainian governments in 1917–20).

However, Ukraine's economic problems in 1992–4 were largely either of its own making or the result of circumstances that should have been foreseen in 1991.[161] Inflation was mainly fuelled by lax monetary and fiscal policies;[162] Ukraine's chronic trading indebtedness was structural and due above all to energy dependency on Russia, which far outweighed any putative export surpluses in items such as grain and coal in which such hope had been invested back in 1991;[163] at the same time, the downward spiral in national production was caused by collapsing supply links as Ukraine cut loose from the hyper-centralised Soviet economy.[164] Moreover, under Kravchuk, Ukraine failed to take any compensatory reform measures, preferring instead to chase a mythical Ukrainian 'third way'. Plans for privatisation were delayed by nationalist fears that 'Russian capital could take over the Ukrainian economy', schemes for restoring economic links with Russia and the rest of the CIS were attacked as 'likely to undermine first Ukraine's economic sovereignty and then its political sovereignty',[165] and plans to trim industrial subsidies and welfare spending were stymied by fears of a social explosion in Russophone eastern Ukraine.[166]

Above all, in the immediate aftermath of independence, the main priority of most nationalists was not reform qua reform, but 'securing the self-sufficiency of the national economy and its independence from the influence of external economic competitors or political manoeuvrings'.[167] They therefore supported Kravchuk's conservative economic policies in 1992–4, but his attempts at 'administrative stabilisation' only made the problem worse by strangling the nascent private sector or forcing it underground.[168] Only Rukh seemed to have deduced from the December 1991 referendum campaign that most nationalists were putting the cart before the horse and that, instead of building a 'strong state' and assuming a prosperous economy would follow, institution-building would be easier if economic reform had first spread prosperity and helped win broader support for the national cause.[169]

On the other hand, many national-democrats, especially those close to the Ukrainian Republican Party, have been influenced by Lypyns'kyi's ideas on the importance of widespread property ownership in cementing support for procedural democracy and a rule of law (see chapter 2), and are fond of repeating his argument that 'Ukrainians have historically had a feeling for ownership, husbandry and entrepreneurial talent', which, moreover, 'they have preserved [better than others] under totalitarianism'.[170] It is therefore claimed that the Ukrainians are more likely than the Russians to take to a privatisation programme designed to create a 'society of property-owners', so long as it does more than just enrich managers and bureaucrats.[171] Furthermore, again in contrast to Russia, Ukrainian nationalist organisations are happy to think of themselves as on the conservative right. A Ukrainian 'red-brown' alliance in opposition to market reforms would be difficult to conceive. On the contrary, many nationalists hoped to build a support base amongst a new national bourgeoisie.[172]

Nevertheless, the economy is likely to remain Ukraine's Achilles' Heel. Even if radical economic reforms are finally introduced (the then new president, Kuchma, finally began to force through a series of liberalisation measures in autumn 1994), nationalists will have to face up to some painful realities further down the line. One is that, contrary to the euphoric expectations of 1991, Ukraine cannot swiftly reorient its economy westward and will remain dependent on Russia for the foreseeable future, both as its main market and as an energy and raw material supplier. Secondly, therefore, the issues of Russian leverage over the Ukrainian economy and the (re)creation of CIS economic structures are likely to remain pertinent for a long time to come. Consequently Ukrainian nationalists, whether justified or not, are always likely to feel that Ukraine's political independence is being undermined by economic neo-colonialism, especially as genuine trade liberalisation and privatisation will expose the Ukrainian economy still further to the economic might of its larger northern neighbour. Third, given the limited appeal of ethno-nationalism in Ukraine, Ukraine's economic performance relative to Russia will be of crucial importance in determining many citizens' attitudes to the new state.

Conclusion

The national issue is likely to remain a long-term point of contention in Ukraine's internal politics. Despite a relatively liberal record on ethnic and national issues in the early 1990s, Ukrainian nationalists are bound to press for Ukrainianisation policies because of the damage they feel that Ukrainian language and culture suffered under both tsarist and Soviet rule. However, non-Ukrainian minorities and possibly many Russophone Ukrainians are equally certain to resist. Nationalists lack the strength or numbers for easy victory, but anti-nationalists are unlikely to be able to force the issue off the agenda. An element of confrontation is therefore more or less guaranteed.

7 The nationalist agenda: external affairs – untying the Russian knot

Since 1991 Ukraine has sought to chart its place in the new post-communist international order.[1] As with many aspects of domestic policy, however, Ukraine has given out confusing signals as to how it sees its role in the world, not so much because of a lack of coherent geostrategic vision in Ukraine as such, but because of a standoff between the irreconcilable views of nationalists and their opponents. The nationalist position on the future course of Ukraine's foreign and defence policy is clear enough, and can be neatly summarised as anti-Russian and pro-European. Nevertheless, Ukraine has been unable to follow Poland or the Baltic states and enact these principles as the basis of an unambiguous foreign policy. Ukraine's large Russian community (which unlike that in Latvia or Estonia is enfranchised) and a substantial number of ethnic Ukrainians do not share the nationalists' vision, and see Ukraine and Russia as intimately linked by a common history of mutual interchange as much as by colonial dependency. Moreover, as argued in chapters 1 and 2, the latter point of view is as much a part of the Ukrainian intellectual tradition as nationalism, with a pedigree stretching back to Gogol, Kostomarov and beyond.[2]

Ukraine and Russia

The root of Ukrainian nationalists' world-view is their compression of the complex relationship between Ukraine and Russia into a basic syllogism.[3] Ukraine is an 'organic part' of Europe and European civilisation, from which centuries of Russian rule have unnaturally separated it. Russia, on the other hand, is by nature an 'Asiatic' despotism and an expansionist imperialist state. As well as denying Ukraine self-determination, Russia has therefore attempted to sever Ukraine from its very essence. Consequently Ukraine's primary foreign policy tasks should be to secure a 'return to Europe' and build a strong independent state free from pernicious Russian influence.[4]

The belief in Ukraine's European past was examined in detail in chapter 6. The second nationalist axiom is that, both in general and with respect to Ukraine in particular, 'imperialism is part of the Russian political tradition. It's in their blood. Only force can restrain Russia's biological tendency toward expansion; they will never do so of their own accord.'[5] Russian imperialism 'may change its form, it may go under the red flag or under the tricolour, it may use the ideology of Marxism or stand under the White Guard banner of Orthodoxy. But its essence, and therefore its name, does not change.'[6] Even more bluntly, 'war is for Russia a natural state of affairs. It simply cannot restrain itself from making war on foreign lands.'[7] Therefore, 'it is impossible to believe in any agreement made with Russia, because from the very beginning of its existence to the present day it has been and remains an empire, the basis of which is contempt for Ukrainian rights and interests, and intolerance of her freedom'.[8] Russia is simply unable to accommodate itself psychologically to the idea of an equal relationship with Ukraine as a separate sovereign entity.[9]

That said, however, modern Ukrainian nationalists have continued the argument between Dontsov and Drahomanov as to whether Ukraine's real enemy is the Russian people per se or merely the Russian imperial system. Moderates such as Ivan Drach have insisted that Ukrainian nationalists should differentiate between Russian democrats and neo-imperialists, warning that 'after the Russia of Yel'tsin comes the Russia of Zhirinovskii'.[10] Rukh and the national-democrats expressed consistent support for Yel'tsin against his opponents, at least up to the beginning of the Chechen war.[11] On the other hand, radicals have argued that all Russians are the same: 'Ukrainian nationalists have always said that the real enemy is not some mythical imperial centre, not the command-administrative system, but Russia, and Russian chauvinism.' The Russian people could not blame their imperial tradition on the tsars or on communism – it was in their blood; 'the Russian people themselves are the creators of the Russian Empire'.[12] Nationalists such as Yurii Badz'o criticised those such as Drahomanov, who

saw Ukraine's future in some kind of union with Russia. They hoped that Ukrainian traditions [and] Ukrainian society would influence Russia, lessen the authoritarianism in the Russian tradition and harmonise the relations between us as neighbours. History has shown that this is impossible. The inertia of Russia's imperialistic attitude toward Ukraine is still powerful. The formation of Ukrainian statehood and the assertion of independence from Russia in all spheres of life is therefore the only guarantee of [our] democracy.[13]

'Away from Moscow!'

The basic tenet of Ukrainian nationalism's world-view is therefore that Ukraine is in fact the geographical 'centre of Europe',[14] if the latter is defined as stretching from the Atlantic to the Urals (although it is not clear how this can be reconciled with the idea of an 'Asiatic' Russia). Nationalists see a 'return to Europe' not merely as a post-communist reflex or an economic necessity, but as part of Ukraine's historical destiny.[15] In so far as Ukraine defines itself against Russia, an orientation toward Europe is an essential differentiating element that provides Ukrainians with a myth of descent to distinguish them from their neighbours. Supposedly therefore, an 'eastward orientation for Ukraine would lead to the loss of national identity, the loss of our European mentality and as a result – the liquidation of the Ukrainian state'.[16] Without, in Khvyl'ovyi's words, 'psychological Europe', Ukraine, especially its Little Russian population, would fall back into the Russian embrace. Furthermore, nationalists would argue that liberation from the Russian tradition is synonymous with the embrace of democracy and the principles of civilised coexistence in international affairs, as both are supposedly alien concepts to Russia.

Hence Ukraine's otherwise inexplicable tendency to oscillate between loyalist Little Russianism and uncompromising nationalism. As before October 1917, in the early phases of the Soviet endgame in 1988 and 1989 most Ukrainians favoured the maintenance of some form of federal or confederal link with Russia and the rest of the USSR. At the time Rukh provided a broad church for both nationalists and Little Russians. On both occasions the independence option was slowly gathering support of its own accord, but it was the sudden implosion of the Russian/Soviet centre which dramatically transformed visions of the politically possible and rendered Moscowcentric strategies unfeasible, with the Lithuanian and August 1991 crises playing a similar role to the Kornilov affair and Bolshevik coup in 1917 in uncovering the impotence of the centre and prompting the rush toward peripheral nationalism.

After 1990, nationalists and Little Russians largely parted company, allowing the former to express their opposition to Gorbachev's proposed Union Treaty in the strongest possible terms. Even moderate national-democrats called for mass civil disobedience and an all-Ukrainian political strike if it were signed, characterising all concessions as simply a cover for the restoration of imperial rule in a different guise.[17] After August 1991, national independence became a non-negotiable absolute for all nationalists. Even minimal links with Russia were rejected because of the existential threat they posed to the revival of Ukraine's 'European tradition', and because it was feared that any such ties would gradually draw the Little Russians back into Russia's cultural orbit. Therefore, although the Belovezhkaia Pushcha agreement in December 1991 led to the dissolution of the USSR, the subsequent establishment of the Commonwealth of Independent States (CIS) was variously denounced as a 'betrayal', a 'trap', and a 'colossal moral-psychological blow to our newly established statehood' that would 'support and even strengthen the imperial attitude toward Ukraine on the part of certain leadership circles in Russia, and leave the Ukrainian people at the mercy of their age-old encroachment on our freedom', leading to the 'reanimation of the empire' in a different form.[18]

The CIS could not be a means of replicating or renewing the USSR. At best it was simply a 'civilised form for [managing] the collapse of the Union'.[19] Even when the Ukrainian Parliament ratified the agreement, it added no less than thirteen substantive amendments,[20] and leading nationalists were calling for Ukraine's departure from the CIS as early as January 1992.[21] This absolutist position has shown no signs of weakening, despite the CIS lasting much longer than many nationalists had predicted. In fact every subsequent crisis in Ukrainian–Russian relations has led to a renewal of the demand for withdrawal. Moreover, as Ukrainian nationalists are against the CIS root-and-branch, they have of course also opposed all its offshoots: the CIS Charter, Parliamentary Assembly, Economic Union and so on. Particularly in 1992–3 therefore Ukraine was usually the Commonwealth's most reluctant and least constructive member.

For most Ukrainian nationalists the CIS is only a holding operation while Ukraine attempts to pursue its 'return to the West'. Nationalists have pressed wherever possible for Ukraine's rapid integration into Europe's overlapping political, economic and security architecture (OSCE, North Atlantic Assembly, EU and WEU, NATO, Council of Europe, etc.). However, as more realistic nationalists are prepared to acknowledge, 'admittance into core European structures is not an immediate possibility'.[22] Ukrainian nationalists may see Ukraine as a natural part of Europe, but its long estrangement from the centre of European affairs means that Ukraine is not often thought of as a natural partner in the chancelleries of the West, where realpolitik is likely to continue to dictate the preservation of the traditional special relationship with Moscow.[23]

Nevertheless, nationalists have continued to argue that Ukraine must pursue whatever advantage it can obtain, following a policy of small steps and seeking gradual integration into pan-European structures.

Inevitably, however, Ukraine is likely to be disappointed with the pace of progress, as it is far from the front of the queue. It may therefore have an ambivalent attitude to, for example, the extension of EU or NATO membership to the Visegrad states. On the one hand, this would extend the borders of either organisation closer to Ukraine. On the other hand, the expansion may stop short of, or even at, the Ukrainian border, and Ukraine would be likely to come under great pressure to join a countervailing security arrangement led by Russia. Ukraine, like Russia, may therefore develop a preference for dealing with broader organisations such as the OSCE.[24]

As a full 'return to Europe' has come to seem increasingly chimerical, many Ukrainian nationalists have chosen to support a policy of integration with Eastern and East-Central Europe alone.[25] 'Since the time of our first national state, Kievan Rus'', it is argued, 'the basic sphere of Ukrainian geopolitical interests has been central Europe and the Black Sea–Mediterranean basin.'[26] One way of breaking away from Russia would therefore be to form a 'Baltic–Black Sea Commonwealth' stretching from Estonia to the Caucasus, which would supposedly provide a 'powerful shield' against the possible renewal of Russian expansionism, and an alternative 'third pillar' of European security.[27] Ukraine's 'territory, along with that of Moldova, Belarus and Lithuania, makes up a vast buffer zone that separates the European states from direct contact with the Russian Federation, which has yet to shake off the marks of empire [nadderzhava]'.[28] Ukraine can therefore become a new cordon sanitaire, substituting for the role France has supposedly traditionally sought for Poland in Eastern Europe, or Germany planned for the whole region in World War I.[29]

Moreover, such a regional alliance would have several historical precedents, such as the abortive Hadiach Treaty of 1658, Mazepa's alliance with Sweden in the 1700s and Georgii Andruz'kyi's plan in the 1840s for an anti-Russian Slav federation. The diplomats of the Ukrainian National Republic made tentative attempts to create just such an alliance in 1919,[30] and the OUN was instrumental in helping to found the Bloc of Anti-Bolshevik Nations in 1943 (an alliance of nationalist groups in the Soviet sphere of influence). The latter reconstituted itself 'on occupied territory' at a congress in Kiev in June 1991, and after the collapse of communism renamed itself the Bloc of European and Asian Nations for Independence and Freedom at a conference in Toronto in November 1992.[31] Stepan Khmara has endorsed a similar goal, calling on Ukraine to lead the formation of a 'CIS without Russia', or 'an anti-Russian, anti-imperialist front of the former republics of the USSR'.[32]

Nationalist groups in Ukraine have therefore long cultivated links with their counterparts elsewhere in Eastern Europe, particularly in the late 1980s when the Ukrainians were anxious to learn from Solidarity's experience in Poland and coordinate their actions with the newly established Baltic Popular Fronts. These contacts bore fruit in July 1994, when the Republican and Democratic Parties helped to launch a 'League of Parties of the Baltic–Black Sea–Adriatic Region' with like-minded parties from Poland, Belarus and the Baltic states.[33] At the state level, however, there has been little progress, despite President Kravchuk taking up the issue in 1992–4. It is not clear whether such a regional grouping would be expected to serve as a clearing house for the gradual extension of economic, political and military links with Western European institutions, or as an alternative to them, creating an anti-Russian alliance in Europe's backyard. Moreover, Ukraine's would-be partners are more interested in pan-European security schemes, and Western Europe is likely to be extremely sceptical of an arrangement that would lock Ukraine into a hostile relationship with Russia. Belarus has shown a marked preference for remaining in the Russian security zone, the Baltic states have concentrated on cultivating their traditional links with their Scandinavian cousins and Ukraine's relations with Poland, its most important neighbour in the west, have cooled somewhat after a promising start in 1990–1[34] (although the defusing of traditional enmity with the Poles, after two Polish–Ukrainian wars in this century alone, is of course a major achievement in itself). Finally, many Ukrainians agree that such a grouping would antagonise Russia unnecessarily (see pp.191–3 below).[35]

The other traditional pole of Ukraine's triadic foreign policy relations is Turkey. Nationalists have argued that Ukraine should strengthen its ties with its southern neighbour, both as a traditional enemy of Russia (as also with Israel and China) and as an alternative escape route to the south.[36] Moreover, Ukraine is most likely to find alternative energy supplies from the Middle East and through the Bosphorus (in the early 1990s nationalists saw the construction of a new oil terminal at Odesa as the answer to many of Ukraine's economic difficulties, and as a touchstone in determining future relations with Russia; see chapter 6).[37] Developing countries to the east and south are also a more likely market for Ukrainian products. Turkey, however, has no wish to worsen its relations with Russia and is extremely reluctant to allow an increase in trade through the Bosphorus, especially tanker traffic. Although Ukraine helped to set up a Black Sea Economic Cooperation project in 1990 and a Parliamentary Assembly of Black Sea Countries in 1993,[38] it is likely to find a diplomatic breakthrough to the south as elusive as an open road to the West.[39]

A second Rus'?

As attempts to forge (or reforge) links with the rest of Europe have proved disappointing, an anti-Western backlash is possible, if unlikely. It is therefore worth analysing an alternative, albeit minority, nationalist foreign policy vision which is both anti-Russian and anti-Western, namely that of the ultra-nationalist Ukrainian National Assembly (UNA).

The UNA would prefer to see Ukraine become an inward-looking power, self-reliant and regionally dominant.[40] As argued in chapter 3, the UNA considers the slogan 'Away from Moscow!' to be simplistic and the search for a place in Europe demeaning. Ukraine should be as wary of the West as it is of Moscow. Both are imperial powers and neither has any real interest in the emergence of a strong Ukrainian state.[41] Instead of a 'return to Europe', the UNA therefore advocates 'Ukrainian pan-Slavism', a 'united Slav state with its centre in Kiev', restoring Kiev to the position of leadership amongst the Eastern Slavs that it supposedly enjoyed at the time of Rus'.[42] As well as incorporating 'ethnically Ukrainian' lands such as the Left Bank of the Dniester, the UNA's version of a modern Greater Ukraine would also involve establishing links with groups such as the Don Cossacks, and support for 'national liberation movements in Russia' in Chechenia or Tatarstan,[43] on the principle that any enemy of Russia is a friend of Ukraine. (The UNSO briefly participated in the Abkhazian and Chechen wars on the side of the Georgian and Chechen governments; in Moldova in 1992 it fought 'in parallel' with Russian irregulars, claiming that 'we can't allow Russians to defend Ukrainians in Dnistrov''ia – we must do it ourselves'.)[44] For groups such as the UNA, Ukraine's long-term aim should therefore be 'the creation of a buffer zone of autonomous or state structures between Russia and Ukraine in the Kuban' and the Don'.[45] The UNA has consistently predicted an implosion of Russian power and even of the Russian state itself. It argues that Ukraine should therefore build up its own military-industrial complex in order to take advantage of the inevitable vacuum in regional security and replace Russia as the key regional superpower. The UNA's deputies were also amongst the handful who opposed Ukraine's adherence to the Nuclear Non-Proliferation Treaty in November 1994 (see pp. 188–91 below).[46]

The UNA's isolationist anti-Europeanism does not really mesh well with the key historical myths of Ukrainian nationalism. However, disillusion with the West could well become a powerful force if Ukraine's economic problems continue to worsen. The element of hyperbole in the UNA's vision may be unrealistic, but is nevertheless flattering to bruised Ukrainian egos. The possibility of Ukraine somehow turning in on itself or becoming a more aggressive regional power cannot therefore be ruled out.

The diaspora issue

Ukraine has also sought to establish a special relationship with its eastern diaspora, the 6.8 million ethnic Ukrainians recorded by the last official Soviet census in 1989 as resident in the other republics of the former USSR. Most (4.4 million) live in the Russian Federation.[47] Large numbers of Ukrainians are concentrated in neighbouring regions of Moldova, Belarus and Russia, but others live further afield in areas such as Omsk and north-western Kazakhstan (Siryi Klyn) and eastern Siberia (Zelenyi Klyn).[48] Neighbouring territories have been subject to Ukrainian penetration for centuries, but migration further afield took place mainly in the late nineteenth and early twentieth centuries, although large numbers continued to leave throughout the Soviet period (for example, during the 1950s 'virgin lands' campaign in Kazakhstan). Ukrainian schools, theatres and other institutions were opened in other Soviet republics in the 1920s, but nearly all were closed in the early 1930s. Nationalists would therefore claim that the consequent mass 'denationalisation' of Ukrainians abroad masks a true figure for Ukrainians in Russia alone of up to ten to twenty million.[49]

It is a standard tenet of modern Ukrainian nationalism that Ukrainians have a moral duty to assist the national 'rebirth' of their brethren abroad, demanding at the very least that 'Ukrainians in Russia [and elsewhere in the former USSR] should have the same ethnic rights as Russians in Ukraine'.[50] Whereas the Russian minority in Ukraine is if anything supposedly overprivileged, Ukrainians in Russia continue to be denied the basic rights to native-language schooling and cultural self-expression that they lost in the 1930s. In negotiations with Russia, the Ukrainians have therefore rejected every Russian attempt to put itself forward as the guardian of the 'Russian-language population' beyond its borders, arguing that it must put its own house in order first.[51] Nationalist pressure resulted in the constitutional duties of the Ukrainian president being redefined in February 1992 to include 'helping to secure the national-cultural, spiritual and linguistic needs of Ukrainians living in other states'.[52]

Others have gone further to argue that the eastern diaspora constitutes a vast reservoir of potential support for the new Ukrainian state. As well as organising practical measures of repatriation and financial support, many nationalists have enjoyed pointing out that 'the Ukrainian diaspora is strongest precisely in those areas where Ukraine's economic dependence on Russia is greatest', such as the Kuzbass and Siberian oil fields, and that political mobilisation of the diaspora in these regions would enable Ukraine to exert countervailing pressure on Russia whenever it attempted to exercise economic and political pressure on Ukraine.[53]

However, despite the best efforts of Ukrainian nationalists, the two diasporas are unlikely ever to be of equal geopolitical importance. The Russian minority in Ukraine is likely to remain a much more central issue in bilateral relations, remaining for many nationalists a huge potential Trojan Horse on Ukrainian territory.[54] Ukraine's eastern diaspora on the other hand lacks many of the basic features that help stimulate political mobilisation.[55] Collective identity amongst Ukrainians living in the former USSR is weak. Ukrainian nationalists are quite right to bemoan the parlous state of the Ukrainian language and culture amongst the eastern diaspora, at least since the reversals of the early 1930s. Outside the Russian Federation many nominal Ukrainians see themselves as part of the general 'Russian-speaking' diaspora. Moreover, even among nationally conscious Ukrainians, other than in perhaps the Kuban' (see pp. 182–3 below), there is little real sense that areas of concentrated Ukrainian settlement are ethnic Ukrainian 'homelands' in the same sense as local Russians might feel about Crimea or Armenians about Nagorno-Karabakh[56] (the best evidence for this is that Ukrainians in eastern Moldova, who outnumber local Russians in a territory that was part of the Ukrainian SSR until 1940, have largely accepted the leadership of the Russophile 'Dniester Republic').[57] Thirdly, there is little sign of loyalty to the Ukrainian homeland manifesting itself in return migration. In the first half of 1993, for example, only between 5,000 and 6,000 Ukrainians returned to Ukraine.[58] It will therefore be even more difficult to mobilise a nationalist movement beyond Ukraine's borders than it is at home.

A Greater Ukraine?

For more radical Ukrainian nationalists the diaspora issue goes beyond mere concern for language and culture. As much of the territory settled by the eastern diaspora remains contiguous to the modern Ukrainian state, many still hark back to Mikhnovs'kyi's vision of a Greater Ukraine stretching from the Carpathians to the Caucasus. Just as nostalgic Russian nationalists would like to restore Russia's borders of 1914 or Hungarians those of 1867, Ukrainian nationalists tend to imagine the nation at its maximum supposed geographical extent, namely after the out-migration stimulated by rural overpopulation and Stolypin's reforms in the period between 1861 and 1914. Given the lack of defined political borders at the time, this has tended to mean the broadest possible definition of 'Ukrainian ethno-linguistic territory' as recorded in the censuses of 1897 and 1926 (despite the establishment of the Ukrainian SSR, the Ukrainian–Russian 'border' was still fluid in the 1920s, and was adjusted substantially westward at Ukraine's expense in 1924–5).[59]

Since Mikhnovs'kyi the idea of a 'Ukrainian Independent United State' (*Ukraïns'ka samostiina soborna derzhava*) has been a key nationalist slogan, but many would argue that the 'unification' (*sobornist'*) of Ukrainian lands was only partially completed in 1939–45.[60] Today's would-be *Ukraïna irredenta* is mainly in the east, on territory that is now part of the Russian Federation, namely the Starodub region north of Chernihiv, the south-eastern parts of Voronezh, Kursk and Rostov oblasts, and the Kuban' region in the north Caucasus. In the west, some radical nationalists would also covet the left bank of the river Dniester in Moldova, the Prešov region in north-east Slovakia, the Chełm and Przemyśl territories in south-east Poland, the Brest region in south-west Belarus, and possibly southern Bukovyna and the area around Maramures in Romania.[61]

As with the territory currently bounded by the Ukrainian state, radical nationalists would argue that Ukrainian lands further afield will always remain Ukrainian because they were first settled by ethnic Ukrainians, regardless of subsequent population movements or changes in political boundaries. The Kuban' for example was supposedly first colonised by the Zaporozhian Cossacks after the destruction of their headquarters in 1775 forced them to settle further afield,[62] and the left bank of the river Dniester (the site of the would-be breakaway 'Dniester Republic' in Moldova) was an integral part of Kievan Rus' from the ninth to the thirteenth centuries, and belonged to the Ukrainian SSR until 1940.[63] Related to the historical argument is the assertion that deliberate falsification of the figures or forcible 'Russification' or 'Romanianisation' has concealed the true extent of 'Ukrainian ethno-linguistic territory' in neighbouring states. Instead of the reported 67,000 Ukrainians in Romania, for example, there are supposedly some 200,000 to 300,000; in Slovakia 203,000 rather than 40,000; in Belarus some 500,000 rather than 230,000.[64] Similarly, it is claimed that the censuses of 1897 and 1926 recorded solid Ukrainian majorities in many parts of the Kuban' and Don territories, before subsequent 'Russification' kicked over the traces of Ukrainian settlement.[65]

National-democratic organisations such as Rukh and Prosvita have sought to promote a Ukrainian national revival in areas such as the Kuban' and Zelenyi Klyn,[66] providing practical assistance with textbooks and Ukrainian newspapers and helping to set up cultural organisations (see chapter 3), but to date have refrained from backing overtly political groups, particularly in sensitive regions such as eastern Moldova.[67] The radical right has no such qualms. The tiny underground Ukrainian National Party, which briefly surfaced in Galicia in October 1989, was the first to call for 'the rebirth of the Ukrainian People's Republic within her ethnic borders', but it was soon followed by other ultra-radical parties such as the DSU and Stepan Khmara's UCRP.[68] The UNA has demanded the 'return' of the left bank of the Dniester from Moldova to Ukraine.[69] Furthermore, such groups have also declared that the time is right 'to take the field of struggle onto Russian territory', arguing that any state which 'fails to pursue active politics abroad will become subject to the active politics of its neighbours'.[70] Ultra-nationalists have often threatened that any Russian destabilisation of Ukrainian politics will be matched by equivalent measures in Russia.[71]

The possibility of Ukraine making serious territorial pretensions against its neighbours can be discounted (the boot is more likely to be on the other foot). Nevertheless, more radical Ukrainian nationalists may well attempt to take advantage of Russian difficulties in troubled regions such as the north Caucasus, and perhaps even further afield, particularly if any serious conflict should develop between Russia and Ukraine.

National defence: establishing armed forces

Despite its economic problems, Ukraine surprised many observers in 1991–2 by seeking to establish extremely large armed forces, second in size in Europe only to Russia's, although the high opportunity costs of maintaining a large standing army have forced Ukraine to scale down its ambitions from an army of 420,000 men to one of around 200,000.[72] The high priority placed on national defence can be explained by several factors. The most obvious is the perception of Russian threat and the possibility of internal instability. Second, as explained above, the relative lack of success in finding friends abroad, even amongst the Ukrainian diaspora, has led to a lack of faith in purely diplomatic solutions to Ukraine's problems. Third, it is axiomatic amongst modern Ukrainian nationalists that Ukraine lost its independence in 1917–20 'because its then leaders (Vynnychenko, Hrushevs'kyi) were blinded by socialist ideals and did not defend the Ukrainian nation' militarily.[73] Fourth, the abortive coup attempt in August 1991 (which supposedly, in the words of the Ukrainian declaration of independence, placed Ukraine in 'mortal danger'), rumours of military intervention to forestall the Belovezhkaia

Pushcha agreement of December 1991[74] and the Moscow events of October 1993 convinced even the national communists that their long-term survival in power was likely to require some military underpinning. In the military field therefore the influence of nationalist principles has been more noticeable than elsewhere.

Nationalist agitation for the establishment of separate Ukrainian armed forces began as early as 1989 amongst radical groups such as the Ukrainian National Party and the Helsinki Union. The latter's 1988 Declaration of Principles demanded the right to form 'republican military formations', although it was envisaged that these would still be part of the Soviet armed forces.[75] Nationalist deputies managed to include in the 1990 declaration of sovereignty the claim that Ukraine 'had the right to' form its own armed forces, and in August 1990 Parliament passed a resolution that Ukrainian conscripts should only serve on Ukrainian territory.[76] However, the possibility of forming truly independent armed forces was first seriously discussed at a conference on the 'External and Internal Security of Ukraine' organised by Rukh and the URP in February 1991. The conference rejected the Baltic option of seeking to expel all Soviet forces from Ukrainian territory and the Moldovan/ Armenian route of building armed forces from scratch, and argued that the only feasible way to build armed forces of sufficient size sufficiently quickly was to take over all Soviet forces stationed in Ukraine.[77]

This was the approach duly taken after independence, on the principle that 'everything that is situated on Ukrainian territory is the property of the Ukrainian people'.[78] Nationalists backed up this claim with the subsidiary argument that, as the dissolution of the USSR into separate sovereign states implied a division of its economic assets and liabilities (see chapter 6), then the same should be true of military bases and hardware. Given its contribution to Soviet GNP and/or its military-industrial sector, the former Soviet forces on Ukrainian territory in December 1991 were simply Ukraine's fair share of the spoils (using such a method, Levko Luk"ianenko calculated that Ukraine was entitled to exactly 30.2 per cent of all Soviet naval resources, making its demand for control over the Black Sea fleet a relatively modest claim).[79]

Ukraine also attempted to 'nationalise' all personnel stationed on Ukrainian territory at that time. The latter were never properly counted, but probably consisted of around 600,000 to 700,000 men. Despite the fact that only a minority were Ukrainians (one report stated that 44 per cent of men and more than 60 per cent of officers were ethnic Russians),[80] nationalists wished at all costs to avoid large numbers of foreign troops, controlled from abroad, remaining on Ukrainian territory, and urged that all military personnel should be encouraged to take the new oath of loyalty. Moreover, a broad-brush approach was the only quick route to an army of substantial size.

Ukraine's radical approach had its disadvantages, however. First, although Ukraine successfully seized the vast majority of arms, tanks, etc. on its territory, this was necessarily a one-off opportunity. Ukraine did not have a self-sufficient arms industry to guarantee future procurement. Second, Ukraine was unable to secure control of the Black Sea fleet, but refused to countenance alternative options of withdrawal, demilitarisation or division.[81] A dangerous mix of military and separatist forces was therefore soon brewing on the Crimean peninsula. Third, many nationalists were soon questioning why a proprietary claim should not also be made over the nuclear weapons on Ukrainian territory, despite the fact that in December 1991 President Kravchuk declared himself commander-in-chief of all conventional forces (only) in Ukraine, and in the Minsk agreement later that month Ukraine had agreed to 'preserve and maintain under united command a common military-strategic space, including control over nuclear weapons' (see pp. 188–91 below).[82]

National defence: Ukrainianising the armed forces

A fourth problem was created by Ukraine's very success in persuading the vast majority of servicemen (the Black Sea fleet excepted) to take the Ukrainian oath in early 1992. The Ukrainians therefore inherited nearly all local units of the Soviet army extant and nationalists were forced to reconsider the benefits of a multi-ethnic army. According to Levko Luk"ianenko in 1992, for example, 'among the 500 officers attached to the ministry of defence, 202 are Ukrainian and 264 Russian. How can we be sure that such a ministry of defence and such an officer corps can build an army that is capable of waging a war against an invasion from the east?'[83] Nationalists also grew increasingly opposed to the presence of what were termed 'foreign forces and foreign bases' on Ukrainian 'territory',[84] in other words the Black Sea fleet, the majority of whose ships and servicemen remained loyal to Russia.

Nationalists therefore began to argue that those who had taken the oath for basically economic motives should be gradually weeded out in favour of patriotic ethnic Ukrainians serving elsewhere in the former USSR (an estimated 200,000 to 300,000 men). Moreover, the Union of Officers of Ukraine (UOU) campaigned hard for leading appointments to go to its members (see chapter 3). Under Kostiantyn Morozov, Ukraine's first minister of defence from 1991 to 1993, some progress was made in Ukrainianising the highest levels of the armed forces,[85] and a decree was passed in April 1993 to enforce the use of the Ukrainian language in the armed forces' administration by the end of 1995. However, widespread resistance to such policies was a key factor in enforcing Morozov's departure in October 1993.[86] Only a few thousand non-Ukrainians could be persuaded to leave (although more left voluntarily for Russia as relative economic conditions worsened), and few Ukrainians were able or willing to return from the diaspora.[87] Under Morozov's successors, Vitalii Radets'kyi and Valerii Shmarov, the influence of the UOU was sharply reduced and the policy of Ukrainianisation effectively suspended in the face of resistance from the multiethnic lower ranks[88] (although successive drafts have brought the ethnic mix of the armed forces closer to that of Ukraine's population as a whole).

Nationalists have also disturbed many in the armed forces by attempting to insist that all servicemen should be educated in the best 'traditions of the Ukrainian people and armed forces'.[89] The main vehicle for this was the Social-Psychological Service set up in 1992 under Volodymyr Muliava.[90] Muliava's thousand or so officers, who had strong links to the UOU, earned themselves few friends by following the didactic traditions of Soviet political commissars (the armed forces' Main Political Administration). Critics were soon accusing the group of simply replacing socialist with nationalist indoctrination, and the service's activities were scaled down and Muliava replaced in autumn 1993 (Muliava remained popular in nationalist circles and was elected as a deputy from Ivano-Frankivs'k in 1994).[91]

Nevertheless, the attempt to foster a new military patriotism through the glorification of Ukraine's military past has continued, albeit skirting around delicate areas of past Ukrainian–Russian confrontation.[92] Considerable care had to be taken with rehabilitating the likes of Mazepa and the armies of the Ukrainian People's Republic, as their struggle was primarily with Moscow,[93] but the most sensitive issue was the UPA. The demand by many Galicians that the UPA be rehabilitated to serve as a model for the new Ukrainian armed forces was clearly unrealistic. Military journals began slowly chipping away at the Soviet image of the UPA as a neo-Nazi German puppet organisation confined to western Ukraine,[94] but had to be extremely wary of alienating the multi-ethnic and trans-regional Ukrainian army (and public opinion at large). Great care was also taken to ensure that the Ukrainian part in Soviet victory in World War II was still celebrated in traditional fashion.[95] Military historians and propagandists have therefore tended to concentrate on safer topics, such as the campaigns of the Zaporozhian Cossacks against a third party, the Crimean Tatars and Ottoman Turks (the argument that the Zaporozhians played the leading role in conquering southern Ukraine and Crimea for Catherine II in the late eighteenth century was also useful in solidifying Ukraine's historical claims to both regions).[96]

National defence: threat perception and force deployment

What were Ukrainian armed forces to be for? Working out an appropriate national security doctrine was initially handicapped by the statement in the 1990 declaration of sovereignty that Ukraine would be 'a permanently neutral state, taking no part in [any] military blocs'.[97] The foreign policy doctrine passed in July 1993 was similarly anodyne, although it gave the impression that the development of links with Western and Central Europe was a greater priority than relations with the CIS.[98] For most Ukrainian nationalists, however, 'political realities in the world are not the stuff of sentimental dreams, but of the national interests of states'.[99] Therefore their first priority has been to set aside such romantic notions and develop a military doctrine based in a realpolitik of well-defined Ukrainian national interests. Moreover, Ukraine supposedly could not afford to be militarily neutral in a situation where 'every one of Ukraine's neighbours has territorial pretensions (historical or political) against her'.[100] A potential Polish claim on Galicia or Hungarian threat to Transcarpathia are admittedly remote possibilities, but Romania's claim to northern Bukovyna and southern Bessarabia and, above all, the potential Russian irredentist threat to a large swathe of eastern and southern Ukraine are to a Ukrainian nationalist very real and potent dangers.[101]

Ukrainian nationalists therefore tend to pay only lip-service to the doctrine of minimum sufficient defence, and have pressed for Ukraine to maintain relatively large armed forces in the face of the perceived Russian threat. Moreover, this threat is assumed to be most likely to manifest itself as a large-scale conventional attack, rather than via internal instability in Ukraine or third-party manipulation (Russian difficulties in the Chechen war notwithstanding). Moreover, the uncertainties surrounding the nuclear issue have also fuelled the demand for large conventional forces, even though some nationalists took a belt-and-braces approach by supporting both conventional and nuclear deterrence (see pp. 188–91 below). Nationalists have criticised plans to reduce the size of the armed forces to some 200,000 to 250,000 by the end of the millennium (still a considerable total), and have advocated maintaining a total strength of 500,000 to 520,000 men.[102] Moreover, nationalists have argued that troops should be redeployed from western and south-western Ukraine (where Soviet military planners had positioned them) to Ukraine's eastern borders to face the threat from Russia, and have urged the development of a rapid-deployment force to deal with hotspots on or near Ukraine's borders.[103]

Ukraine's Military Doctrine, finally adopted by Parliament in October 1993 after nationalist criticism resulted in the rejection of two earlier drafts in October 1992 and April 1993, was strongly influenced by such thinking. Although the doctrine declared that Ukraine had no fundamental quarrels with any of its neighbours and that Ukrainian national security policy was fundamentally defensive in nature, it nevertheless affirmed that 'Ukraine will regard as a potential enemy any state whose policy consistently threatens its military security, interferes in its internal affairs or aspires to control its territory or infringe its national interests', an obvious reference to Russia. Moreover, the doctrine declared that Ukraine would seek to become 'an influential power' in the region, and implausibly committed the state to an expensive procurement campaign, including the latest high-technology weapons and 'ocean-going ships', rather than mere coastal defence. The doctrine also referred to the need for 'patriotic-military education of pre-conscription youth and all personnel'.[104]

Ukrainian defence strategy may well, however, prove to be misguided as well as ruinously expensive. Russia is unlikely to have the capacity to launch a large-scale conventional assault for many years to come. Ukrainian nationalists may consider that a military build-up will help purchase psychological security, but they may also find that a policy of military confrontation with Russia becomes self-fulfilling, and that an imagined threat becomes a real one. On the other hand, economic realities and the continued multi-ethnic basis of the Ukrainian army may well combine to rule out any regional arms race on practical grounds, and no doubt it would be wiser if Ukraine's Military Doctrine recognised this fact.

The nuclear weapons issue

Much attention has been paid in the West to Ukraine's alleged backsliding over the question of nuclear arms.[105] Before independence nearly all nationalists, apart from extremist groups such as the UNA-UNSO,[106] advocated a non-nuclear Ukraine in order to reassure the rest of the world that they had nothing to fear from Ukrainian independence (and because in the immediate aftermath of the Chornobyl' disaster Ukrainian public opinion was strongly anti-nuclear). However, after 1991 rapid reversals of policy in the face of the perceived security threat from Russia and the supposed economic and diplomatic benefits of nuclear status earned Ukraine considerable international opprobrium.[107] (Ukraine had neither recognised ownership nor operational control over former Soviet nuclear weaponry on its territory, but enjoyed de facto administrative control.) Moreover, although Ukraine signed the NPT (nuclear non-proliferation treaty) in 1994, it should not be assumed that all its doubts had been laid to rest.

The 1990 declaration of sovereignty committed Ukraine 'not to accept, not to produce and not to acquire nuclear weapons', and this was subsequently reinforced by a declaration of Ukraine's non-nuclear status in October 1991[108] and Leonid Kravchuk's apparent promise to adhere to the NPT at the Lisbon summit in May 1992. All tactical nuclear weapons were indeed transferred from Ukraine to Russia for destruction by May 1992. The 179 ICBMs (and 30 strategic Bear-H and Blackjack bombers) that remained on Ukrainian territory could not be removed so quickly, however, and the subsequent pause allowed the nationalist critique of 'one-sided, timid and ill-conceived nuclear disarmament'[109] to gather momentum.

Nationalist thinking was divided into two camps. Moderate nationalists argued that Ukraine should only disarm if three key conditions were met. Firstly, 'Ukraine must have firm guarantees from the nuclear states, the United Nations Security Council and NATO concerning national security and non-interference in her internal affairs.' Secondly, Ukraine needed 'financial resources and technological assistance for the dismantling of nuclear warheads and their carriers (with such dismantling to take place on the territory of Ukraine)'. Thirdly, 'Ukrainian disarmament is possible only in parallel with the disarmament of other nuclear states', as 'part of the process of general European and global nuclear disarmament'[110] (as Russia was usually named as one of the above 'nuclear states', this last condition would amount to more or less permanent retention of nuclear arms, as there is little likelihood of Russia disarming before Ukraine). As many other adherents to the NPT have pointed out, the treaty requires the nuclear states to work toward their own gradual disarmament.

More radical nationalists went beyond conditionality to argue that Ukraine should keep its nuclear arsenal more or less indefinitely,[111] arguing that nuclear disarmament would be 'a sign of the weakness of Ukraine' that would leave it 'a defenceless puppet in foreign hands, subject to the will of other states'. Moreover, while 'a nuclear Ukraine is a powerful, modern superpower', 'a non-nuclear Ukraine [would be] a mere second-rate and dependent' state.[112] Nuclear status would guarantee Ukraine a place at international conference tables that it would otherwise never obtain. Financial assistance would always be welcome, but just as Russia could not be trusted to refrain from attacking Ukraine, the West could not be relied on to spill its own soldiers' blood in Ukraine's defence. Therefore no external security guarantees could possibly substitute for a nuclear shield against Russia.

Moreover, opposition to nuclear disarmament was not confined to nationalist circles. Many independents shared nationalist reservations that the policy lacked realpolitik, while leftists thought that preserving Ukraine's nuclear capacity would help to restore both superpower cooperation with Russia and Ukraine's military-industrial potential.[113] In April 1993, 162 Ukrainian deputies signed a motion urging President Kravchuk openly to declare Ukraine a nuclear state (that is to assert Ukrainian ownership and control of the weapons), and opinion polls indicated that around a quarter to a third of the population, mainly in western and central Ukraine, were prepared to countenance a nuclear Ukraine.[114]

It therefore took two years of political struggle before Ukraine signed the January 1994 trilateral disarmament treaty in Moscow with Russia and the United States, by which it promised to dismantle all remaining weaponry in return for financial assistance and security assurances,[115] which were reiterated by all the Western nuclear states at the OSCE summit in Budapest in December 1994.[116] In February 1994 Ukraine ratified the START-1 treaty and the NPT the following November.[117]

Both treaties were ratified by impressive majorities (START-1 by 260 votes to 3, the NPT by 301 to 8). It should not be assumed however that nationalist reservations had dissipated overnight. *Force majeure* lay behind the climb-down rather than any genuine change of heart. By late 1993 it was becoming clear that stalling the nuclear disarmament process was beginning to threaten more deeply cherished nationalist priorities, especially the diplomatic 'return to Europe', the hope of economic assistance and the desire to obtain security guarantees against Russia. As regards the latter, the building of conventional defence had been the first priority since 1991 and it was increasingly clear that the construction of a nuclear capability could only be at the expense of the rest of the already woefully inadequate military budget. On the other hand, after the Massandra summit in September 1993, nationalists came to realise that the involvement of the Western powers, the United States above all, in the disarmament negotiation process would help Ukraine to obtain security guarantees which, although still vague and far from legally binding, it could never have obtained in direct negotiations with Russia alone.[118]

Moreover, nationalists carefully constructed a fall-back position. The 1994 Trilateral Agreement envisaged that the disarmament process could take up to seven years, leaving nationalists free to demand its suspension if relations with Russia were to deteriorate significantly. Similarly, the November 1994 resolution on the NPT referred to 'the threat to use force against the territorial unity . . . of Ukraine on the part of any nuclear state' and 'the exercise of economic pressure' as 'exceptional circumstances' that could conceivably lead Ukraine to rethink its obligations under the treaty.[119] Lastly, the security 'assurances' that Ukraine obtained in January and December 1994 from Russia and the West were far from being 'guarantees'. Ukrainian nuclear disarmament is therefore likely to be a long-running saga.

Little Russianism

The nationalist foreign policy agenda, as with its equivalent in domestic politics, is opposed by a strong counter-lobby which argues that it is more natural for Ukraine to make its way in the world in alliance with Russia than in opposition to its influence. Moreover, if Ukraine were to attempt to define its independence in a manner that too obviously excluded Russia and Russian interests, then the political reaction in Russia might well further politicise Ukraine's Russian or Russophone population in opposition to the nationalist vision.

The left-wing poet Borys Oliinyk, who was one of the original leaders of Rukh and became chairman of the parliamentary foreign affairs committee in 1994, has criticised the growing tendency amongst Ukrainian nationalists to find constant fault with the Russian 'elder brother', and stylise Ukraine as a 'victimised [pohromnyts'kyi – literally "pogromised"] country'. In historical fact, he has asked

was it the Russian people who themselves chose the name 'elder brother'? Was it the Russian people who issued the Valuiev and Ems Ukazy, which banned the Ukrainian language? Was it the Russian people who drowned itself in luxury? Was it the Russian people who alongside our own fell on the field of battle against fascism? . . . Was it the Russian people who alongside our own liberated from the fascists a despoiled Ukraine that has now become a sovereign, independent state? . . . Leaders come and go, but peoples always remain. Our love and respect for the Russian people cannot be shifted by any earthly or cosmic force.[120]

As Drahomanov argued in the nineteenth century, Ukrainians should not mistake the actions of the imperial authorities for those of the Russian people as whole. Nevertheless, the anti-nationalist camp contains several strands. At one extreme to nationalist 'Europeanism' is the 'Eurasian' lobby, which argues, as President Kuchma stated in his inauguration speech in July 1994, that 'Ukraine is historically part of the Eurasian economic and cultural space' alongside Russia and Belarus.[121]

The concept of Eurasianism was first propagated in the 1920s by Russian émigrés such as Georgii Vernadskii and Nikolai Trubetskoi, who were sympathetic to the Bolsheviks' attempt to reconstruct the tsarist empire and to their anti-Western ideology, but argued that the new Russia should be a 'symphonic union' of the Eastern Slavs (above all the twin 'Asiatic sisters' of Russia and Ukraine) rather than a socialist internationalist state.[122] Modern-day 'Eurasianists' in Ukraine do not go so far as to dissolve Ukrainian history into that of Russia, nor would they necessarily echo the anti-Western and Messianic themes of the 1920s, but they agree that because of close ethnic and religious ties and centuries of common history Ukraine's natural destiny remains in the East Slavic world rather than in chasing some chimerical 'Europe'. According to the 'Eurasianists', it is Galicia, with its Habsburg–Polish past, whose path of development and current political preferences have been exceptional rather than eastern or southern Ukraine. 'In the Donbass' at least, it is argued, 'local Ukrainians are much closer to Russians or local Greeks than to their ethnic cousins from L'viv.'[123] Left-wing and regional lobbies in Ukraine have therefore supported proposals for economic and even political reunion, usually between the Slavic triad of Ukraine, Russia and Belarus, although sometimes with the addition of Kazakhstan, in essence echoing Alexander Solzhenitsyn's vision of the post-Soviet future.[124] Many left-wingers have also argued for Ukraine and Russia to coordinate (or simply to merge) their military efforts as the only way to restore the old Soviet military-industrial complex to its former glory.

The more moderate anti-nationalist position may be more properly labelled 'Little Russianism'.[125] Its adherents remain firmly in favour of an independent Ukraine, but either have no desire to leave the Russian cultural and historical space and/or argue that East European political realities are such that Russia must remain Ukraine's main diplomatic, military and trading partner for the foreseeable future.[126] According to Oliinyk again, 'we are determined by fate to live side by side with Russia'.[127] Ukraine has one foot in both East and West, but in contrast to the nationalists who argue that this is the artificial result of centuries of Russian imperial domination, it is accepted that this is a natural consequence of Ukraine's historical development that cannot be gainsaid (these ideas were first raised at the Democratic Congress organised in Kharkiv in January 1991; see chapter 3).

In Kuchma's alternative formulation therefore, 'Ukraine can become a bridge between East and West', whilst remaining an independent state with links to both camps.[128] As well as cooperating wherever possible with Western institutions, Ukraine should seek to play a more constructive role in the CIS.[129] As is often also said of the United Kingdom and the European Union, it is better for Ukraine to be inside the CIS shaping its decisions than to be outside and still subject to policies decided by others. In the words of the centrist New Ukraine lobby, 'the defence of Ukraine's national interests is best carried out through the CIS. This will allow Ukraine to unite in negotiations with other states who must also defend their own national interests against the demands of the Russian leadership.'[130]

Conclusion

It has not been easy for the new Ukrainian state to find its place in the world. Nationalist solutions to defence and foreign policy dilemmas may seem seductive and straightforward, but are often impractical. Ukraine has no obvious escape routes from its external difficulties. However, the nationalist foreign policy agenda has little to do with practical concerns and everything to do with the psychological need to disentangle Ukraine from Russia. As Russia is likely to remain the hegemonic regional power for the foreseeable future, Ukrainian nationalists are likely to continue to press their case.

8 Conclusions: nationalism and national consolidation

This last chapter will attempt to draw some conclusions, and to examine how possible scenarios for the future development of Ukrainian nationalism may affect the Ukrainian state as a whole.

Historical continuities

The main theme of this work has been the lack of an established tradition of Ukrainian statehood and the consequent sharp historical differences both between and within the Ukrainian regions. Regional divisions helped determine the fate of the national movement in both 1917–20 and 1941–4, and have shown no sign of diminishing in importance in the 1990s. Furthermore chapter 5 demonstrated that regional cleavages remained remarkably stable throughout the period 1989–94 and are still the most salient influence on contemporary politics. The most striking fact about modern Ukrainian politics in general, and support for Ukrainian nationalism in particular, is the continuing importance of past historical divides.

In part this is an argument about the relative stability of political culture over time, or about the defining importance that the historical legacy takes on when traditions of political culture are relatively weak, and about the central importance of local myths of descent in facilitating ethno-nationalist mobilisation. Political culture is not an unchanging absolute, and elites may manipulate myths and symbols, but the former is not completely malleable and the latter cannot simply be 'invented'.[1] Pre-Soviet historical traditions were of course forced underground during the communist period which developed a political culture of its own,[2] but in western Ukraine at least the relatively short period of Soviet rule was unable to eradicate the strong Ukrainian tradition which developed under the Habsburgs and in interwar Poland. Postwar repression was unable to extinguish the older generation's memories and life experiences from the turbulent 1930s, 1940s and 1950s, including war and attempted national revolution, the deportations of the late

194

1940s and the long coda of the UPA campaign lasting into the mid-1950s.[3] Despite the hostility of the Soviet state, social memory and the socialisation of new generations helped to nurture traditional patterns of political culture and national myths and symbols in the private sphere, which were resuscitated with surprising ease in the late 1980s. If anything, national identity in the west, in Galicia at least, is over-determined and out of step with the rest of Ukraine. Moreover, western Ukraine is the only region to have a strong authoritarian nationalist tradition (although the far right has also found some support in Kiev), and the conflict between democratic and authoritarian nationalism has reemerged in the 1990s, echoing the interwar conflict between the UNDO and the OUN and the disputes in the mid-1940s between the Banderites and the UHVR.

In most of eastern and southern Ukraine on the other hand, pre-Soviet history was more complicated and the relationship with Russia more intimate. In neither the Kievan nor the Cossack eras did Ukrainian settlement extend throughout the region. Although nationalists have promoted the Zaporozhian myth as a means of solidifying Ukrainian identity in the east and south, they face an uphill struggle to convince the local population that the extent of Zaporozhian settlement was as wide as is now argued.[4] Without plausible local myths of descent and with only a limited cultural legacy from the Cossack period, both national consciousness and the national movement were weak in 1917–20 and 1941–4, and remain so today. Political and national-cultural socialisation came about almost entirely under the period of Soviet rule, resulting in a complicated overlay of Ukrainian, Russian, Soviet and localist loyalties. (Many local Ukrainians could still be plausibly described as *tuteshni*, those whose identity is primarily to locality, from *tut* or 'here').[5] In time the local population may develop a form of state-centred civic patriotism, but it has little natural affinity with west Ukrainian ethno-nationalism.

Central Ukraine also has its own specific character. It is the site of longest continuous Ukrainian settlement, and is the only region to have played a role in all the key episodes of Ukrainian history (the Cossacks were not a west Ukrainian phenomenon). However, the region fell under Russian control in either 1654 (the Left Bank) or 1793–5 (the Right) rather than 1939–45, that is in the pre-modern era when local elites were particularly vulnerable to assimilation. A national revival of sorts began in the quarter-century before 1917, but links between the tiny national intelligentsia and the broad mass of illiterate and parochial peasants were not strong. The 1917 Constituent Assembly results showed the possibility of convergence between the two groups, but the opportunity was lost in 1918–19. It seemed for a time that the Ukrainianisation campaign of the 1920s might provide a second chance, but it was cut short. The peasantry was then subjected to the twin blows of collectivisation and the Great Famine, while the old intelligentsia suffered particularly heavily in the purges. Although there were some stirrings of support for the national movement in 1941–3 and in the 1960s when Kiev emerged as a leading centre of dissent, the gap between the intelligentsia and the countryside remained wide. The national movement's failure to win significant support outside the main central cities in 1989–94 and the polarisation between Left and Right Bank in the 1994 presidential elections were considerable setbacks in the one region where nationalists had best hopes of making progress.

Continuity is also evident in patterns of political development. The weakness of the Ukrainian national movement has meant that its best opportunities have come when the power of Moscow or St Petersburg was in decline. During periods when 'the Russian state gathers strength, Ukrainian independence is lost ... and vice versa. Weakness and cataclysm in Russia provide Ukraine with the chance to declare independence', which periods of imperial recovery have then taken away.[6] Ukrainian nationalism therefore waxed in periods of imperial weakness such as 1917–18, 1941–4 and the late 1980s, but on the first two occasions waned when the empire subsequently recovered its strength. During the early phases of national revival, as before October 1917 and in 1987–9, Ukrainians have proceeded cautiously, first confining themselves to a largely cultural agenda and then to modest political demands for a federal or confederal link with Russia. Only relatively late in the day, emboldened and empowered by collapsing central power, have they moved to seize outright independence.

On the other hand, the long-term division of Ukrainian lands has tended to leave the various branches of the national movement unsynchronised and out of step. Specifically, the national movement in Galicia has since the 1890s been much more radical than that in the rest of Ukraine, but the attempt by Galicians to promote their homeland as 'the Ukrainian Piedmont' has not necessarily won widespread acceptance elsewhere. The consequent sense of frustration has therefore increased the attraction of maximalist and ultra-radical nationalism to many west Ukrainians, determined to think 'beyond the limits of the possible' and condemn the caution of their fellow countrymen. In particular, 'Ukrainianisation' has become a panacea, a means of creating unity out of diversity, and language politics in particular has taken on central importance as a means of transcending regional and ethnic cleavages, without adequate consideration of why they exist in the first place.

Just as Mikhnovs'kyi and Dontsov denounced moderates such as Drahomanov and Hrushevs'kyi in the 1900s and 1920s, and Valentyn Moroz attacked Ivan Dziuba in the 1970s, so contemporary ultra-radicals have wrongly diagnosed the weakness of the Ukrainian national movement as due to the timidity of moderate nationalist leaders, rather than historical and regional factors,[7] and have turned on the 'national-democrats', thereby dividing the national movement from within. Inter- and intra-party struggle within the nationalist camp has therefore been bitter (see chapter 3), resulting in a diminution of overall influence.

Nationalist ideology

Partly as a consequence of this pattern of historical development, Ukrainian nationalism has appeared in a variety of ideological guises. Chapters 1 and 2 argued that, because of the many discontinuities in Ukrainian history, the Ukrainian national movement has never developed as a continuum. Different forms of nationalism have appeared at different times and in different regions (liberal federalism before 1917, integral nationalism in the 1920s, the civic nationalism of the *shistdesiatnyky*), but none has ever established itself as the dominant tradition. Contemporary nationalism reflects this diversity of choice.[8]

Most national-democrats have taken their ideological inspiration from Hrushevs'kyi or Lypyns'kyi rather than Mikhnovs'kyi or Dontsov. Rukh has tried its best to remain loyal to postwar civic nationalism, while more radical nationalists in the URP and the Congress of National-Democratic Forces have advocated a form of 'ethnic-led territorialism'. However, as all national-democrats are agreed on the importance of promoting Ukrainianisation and 'the Ukrainian character of Ukrainian statehood' the difference is not as great as it appears. Nevertheless, the appearance of supposedly 'post-nationalist' groups, such as New Wave in L'viv in 1993 or the Reform faction in the 1994 Parliament, has shown that a modern Ukrainian liberal nationalism is still possible.[9]

The ultra-nationalist fringe is characterised by a similar diversity of choice. The Congress of Ukrainian Nationalists, whilst trying to present a modernised image, still has one foot in the 1930s and 1940s. For those for whom one foot is not enough, organisations such as the DSU and OUN in Ukraine openly model themselves on the 1930s OUN. The Ukrainian National Assembly, on the other hand, has tried to play on post-communist anomie to construct a uniquely Ukrainian mixture of militarism, authoritarianism and pan-Slavism. Despite such disagreements, however, nearly all ultra-nationalists share an idealised version of the wartime UPA and the Dontsovite past, brushing aside the compromises that were made in 1943–4.

This ideological diversity is matched (or rather exceeded) by the proliferation of nationalist parties and organisations (see chapter 3). However, organisational disunity and party-political conflict often masks a surprising level of underlying agreement. The key themes that are most common in Ukrainian nationalist discourse – the special rights of ethnic Ukrainian indigenes, the unique status and special suffering of the Ukrainian people, and the inevitability of cultural and political conflict with Russia – tend to cut across party divisions and ideological categories. In this respect, Ukrainian nationalism is hardly unique. The importance of 'national homeland', the mythologising of national suffering and the demonisation of the traditional ethnic 'other' are common elements in most ethno-nationalist movements.[10]

Minority status

The other key argument of this work has been that historical and regional differences have combined to make nationalist political mobilisation in Ukraine much more difficult than in many other parts of the former communist world, such as Transcaucasia or the Baltic states. Ukraine's unique feature is the existence of deep divisions within the titular nationality group as well as between different ethnic groups. As outlined in chapter 1, Ukrainian society is divided into three roughly equal parts. As well as the massive ethnic Russian minority (22 per cent of the population) the nominal Ukrainian majority is itself divided into Ukrainophones (some 40 per cent of the total population) and Russophones (33–4 per cent).

Nationalism has therefore always had to compete with Little Russianism for Ukrainians' loyalties. Even in western Ukraine the national movement faced a strong challenge from the rival Russophile movement until as late as the 1880s. In the 1920s Dontsov and Khvyl'ovyi denounced the failure of so many ethnic Ukrainians to liberate themselves from the Russian cultural space and embrace 'psychological Europe', and this theme has been taken up with enthusiasm by nationalists in the 1990s, but for many Ukrainians Little Russianism remains a natural identity. However, Ukrainian nationalists have in practice done little to bring them on board. As argued in chapter 6, the ethno-nationalist premises of Ukrainian nationalist argument tend to breed the assumption that the non-nationalist majority will simply fall in line. However, although most nationalists have themselves stressed the importance of an all-inclusive state-building project, they tend not to realise that many of their key concepts are in fact essentially ethno-nationalist and that they are therefore engaged in a self-limiting project of ethno-nationalist mobilisation.[11] However, without the support of the non-nationalist majority, the Ukrainian state rests on a dangerously narrow base.

This has been disguised by the fact that political mobilisation is much stronger amongst Ukrainophone Ukrainians than amongst Russophone Ukrainians, who have yet to develop strong political organisations of their own. The relative vacuum in the political centre has encouraged the nationalists to pursue their nationalising project, but has also deluded them about their relative chances of success. Ukrainian nationalists have tended to blame their political weakness on the 'denationalised' population in eastern and southern Ukraine, and in the countryside, deriding their Little Russian 'inferiority complex', 'sausage mentality' and indifference to the fate of their own nation,[12] but are likely to be surprised by the resilience of Russophone resistance to Ukrainianisation policies. The perception that the Ukrainian state is engaged in a nationalising project may have declined somewhat after Leonid Kuchma's victory in the 1994 presidential election, but so long as Ukrainianisation continues to be a key part of the nationalist agenda the risk of estrangement between Ukrainophones and Russophones remains real.

However, although west and east may be out of step, both nationalists and anti-nationalists seem fated to struggle against one another within the same state. Galician nationalists tend to be messianic, seeing themselves as the true keepers of the national faith held in trust for the rest of apostate Ukraine, and the geopolitical situation of western Ukraine makes the idea of voluntary Galician separatism nonsensical. Although anti-nationalists in the east and south often argue that Ukraine without Galicia would be better placed to normalise relations with Russia, the Galicians have nowhere to go and their sense of identity is inescapably bound up with their links to the rest of Ukraine. On the other hand, most Russians in eastern and southern Ukraine think of themselves as indigenes and are unlikely to contemplate separatism if that would cut them off from Kiev and central Ukraine. The balance of population and traditions of east Ukrainian political representation in Kiev also make Russian (or Russophone) separatism less likely. Moreover, Russia may be happy to exercise influence in eastern and southern Ukraine, but it is far from clear that its interests would be served by re-absorbing these regions. A truncated Ukraine would be much less stable and in all likelihood violently anti-Russian, both because of its more concentrated ethnic make-up and historical character, and in reaction to the very fact of its truncation.

State nationalism and civic patriotism

What then are the prospects for bridging these divides and developing an overarching state-centred or civic nationalism, either at the elite or mass level? Chapter 4 described how the nationalist movement received crucial reinforcements in 1990–1 from the national communist wing of the CPU, with Leonid Kravchuk and Ivan Pliushch making a vital contribution both to the winning of independence and to the subsequent promotion of the national idea. However, the Ukrainian national communists were never as strong as their equivalents in Lithuania or Poland, they failed to develop durable political organisations and the 1994 elections demonstrated a considerable loss of unity amongst their ranks. Furthermore, they were not able to bring the whole of the old left with them. Whereas the Democratic Labour Party in Lithuania and the Democratic Left Alliance in Poland are now regarded as safe custodians of the national state and caused few alarms when they returned to power in 1992 and 1993, the reborn Communist Party of Ukraine remains violently anti-nationalist.

Nevertheless, it remains possible that raison d'état will over time help to consolidate elite loyalties to the new Ukrainian state. Independence has brought Ukrainian elites considerable benefits, including international prestige, freedom from Moscow's tutelage, protection of their own backyard from outsider competition and the enhanced ability to build political constituencies through the control of local institutions and resources.[13] Moreover, as custodians of the state, they may well be moulded by their office and come to see themselves as advocates of Ukraine's particularistic national interests, regardless of their regional or ethnic origin. Examples of such behaviour are not hard to find. Kostiantyn Morozov, an ethnic Russian who served as Ukraine's first defence minister from 1991 to 1993, became an ardent nationalist, if anything *plus royaliste que le roi*, who resigned in protest against Kravchuk's willingness to surrender most of the Black Sea fleet to Russia.[14] Ukrainian deputies have voted in surprisingly large numbers to take a tough line against Crimea, as in March 1995 when 246 voted against 55 to abolish the Crimean presidency and constitution, a majority that must have cut across party, ethnic and linguistic boundaries.[15] Most significantly of all, once installed in office, Leonid Kuchma, given that he could be more confident of Russophone support, in many instances took a tougher line with Russia than his predecessor Kravchuk.[16]

As regards the mass of the population, particularly the Russophones and/or Little Russians, unless the Ukrainian state adopts a more flexible attitude to national myths and symbols, economic nationalism rather than ethno-nationalism is probably the best hope of solidifying support. The loyalty of the non-nationalist majority to the Ukrainian state is likely to remain conditional on the prospects for economic recovery, or more precisely Ukraine's economic performance relative to that of Russia (that is regression in Russia would be as likely to strengthen loyalty to Ukraine as Ukrainian economic improvement). The 1991 referendum campaign showed that such support could be assembled, but subsequent severe economic difficulties have shown how easily it can be dissipated. Moreover, Ukraine's complex ethno-regional politics are also likely to make substantive economic reforms difficult. Any Ukrainian government is likely to find it difficult to implement rigorous reforms and austere budgets over the heads of regional protests. The achievement of a social consensus to smooth the crucial early phases of reform, difficult enough in relatively homogeneous nation-states like Poland or the Czech Republic,[17] is likely to prove even more elusive in Ukraine.[18]

Radicalisation: 'Weimar Ukraine?'

The opposite possibility is that severe socio-economic crisis or a sharp deterioration in relations with Russia could lead to a surge in support for Ukrainian nationalism that enabled it to transcend its inherited historical limitations. Ultra-nationalist groups such as the UNA-UNSO have openly looked forward to what they call the 'Weimar scenario',[19] arguing that 'the Ukrainian revolution [will have] two phases: the first is national-democratic (the establishment of the Ukrainian Weimar republic, the sale and/or dispersal of everything into small pieces), and the second is the decisive entry of organised nationalism onto the scene ... we are people of the second wave'.[20] Valentyn Moroz, the veteran 1970s dissident, argued as early as 1992 that 'the democratic resources of the Ukrainian revival are now depleted ... the next stage must be nationalist'.[21]

Ukraine is not Weimar Germany. It has not lost an empire; it has no 'stab in the back' myth; it has no middle class angry and disoriented by the loss of wealth and social prestige. Ukraine has a large diaspora, but it remains politically under-mobilised and it is unlikely to force the question of border revision onto the agenda (see chapter 7). Russia is of course the more apposite case for comparison with Weimar Germany, but modern Ukraine arguably meets three of the four conditions listed by one author as conducive to the growth of fascistic movements, namely a strong 'native current of ultra-nationalism' (albeit a strongly contested one), 'an inadequate consensus on liberal values' and the fact that it is a 'modern society undergoing a structural crisis'.[22]

However, the fourth factor, 'favourable contingency', is critical. A sharper sense of national identity is often forged from crisis conditions or in confrontation with another nation. Should Russia itself develop a 'Weimar syndrome' and embrace confrontational and neo-imperial ultra-nationalism then a Ukrainian reaction is highly probable, at least in western Ukraine. On the other hand, it is extremely unlikely that eastern and southern Ukraine would go along with such a movement. A serious crisis in Russian–Ukrainian relations would also trigger a crisis within Ukraine itself. Short of such an outcome, therefore, the need to maintain internal unity should, it is to be hoped, act as a restraint on all but the wildest west Ukrainians.

Conclusion

The situation in Ukraine is therefore finely poised. A delicate balance of forces means that only the foolhardy would attempt to predict the future. Nevertheless, the major themes outlined in this work are likely to remain a constant feature of Ukrainian politics into the next millennium. Moreover it can be safely asserted that events in Ukraine will have an immense impact on the prospects for political stability in both Eastern and Central Europe, and that the national question will remain of central importance in determining how events unfold.

Notes

1 UKRAINE: HISTORICAL ROOTS OF DIVERSITY

1 For a discussion of Ukraine's different regions, see F. D. Zastavnyi, *Ukraïns'ki etnichni zemli* (L'viv: Svit, 1993); M. F. Dmytriienko, 'Administratyvno-terytorial'nyi podil ukraïns'kykh zemel': istoriia, proekty, real'nist' (XIX–pochatok XX st.)', in V. S. Trubenko and V. I. Horbyk (eds.), *Istorychno-heohrafichni doslidzhennia v Ukraïni* (Kiev: Naukova dumka, 1994), pp. 23–46; Viktor Vovk and Oleksii Mustafin, 'Bogataia mnogoobraziem, sil'naia edinstvom', *Kyïvs'kyi sotsial-demokrat*, no. 1 (October), 1991; Roman Szporluk, 'Russians in Ukraine and the Problems of Ukrainian Identity in the USSR', in Peter J. Potichnyj (ed.), *Ukraine in the 1970s* (Oakville, Ont.: Mosaic Press, 1975), pp. 195–217; and Paul Robert Magocsi, *Ukraine: A Historical Atlas* (Toronto: University of Toronto Press, 1985).

2 'Ethno-nationalism' is here defined as 'identification with and loyalty to one's nation', where 'nation connotes a group of people who believe they are ancestrally related': Walker Connor, *Ethnonationalism: The Quest For Understanding* (Princeton: Princeton University Press, 1994), p. xi. As in Connor's usage, it can be assumed that the term 'nationalism' is synonymous with ethno-nationalism unless otherwise indicated. The prospects for the development of a broader state-centred nationalism in Ukraine are discussed in chapter 8.

3 Mykhailo Horyn', *Respublikans'ki chetverhy*, no. 2 (February), 1995, p. 8.

4 For a review of recent works on Ukrainian history, see David Saunders, 'Modern Ukrainian History', *European History Quarterly*, vol. 18 (1988), pp. 473–9; and vol. 21 (1991), pp. 81–95. The standard history of Ukraine is Orest Subtelny, *Ukraine: A History* (Toronto: University of Toronto Press, 2nd edn, 1994). See also Andreas Kappeler *Kleine Geschichte der Ukraine* (Munich: C. H. Beck, 1994); Volodymyr Kubijovyc and Danylo Husar Struk (eds.), *The Encyclopaedia of Ukraine* (Toronto: University of Toronto Press, 1984–93), 5 vols.; Nicholas L. Fr.-Chirovsky, *An Introduction to Ukrainian History* (New York: Philosophical Library, 1981 and 1984), 2 vols.; W. E. D. Allen, *The Ukraine: A History* (Cambridge: Cambridge University Press, 1941); Władysław A. Serczyk, *Historia Ukrainy* (Wrocław: Zakład Narodowy im. Ossolinskich, 1979); Ivan Kryp"iakevych, *Istoriia Ukraïny* (L'viv: Svit, 1992; reprint of 1938 edn); and Dmytro Doroshenko, *Narys istoriï Ukraïny* (Kiev: Globus, 1991; reprint of 1932 edn).

5 A. A. Hors'kyi, 'Shche raz pro rol' normanniv u formuvanni Kyïvs'koï Rusi', *Ukraïns'kyi istorychnyi zhurnal*, no. 1, 1994, pp. 3–9.

6 V. F. Soldatenko and Yu. V. Syvolov, 'Vytoky i peredvisnyky ukraïns'koï ideï', in Soldatenko (ed.), *Ukraïns'ka ideia. Pershi rechnyky* (Kiev: Znannia, 1994), pp. 5–25, at p. 11. Cf. B. A. Rybakov, *Gerodotova Skiffia: istoriko-geograficheskii analiz* (Moscow: Nauka, 1979).

7 Subtelny, *Ukraine*, p. 25.

8 Omeljan Pritsak, *The Origins of Rus'* (Cambridge, Mass.: Harvard Ukrainian Research Institute, 1981), vol. I.

9 O. B. Holovko, 'Slov"iany Pivnichnoho Prychornomor"ia doby Kyïvs'koï Rusi ta problema vytokiv ukraïns'koho kozatstva', *Ukraïns'kyi istorychnyi zhurnal*, no. 11, 1991, pp. 24–35.

10 For some recent works on religious history in Ukraine, see J. Madey, 'Church, History of the Ukrainian', in Kubijovyc and Struk, *Encyclopaedia of Ukraine*, vol. I, pp. 472–85; Geoffrey A. Hosking (ed.), *Church, Nation and State in Russia and Ukraine* (London: Macmillan, 1991); Ivan Wlasowsky, *Outline History of the Ukrainian Orthodox Church* (South Bound Brook, N. J., 1974–9), 2 vols.; O. S. Onyshchenko (ed.), *Istoriia khrystyians'koï˙ tserkvy na Ukraïni: relihiieznavchyi dovidkovyi narys* (Kiev: Naukova dumka, 1992); Kost' Panas, *Istoriia ukraïns'koï˙ tserkvy* (L'viv: Transintekh, 1992); Ivan Ohiienko, *Ukraïns'ka tserkva* (Kiev: Ukraïna, 1993; reprint of 1942 Prague edn); N. Tsisyk (ed.), *Ukraïns'ke vidrodzhennia i natsional'na tserkva* (Kiev: Pam"iatky Ukraïny, 1990); and the more popular Volodymyr Mokryi, *Tserkva v zhytti ukraïntsiv* (L'viv: Prosvita, 1993). See also the special issue of *Harvard Ukrainian Studies*, vol. 12/13, 1988/1989, marking the millennium of 988; and J. I. Fennell, *The History of the Russian Orthodox Church to 1448* (London: Longman, 1995).

11 On the problem of Ukraine's open borders, see Ivan Dziuba, 'Ukraïna i svit', in Ihor Ostash (ed.), *Quo vadis, Ukraïno?* (Kiev: Maiak, 1992), pp. 10–36; and Joseph L. Wieczynski, *The Russian Frontier: The Impact of Borderlands upon the Course of Early Russian History* (Charlottesville: University Press of Virginia, 1976), especially chapter 2.

12 Jaroslaw Pelenski, 'The Contest over the "Kievan Inheritance" in Russian–Ukrainian Relations: The Origins and Early Ramifications', in Peter J. Potichnyj *et al.* (eds.), *Ukraine and Russia in Their Historical Encounter* (Edmonton, Ont.: Canadian Institute of Ukrainian Studies, hereafter CIUS, 1992), pp. 3–19; Mikhail V. Dmitriev, 'Ukraine and Russia', *Canadian Slavonic Papers*, vol. 35, nos. 1–2 (March–June 1993), pp. 131–47 (a review of Potichnyj, *Ukraine and Russia*); and Zenon E. Kohut, 'History as a Battleground: Russian–Ukrainian Relations and Historical Consciousness in Contemporary Ukraine', in S. Frederick Starr (ed.), *The Legacy of History in Russia and the New States of Eurasia* (London: M. E. Sharpe, 1994), pp. 123–45.

13 Stephen Velychenko, *National History as Cultural Process: The Interpretation of Ukraine's Past in Polish, Ukrainian and Russian Historiography* (Edmonton, Ont.: CIUS, 1992), pp. 84–91; and Lowell Tillet, *The Great Friendship: Soviet Historians on the Non-Russian Nationalities* (Chapel Hill: University of North Carolina Press, 1969). For two modern Russian views of post-Rus'

history, see L. N. Gumilev, *Ot Rusi k Rossii: ocherki etnicheskoi istorii* (Moscow: Ekopros, 1992); and Boris Rybakov, *Kievan Rus* (Moscow: Progress, 1989).

14 Mykhailo Hrushevs'kyi, 'The Traditional Scheme of "Russian" History and the Problem of a Rational Organisation of the History of the Eastern Slavs', reprinted in *From Kievan Rus' to Modern Ukraine: Formation of the Ukrainian Nation* (Cambridge, Mass.: Ukrainian Studies Fund, 1984), pp. 355–64.

15 Volodymyr Kisyk, 'Pro shliakhy rozvytku tserkvy v Ukraïni i Rosiï (XI–XVI st.)', *Ukraïns'kyi istorychnyi zhurnal*, no. 2–3 (February–March), 1993, pp. 76–85; V. I. Ul'ianovs'kyi, *Istoriia tserkvy ta relihiinoï dumky v Ukraïni* (Kiev: Lybid', 1994), vol. I, pp. 43–78.

16 In order to avoid predating the emergence of modern Ukrainian national consciousness, it is more exact to refer to southern Rus' and its 'Ruthenian' inhabitants, rather than 'Ukraine' and 'Ukrainians' in this period.

17 Omeljan Pritsak, 'Kievan Rus' and Sixteenth–Seventeenth Century Ukraine', in Ivan L. Rudnytsky (ed.), *Rethinking Ukrainian History* (Edmonton, Ont.: CIUS, 1981), pp. 1–28 addresses the problem of continuity between the Rus' and Lithuanian periods.

18 Jaroslaw Pelenski, 'The Incorporation of the Ukrainian Lands of Old Rus' into Crown Poland (1569)', *American Contributions to the Seventeenth International Congress of Slavists* (The Hague, 1973), pp. 19–52.

19 Mikhail Dmitriev, 'The Religious Programme of the Union of Brest in the Context of the Counter-Reformation in Eastern Europe', *Journal of Ukrainian Studies*, vol. 17, nos. 1–2 (Summer–Winter 1992), pp. 29–43; N. M. Yakovenko, *Ukraïns'ka shliakhta kintsia XIV do seredyny XVII st. (Volyn' i Tsentral'na Ukraïna)* (Kiev: Naukova dumka, 1993).

20 Vasyl' Ivanyshyn, 'Ukraïns'ka tserkva i protses natsional'noho vidrodzhennia', in Tsisyk, *Ukraïns'ke vidrodzhennia*, pp. 23–62; Oleh Mal'chevs'kyi, 'Polonizatsiia ukraïns'koï shliakhty (1569–1648 rr.)', in Yaroslav Dashkevych *et al.* (eds.), *Ukraïna v mynulomu* (Kiev: Academy of Sciences, 1992), vol. I, pp. 37–53.

21 Oleksa Myshanych (ed.), *Ukraïns'ke barokko* (Kiev: Academy of Sciences, 1993).

22 Frank E. Sysyn, 'The Formation of Modern Ukrainian Religious Culture: The Sixteenth and Seventeenth Centuries', in Hosking, *Church, Nation and State*, pp. 1–22, at p. 17.

23 The word 'Cossack' is derived from Turkic, and means 'free' or 'masterless' men. The Ukrainian Cossacks supposedly developed separately from other Cossack groups around the Don and in the northern Caucasus.

24 Linda Gordon, *Cossack Rebellions: Social Turmoil in the Sixteenth-Century Ukraine* (Albany: New York University Press, 1983); Frank E. Sysyn, *Between Poland and the Ukraine: The Dilemma of Adam Kysil, 1600–1653* (Cambridge, Mass.: Harvard University Press, 1985); and Yurii Kosenko (ed.), *Zaporozhtsi* (Kiev: Mystetstvo, 1993).

25 On the Cossacks' relatively democratic forms of government, see A. H. Sliusarenko and M. V. Tomenko, *Istoriia ukraïns'koï konstytutsiï* (Kiev: Znannia, 1993), chapter 1; and V. A. Smolii, 'Ukraïns'ka kozats'ka derzhava', *Ukraïns'kyi istorychnyi zhurnal*, no. 4, 1991, pp. 5–19.

26 John Basarab, *Pereiaslav 1654: A Historiographical Survey* (Edmonton, Ont.: CIUS, 1982); Ivan L. Rudnytsky, 'Pereiaslav: History and Myth', in his *Essays in Modern Ukrainian History* (Edmonton, Ont.: CIUS, 1987), pp. 77–89; Olena Apanovych, *Ukraïns'ko-Rosiis'kyi dohovir 1654r. Mify i real'nist'* (Kiev: Varta, 1994); and V. A. Smolii and V. S. Stepankov, *Bohdan Khmel'nyts'kyi: khronika zhyttia ta diial'nosti* (Kiev: Naukova dumka, 1994). See also Frank E. Sysyn, 'Ukrainian–Polish Relations in the Seventeenth Century: The Role of National Consciousness and National Conflict in the Khmelnytsky Movement', in Peter J. Potichnyj (ed.), *Poland and Ukraine: Past and Present* (Edmonton, Ont.: CIUS, 1980), pp. 58–82.

27 Stephen Velychenko, *Shaping Identity in Eastern Europe and Russia: Soviet and Polish Accounts of Ukrainian History, 1914–1991* (New York: St Martin's Press, 1993), p. 158.

28 On the concept of *Slavia Orthodoxa*, see Iaroslav Isaievych, 'Early Modern Belarus, Russia and Ukraine: Culture and Cultural Relations', *Journal of Ukrainian Studies*, vol. 17, nos. 1–2 (Summer–Winter 1992), pp. 17–28, at pp. 20–2.

29 Edward L. Keenan, 'On Certain Mythical Beliefs and Russian Behaviors', in Starr, *Legacy of History*, pp. 19–40, especially pp. 21–5; and Keenan, 'Muscovite Perceptions of Other East Slavs Before 1654 – An Agenda for Historians', in Potichnyj *et al.*, *Ukraine and Russia*, pp. 20–38, at pp. 25 and 34. See also Serhii Plokhy, 'The Symbol of Little Russia: The Pokrova Icon and Early Modern Ukrainian Political Ideology', *Journal of Ukrainian Studies*, vol. 17, nos. 1–2 (Summer–Winter 1992), pp. 171–88.

30 D. I. Bahalii (Bagelei), *Istoriia Slobids'koï Ukraïny* (Kharkiv: Del'ta, 1993; reprint of 1918 edn). Slobids'ka means 'free'; 'New Serbia' was originally settled by Serb migrants.

31 V. A. Pirko, 'Zaselenie v XVI–XVIII v v.', in A. A. Slin'ko (ed.), *Novye stranitsy v istorii Donbassa* (Donets'k: Donets'k University Press, 1992), pp. 26–43. Cf. Petro Lavriv, *Istoriia pivdenno-skhidnoï Ukraïny* (L'viv: Slovo, 1992), pp. 68–71.

32 David Saunders, *The Ukrainian Impact on Russian Culture* (Edmonton, Ont.: CIUS, 1985).

33 Orest Subtelny, *The Mazepists: Ukrainian Separatism in the Early Eighteenth Century* (Boulder: East European Monographs, 1981).

34 Marc Raeff, 'Ukraine and Imperial Russia: Intellectual and Political Encounters from the Seventeenth to the Nineteenth Century', in Potichnyj *et al.*, *Ukraine and Russia*, pp. 69–85. Russia's tactics varied in different corners of the empire, but Ukrainian elites were deliberately coopted. See David Laitin, 'The National Uprisings in the Soviet Union', *World Politics*, vol. 44 (October 1991), pp. 139–77.

35 Zenon E. Kohut, *Russian Centralism and Ukrainian Autonomy: Imperial Absorption of the Hetmanate, 1760s–1830s* (Cambridge, Mass.: Harvard University Press, 1980). O. L. Oliinyk, 'Shche raz pro prychyny likvidatsiï Zaporoz'koï Sichi', *Ukraïns'kyi istorychnyi zhurnal*, no. 2, 1992, pp. 33–9 rejects the argument that the Sich was only liquidated because Catherine II's conquest of the northern Black Sea coast rendered it superfluous to the task of imperial defence.

36 Under the tsars, *Novorossiia* was eventually divided into three guberniias: Kherson, Taurida and Yekaterinoslav, which extended into what is now the south of Kirovohrad and Zaporizhzhia oblasts and as far as the southern Donbas.

37 Zenon E. Kohut, 'The Development of a Little Russian Identity and Ukrainian Nationbuilding', *Harvard Ukrainian Studies*, vol. 10 (1986), pp. 559–76; Frank E. Sysyn, 'The Khmelnytsky Uprising and Ukrainian Nation-Building', *Journal of Ukrainian Studies*, vol. 17, nos. 1–2 (Summer–Winter 1992), pp. 141–70.

38 B. Kravtsiv, 'Mala Rus'', in Volodymyr Kubiiovych (ed.), *Entsyklopediia Ukraïnoznavstva* (L'viv: Shevchenko Society, 1994), vol. IV, pp. 1446–7; and F. D. Zastavnyi, 'Pokhodzhennia nazvy "Ukraïna"', in his *Heohrafiia Ukraïny* (L'viv: Svit, 1994), pp. 5–10.

39 Edward C. Thaden, *Russia's Western Borderlands, 1710–1870* (Princeton: Princeton University Press, 1984); P. S. Wandycz, *The Lands of Partitioned Poland, 1795–1918* (Seattle: University of Washington Press, 1974); and Daniel Beauvois, *The Noble, the Serf and the Revizor: The Polish Nobility Between Tsarist Imperialism and the Ukrainian Masses (1831–1863)* (Chur, Switzerland: Harwood Academic Publishers, 1991). The tsarist guberniia of Volhynia was roughly equivalent to the modern-day oblasts of Rivne and Volyn', although it also included the west of what is now Zhytomyr oblast and the northern part of Khmel'nyts'kyi oblast.

40 Northern Bukovyna, the core of what is now Chernivtsi oblast, was part of the kingdom of Galicia-Volhynia until the fourteenth century, then part of the Moldovan kingdom, before falling under Ottoman rule until 1774.

41 John-Paul Himka, 'The Greek Catholic Church and Nation-Building in Galicia, 1772–1918', *Harvard Ukrainian Studies*, vol. 8, no. 3/4 (December 1984), pp. 426–52; Himka, 'The Greek Catholic Church in Nineteenth-Century Galicia', in Hosking, *Church, Nation and State*, pp. 52–64; and his *The Greek Catholic Church and Ukrainian Society in Austrian Galicia* (Cambridge, Mass.: Ukrainian Studies Fund, forthcoming).

42 Paul Robert Magocsi, *Galicia: A Historical Survey and Bibliographical Guide* (Toronto: University of Toronto Press, 1983); Magocsi, 'A Subordinate or Submerged People: The Ukrainians of Galicia Under Habsburg and Soviet Rule', in Richard L. Rudolph and David F. Good (eds.), *Nationalism and Empire: The Habsburg Empire and the Soviet Union* (New York: St Martin's Press, 1992), pp. 95–108; Ivan L. Rudnytsky, 'The Ukrainians in Galicia Under Austrian Rule', in his *Essays in Modern Ukrainian History*, pp. 315–52; Christine D. Worobec, ' "Galicians into Ukrainians": Ukrainian Nationalism Penetrates Nineteenth-Century Rural Austrian Galicia', *Peasant Studies*, vol. 16, no. 3 (Spring 1989), pp. 200–9; and John-Paul Himka, *Galician Villagers and the Ukrainian National Movement in the Nineteenth Century* (New York: St Martin's Press, 1988). Worobec's article is a review of Himka's book. Andrei S. Markovits and Frank E. Sysyn (eds.), *Nationbuilding and the Politics of Nationalism: Essays on Austrian Galicia* (Edmonton, Ont.: CIUS, 1982) collects many of the above essays amongst other contributions.

43 One source calculates that the Ukrainian share of the local population

actually fell from 69 per cent to 33 per cent between 1775 and 1910, while the Romanian percentage rose from 20 per cent to 41 per cent: Zastavnyi, *Ukrains'ki etnichni zemli*, pp. 133–4.

44 For the Rusyn point of view, see Paul Robert Magocsi, *The Shaping of a National Identity: Subcarpathian Rus' 1848–1948* (London: Harvard University Press, 1978); and Magocsi, 'Magyars and Carpatho-Rusyns: On the Seventieth Anniversary of the Founding of Czechoslovakia', *Harvard Ukrainian Studies*, vol. 14, no. 3/4 (December 1990), pp. 427–60. For the Ukrainian side, see Ivan L. Rudnytsky, 'Carpatho-Ukraine: A People in Search of Their History', in his *Essays in Modern Ukrainian History*, pp. 353–73; and Oleksa V. Mysanyc, 'From Subcarpathian Rusyns to Transcarpathian Ukrainians', in Magocsi (ed.), *The Persistence of Regional Culture: Rusyns and Ukrainians in their Carpathian Homeland and Abroad* (New York: East European Monographs, distributed by Columbia University Press, 1993), pp. 7–52. In the same series, see also Alexander Bonkalo, *The Rusyns* (1990).

45 Athanasius B. Pekar, *The History of the Church in Carpathian Rus'* (New York: East European Monographs, distributed by Columbia University Press, 1992).

46 Zenon E. Kohut, 'Problems in Studying the Post-Khmelnytsky Ukrainian Elite (1650s to 1830s)', in Rudnytsky, *Rethinking Ukrainian History*, pp. 103–19.

47 Bohdan Krawchenko, *Social Change and National Consciousness in Twentieth-Century Ukraine* (Oxford: St Anthony's/Macmillan, 1985), introduction; Krawchenko, 'The Social Structure of Ukraine at the Turn of the Twentieth Century', *East European Quarterly*, vol. 16, no. 2 (June 1982), pp. 171–81; and Krawchenko, 'The Social Structure of Ukraine in 1917', *Harvard Ukrainian Studies*, vol. 14, no. 1/2 (June 1990), pp. 97–112.

48 On the eastward emigration, see Ihor Stebelsky, 'Ukrainian Migration to Siberia Before 1917: The Process and Problems of Losses and Survival Rates', in Bohdan Krawchenko (ed.), *Ukrainian Past, Ukrainian Present* (London: Macmillan, 1993), pp. 55–69; F. D. Zastavnyi, *Skhidna ukrains'ka diaspora* (L'viv: Svit, 1992); Rostyslav Sossa, *Ukraïntsi: skhidna diaspora* (Kiev: Mapa, 1993); and Olena Koval'chuk, 'Pereselennia selian ukraïns' kykh gubernii Rosiis'koï imperii (druha polovyna XIX–pochatok XX st.)', *Ukrains'ka diaspora*, vol. 1, no. 1 (Kiev and Chicago: Intel, 1992), pp. 30–42.

49 Dorothy Atkinson, *The End of the Russian Land Commune, 1905–1930* (Stanford: Stanford University Press, 1983); and Judith Pallot, *Social Change and Peasant Landholding in Pre-Revolutionary Russia* (Oxford: School of Geography Research Paper, 1982). For figures on land use in Ukraine, see Steven L. Guthier, 'The Popular Basis of Ukrainian Nationalism in 1917', *Slavic Review*, vol. 38, no. 1 (March 1979), pp. 30–47, n. 9.

50 A. L. Zinchenko, 'Z istorii selians'koho rukhu na pravoberezhnii Ukraïni u XVIII–pershii polovyni XIX st.', *Ukrains'kyi istorychnyi zhurnal*, no. 1, 1991, pp. 36–45.

51 Patricia Herlihy, *Odessa: A History, 1794–1914* (Cambridge, Mass.: Harvard Ukrainian Research Institute, 1986).

52 Theodore H. Friedgut, *Iuzovka and Revolution. Vol. I: Life and Works in*

Russia's Donbass, 1869–1924, and *Vol. II: Politics and Revolution in Russia's Donbass, 1869–1924* (Princeton: Princeton University Press, 1989 and 1994).

53 Olga Andriewsky, *The Politics of National Identity: The Ukrainian Question in Russia, 1904–1912* (Ph.D, Harvard University, 1991).

54 On the events of 1917–21, see Subtelny, *Ukraine,* chapters 18 and 19; Jurij Borys, *The Sovietisation of Ukraine, 1917–1923* (Edmonton, Ont.: CIUS, 1980, rev. edn); John Reshetar, *The Ukrainian Revolution, 1917–1920: A Study in Nationalism* (Princeton: Princeton University Press, 1952); Taras Hunchak (Hunczak) (ed.), *The Ukraine, 1917–1921: A Study in Revolution* (Cambridge, Mass.: Harvard Ukrainian Research Institute, 1977); Oleh Pidhainy, *The Ukrainian Republic in the Great East European Revolution* (Toronto: New Review Books, 1966–75), vols. I–VI; Ronald Grigor Sumy, 'Nationalism and Class in the Russian Revolution: A Comparative Survey', in Edith Frankel *et al.* (eds.), *Revolution in Russia: Reassessments of 1917* (Cambridge: Cambridge University Press, 1992), at pp. 226–30; and Richard Pipes, *The Formation of the Soviet Union: Communism and Nationalism, 1917–1923* (Cambridge, Mass.: Harvard University Press, 1957).

55 Michael Malet, *Nestor Makhno in the Russian Civil War* (London: Macmillan, 1982); Michael Palij, *The Anarchism of Nestor Makhno, 1918–1921: An Aspect of the Ukrainian Revolution* (Seattle: University of Washington Press, 1976); and V. F. Verstiuk, *Makhnovshchyna: selians'kyi povstans'kyi rukh na Ukraïni (1918–1921)* (Kiev: Naukova dumka, 1991). Arthur E. Adams, 'The Great Ukrainian Jacquerie', in Hunczak, *Ukraine, 1917–1921,* pp. 247–70 argues that the vast majority of Ukrainian peasants preferred to keep themselves to themselves.

56 Ihor Kamenetsky, 'Hrushevsky and the Central Rada', in Hunczak, *Ukraine, 1917–1921,* pp. 33–60; and S. V. Kul'chyts'kyi, 'Tsentral'na Rada. Utvorennia UNR', *Ukraïns'kyi istorychnyi zhurnal,* nos. 5 and 6, 1992, pp. 71–88 and 73–94. Yu. D. Pryliuk (ed.), *Konstytutsiini akty Ukraïny. 1917–1920. Nevidomi konstytutsiï Ukraïny* (Kiev: Filosofs'ka i sotsiolohichna dumka, 1992) is a collection of many important documents from the period.

57 Taras Hunczak, 'The Ukraine Under Hetman Pavlo Skoropadskyi', in Hunczak, *Ukraine, 1917–1921,* pp. 61–81; and S. V. Kul'chyts'kyi, 'Ukraïns'ka derzhava chasiv Het'manshchyna', *Ukraïns'kyi istorychnyi zhurnal,* no. 7–8, 1992, pp. 60–79.

58 Martha Bohachevsky-Chomiak, 'The Directory of the Ukrainian National Republic', in Hunczak, *Ukraine, 1917–1921,* pp. 82–103; and V. S. Horak, 'Dyrektoriia: potentsial i mozhlyvosti politychnoho vyzhyvannia', in I. S. Khmil' with V. S. Horak, O. M. Maiboroda and V. M. Tkachenko (eds.), *Ukraïna XX st. Problemy natsional'noho vidrodzhennia* (Kiev: Naukova dumka, 1993), pp. 74–90.

59 Friedgut, *Iuzovka and Revolution: Vol. II: Politics and Revolution,* pp. 124, 292, 309 and 334. Cf. Rex A. Wade, 'Ukrainian Nationalism and "Soviet Power": Kharkiv 1917', in Krawchenko, *Ukrainian Past, Ukrainian Present,* pp. 70–83.

60 The five central Ukrainian guberniias, plus Kharkiv, Yekaterinoslav, Kherson and Taurida (excluding Crimea). The Second Universal had added little to the First.

61 V. F. Soldatenko, 'Stanovlennia ukraïns'koï derzhavnosti i problema zbroinykh syl (berezen' 1917 r.–kviten' 1919 r.)', *Ukraïns'kyi istorychnyi zhurnal*, nos. 5 and 6, 1992, pp. 38–51 and 26–39.

62 Stephen Horak, *The First Peace Treaty of World War I: Ukraine's Treaty with the Central Powers of February 9, 1918* (Boulder: East European Monographs, 1988).

63 R. Ya. Pyrih and F. M. Prodaniuk, 'Pavlo Skoropads'kyi: shtrykhy do politychnoho portreta', *Ukraïns'kyi istorychnyi zhurnal*, no. 9, 1992, pp. 91–105.

64 Magocsi, *Ukraine: A Historical Atlas*, p. 21.

65 Jaroslav Pelenski, 'Hetman Pavlo Skoropadsky and Germany (1917–1918) as Reflected in His Memoirs', and Peter Borowsky, 'Germany's Ukrainian Policy During World War I and the Revolution of 1918–1919', both in Hans-Joachim Torke and John-Paul Himka (eds.), *German–Ukrainian Relations in Historical Perspective* (Edmonton, Ont.: CIUS, 1994), pp. 69–83 and 84–94 deny that Skoropads'kyi was a German puppet. Vasyl' Dmytryshyn, 'Povalennia nimtsiamy Tsentral'noï Rady u kvitni 1918 roku: novi dani z nimets'kykh arkhiviv', *Politolohichni chytannia*, no. 1, 1994, pp. 104–20 makes the opposite case.

66 S. M. Derev"ianko and A. M. Panchuk, 'ZUNR v ukraïns'kii istoriohrafiï', *Ukraïns'kyi istorychnyi zhurnal*, no. 2, 1995, pp. 28–36; O. Yu. Karpenko, 'Lystopadova 1918 r. Natsional'no-demokratychna revoliutsiia na zakhidnoukraïns'kykh zemliakh', *Ukraïns'kyi istorychnyi zhurnal*, no. 1, 1993, pp. 16–28.

67 Taras Hunczak, *Symon Petliura and the Jews: A Reappraisal* (Toronto: Ukrainian Historical Association, 1985), reprinted as Taras Hunchak, *Symon Petliura ta yevreï* (Kiev: Lybid', 1993); Jonathan Frankel, 'The Dilemmas of Jewish Autonomism: The Case of Ukraine, 1917–1920', in Peter J. Potichnyj and Howard Aster (eds.), *Ukrainian–Jewish Relations in Historical Perspective* (Edmonton, Ont.: CIUS, 1988), pp. 263–79, at p. 275.

68 Taras Hunczak (ed.), *Ukraine and Poland in Documents, 1918–1922* (New York: Shevchenko Scientific Society, 1983), 2 vols.

69 I. M. Nowosiwsky, *Bukovinan Ukrainians: A Historical Background. Their Self-Determination in 1918* (New York: Shevchenko Scientific Society, 1970).

70 Magocsi, *Shaping of a National Identity*, pp. 76–102.

71 Bohdan Nahaylo, 'Ukrainian National Resistance in Soviet Ukraine During the 1920s', *Journal of Ukrainian Studies*, vol. 15, no. 2 (Winter 1990), pp. 1–18.

72 See Andrew Wilson, 'Ukraine: Between Eurasia and the West', in Thomas G. Fraser and Seamus Dunn (eds.), *Europe and Ethnicity: The Legacy of World War I* (London: Routledge, 1996), pp. 110–37; Mark von Hagen, 'The Dilemmas of Ukrainian Independence and Statehood, 1917–1921', *Harriman Institute Forum*, vol. 7, no. 5 (January 1994), pp. 7–11; and I. L.

Hoshuliak, 'Pro prychyny porazky Tsentral'noï Rady', *Ukraïns'kyi istorychnyi zhurnal*, no. 1, 1994, pp. 31–44.

73 Geoff Ely, 'Remapping the Nation: War, Revolutionary Upheaval and State Formation in Eastern Europe, 1914–1923', in Potichnyj and Aster, *Ukrainian–Jewish Relations*, pp. 205–46; and Alexander J. Motyl, *Sovietology, Rationality, Nationality: Coming to Grips with Nationalism in the USSR* (New York: Columbia University Press, 1990), chapter 7.

74 Reshetar, *Ukrainian Revolution*; Krawchenko, *Social Change and National Consciousness*; and Guthier, 'Popular Basis of Ukrainian Nationalism'.

75 John-Paul Himka, 'Western Ukraine in the Interwar Period', *Nationalities Papers*, vol. 22, no. 2 (Fall 1994), pp. 347–63.

76 Bohdan Budurowycz, 'Poland and the Ukrainian Problem', *Canadian Slavonic Papers*, vol. 25, no. 4 (December 1983), pp. 473–500.

77 Subtelny, *Ukraine*, p. 427–30.

78 M. M. Behesh and V. Ye. Zadorozhnyi, 'Karpats'ka Ukraïna v 1938–1939 rr.: deiaki aspekty sotsial'no-ekonomichnoho i politychnoho rozvytku', *Ukraïns'kyi istorychnyi zhurnal*, no. 2, 1995, pp. 42–51.

79 Hoshuliak, 'Pro prychyny porazky Tsentral'noï Rady', pp. 36–7; Adams, 'Great Ukrainian Jacquerie', in Hunczak, *Ukraine, 1917–1921*, pp. 259–60.

80 The abbreviation 'CPU' is used for convenience, although a separate Communist Party of Ukraine has never existed as such (see chapter 4). The CPU was known as the Communist Party (Bolshevik) of Ukraine until 1952.

81 Dominique Arel, *Language and the Politics of Ethnicity: The Case of Ukraine* (Ph.D, University of Illinois at Urbana-Champaign, 1993), p. 146. See also George Y. Shevelov, *The Ukrainian Language in the First Half of the Twentieth Century (1900–1941)* (Cambridge, Mass.: Harvard Ukrainian Research Institute, 1989).

82 Bohdan R. Bociurkiw, 'The Rise of the Ukrainian Autocephalous Orthodox Church, 1919–1922', in Hosking, *Church, Nation and State*, pp. 228–49; Bociurkiw, 'The Ukrainian Orthodox Church, 1920–1930: A Case Study in Modernisation', in Dennis Dunn (ed.), *Religion and Modernisation in the Soviet Union* (Boulder: Westview, 1977), pp. 316–47; Frank E. Sysyn, 'The Ukrainian Orthodox Question in the USSR', *Religion in Communist Lands*, vol. 2, no. 3 (Winter 1983), pp. 251–63; and the series of articles by Oleksandr Voronyn, 'Avtokefaliia ukraïns'koï pravoslavnoï tserkvy', in *Literaturna Ukraïna*, beginning in issue no. 41, 1991.

83 Bociurkiw, 'Rise of the Ukrainian Autocephalous Orthodox Church', p. 242.

84 Yurii Shapoval, 'Stalinizm i Ukraïna', *Ukraïns'kyi istorychnyi zhurnal*, no. 12, 1990, nos. 2, 4–8, 10–12, 1991 and nos. 1–12, 1992; V. M. Danylenko, H. V. Kas'ianov and S. V. Kul'chyts'kyi, *Stalinizm na Ukraïni: 20–30-ti roky* (Kiev: Lybid', 1991); Robert S. Sullivant, *Soviet Politics and the Ukraine, 1917–1957* (New York: Columbia University Press, 1962); L. A. Shevchenko, 'Kul'turno-ideolohichni protsesy v Ukraïni u 40–50-kh rr.', *Ukraïns'kyi istorychnyi zhurnal*, no. 7–8, 1992, pp. 39–48; and David R. Marples, *Stalinism in Ukraine in the 1940s* (London: Macmillan, 1992).

85 Heorhii Kas'ianov, *Ukraïns'ka inteligentsiia 1920-kh–30-kh rokiv: sotsial'nyi*

portret ta istorychna dolia (Kiev: Globus: 1992); Kas'ianov and V. M. Danylenko, *Stalinizm i ukraïns'ka inteligentsiia (20–30-i roky)* (Kiev: Naukova dumka, 1991).

86 Bohdan R. Bociurkiw, 'The Soviet Destruction of the Ukrainian Auto-cephalous Orthodox Church, 1929–1930', *Journal of Ukrainian Studies*, vol. 12, no. 1 (Summer 1987), pp. 3–21; and Bociurkiw, 'Soviet Religious Policy in Ukraine in Historical Perspective', in M. S. Pap (ed.), *Russian Empire: Some Aspects of Tsarist and Soviet Colonial Practices* (Cleveland, Ohio: John Carroll University Press, 1985), pp. 95–112.

87 On the famine, see Robert Conquest, *The Harvest of Sorrow: Soviet Collectivisation and the Terror Famine* (London: Hutchinson, 1986); S. V. Kul'chyts'kyi and Serhii Maksudov, 'Vtraty naselennia Ukraïny vid holodu 1933 r.', *Ukraïns'kyi istorychnyi zhurnal*, no. 2, 1991, pp. 3–10; and Kul'chyts'kyi (ed.), *Kolektyvizatsiia i holod na Ukraïni. Zbirnyk dokumentiv i materialiv* (Kiev: Naukova dumka, 1992). Serhii Pirozhkov, 'Population Loss in Ukraine in the 1930s and the 1940s', in Krawchenko, *Ukrainian Past, Ukrainian Present*, pp. 84–96, at p. 89, cites a total figure of 5.8 million 'direct and indirect' deaths from the famine and the purges in the 1930s.

88 Pirozhkov, 'Population Loss in Ukraine', p. 93. Taras Hunczak, 'Between Two Leviathans: Ukraine During the Second World War', in Krawchenko, *Ukrainian Past, Ukrainian Present*, pp. 97–106, at p. 104 gives a round figure of 10 million for war deaths.

89 On Ukraine during World War II, see Yurii Boshyk (ed.), *Ukraine During World War II: History and Its Aftermath* (Edmonton, Ont.: CIUS, 1986); Marples, *Stalinism in Ukraine*; and Volodymyr Kosyk, *Ukraïna i Nimech-chyna u druhii svitovii viini* (L'viv: Shevchenko Society, 1993).

90 Yaroslav Bilinsky, 'The Incorporation of Western Ukraine and Its Impact on Politics and Society in Soviet Ukraine', in Roman Szporluk (ed.), *The Influence of Eastern Europe and the Soviet West on the USSR* (New York: Praeger, 1975), pp. 180–228.

91 Ustina Markus, *Soviet Counterinsurgency: The Guerrilla Wars in the Western Republics* (Ph.D, London School of Economics and Political Science, University of London, 1992), chapters 3 and 7; O. S. Rubl'ov and Yu. A. Cherchenko, *Stalinshchyna i dolia zakhidnoukraïns'koï inteligentsiï* (Kiev: Naukova dumka, 1994), chapters 5 and 6.

92 Ihor Vynnychenko, *Ukraïna 1920–1980-kh: deportatsiï, zaslannia, vyslannia* (Kiev: Rada, 1994), pp. 40–86; I. Hrat, 'The Moscow Patriarchate and the Liquidation of the Eastern-Rite Catholic Church in Ukraine', *Religion in Communist Lands*, vol. 13, no. 2 (Summer 1985), pp. 182–8.

93 Krawchenko, *Social Change and National Consciousness*; Krawchenko, 'The Impact of Industrialisation on the Social Structure of Ukraine', *Canadian Slavonic Papers*, vol. 22, no. 3 (September 1980), pp. 338–57; George O. Liber, *Soviet Nationality Policy, Urban Growth and Identity Change in the Ukrainian SSR, 1923–1934* (Cambridge: Cambridge University Press, 1992), chapters 3 and 6; and Wsevolod Isajiw, 'Urban Migration and Social Change in Contemporary Soviet Ukraine', *Canadian Slavonic Papers*, vol. 22, no. 1 (March 1980), pp. 58–86.

94 Bohdan Krawchenko, 'Ukraine: The Politics of Independence', in Ian Bremmer and Ray Taras (eds.), *Nations and Politics in the Soviet Successor States* (Cambridge: Cambridge University Press, 1993), pp. 75–98.

95 Ivan L. Rudnytsky, 'Soviet Ukraine in Historical Perspective', in his *Essays in Modern Ukrainian History*, pp. 463–75; and Kenneth Farmer, *Ukrainian Nationalism in the Post-Stalin Era: Myths, Symbols and Ideology in Soviet Nationality Policy* (The Hague: Martinus Nijhoff, 1980).

96 Danylenko, Kas'ianov and Kul'chyts'kyi, *Stalinizm na Ukraïni*, p. 323; Kas'ianov, *Ukraïns'ka inteligentsiia 1920-kh–30-kh rokiv*, p. 172.

97 Kas'ianov, *Ukraïns'ka inteligentsiia 1920-kh–30-kh rokiv*, p. 172; Y. A. Kurnusov, 'The Ukrainian Intelligentsia: The Process of Formation and Development', *East European Quarterly*, vol. 24, no. 2 (Summer 1990), pp. 201–18. Cf. Richard Pipes, 'The Historical Evolution of the Russian Intelligentsia', in Pipes (ed.), *The Russian Intelligentsia* (New York: Columbia University Press, 1961), pp. 47–62, or Alexander Solzhenitsyn's concept of *obrazovanshchina*.

98 Robert J. Kaiser, *The Geography of Nationalism in Russia and the USSR* (Princeton: Princeton University Press, 1994), pp. 138–47 and 378–94.

99 See the chapters by Ioan Chiper, 'Bessarabia and Northern Bukovina', pp. 107–27, Istvan Madi, 'Carpatho-Ukraine', pp. 128–42, and Wojciech Materski, 'Eastern Poland', pp. 143–55, in Tuomas Forsberg (ed.), *Contested Territory: Border Disputes at the Edge of the Former Soviet Empire* (Aldershot: Edward Elgar Publishing, 1995).

100 On Polish losses, see Halyna Shcherba, 'Deportatsiï naselennia z pol's'ko-ukraïns'koho pohranychchia 40-kh rokiv', in S. Holovko *et al.* (eds.), *Ukraïna–Pol'shcha: istorychna spadshchyna i suspil'na svidomist'* (Kiev: Lybid', 1993), pp. 248–55. On the Jews, see Volodymyr Kubijovyc and Vasyl' Markus, 'Jews', in Kubijovyc and Struk, *Encyclopaedia of Ukraine*, vol. II, pp. 385–93. There were 2.68 million Jews living on what is now Ukrainian territory in 1897 (9.3 per cent of the total population), and 2.72 million in the late 1920s (Soviet 1926 census, Polish 1931 census, Romanian and Czechoslovak 1930 censuses). Only 840,311 (2.0 per cent of the population) remained in 1959, and a mere 486,326 (0.9 per cent) in 1989. Emigration to Israel in the early 1990s is estimated to have halved the 1989 figure.

101 All information from the 1989 Soviet census is derived from Zastavnyi, *Heohrafiia Ukraïny*.

102 Vladimir Socor, 'Moldovian Lands Between Romania and Ukraine: The Historical and Political Geography', *Report on the USSR*, RL 473/90, 16 November 1990.

103 Arel, *Language and the Politics of Ethnicity*, chapter 3; Roman Szporluk, 'The Strange Politics of Lviv: An Essay in Search of an Explanation', in Zvi Gitelman (ed.), *The Politics of Nationality and the Erosion of the USSR* (London: Macmillan, 1992), pp. 215–31.

104 Michael F. Hamm, *Kiev: A Portrait, 1800–1917* (Princeton: Princeton University Press, 1993), p. 104. Hamm records only 'major ethnic groups': Arel, *Language and the Politics of Ethnicity*, p. 114. Cf. Roman Szporluk, 'Urbanisation in Ukraine Since the Second World War', in Rudnytsky,

Rethinking Ukrainian History, pp. 180–202; and Krawchenko, *Social Change and National Consciousness*, chapter 5.

105 The term 'Russification' has been avoided because it implies a prior loyalty to Ukrainian language and culture, which may not necessarily have existed.

106 Kaiser, *Geography of Nationalism*, pp. 33–93 and 385. Moreover, Ukrainian migration continued to be balanced by Russian arrivals from further afield.

107 Arel, *Language and the Politics of Ethnicity*, p. 133. Assimilation can occur at many levels. Use of Russian as one's native language may well, but not necessarily, also lead to assimilation to Russian culture.

108 By September 1993, some 260,000 Crimean Tatars had returned to the peninsula, raising the Tatars' percentage of the local population to 10 per cent: Andrew Wilson, *The Crimean Tatars* (London: International Alert, 1994), pp. 36–8.

109 Arel, *Language and the Politics of Ethnicity*, p. 352. Cities such as Kharkiv and Mykolaïv which are still surrounded by a large rural Ukrainian hinterland may potentially be partial exceptions to this statement.

110 Arel, *Language and the Politics of Ethnicity*, pp. 153–5.

111 Ibid., p. 160; Serhii Tsapok, 'Enhvo-linhvistychna sytuatsiia v Ukraïni', *Slovo*, no. 22 (December), 1991.

112 Roman Solchanyk, 'Language Politics in the Ukraine', in Isabelle T. Kreindler (ed.), *Sociolinguistic Perspectives on Soviet National Languages* (Berlin: Mouton de Gruyter, 1985), pp. 57–105.

113 T. M. Rudnyts'ka, 'Natsional'ni hrupy i movni protsesy v Ukraïni', *Filosofs'ka i sotsiolohichna dumka*, no. 5, 1991, pp. 145–55, table 2.

114 See also Ivan Lysiak-Rudnyts'kyi, 'Rusyfikatsiia chy malorosiianizatsiia?', *Journal of Ukrainian Graduate Studies*, Spring 1978, pp. 78–84.

115 Valerii Khmel'ko, 'Dva berehy – dva sposoby zhyttia', *Demoz*, no. 1, 1995, pp. 17–20, at p. 18. See also Khmel'ko, 'Tretii rik nezalezhnosti: shcho vyiavyly druhi prezydents'ki vybory', *Ukraïna segodnia*, no. 6, 1994; and Valerii Khmel'ko, with assistance from Andrew Wilson, 'The Political Orientations of Different Regions and Ethno-Linguistic Groups in Ukraine Since Independence' (forthcoming). 'Language of convenience' was identified by the interviewee's free choice as to whether the interview was conducted in Ukrainian or in Russian. Ukrainophone Russians account for only 1–2 per cent of the population.

116 Some 25–6 per cent of the adult population consider themselves in some way both Ukrainian and Russian. See Khmel'ko and Wilson, 'Political Orientations'.

117 The regional division is not exact, as modern oblast boundaries do not always coincide with historical divides. Kharkiv and Dnipropetrovs'k (historically Slobids'ka Ukraine and the northern reaches of the Sich) could be placed with the Left Bank, but in terms of ethno-linguistic balance they have more in common with the other oblasts of the east. Coastal Zaporizhzhia was historically a part of *Novorossiia* (southern Ukraine), but its urban areas have more in common with the east. Kirovohrad was historically a transitional region between the central Ukrainian heartland and the open steppe of the south.

118 The following works have appeared on contemporary Ukraine to date:

Taras Kuzio and Andrew Wilson, *Ukraine: Perestroika to Independence* (London: Macmillan, 1994); Alexander J. Motyl, *Dilemmas of Independence: Ukraine After Totalitarianism* (New York: Council of Foreign Relations Press, 1993); Taras Kuzio, *Ukraine: The Unfinished Revolution* (London: Institute for European Defence and Strategic Studies, 1992); David Marples, *Ukraine Under Perestroika: Ecology, Economics and the Workers' Revolt* (London: Macmillan, 1991); Roman Solchanyk (ed.), *Ukraine: Chernobyl' to Sovereignty* (London: Macmillan, 1992; a collection of interviews); Bohdan Nahaylo, *The New Ukraine* (London: Royal Institute for International Affairs, 1992); Krawchenko, 'Ukraine: The Politics of Independence'; Volodymyr Lytvyn, *Politychna arena Ukraïny: diiovi osoby ta vykonavtsi* (Kiev: Abrys, 1994); and Anatol' Kamins'kyi, *Na perekhidnomu etapi: 'hlasnist'', 'perebudova' i 'demokratyzatsiia' na Ukraïni* (Munich: Ukrainian Free University, 1990).

119 As Johann Arnason, *The Future That Failed: Origins and Destinies of the Soviet Model* (London: Routledge, 1993), p. 212 has pointed out, 'the fact that the nation-state has become the main beneficiary of the demise of the Soviet model should not lead us to mistake it for the historical subject of the transformation'.

120 For emphasis on the former, see Benedict Anderson, *Imagined Communities* (London: Verso, 1983); for the latter, Anthony D. Smith, *The Ethnic Origins of Nations* (Oxford: Basil Blackwell, 1986).

121 Józef Chlebowczyk, *On Small and Young Nations in Europe: Nation-Forming Processes in Ethnic Borderlands in East-Central Europe* (Warsaw: Polish Historical Library, no. 1, 1980).

2 UKRAINIAN NATIONALISM IN THE MODERN ERA

1 See Michael F. Hamm, 'Polish Kiev', chapter 3 in *Kiev: A Portrait*, pp. 55–81.

2 Ibid., p. 116.

3 Miroslav Hroch, *Social Preconditions of a National Revival in Europe* (Cambridge: Cambridge University Press, 1985); V. H. Sarbei, 'Etapy formuvannia ukraïns'koï natsional'noï samosvidomosti (kinets' XVIII–pochatok XX st.)', *Ukraïns'kyi istorychnyi zhurnal*, no. 7–8, 1993, pp. 3–16. Cf. Omeljan Pritsak and John S. Reshetar Jr, 'The Ukraine and the Dialectics of Nation-Building', in Donald W. Treadgold (ed.), *The Development of the USSR: An Exchange of Views* (Seattle: University of Washington Press, 1964) who list five stages of development. For a critique of Hroch's model, see Ernest Gellner, *Encounters with Nationalism* (Oxford: Blackwell, 1994), chapter 14.

4 Paul Robert Magocsi, 'The Ukrainian National Revival: A New Analytical Framework', *Canadian Review of Studies in Nationalism*, vol. 16, nos. 1–2 (1989), pp. 45–62.

5 Roman Szporluk's review of Taras Hunchak (Hunczak), *Ukraine, 1917–1921*, in *Annals of the Ukrainian Academy of Arts and Sciences in the United States*, vol. 14 (1978–80) argues that the national movement had been gathering strength before 1917.

6 See Roman Szporluk, *Ukraïna: korotka istoriia* (Kiev: Taki spravy, 1992); Andreas Kappeler, 'The Ukrainians of the Russian Empire, 1860–1914', in his edited volume *The Formation of National Elites* (New York: New York University Press, 1992), pp. 105–32; David Saunders, 'What Makes a Nation a Nation? Ukrainians Since 1600', *Ethnic Studies*, vol. 10 (1993), pp. 101–24; Ivan L. Rudnytsky, 'The Role of the Ukraine in Modern Society', in Treadgold, *Development of the USSR*, pp. 211–74; Rudnytsky, 'Trends in Modern Ukrainian Political Thought', and 'The Intellectual Origins of Modern Ukraine', both in his *Essays in Modern Ukrainian History*, pp. 91–141.

7 Mykhailo Hrushevs′kyi, 'Ukrainskii P′emont', *Ukrainskii vestnik*, no. 2, 1906.

8 In the early nineteenth century, 'Little Russianism' implied local *Landespatriotismus* and the desire to defend the Pereiaslav 'contract', but also loyalty to the empire. It did not have the pejorative overtones it was later to acquire.

9 D. I. Bagalei, *Istoriia Khar′kova za 250 let* (Kharkiv: Khar′kovskoe gorodskoe obshchestvennoe upravlenie, 1905), 2 vols.

10 Richard H. Marshall Jr and Thomas E. Bird (eds.), *Hryhorij Savyc Skovoroda: An Anthology of Critical Articles* (Edmonton, Ont.: CIUS, 1994); Hryhorii Skovoroda, *Tvory v dvokh tomakh* (Kiev: Academy of Sciences, 1961); Dmitrij Tschizewskij, *Skovoroda: Dichter, Denker, Mystiker* (Munich: Wilhelm Fink, 1974); and V. M. Nichyk (ed.), *Skovoroda, Hryhorii. Doslidzhennia, rozvidky, materialy* (Kiev: Naukova dumka, 1992).

11 Hamm, *Kiev: A Portrait*, pp. 68 and 95 talks of 90–100 members. Subtelny, *Ukraine*, p. 236 talks of 'a dozen core members and perhaps several dozen sympathisers'. On the Brotherhood, see P. S. Sokhan′ (ed.), *Kyrylo-Mefodiïvs′ke tovarystvo u tr′okh tomakh* (Kiev: Naukova dumka, 1990), 3 vols., a collection of all available documents on the society; David Saunders, 'The Kirillo-Methodian Society', *Slavonic and East European Review*, vol. 71, no. 4 (October 1993), pp. 684–92; and S. N. Luckyj, *Young Ukraine: The Brotherhood of Saints Cyril and Methodius, 1845–1847* (Ottawa and Paris: University of Ottawa Press, 1991).

12 M. I. Kostomarov, *Tvory v dvokh tomakh* (Kiev: Dnipro, 1990), 2 vols.; Orest Pelech, 'The State and the Ukrainian Triumvirate in the Russian Empire, 1831–1847', in Krawchenko, *Ukrainian Past, Ukrainian Present*, pp. 1–17; Yu. A. Pinchuk, 'Do otsinky naukovoï i hromads′koï diial′nosti M. I. Kostomarova', *Ukraïns′kyi istorychnyi zhurnal*, no. 3, 1992, pp. 3–12; Pinchuk, *Mykola Ivanovych Kostomarov* (Kiev: Naukova dumka, 1992); and Ihor Mykhailyn, 'Mykola Kostomarov: Paradoks', *Literaturna Ukraïna*, 4 June 1992.

13 The most readily available works on Shevchenko are George Grabowicz, *The Poet as Mythmaker: A Study of Symbolic Meaning in Taras Shevchenko* (Cambridge, Mass.: Harvard University Press, 1982); Pavlo Zaitsev, *Taras Shevchenko: A Life*, trans. and edited by George S. N. Luckyj (Toronto: University of Toronto Press, 1988); and Luckyj (ed.), *Shevchenko and the Critics, 1861–1980* (Toronto: University of Toronto Press, 1980), a collection of the best articles on the subject.

14 Panteleimon Kulish, *Tvory v dvokh tomakh* (Kiev: Dnipro, 1989), 2 vols. See also Friedrich Scholz's edition of Kulish's *Zapiski o yuzhnoi Rusi* (Heidelberg: Carl Winter, 1989); and George Luckyj, *Panteleimon Kulish: A Sketch of Life and Times* (Boulder: 1983).

15 Mykola Kostomarov, *Dve russkie narodnosti* (Kiev: Maidan, 1991; a reprint of the 1861 edn).

16 See also John Hutchinson, 'Moral Innovators and the Politics of Regeneration: The Distinctive Role of Cultural Nationalists in Nation-Building', in Anthony D. Smith (ed.), *Ethnicity and Nationalism* (Leiden: E. J. Brill, 1992), pp. 101–17.

17 Subtelny, *Ukraine*, p. 234.

18 Pritsak and Reshetar, 'Ukraine and the Dialectics of Nation-Building', n. 64.

19 L. I. Yevselevs'kyi and S. Ya. Faryna, *Prosvita v Naddniprians'kii Ukraïni* (Kiev: Prosvita, 1993); Oleksandr Konovets', *Prosvitnyts'kyi rukh v Ukraïni (XIX–persha tretyna XX st.)* (Kiev: Khreshchatyk, 1992); and Alla Serediak, 'Dial'nist' tovarystva Prosvita v 1868–1914 rr.', in Roman Ivanychuk, Teofil' Komarynets', Ihor Mel'nyk and Alla Serediak (eds.), *Narys istoriï Prosvity* (L'viv: Prosvita, 1993), pp. 18–41.

20 P. Ya. Miroshnychenko, *T. Shevchenko i selians'ka pravda* (Kiev: Ministry of Higher Education, 1992).

21 George Y. Shevelov, 'Evolution of the Ukrainian Literary Language', in Rudnytsky, *Rethinking Ukrainian History*, pp. 216–31, at p. 227. The populists' version of Ukrainian was accepted as standard 'Ruthenian' in Galicia in the 1860s and 1870s (resulting in some Westernisation), where it was preserved and developed, before returning (legally) to Russian Ukraine in the wake of the 1905 revolution. Full systematisation only occurred in the 1920s, however: N. D. Babych, *Istoriia ukraïns'koï literaturnoï movy* (L'viv: Svit, 1993), pp. 5–8; R. G. A. de Brey, *Guide to the Slavonic Languages* (London: J. M. Dent and Sons, 1951), pp. 70–3; Vasyl' Chaplenko, *Istoriia novoï ukraïns'koï literaturnoï movy* (New York and Munich: Fremdsprachendruckerei Dr. Peter Belej, 1970).

22 O. Ohloblyn, 'Antonovych, Volodymyr', Kubijovyc and Struk, *Encyclopaedia of Ukraine*, vol. I, pp. 85–6.

23 Thomas M. Prymak, *Mykhailo Hrushevsky: The Politics of National Culture* (Toronto: University of Toronto Press, 1987); Stephen M. Horak, 'Mykhailo Hrushevs'kyi: Portrait of a Historian', *Canadian Slavonic Papers*, vol. 10, no. 3, pp. 341–56; Lubomyr R. Wynar, *Mykhailo Hrushevs'kyi: Ukrainian–Russian Confrontation in Historiography* (Toronto: Ukrainian Historical Association, 1988); the special issue of *Ukraïns'kyi istoryk* on Hrushevs'kyi, vol. 28–9 (1991–2); O. L. Kopylenko, *'Ukraïns'ka ideia' M. Hrushevs'koho: istoriia i suchasnist'* (Kiev: Lybid', 1991); and A. P. Demydenka (ed.), *Velykyi Ukraïnets'. Material z zhyttia ta diial'nosti M. S. Hrushevs'koho* (Kiev: Veselka, 1992). Hrushevs'kyi's main work, *Istoriia Ukraïny–Rusi*, is being reprinted by Naukova dumka/CIUS.

24 Drahomanov's selected works are published as Mykhailo Drahomanov, *Vybrane* (Kiev: Lybid', 1991). See also P. M. Fedchenko, *Mykhailo*

Drahomanov (Kiev: Dnipro, 1991); Ivan L. Rudnytsky, 'Drahomanov as a Political Theorist', in his *Essays in Modern Ukrainian History*, pp. 203–53; the collected articles on Drahomanov in *Filosofs'ka i sotsiolohichna dumka*, no. 9, 1991; Mykola Tomenko, 'Politychni pohliady Mykhaila Drahomanova ta Dmytra Dontsova', *Slovo*, no. 21 (December), 1991; O. I. Kyian, 'M. P. Drahomanov i Rosiis'kyi liberalizm', *Ukraïns'kyi istorychnyi zhurnal*, no. 4, 1992, pp. 31–9; R. P. Ivanov, *Mykhailo Drahomanov u suspil'no-politychnomu rusi Rosiï ta Ukraïny* (Kiev: Kiev University Press, 1971); and R. Zadesnians'kyi, *Natsional'no-politychni pohliady M. Drahomanova, ikh vplyv ta znachinnia* (Toronto: Basilica Press, 1980).

25 David Saunders, 'Russia's Ukrainian Policy (1847–1905): A Demographic Approach', *European History Quarterly*, vol. 25, no. 2 (April 1995), pp. 183–210; and Saunders, 'Russia and Ukraine Under Alexander II: The Valuev Edict of 1863', *International History Review*, vol. 17, no. 1 (February 1995), pp. 23–50.

26 On Ukrainian political parties in the early twentieth century, see Jurij Borys, 'Political Parties in the Ukraine', in Hunchak, *Ukraine, 1917–1921*, pp. 128–58; George Yury Boshyk, *The Rise of Ukrainian Political Parties in Russia, 1900–1907: With Special Reference to Social Democracy* (Ph.D, University of Oxford, 1981); Oleksandr Fed'kov (ed.), *Samostiina Ukraïna: zbirnik prohram ukraïns'kykh politychnykh partii pochatku XX stolittia* (Ternopil': Redaktsiino-vydavnychyi viddil upravlinnia po presi, 1991); V. S. Zhuravs'kyi (ed.), *Bahatopartiina ukraïns'ka derzhava na pochatku XX st. Prohramni dokumenty pershykh ukraïns'kykh politychnykh partii* (Kiev: Poshuk, 1992); V. F. Shevchenko (ed.), *Ukraïns'ki politychni partiï kintsia XIX–pochatku XX stolittia* (Kiev: Feniks, 1993); and V. F. Zhmyr, D. B. Yanevs'kyi, D. Tabachnyk and V. Rybchuk, 'Problema bahatopartiinosti', *Filosofs'ka i sotsiolohichna dumka*, nos. 9 and 10, 1990, pp. 3–17 and 17–36 respectively.

27 Heorhii Kas'ianov, *Ukraïns'ka inteligentsiia na rubezhi XIX–XX stolit'* (Kiev: Lybid', 1993), p. 48. See also Yu. O. Kurnosov *et al.*, *Narysy istoriï ukraïns'koï inteligentsiï (persha polovyna XX st.)* (Kiev: Academy of Sciences, 1994), vol. I, pp. 60–73.

28 Terrence Emmons, *The Formation of Political Parties and the First National Elections in Russia* (Cambridge, Mass.: Harvard University Press, 1983), pp. 176, 332–5 and 340.

29 Kas'ianov, *Ukraïns'ka inteligentsiia na rubezhi*, pp. 54 and 56. The UDRP won thirty of the Ukrainian seats in the second Duma: Borys, 'Political Parties in the Ukraine', p. 131. See also O. O. Konyk, 'Selians'ki deputaty z Ukraïny v I i II Derzhavnykh dumakh Rosiis'koï imperiï', *Ukraïns'kyi istorychnyi zhurnal*, no. 1, 1995, pp. 58–66.

30 In the period 1905–16 a total of 1,941 civic organisations were founded in Russian Ukraine, compared to 682 in the entire proceeding century: Mykhailo Pashkov, 'Formuvannia systemy hromads'kykh ob"iednan' v Ukraïni yak atrybuta latentnoï derzhavnosti', *Politolohichni chytannia*, no. 2, 1992, pp. 75–100, at p. 87.

31 Kas'ianov, *Ukraïns'ka inteligentsiia nz rubezhi*, p. 61; and Yevselevs'kyi and Faryna, *Prosvita*, pp. 32–61.

32 Hamm, *Kiev: A Portrait*, pp. 113–4.
33 The Russian chauvinist 'Union of the Russian People' had 190,000 members in Ukraine in 1905–7, half their estimated overall total: I. H. Samartsev, 'Chornosotentsi na Ukraïni (1905–1917 rr)', *Ukraïns'kyi istorychnyi zhurnal*, no. 1, 1992, pp. 90–8, at p. 91. Kiev's most prominent newspaper, founded in 1864, was the chauvinistic and anti-Semitic *Kievlianin*.
34 Yu. A. Levenets', 'Livoradykal'ni partiï v Ukraïni naperedodni zhovtnevoho perevorotu', *Ukraïns'kyi istorychnyi zhurnal*, no. 3, 1992, pp. 23–31; and Heorhii Kas'ianov, 'Ukraïns'kyi sotsializm: liudy, partiï, ideï (pochatok XX storichchia)', *Politolohichni chytannia*, no. 2, 1992, pp. 101–14.
35 Kas'ianov, *Ukraïns'ka inteligentsiia na rubezhi*, p. 70.
36 Cf. O. P. Reient, 'Stavlennia proletariatu Ukraïny do Tsentral'noï Rady', *Ukraïns'kyi istorychnyi zhurnal*, no. 4, 1994, pp. 3–18.
37 Borys, 'Political Parties in the Ukraine', p. 133.
38 Hamm, *Kiev: A Portrait*, pp. 179–88.
39 The USDWP had 5,000 members in 1907: Zhmyr *et al.*, 'Problema bahatopartiinosti', no. 9, p. 4.
40 Kas'ianov, *Ukraïns'ka inteligentsiia na rubezhi*, pp. 96–109.
41 I. F. Kuras, F. H. Turchenko and T. S. Herashchenko, 'M. I. Mikhnovs'kyi: postat' na tli epokhy', *Ukraïns'kyi istorychnyi zhurnal*, nos. 9 and 10, 1992, pp. 76–91 and 63–79; Ivan Lysiak-Rudnyts'kyi, 'Natsionalizm', in his *Mizh istoriieiu i politykoiu* (Munich: Suchasnist', 1973), pp. 233–49.
42 Ivan L. Rudnytsky, 'Franciszek Duchinski and His Impact on Ukrainian Political Thought', in his *Essays in Modern Ukrainian History*, pp. 187–201.
43 Taras Hunchak (Hunczak) and Roman Solchanyk (Sol'chanyk) (eds.), *Ukraïns'ka suspil'no-politychna dumka v 20 stolitti: dokumenty i materialy* (Munich: Suchasnist', 1983), vol. I, pp. 61–72, at pp. 70 and 71.
44 Kas'ianov, *Ukraïns'ka inteligentsiia na rubezhi*, p. 105.
45 I. S. Khmil', 'Vyznachal'na ideia natsional'nykh syl Ukraïny do zhovtnia 1917 r.', in Khmil' *et al.*, *Ukraïna XX st.*, pp. 50–73, at p. 66.
46 Herlihy, *Odessa*, pp. 285–6; and Friedgut, *Iuzovka and Revolution: Vol. II: Politics and Revolution*, pp. 52, 124 and 347.
47 Kas'ianov, *Ukraïns'ka inteligentsiia na rubezhi*, pp. 35–6.
48 Omeljan Pritsak, 'Prolegomena to the National Awakening of the Ukrainians During the Nineteenth Century', in Roland Sussex and J. C. Eade (eds.), *Culture and Nationalism in Nineteenth-Century Eastern Europe* (Columbus, Ohio: Slavicaj, 1985), pp. 96–110.
49 Kaiser, *Geography of Nationalism*, p. 43.
50 Kas'ianov, *Ukraïns'ka inteligentsiia na rubezhi*, pp. 68, 45 and 155.
51 Jan Kozik, *The Ukrainian National Movement in Galicia: 1815–1849* (Edmonton, Ont.: CIUS, 1986); Peter Brock, 'Ivan Vahylevych (1811–1866) and the Ukrainian National Identity', *Canadian Slavonic Papers*, vol. 14, no. 2 (1972), pp. 153–90; and I. H. Samartsev, 'Halyts'ki budyteli', in Soldatenko, *Ukraïns'ka ideia*, pp. 97–111.
52 In the 1913 elections to the Viennese parliament the Russophiles elected only one deputy in eastern Galicia, and the Ukrainian parties thirty-one: Taras Hunchak, *Ukraïna persha polovyna XX stolittia* (Kiev: Lybid', 1993),

p. 60. Ironically this was the era of greatest support from the Russian state for the Russophiles.

53 Himka, 'Greek Catholic Church in Nineteenth-Century Galicia', p. 56.

54 Paul Robert Magocsi (ed.), *Morality and Reality: The Life and Times of Andrei Sheptyts'kyi* (Edmonton, Ont.: CIUS, 1989), especially the chapters by John-Paul Himka and Bohdan Budurowycz on 'Sheptyts'kyi and the Ukrainian National Movement Before 1914' and 'Sheptyts'kyi and the Ukrainian National Movement After 1914', respectively, pp. 29–74.

55 Stephen M. Horak, 'The Shevchenko Scientific Society (1873–1973): Contribution to the Birth of a Nation', *East European Quarterly*, no. 7 (1973), pp. 249–64.

56 Ivanychuk *et al.*, *Narys istorii'Prosvity*, p. 213.

57 Subtelny, *Ukraine*, p. 324.

58 Himka, *Galician Villagers and the Ukrainian National Movement*.

59 Hunchak and Solchanyk, *Ukrains'ka suspil'no-politychna dumka*, vol. I, pp. 26–33; John-Paul Himka, 'Young Radicals and Independent State-hood: The Idea of a Ukrainian Nation-State, 1890–1895', *Slavic Review*, no. 2, 1982, pp. 219–35.

60 Hunchak and Solchanyk, *Ukrains'ka suspil'no-politychna dumka*, vol. I, pp. 80–7; O. S. Zabuzhko, *Filosofiia ukrains'koi'idei'ta yevropeis'koi'kontekst: frankivs'kyi period* (Kiev: Osnovy, 1993); Bohdan Chervak, *Napered Ukraintsi* (Kiev: Oleny Telihy, 1994); *Ivan Franko i svitova kul'tura. Materialy mizhnarodnoho sympoziumu YuNESKO* (Kiev: Naukova dumka, 1990), 3 vols.; E. Winter and P. Kirchner, *Ivan Franko. Beiträge zur geschichte und kultur des Ukraine* (Berlin: Akademie Verlag, 1963); and M. O. Moroz (ed.), *Ivan Franko: Bibliohrafichnyi pokazhchyk, 1956–1984* (Kiev: Naukova dumka, 1987).

61 Before 1907 the electorate was divided into fixed estates, with the 'village estate' in which the Ukrainian population was concentrated being deliber-ately underrepresented.

62 John-Paul Himka, 'Sheptyts'kyi and the Ukrainian National Movement Before 1914', pp. 29–46.

63 T. B. Ciuciura and V. Markus, 'Elections', in Kubijovyc and Struk, *Encyclopaedia of Ukraine*, vol. I, pp. 806–8; and Subtelny, *Ukraine*, p. 332.

64 Subtelny, *Ukraine*, p. 334.

65 On the composition of the various Ukrainian governments in 1917–20, and the changing balance between the parties, see Pryliuk, *Konstytutsiini akty Ukrainy*, pp. 8–37. On the divisions between and within the political parties, see Rudolf A. Mark, 'Social Questions and National Revolution: The Ukrainian National Republic in 1919–1920', *Harvard Ukrainian Studies*, vol. 14, nos. 1–2 (June 1990), pp. 113–31.

66 Ivan L. Rudnytsky, 'The Fourth Universal and Its Ideological Antecedents', in his *Essays in Modern Ukrainian History*, pp. 389–416; Mykhailo Hrush-evs'kyi, 'Vil'na Ukraina', in Hunchak and Solchanyk, *Ukrains'ka suspil'no-politychna dumka*, vol. I, pp. 268–82; and V. A. Potul'nyts'kyi, 'Ideia federalizmu v tvorchosti narodnykiv', a chapter in his *Istoriia ukrains'koi' politolohii'* (Kiev: Lybid', 1992), pp. 75–107.

67 Zhuravs'kyi, *Bahatopartiina ukrains'ka derzhava*, p. 13. Zhmyr *et al.*,

'Problema bahatopartiinosti', no. 9, p. 14 estimate party membership at between 75,000 and 350,000.

68 The vast majority of the Rada's members, 86 per cent, were from the small-town or rural intelligentsia: Olena Balyts'ka, 'Deiaki pytannia derzhavot-vorchoï diial'nosti ukraïns'koï inteligentsiï', *Rozbudova derzhavy*, no. 11 (November), 1993, p. 29.

69 Borys, 'Political Parties in the Ukraine', p. 141.

70 Vynnychenko's classic study of the revolution *Vidrodzhennia natsiï* ('The rebirth of the nation'), originally written in 1920, was republished in 1990 in Kiev by the Vydavnytstvo politychnoï literatury Ukraïny in three volumes. See also Symon Petliura, *Statti* (Kiev: Dnipro, 1993); and L. V. Holota (ed.), *Symon Petliura: vybrani tvory ta dokumenty* (Kiev: Dovira, 1994).

71 Hunchak, *Ukraïna persha polovyna XX stolittia*, p. 116.

72 Pryliuk, *Konstytutsiini akty Ukraïny*, p. 10.

73 George O. Liber, 'Ukrainian Nationalism and the 1918 Law on National-Personal Autonomy', *Nationalities Papers*, vol. 15, no. 1 (Spring 1987), pp. 22–42.

74 A. Zhukovsky, 'Constituent Assembly of Ukraine', Kubijovyc and Struk, *Encyclopaedia of Ukraine*, vol. I, pp. 567–8.

75 Liber, *Soviet Nationality Policy*, p. 17–18.

76 Zhmyr *et al.*, 'Problema bahatopartiinosti', no. 10, pp. 17, 18, 28 and 29. On the Mensheviks in Ukraine, see S. Volyn, *Men'sheviki na Ukraine (1917–1921)* (Benson, Vt.: Chalidze Publications, 1990).

77 Zhmyr *et al.*, 'Problema bahatopartiinosti', no. 10, p. 17 refer to 60,000 Bolsheviks in spring 1917. Borys, 'Political Parties in the Ukraine', p. 148 gives a figure of 23,000 Bolsheviks in Ukraine as of August 1917. Subtelny cites a much lower figure of 4,364 Bolsheviks in Ukraine as of July 1918: *Ukraine*, p. 364.

78 Hoshuliak, 'Pro prychyny porazky Tsentral'noï Rady', p. 34.

79 Reshetar, *Ukrainian Revolution*; Arthur E. Adams, 'The Great Ukrainian Jacquerie', in Hunchak, *Ukraine, 1917–1921*, pp. 247–70; and Mark, 'Social Questions and National Revolution'.

80 Guthier, 'Popular Basis of Ukrainian Nationalism', p. 32.

81 Ibid., pp. 36–7.

82 Dontsov's two main works are *Natsionalizm*, written in 1926 (London: Ukraïns'ka vydavnycha spilka, 3rd edn, 1966), and *Dukh nashoï davnyny*, written in 1944 (Munich: Vidrodzhennia, 2nd edn, 1951). The fullest commentary on his work is M. Sosnovs'kyi, *Dmytro Dontsov: politychnyi portret* (New York: Trident International, 1974). See also V. S. Lisovyi, 'Drahomanov i Dontsov', *Filosofs'ka i sotsiolohichna dumka*, no. 9, 1991, pp. 83–101; and Tomenko, 'Politychni pohliady Mykhaila Drahomanova ta Dmytra Dontsova'. For the general intellectual climate of the time, see Taras Hunchak (Hunczak), 'Ukraïns'ka politychna dumka 1920-ykh rokiv: monarkhizm, natsionalizm, natsional-komunizm', *Literaturna Ukraïna*, 20 June 1991.

83 Sosnovs'kyi, *Dmytro Dontsov*, pp. 232–8.

84 Dmytro Dontsov, *Rosiia chy Evropa?* (Kiev: reprint by the Union of

Ukrainian Youth, 1992); Dontsov, *Istoriia rozvytku ukraïns'koï derzhavnoï idei* (Kiev: Znannia, 1991).

85 Lypyns'kyi's main work is *Lysty do brativ-khliborobiv* (Vienna, 1926). For a study of his philosophy, see the special issue of *Harvard Ukrainian Studies*, vol. 9, no. 3/4 (December 1985) on 'The Political and Social Ideas of Vjacheslav Lypyns'kyj'; Ivan L. Rudnytsky, 'Viacheslav Lypynsky: Statesman, Historian and Political Thinker', and 'Lypynsky's Political Views from the Perspective of Our Time', both in his *Essays in Modern Ukrainian History*, pp. 437–61; Alexander J. Motyl, 'Viacheslav Lypyns'kyi and the Ideology and Politics of Ukrainian Monarchism', *Canadian Slavonic Papers*, vol. 27, no. 1 (March 1985), pp. 31–48; Yaroslav Pelens'kyi (ed.), *V"iacheslav Lypyns'kyi. Istoryko-politolohichna spadshchyna i suchasna Ukraïna* (Kiev and Philadelphia: Academy of Sciences *et al.*, 1994); Dmytro Chyzhevs'kyi, 'Viacheslav Lypyns'kyi yak filosof istoriï', *Filosofs'ka i sotsiolohichna dumka*, no. 10 (October), 1991, pp. 51–62; and V. Potul'nyts'kyi, 'Politychna doktryna V. Lypyns'koho', *Ukraïns'kyi istorychnyi zhurnal*, no. 9, 1992, pp. 37–44.

86 The 1920s poet Dmytro Zahul, quoted in Myroslav Shkandrij, *Modernists, Marxists and the Nation: The Ukrainian Literary Discussion of the 1920s* (Edmonton, Ont.: CIUS, 1992), p. 76.

87 Rudnytsky, 'Lypynski's Political Views', p. 448.

88 Mykola Chubatyi, *Osnovy derzhavnoho ustroiu Zakhidn'o-Ukraïns'koï Respubliky* (L'viv, 1920).

89 Oleksandr Zaitsev, 'Predstavnyky ukraïns'kykh politychnykh partii zakhidnoï Ukraïny v parlamenti Pol'shchi (1922–1939 rr.)', *Ukraïns'kyi istorychnyi zhurnal*, no. 1, 1993, pp. 72–84, at p. 73.

90 Budurowycz, 'Poland and the Ukrainian Problem', p. 479. Twenty Ukrainian deputies were elected in the less radical region of Volhynia.

91 Mykola Rozhyk, 'Ukraïns'ke natsional'no-demokratychne ob"iednannia', *Respublikanets'*, no. 6 (October), 1993, pp. 16–21.

92 Bohdan Budurowycz, 'Sheptyts'kyi and the Ukrainian National Movement After 1914', pp. 47–74. The Uniates also supported the Ukrainian Catholic Union formed in January 1931, and Sheptyts'kyi maintained contacts with most Ukrainian political groups, except the Organisation of Ukrainian Nationalists (although he had links with Mel'nyk), as he viewed divisive party politics with disdain.

93 Zaitsev, 'Predstavnyky ukraïns'kykh politychnykh partii', pp. 75–6; Budurowycz, 'Poland and the Ukrainian Problem', pp. 435 and 481–2. Ciuciura and Markus ('Elections') record forty-eight Ukrainian seats in 1928. See also Janusz Radziejowski, *The Communist Party of Western Ukraine* (Edmonton, Ont.: CIUS, 1983), p. 175, table 1.

94 Zaitsev, 'Predstavnyky ukraïns'kykh politychnykh partii', p. 78. UNDO won seventeen seats. On the 'pacification' campaign, see M. Shvahuliak, *Patsyfikatsiia: pol's'ka represyvna aktsiia u Halychyni 1930 r. i ukraïns'ka suspil'nist'* (L'viv: Instytut ukraïnoznavstva im. I. Krypiakevycha, 1993), which argues that Ukrainian terrorism was as much a cause of the Polish action as its consequence.

95 Ibid., p. 80. UNDO won thirteen seats.

96 As argued by Oleksandr Zaitsev, 'Natsionalizm i natsional'na demokratiia: vytoky konfliktu (1920–1930-i rr.)', *Suchasnist'*, February 1994, pp. 70–6. According to Subtelny and Zhukovs'kyi, *Narys istorii Ukraïny* (L'viv: Shevchenko Society, 1992), p. 110, 'the OUN was the only real political force in western Ukraine' by 1939.

97 Zaitsev, 'Predstavnyky ukraïns'kykh politychnykh partii', p. 76.

98 The standard work on the CPWU is Radziejowski, *Communist Party of Western Ukraine*. See also Roman Solchanyk, 'The Comintern and the Communist Party of Western Ukraine', *Canadian Slavonic Papers*, vol. 22, no. 2 (1981), pp. 181–97; and Yurii Slavka and Oleksandr Zaitsev, 'Istoriia KPZU: sproba novoho osmyslennia', *Holos Ukraïny*, 13, 22, 29 and 30 May 1991.

99 Lysiakh-Rudnyts'kyi, 'Natsionalizm'; and Alexander J. Motyl, *The Turn to the Right: The Ideological Origins and Development of Ukrainian Nationalism, 1919–1929* (Boulder: East European Monographs, 1980), p. 172 both stress that the new ultra-nationalism was largely a reaction to the defeats of 1917–20. Kas'ianov, *Ukraïns'ka inteligentsiia na rubezhi*, p. 97 argues that many of its key ideas were already current in the 1900s.

100 Motyl, *Turn to the Right*; Zinovii Znysh, *Stanovlennia OUN* (Kiev: Oleny Telihy, 1994); V. P. Troshchyns'kyi, *Mizhvoienna ukraïns'ka emihratsiia v Yevropi yak istorychne i sotsial'no-politychne yavyshche* (Kiev: Intel, 1994), chapters 4 and 5; and Oleh Bahan, *Natsionalizm i natsionalistychnyi rukh: istoriia ta idei* (Drohobych: Vidrodzhennia, 1994).

101 Subtelny, *Ukraine*, pp. 446–8.

102 Ibid., pp. 448–9.

103 Subtelny, *Ukraine*, p. 450; and Zastavnyi, *Ukraïns'ki etnichni zemli*, p. 78. For a Ukrainian view of the events of 1938–9 in Transcarpathia, see Stepan Rosokha, *Soim Karpats'koï Ukraïny* (L'viv: Memorial/Vil'na Ukraïna, 1991).

104 John A. Armstrong, *Ukrainian Nationalism* (Englewood, Colo.: Ukrainian Academic Press, 2nd edn, 1990). See also Volodymyr Kubijovyc, *Western Ukraine Within Poland, 1920–1939* (Chicago: Ukrainian Research and Information Institute, 1963).

105 Armstrong, *Ukrainian Nationalism*, p. 125.

106 Hunchak and Solchanyk, *Ukraïns'ka suspil'no-politychna dumka*, vol. II, pp. 329, 401 and 422. See also Mykola Stsibors'kyi, *Natsiokratiia* (Prague: Proboem, 1942).

107 For Bandera's own account of his life and political activity, see Stepan Bandera, *Perspektyvy ukraïns'koï revolutsiï* (Toronto: Vydannia Orhanizatsiï ukraïns'kykh natsionalistiv, 1978).

108 Mykola Behesh, 'Solidarnist' ukraïntsiv Skhidnoï Halychyny z natsional'no-vyzvol'noiu borot'boiu zakarpats'kykh ukraïntsiv (1938–1939)', *Suchasnist'*, February 1995, pp. 84–90.

109 For two overviews, see David R. Marples, 'Wartime Collaboration in Ukraine: Some Preliminary Questions and Responses', in his *Stalinism in Ukraine*, pp. 64–81; and John A. Armstrong, 'Collaboration in World War II: The Integral Nationalist Variant in Eastern Europe', *Journal of Modern History*, vol. 40 (1968), pp. 396–410. Ukrainians from both east and west also served in the Vlasovite army.

110 Wolfdieter Bihl, 'Ukrainians in the Armed Forces of the Reich: The 14th *Waffen* Grenadier Division of the SS', in Torke and Himka, *German–Ukrainian Relations*, pp. 138–62, at p. 141.

111 Peter J. Potichnyj, 'Ukrainians in World War II Military Formations: An Overview', and Myroslav Yurkevich, 'Galician Ukrainians in German Military Formations and in the German Administration', both in Boshyk, *Ukraine During World War II*, pp. 61–6 and 68–87.

112 Despite its name, the SS-Galicia was a front-line division rather than an adjunct of the SS. See Bihl, 'Ukrainians in the Armed Forces of the Reich'; and the revisionist history by Mykhailo Slaboshpyts'kyi and Valerii Stetsenko (eds.), *Ukraïns'ka dyviziia 'Halychyna'* (Kiev and Toronto: Visti z Ukraïny, 1994).

113 Many Jews were peddlars or grain merchants, or sold alcohol.

114 See Potichnyj and Aster, *Ukrainian–Jewish Relations*; and their *Jewish–Ukrainian Relations: Two Solitudes* (Oakville, Ont.: Mosaic Press, 1983).

115 'Postanovy II (krakivs'koho) Velykoho Zboru Orhanizatsiï Ukraïns'kykh Natsionalistiv', in Hunchak and Solchanyk, *Ukraïns'ka suspil'no-politychna dumka*, vol. III, pp. 7–22, at p. 15.

116 The eyewitness account by David Kahane, *Lvov Ghetto Diary* (Amherst: University of Massachusetts Press, 1990), pp. 6–7, 10–13, 86–7 and 136 condemns those Ukrainians who took part in the July 1941 pogrom, but praises Sheptyts'kyi for his efforts in defence of the Jews, at pp. 57–9, 119–25 and 138–9. Sheptyks'kyi's open letter 'Thou Shalt Not Murder' is reprinted on pp. 158–62. For a generally critical account of the Ukrainian record, see Aharon Weiss, 'Jewish–Ukrainian Relations in Western Ukraine During the Holocaust', in Potichnyj and Aster, *Ukrainian–Jewish Relations*, pp. 409–20. B. F. Sabrin, *Alliance for Murder: The Nazi–Ukrainian Nationalist Partnership in Genocide* (New York: Sarpedon/Shapolsky, 1991) is somewhat tendentious. The case for the Ukrainian defence is made by M. V. Koval', 'Natsysts'kyi henotsyd shchodo yevreïv ta ukraïns'ke naselennia (1941–1944 rr.)', *Ukraïns'kyi istorychnyi zhurnal*, no. 2, 1992, pp. 25–32; Yaroslav Bilinsky, 'Methodological Problems and Philosophical Issues in the Study of Jewish–Ukrainian Relations During the Second World War', in Potichnyj and Aster, *Ukrainian–Jewish Relations*, pp. 373–407; and Taras Hunchak (Hunczak), 'Ukrainian–Jewish Relations During the Soviet and Nazi Occupations', in Boshyk, *Ukraine During World War II*, pp. 39–57. See also Wolodymyr Kosyk, *The Third Reich and the Ukrainian Question: Documents, 1934–1944* (London: Ukrainian Publishers Ltd., 1991), and Kosyk, *The Third Reich and Ukraine* (New York: Peter Lang, 1993).

117 Levko Shankovs'kyi, *Pokhidni hrupy OUN* (Munich: Ukraïns'kyi samostiinyk, 1958).

118 Armstrong, *Ukrainian Nationalism*, p. 239.

119 M. V. Koval', ' "Prosvita" v umovakh "novoho poriadku" (1941–1944 rr.)', and 'Dolia ukraïns'koï kul'tury za "novoho poriadku" (1941–1944 rr.)', *Ukraïns'kyi istorychnyi zhurnal*, no. 2, 1995, pp. 37–42 and no. 11–12, 1993, pp. 15–38.

120 Armstrong, *Ukrainian Nationalism*, p. 227.

121 Zenon Horodys'kyi, *Ukraïns'ka natsional'na rada: istorychnyi narys* (Kiev: KM Academia, 1993).
122 Armstrong, *Ukrainian Nationalism*, chapters 8 and 12. Alexius was killed in May 1943.
123 Taras Kuzio, 'OUN v Ukraïni. Dmytro Dontsov i zakordonna chastyna OUN', *Za vil'nu Ukraïnu*, nos. 59 and 60, 1991. See also Armstrong, *Ukrainian Nationalism*, chapters 9 and 10.
124 'Materiialy III nadzvychainoho Velykoho Zboru Orhanizatsiï Ukraïns'kykh Natsionalistiv (S. Bandery)', in Hunchak and Solchanyk, *Ukraïns'ka suspil'no-politychna dumka*, vol. III, pp. 57–63, at pp. 68, 66 and 67. See also Peter J. Potichnyj and Yevhen Shtendera, *Political Thought of the Ukrainian Underground, 1943–1951* (Edmonton, Ont.: CIUS, 1986), pp. 333–53.
125 Hunchak and Solchanyk, *Ukraïns'ka suspil'no-politychna dumka*, vol. III, p. 65.
126 'Platform of the Supreme Ukrainian Liberation Council', Potichnyj and Shtendera, *Political Thought of the Ukrainian Underground*, pp. 359–64, at p. 362; and volume VIII in the series *Litopys UPA* by the same authors, p. 37. See also *Ukraïns'ka holovna vyzvol'na rada: dokumenty* (New York, L'viv and Kiev: UHVR, 1994), and the articles by Petro Poltava in Hunchak and Solchanyk, *Ukraïns'ka suspil'no-politychna dumka*, vol. II, pp. 106–37.
127 Peter J. Potichnyj (ed.), *Litopys ukraïns'koï povstans'koï armiï* (Toronto: Litopys UPA, 1978–84), 10 vols. collects all major documentation on the UPA. The early volumes in the series are reviewed by John A. Armstrong, 'The Chronicle of the Ukrainian Insurgent Army', *Harvard Ukrainian Studies*, vol. 14, no. 1 (June 1990), pp. 171–5. See also Yaroslav Bilinsky, *Bol'shevizm i vyzvol'na borot'ba* (London: Zakordonna chastyna OUN, 1957); Boshyk, *Ukraine During World War II*, pp. 61–104; M. V. Koval', '1941–1945 roky na Ukraïni', *Ukraïns'kyi istorychnyi zhurnal*, no. 6, 1991, pp. 3–23; Mykola Lebid', *Ukraïns'ka povstans'ka armiia* (Munich: Vydavnytstvo UHVR, 1946); Marples, *Stalinism in Ukraine*, pp. 72–9; Petro Mirchuk, *Ukraïns'ka povstans'ka armiia, 1942–1952* (Munich: Cicero, 1953, reprinted in the Rukh paper *Narodna hazeta*, no. 20–1, December 1991) and Mirchuk, *Narys istoriï OUN 1920–1939* (Munich: Ukraïns'ke vydavnytstvo, 1968); Andrii Mykulyn, *OUN v svitli postanov velykykh zboriv, konferentsiv ta inshykh dokumentiv z borot'by 1929–1955 r.* (London: Zakordonna chastyna OUN, 1955); and Petro Poltava, *Zbirnik pidpil'nykh pysan'* (Munich: Ukraïns'kyi samostiinyk, 1959). As much of the above is polemical, Armstrong, *Ukrainian Nationalism* is still the best study.
128 Peter J. Potichnyj, 'The Ukrainian Insurgent Army (UPA) and the German Authorities' in Torke and Himka, *German–Ukrainian Relations*, pp. 163–77, at p. 170.
129 Markus, *Soviet Counterinsurgency*, p. 61. Marples, *Stalinism in Ukraine*, p. 58 cites estimates from 10,000 to 200,000, while Subtelny gives a figure of 30,000–40,000: *Ukraine*, p. 474. Yurkevich, 'Galician Ukrainians', p. 73 also cites a 'peak' figure of 40,000. On the partisan struggle in Volhynia and the short-lived 'Olevs'k Republic', see Taras Bul'ba-Borovets', *Armiia bez derzhavy* (L'viv: Poklyk sumlinnia, 1993).
130 Potichnyj, 'Ukrainian Insurgent Army', and Taras Hunchak (Hunczak),

'OUN–German Relations, 1941–1945', both in Torke and Himka, *German–Ukrainian Relations*, pp. 163–77 and 178–86.

131 Subtelny, *Ukraine*, pp. 472–3.

132 Taras Kuzio, 'Panorama politychnykh partii ta orhanizatsii ukraïns'koï emihratsiï', *Za vil'nu Ukraïnu*, 3 October 1991.

133 Heorhii Kas'ianov, ' "Sprava yuristiv" ta inshi: zvorotnyi bik "vidlyhy" ', *Vyzvol'nyi shliakh*, December 1993, pp. 1497–1505, at p. 1488.

134 On the history of Luk"ianenko's various trials and incarcerations, and letters to and from him in prison, see Stepan Sydovs'kyi (ed.), *Zashyty ukraïns'koho samvydavy, vypusk 11. Zupynit' kryvosuddia! Sprava Levka Luk"ianenka* (Munich: Suchasnist', 1980).

135 As Luk"ianenko stressed in his autobiographical address to the Ukrainian Supreme Council on 29 May 1990, when putting himself forward for the post of chairman of the Supreme Council, *Persha sesiia Verkhovnoï Rady URSR dvanadtsiatoho sklykannia*, bulletin no. 22, p. 7. See also Levko Luk"ianenko, 'Do istoriï ukraïns'koho pravozakhysnoho rukhu', *Vyzvolennia '91*, nos. 1–3 (February–March), 1991.

136 Author's interview with Luk"ianenko, 23 October 1994. The UWPU programme can be found in Levko Luk"ianenko, *Ne dam zahynut' Ukraïni!* (Kiev: Sofiia, 1994), pp. 8–34.

137 M. Prskop, 'Dissident Movement', in Kubijovyc and Struk, *Encyclopaedia of Ukraine*, vol. I, pp. 677–80, at p. 678; Kas'ianov, ' "Sprava yuristiv" ', p. 1500.

138 Interview with Luk"ianenko in *Ukraïna*, no. 39, 1990.

139 Heorhii Kas'ianov, *Nezhodni: ukraïns'ka inteligentsiia v rusi oporu 1960–1980-kh rokiv* (Kiev: Lybid', 1995); Yu. O. Kurnosov, *Inakomyslennia v Ukraïni (60-ti-persha polovyna 80-kh rr. XX st.)* (Kiev: Institute of History, 1994); Yevhen Sverstiuk, 'Shistdesiatnyky i Zakhid', in *Bludni syny Ukraïny* (Kiev: Znannia, 1993), pp. 23–33; Michael Brown (ed.), *Ferment in the Ukraine* (London: Macmillan, 1971); Julian Birch, 'The Nature and Sources of Dissidence in Ukraine' in Potichnyj, *Ukraine in the 1970s*, and Birch, *The Ukrainian Nationalist Movement in the USSR Since 1956* (London: Ukrainian Information Service, 1971); Liudmila Alekseeva, 'Ukrainskoe natsional'noe dvizhenie', *Istoriia inakomysliia v SSR* (Vilnius and Moscow: Vest', 3rd edn, 1992), pp. 7–35; *Ukraïns'ka inteligentsiia pid sudom KGB* (Munich: Suchasnist', 1970); and Jaroslaw Bilocerkowycz, *Soviet Ukrainian Dissent: A Study of Political Alienation* (Boulder: Westview Press, 1988).

140 Luk"ianenko, 'Do istoriï ukraïns'koho pravozakhysnoho rukhu', *Vyzvolennia '91*, no. 2, p. 1.

141 Heorhii Kas'ianov, 'Shistdesiatnyky. Dysydenty. Neformaly. Znaiomi neznaiomi', *Viche*, nos. 10 and 11 (October and November), 1994, pp. 106–18 and 138–46, at p. 109 in no. 10; and Kas'ianov, *Nezhodni*, p. 119.

142 Les' Taniuk, *Khto z"ïv moie m"iaso?* (Drohobych: Vidrodzhennia, 1994), pp. 283–96.

143 Hunchak and Solchanyk, *Ukraïns'ka suspil'no-politychna dumka*, vol. III, pp. 175–86.

144 His account of the 1965–6 trials is available as V"iacheslav Chornovil, *The*

Chornovil Papers (New York: McGraw-Hill, 1968), or as V"iacheslav Chornovil and Borys Penson, *Khronika taborobykh budniv* (Kiev: Taki spravy, 1991; and Munich: Suchasnist', 1976).

145 On Ukrainian political prisoners in the 1960s and 1970s, see Slava Stets'ko (ed.), *Revolutionary Voices: Ukrainian Political Prisoners Condemn Russian Colonialism* (Munich: Press Bureau ABN, 1969); and *Ukrainian Political Prisoners in the Soviet Union: A Biographical List*, with a preface by Valentyn Moroz (Toronto: Canadian League for the Liberation of Ukraine, 1979).

146 Kas'ianov, *Nezhodni*, p. 63.

147 Ivan Dziuba, *Internationalism or Russification?* (London: Weidenfeld and Nicolson, 1968), p. 213.

148 See, in English, *The Ukrainian Herald: Issue 4* (Munich: ABN Press Bureau, 1972); and Yaroslav Bilinsky (ed.), *The Ukrainian Herald: Issue 6* (Baltimore: Smoloskyp, 1977). Issues 1–6 are available in Ukrainian as *Ukraïns'kyi visnyk* (Baltimore: Smoloskyp, 1971–2).

149 Khmara's dissident works were reprinted as *S'ohodni pro mynule* (L'viv: Poklyk sumlinnia, 1993).

150 Kas'ianov, *Nezhodni*, pp. 90–5.

151 Yaroslav Bihun (ed.), *Boomerang: The Works of Valentyn Moroz* (Baltimore: Smoloskyp, 1974).

152 Roman Szporluk, 'The National Question', in Timothy J. Colton and Robert Levgold (eds.), *After the Soviet Union: From Empire to Nations* (New York: W. W. Norton, 1992), pp. 84–112, at p. 102.

153 Ivan L. Rudnytsky, 'The Political Thought of Soviet Ukrainian Dissidents', in his *Essays in Modern Ukrainian History*, pp. 477–89; and George S. N. Luckyj, 'Polarity in Ukrainian Intellectual Dissent', *Canadian Slavonic Papers*, vol. 14, no. 2 (Summer 1972), pp. 269–79.

154 Other groups included the United Party for the Liberation of Ukraine uncovered in Ivano-Frankivs'k in December 1958, the Ob"ednannia ('Union') group in 1960 and the Khodorovs'ka group arrested in 1962: Luk"ianenko, 'Do istoriï ukraïns'koho pravozakhysnoho rukhu', *Vyzvolennia '91*, no. 1.

155 Nina Strokata, 'Ukraïns'kyi natsional'nyi front, 1962?–1967', *Suchasnist'*, June 1985, pp. 67–75.

156 Hunchak and Solchanyk, *Ukraïns'ka suspil'no-politychna dumka*, vol. III, pp. 376–8.

157 For example Yosyp Terelia, *Tsarstvo dukha* (Uzhhorod: Karpats'kyi krai, 1994), a work first written in the camps in 1970.

158 See the biography of Badz'o in *Volia*, no. 5 (April), 1991; and his 'Open Letter to the Soviet Leaders', *Journal of Ukrainian Studies*, vol. 9, nos. 1 and 2 (1984), pp. 74–94 and 47–70.

159 Leonid Pliushch, *History's Carnival: A Dissident's Autobiography* (London: Collins and Harvill, 1977); Marite Sapiets, Peter Reddaway and Caryl Emerson (translators and eds.), *The Case of Leonid Plyushch* (London: C. Hurst, 1976); and Danylo Shumuk, *Life Sentence: Memoirs of a Ukrainian Political Prisoner* (Edmonton, Ont.: CIUS, 1984).

160 I. Hvat, 'The Ukrainian Catholic Church, the Vatican and the Soviet Union During the Pontificate of Pope John Paul II', *Religion in Communist*

Lands, vol. 11, no. 3 (Winter 1983), pp. 264–79; and Bohdan R. Bociurkiw, 'The Ukrainian Catholic Church in the USSR Under Gorbachev', *Problems of Communism*, vol. 39, no. 6 (November–December), 1990, pp. 1–19.

161 Ivan Hel', 'Etnotsyd – holovna meta stratehiv Moskvy', in Bohdan Zalizniak (ed.), *Hrani kul'tury* (L'viv: Atlas, 1993), pp. 40–2.

162 Taras Kuzio, 'Workers' Opposition in Ukraine', *Labour Focus on Eastern Europe*, vol. 5, nos. 5–6 (1982–3), pp. 30–1; and Liudmila Alekseeva, *Soviet Dissent: Contemporary Movements for National, Religious and Human Rights* (Middletown, Conn.: Wesleyan University Press, 1985).

163 Levko Luk''ianenko, 'Zhyttepys', in his *Spovid' u kameri smertnykiv* (Kiev: Vitchyzna, 1991), pp. 8–34, at p. 25. Kurnosov, *Inakomyslennia v Ukraïni*, p. 186 estimates the figure at 30–40 per cent in the 1970s.

164 Ibid., pp. 23 and 25; author's interview with Luk''ianenko, 23 October 1994.

165 Luk''ianenko, 'Do istoriï ukraïns'koho pravozakhysnoho rukhu', *Vyzvolennia '91*, no. 2, p. 1.

166 Ibid.

167 Kurnosov, 'Borot'ba za hratamy', in his *Inakomyslennia v Ukraïni*, pp. 178–215.

168 Hunchak and Solchanyk, *Ukraïns'ka suspil'no-politychna dumka*, vol. III, pp. 370–5, at p. 374.

169 Author's interview with Roman Koval', 5 May 1992.

170 Interview with Rudenko in *Literaturna Ukraïna*, 30 April 1992.

171 Luk''ianenko, 'Do istoriï ukraïns'koho pravozakhysnoho rukhu', *Vyzvolennia '91*, no. 3, p. 2; author's interview with Luk''ianenko, 23 October 1994.

172 'Nashi zavdannia', in Osyp Zinkevych (ed.), *Ukraïns'ka hel'sinks'ka hrupa 1978–1982: dokumenty i materiialy* (Toronto: Smoloskyp, 1983), pp. 21–8. See also Lesya Verba and Bohdan Yasen (eds.), *The Human Rights Movement in the Ukraine: Documents of the UHG, 1976–1980* (Toronto: Smoloskyp, 1980), p. 20; Victor Haynes, 'The Ukrainian Helsinki Group: A Postmortem', *Journal of Ukrainian Studies*, vol. 8, no. 2 (Winter 1983), pp. 102–13, which surveys the literature on the UHG; and for an autobiography of one of the UHG's leading members, Oksana Meshko, *Mizh smertiu i zhyttiam* (Kiev: Yava, 1991).

173 Roman Koval', 'Ukraïns'ki demokraty i demokraty Ukraïny', in his *Chy mozhlyve Ukraïno-Rosiis'ke zamyrennia?* (Stryi: Myron Tarnavs'kyi, 1991), pp. 57–66, at p. 57.

174 Haynes, 'Ukrainian Helsinki Group', p. 105.

175 *Holos vidrodzhennia*, December 1989.

176 Levko Luk''ianenko, *Shcho dali?* (Translated as *What Next?*) (London: Ukrainian Central Information Service, Ukrainian version 1989, English version 1990), p. 37 (English version).

177 Bilocerkowycz, *Soviet Ukrainian Dissent*, p. 81.

178 Bohdan Krawchenko and Jim A. Carter, 'Dissidents in Ukraine Before 1972: A Summary Statistical Profile', *Journal of Ukrainian Studies*, vol. 8, no. 2 (Winter 1983), pp. 85–8.

3 CHANNELS OF NATIONALIST DISCOURSE: POLITICAL PARTIES, CIVIL SOCIETY AND RELIGION

1 Geoffrey A. Hosking, 'The Beginnings of Independent Political Activity', in Hosking, Jonathan Aves and Peter J. S. Duncan (eds.), *The Road to Post-Communism: Independent Political Movements in the Soviet Union, 1985–1991* (London: Pinter, 1992), pp. 1–28.

2 V. M. Lytvyn and A. H. Sliusarenko, 'Na politychnii areni Ukraïny (90-ti rr.). Rozdumy istorykiv', *Ukraïns'kyi istorychnyi zhurnal*, no. 1, 1994, pp. 9–30, at pp. 14–15.

3 Mykola Riabchuk, 'Ukrainskaia literatura i malorossiskii "imidzh"', *Druzhba narodov*, no. 5, 1988, pp. 250–4; and his interview in Solchanyk, *Ukraine: From Chernobyl' to Sovereignty*, pp. 19–30.

4 Bohdan Nahaylo, 'Informal Ukrainian Culturological Club Helps to Break New Ground for *Glasnost'* and ' "Informal" Ukrainian Culturological Club Under Attack', *Radio Liberty Research*, RL 57/88, 8 February 1988 and RL 477/87, 23 November 1987 respectively.

5 Maria Drohobychy, 'The Lion Society: Profile of a Ukrainian Patriotic "Informal" Group', *Radio Liberty Research*, RL 325/88, 18 July 1988.

6 Bohdan Nahaylo, 'Ukrainian Association of Independent Creative Intelligentsia Formed', *Radio Liberty Research*, RL 489/87, 25 November 1987. Chornovil and Mykola Rudenko, formerly of the UHG, were key members.

7 'Kyïvs'ki neformaly: khto vony?', *Radians'ka Ukraïna*, 2 September 1989.

8 Bociurkiw, 'Ukrainian Catholic Church'.

9 Bohdan Horyn', 'Nash shliakh do URP', *Respublikanets'*, no. 1, October 1990; Kamins'kyi, *Na perekhidnomu etapi*, pp. 315–78.

10 V"iacheslav Chornovil, *Komentar do proiektu 'decliaratsiï pryntsypiv'*, UHU document dated 21 October 1989.

11 Taras Kuzio (ed.), *Dissent in Ukraine Under Gorbachev: A Collection of Samizdat Documents* (London: Ukrainian Press Agency, 1989), articles 2 and 4 of the UHU Declaration of Principles.

12 Levko Luk"ianenko, 'Zvitna dopovid' z"ïzdovi Ukraïns'koï hel'sins'koï spilky', *Viruiu v Boha i v Ukraïnu* (Kiev: Pam"iatky Ukraïny, 1991), pp. 282 and 283.

13 Ibid., p. 285–6; and Luk"ianenko's address to the first Rukh congress, pp. 296–305 (also in *Suchasnist'*, December 1989).

14 Kuzio, *Dissent in Ukraine Under Gorbachev*, preamble of the UHU Declaration of Principles.

15 Author's interview with Oleh Pavlyshyn, then deputy leader of the URP, 27 January 1992.

16 The UHU always had good links with its Baltic counterparts: V"iacheslav Chornovil, 'Persha dyplomatychna misiia demokratychnoho bloku', *Moloda Ukraïna*, no. 8, 1990.

17 Kuzio, *Dissent in Ukraine Under Gorbachev*, articles 1 and 5–20 of the UHU Declaration of Principles.

18 Marples, *Ukraine Under Perestroika*, chapter 5; Marples, 'The Greening of Ukraine: Ecology and the Emergence of *Zelenyi svit*, 1986–1990', in Judith B. Sedaitis and Jim Butterfield (eds.), *Perestroika from Below: Social*

Movements in the Soviet Union (Boulder: Westview, 1992), pp. 133–44; and V. Lytvyn, 'Asotsiiatsiia "zelenyi svit" i partiia zelenykh Ukraïny', *Polityka i chas*, no. 9 (June), 1991, pp. 53–7.

19 Author's interview with Mykola Pryluts'kyi, editor of *Zelenyi svit* (the journal of the organisation Zelenyi svit), 22 January 1992.

20 David R. Marples, 'Mass Demonstration in Kiev Focuses on Ecological Issues and Political Situation in Ukraine', *Report on the USSR*, RL 525/88, 7 December 1988.

21 *Lenins'ka molod*, 31 December 1988. Ridna mova took its name from a similar organisation active in Galicia before 1939.

22 *Pravda Ukrainy*, 12 February 1989; Bohdan Nahaylo, 'Inaugural Congress of Ukrainian Language Society Turns Into Major Political Demonstration', *Report on the USSR*, RL 103/89, 13 February 1989.

23 David R. Marples, 'The Shevchenko Ukrainian Language Society: An Interview with Dmytro Pavlychko', *Report on the USSR*, RL 340/89, 29 June 1989.

24 *Materialy pro rozvytok mov v ukraïns'kii RSR* (Kiev: Prosvita, 1991).

25 *Radians'ka Ukraïna*, 5 March 1989.

26 Roman Solchanyk, 'Democratic Front to Promote Perestroika Formed in Ukraine' and 'Lviv Authorities Begin Criminal Proceedings Against Ukrainian Activists', *Radio Liberty Research*, RL 324/88, 17 July 1988 and RL 327/88, 26 July 1988 respectively; and Yurii Kyrychuk, 'Narys istoriï UHS-URP', *Respublikanets'*, no. 2 (November–December), 1991, p. 86.

27 *Robitnycha hazeta*, 4 October 1988; *Radians'ka osvita*, 30 September 1988; Oleksa Haran', *Vid stvorennia Rukhu do bahatopartiinosti* (Kiev: Znannia, 1992), p. 5.

28 Haran', *Ukraïna bahatopartiina* (Kiev: Pam"iatky Ukraïny, 1991), p. 7; Ivan Salii, *Ya povertaius'* (Kiev: Dovira, 1993), pp. 13–16 and 159. The Ukrainian Komsomol paper also carried an appeal for the creation of a Popular Front: *Lenins'ka molod*, 28 July 1988.

29 *Vechirnii Kyïv*, 1 December 1988.

30 'The Beginnings of "Rukh": An Interview with Pavlo Movchan', in Solchanyk, *Ukraine: From Chernobyl' to Sovereignty*, pp. 7–18; Bohdan Nahaylo, 'Kiev's "Popular Movement" for the Support of Restructuring" Allowed to Meet – Behind Closed Doors', *Report on the USSR*, RL 468/88, 2 November 1988; Charles F. Furtado Jr and Michael Hechter, 'The Emergence of Nationalist Politics in the USSR: A Comparison of Estonia and the Ukraine', in Alexander J. Motyl (ed.), *Thinking Theoretically About Soviet Nationalities: History and Comparison in the Study of the USSR* (New York: Columbia University Press, 1992), pp. 169–204; Viktor Teren, 'Musymo pochynaty spochatku', *Samostiina Ukraïna*, no. 13 (March), 1992; Mykola Porovs'kyi, 'Viriu, shcho Rukh ozhyve' and 'Do istoriï Rukhu', *Rozbudova derzhavy*, no. 5 (May), 1993.

31 *Literaturna Ukraïna*, 7 November 1988; *Moloda hvardiia*, 25 November 1988.

32 Lytvyn and Sliusarenko, 'Na politychnii areni Ukraïny', pp. 18 and 20; Vitalii Vrublevskii, *Vladimir Shcherbitskii: pravda i vymysly* (Kiev: Dovira, 1993), p. 252.

33 Oliinyk, a writer and head of the Ukrainian Cultural Fund, had been one of the original sponsors of the initiative, but eventually dissociated himself. See his letter in *Radians'ka Ukraïna*, 8 March 1989. In November 1992 Oliinyk was elected to the Supreme Council; he is still, in 1995, a leading figure in the revived CPU.

34 CSACOU (Central State Archives of Civic Organisations of Ukraine; formerly the archive of the Communist Party in Ukraine): f. 1, op. 11, delo 1911, pp. 88–90 (f. 1 is the general department). The author consulted the archives in spring 1995. See also *Literaturna Ukraïna*, 15 and 22 December 1988.

35 *Literaturna Ukraïna*, 16 February 1989. The programme was drawn up by Drach, Donchyk, Oliinyk, Yurii Mushketyk, V"iacheslav Briukhovets'kyi and others: Ivan Drach, *Rukh ne vycherpav sebe i maie maibutnie*, interview published at the third Rukh congress in February 1992.

36 CSACOU, f. 1, op. 11, delo 1911, pp. 121–3; delo 1865, pp. 20–35; Solchanyk, *Ukraine: From Chernobyl' to Sovereignty*, p. 14; *Radians'ka Ukraïna*, 6 April 1989.

37 Author's interview with Myroslav Popovych, Rukh's spokesman in 1989, 23 January 1992.

38 CSACOU, f. 1, op. 11, delo 2059; *Pravda Ukrainy*, 18 February and 19 March 1989; *Radians'ka Ukraïny*, 7 February 1989; Roman Solchanyk, 'Party and Writers at Loggerheads over Popular Front' and 'Shcherbitsky Assails Popular Front and Helsinki Union', *Report on the USSR*, RL 237/89, 22 May 1989 and RL 256/89, 9 June 1989 respectively.

39 George Sajewych and Andrew Sorokowski (eds.), *The Popular Movement of Ukraine for Restructuring – Rukh: Programme and Charter* (Ellicott City, Md.: Smoloskyp, 1989), p. 4. The figures refer to the number of delegates at Rukh's first congress, who were elected in proportion to local membership.

40 *Literaturna Ukraïna*, 21 and 28 September, and 5 October 1989.

41 Emphasis added. *Literaturna Ukraïna*, 28 September 1989 (as with all other references to the programme).

42 Author's interviews with Myroslav Popovych and Volodymyr Cherniak, 23 January and 1 August 1992.

43 O. V. Haran', *Ubyty drakona. Z istoriï Rukhu ta novykh partii Ukraïny* (Kiev: Lybid', 1993), pp. 48–70.

44 Vladimir Paniotto, 'The Ukrainian Movement for Perestroika – "Rukh": A Sociological Survey', *Soviet Studies*, vol. 43, no. 1 (1991), pp. 177–81, at pp. 178–9. Respondents were allowed to choose two options from a list of fourteen.

45 Thomas F. Remington, 'Conclusion: Partisan Competition and Democratic Stability', in Remington (ed.), *Parliaments in Transition: The New Legislative Politics in the Former USSR and Eastern Europe* (Boulder: Westview, 1994), pp. 217–31, at p. 218.

46 Yevhen Boltarovych, 'L'vivshchyna: politychni syly i politychnyi spektr', *Respublikanets'*, no. 2, 1991. On Rukh's activity in Ternopil', see *Vil'ne zhyttia*, 27 March 1990; for L'viv, see the interview with local head Orest' Vlokh in *Radians'ka Ukraïna*, 19 May 1990; and for Ivano-Frankivs'k, see *Prykarpats'ka pravda*, 3 April 1990.

47 Ivan Drach, 'Pro nezalezhnist', yakoï shche nemae', *Literaturna Ukraïna*, 30 August 1990.

48 Theodore H. Friedgut, 'Pluralism and Politics in an Urban Soviet: Donetsk, 1990–1991', in Carl R. Saivetz and Anthony Jones (eds.), *In Search of Pluralism: Soviet and Post-Soviet Politics* (Boulder: Westview, 1994), pp. 45–61; Haran', *Ubyty drakona*, p. 66; author's interview with Volodymyr Filenko, co-leader of the PDRU, 10 February 1992.

49 *Literaturna Ukraïna*, 8 March 1990.

50 *Visnyk Rukhu*, no. 7 (November), 1990; *Druhi vseukraïns'ki zbory Narodnoho Rukhu Ukraïny – dokumenty* (Kiev: Rukh, 1991); *Literaturna Ukraïna*, 8 November 1990; *Vechirnii Kyïv*, 26 October 1990; and *Radians'ka Ukraïna*, 11 and 13 November 1990.

51 The high-water mark of nationalist political mobilisation was the 'human chain' formed between L'viv and Kiev in January 1990: Bohdan Nahaylo, 'Human-Chain Demonstration in Ukraine: A Triumph for "Rukh" ', *Report on the USSR*, RL 57/90, vol. 2, no. 5, 2 February 1990.

52 *Visnyk Rukhu*, no. 7, 1990, p. 33.

53 *Suchasni politychni partiï ta rukhy na Ukraïni* (Kiev: Institut politychnykh doslidzhen', 1991), p. 230; Sajewych and Sorokowski, *Popular Movement of Ukraine for Restructuring – Rukh*, p. 4; *Visnyk Rukhu*, no. 7, 1990, p. 14. A total of 72 per cent of the delegates had higher education; 30 per cent belonged to the 'cultural intelligentsia', 53 per cent to the 'technical intelligentsia'.

54 Ivan Drach, 'Politychna sytuatsiia na Ukraïni i zavdannia Rukhu', *Literaturna Ukraïna*, 8 November 1990.

55 Mykhailo Horyn', 'Pro robotu sekretariatu Rukhu', *Visnyk Rukhu*, no. 7, 1990, p. 44.

56 'Ukhvala druhykh vseukraïns'kykh zboriv Narodnoho Rukhu Ukraïny', *Druhi vseukraïns'ki zbory NRU*, p. 41.

57 'Prohrama Narodnoho Rukhu Ukraïny', *Druhi vseukraïns'ki zbory NRU*, p. 4. Terms such as 'sovereignty' and 'independence' were again not well defined, but the general thrust of Rukh's programme was now clear.

58 A broad-based coalition including all parties bar the far right and the CPU was tentatively proposed in January 1991 under the name 'Sovereign Democratic Ukraine' but fell apart under the strains of Gorbachev's March 1991 referendum campaign (see chapter 5 of this volume): *Protokoly 6 & 7. Zasidannia Politychnoï Rady Narodnoho Rukhu Ukraïny*, 30 January and 4 February 1991; *Uhoda mizh politychnymy partiiamy ta hromads'kymy orhanizatsiiamy pro politychnu koalitsiiu (blok) Suverenna Demokratychna Ukraïna*, Rukh document dated 4 February 1991.

59 On the development of Ukrainian political parties, see Andrew Wilson, 'Ukraine', in Bogdan Skajkowski (ed.), *Political Parties of Eastern Europe, Russia and the Successor States* (London: Longman, 1994), pp. 577–604; Andrew Wilson and Artur Bilous, 'Political Parties in Ukraine', *Europe–Asia Studies*, vol. 45, no. 4 (1993), pp. 693–703; Artur Bilous, *Politychni ob"iednannia Ukraïny* (Kiev: Ukraïna, 1993); Haran', *Ukraïna bahatopartiina*; Haran', *Vid stvorennia Rukhu do bahatopartiinosti*; Haran, *Ubyty drakona*; V. Lytvyn, 'Pro suchasni Ukraïns'ki partiï, ïkhnikh prykhyl'nykhiv

ta lideriv', *Politolohichni chytannia*, no. 1, 1992, pp. 62–101; and A. H. Sliusarenko and M. V. Tomenko, *Novi politychni partiï Ukraïny* (Kiev: Znannia, 1990).

60 For the founding congress of the Union of Workers and its programme see *Robitnycha hazeta*, 27 February, 3 March and 14 September 1990. On the Intermovement, see Roman Solchanyk, ' "Intermovement" Formed in Donbass', *Report on the USSR*, RL 513/90, 21 December 1990; and *Robitnycha hazeta*, 2 December 1990.

61 'Pro stan i tendentsiï rozvytku robitnychnoho rukhu v respublitsi': CSACOU, f. 1, op. 11, delo 2279, pp. 157–62, dated 2 July 1991.

62 Declaration of the first all-Ukrainian conference of the Social Democratic Party of Ukraine, 24–5 November 1990, *Pro stavlennia do Narodnoho Rukhu Ukraïny*; Myroslav Popovych, 'Filosofiia hromads'kykh rukhiv: pro Narodnyi Rukh Ukraïny za perebudovu', *Nauka i suspil'stvo*, no. 2, 1990.

63 *Holos*, no. 21, 1990; *Partiia demokraticheskogo vozrozhdeniia Ukrainy – materialy uchreditel'nogo s"ezda* (Kiev: UkrNIINTI, 1991); *Literaturna Ukraïna*, 13 December 1990; V. Lytvyn (Litvin), 'Partiia demokraticheskogo vozrozhdeniia Ukrainy', *Politika i vremia*, no. 1 (January), 1991, pp. 84–6.

64 'Kontseptsiia dohovoru pro utvorennia Yevropeis'ko-Aziats'koï spivdruzhnosti derzhav', *Al'ternatyva*, no. 2, 1991; *Literaturna Ukraïna*, 7 February 1991; *Holos Ukraïny*, 20 February 1991; and *Za vil'nu Ukraïnu*, 19 February 1991. Cf. the concept for a loose confederation put forward by Ukrainian academics in *Literaturna Ukraïna*, 27 September 1990, and *Vechirnii Kyïv*, 25 December 1990.

65 *Ustanovchyi z"ïzd Ukraïns'koï respublikans'koï partiï* (Kiev: RUKHinform, 1990). See also *Tsentral'na rada*, no. 5 (June), 1990; *Radians'ka Ukraïna*, 16 May 1990; *Halychyna*, 2 June 1990; and *Za vil'nu Ukraïnu*, 17 July 1990.

66 Of the URP leadership in December 1991, the following had been political prisoners: Levko Luk"ianenko, Mykhailo and Bohdan Horyn', Stepan Khmara, Levko Horokhivs'kyi, Oles' Shevchenko, Petro Rozumnyi, Vasyl' Ovsienko and Volodymyr Andrushkoi, *Samostiina Ukraïna*, no. 19 (December), 1991. The first five were all deputies. Levko Luk"ianenko, 'URP na suchasnomu etapi', *Samostiina Ukraïna*, no. 5 (January), 1992 accepted that in 1990–1 the party had a 'bunker mentality'.

67 *Ustanovchyi z"ïzd URP*, p. 82; Kyrychuk, 'Narys istoriï UHS-URP', p. 95.

68 *URP-zasidannia rady partiï: Protokol N2-R*, 17–18 November 1990; Roman Koval', *Rezolutsiï u zv"iazku z zahostrenniam politychnoï sytuatsiï*, 17 November 1990; author's interviews with the URP's leaders, 20 August 1991; Les' Taniuk and G. P. Krymchuk (eds.), *Khronika oporu* (Kiev, Dnipro, 1991), pp. 203–4.

69 Bohdan Horyn', 'Nash shliakh do URP', p. 6.

70 Kyrychuk, 'Narys istoriï UHS-URP', p. 91; *Visnyk Rukhu*, no. 7, 1990.

71 *Protokol no. 9. Zasidannia politychnoï rady Narodnoho Rukhu Ukraïny*, 10 March 1991 records such complaints against the URP's Mykhailo Horyn'.

72 Author's interviews with Petro Rozumnyi, 26 January 1992 and Roman Koval', 5 May 1992. For the views of the radicals, see Roman Koval', 'URP

na novomu etapi', *Prapor antykomunizmu,* no. 4, 1990; Volodymyr Yavors'kyi, 'Davaite hovoryty po suti', *Prapor antykomunizmu,* no. 5, 1990; and Serhii Zhyzhko, 'My vyzvolymos'', *Vyzvolennia '91,* no. 1 (February), 1991. A radical group appeared in L'viv in December 1990 and called for the URP to copy 'the ideological-political struggle of the OUN': *Zvernennia do chleniv URP. Initsiiatyvnyi komitet po stvorenniu radykal'noi' hrupy URP,* URP document dated 15 December 1990.

73 On the February conference, see *Ideolohiia i taktyka URP: materiialy teoretychnoi'konferentsii'* (Kiev: URP, 1991); *Vyzvolennia '91,* no. 4 (March), 1991; and *Sil's'ki visti,* 27 February 1991. On the second congress, see *II z"izd Ukrains'koi'respublikans'koi'partii',* ed. B. Proniuk (Kiev: URP, 1991); *Za vil'nu Ukrainu,* 7 and 11 June 1991; *Ratusha* (an interview with Khmara), 17–18 June 1991; *Samostiina Ukraina,* nos. 6, 7 and 9 (June–July), 1991; and *Nezalezhnist',* no. 9 (June), 1991.

74 Levko Luk"ianenko, 'URP na suchasnomu etapi'.

75 *Materiialy tret'oho z"izdu Ukrains'koi' respublikans'koi' partii'* (Kiev: URP, 1992); *Samostiina Ukraina,* no. 29 (May), 1992; *Holos Ukrainy,* 7 May 1992; and *Post-postup,* nos. 15 and 19, 1992. At the URP's Grand Council on 1 August 1992, 5–10 per cent of the party membership of 12,000 was reported to have left: author's notes at meeting.

76 Mykhailo Horyn', 'Ukrains'ka respublikans'ka partiia – partiia budivnycha', *Rozbudova derzhavy,* no. 3 (August), 1992.

77 *Pozacherhovyi z"izd Ukrains'koi' respublikans'koi' partii'* (Kiev: URP, 1994), pp. 13 and 20. Three of the URP's deputies were elected in by-elections in late 1994.

78 According to a survey by the party secretariat of the URP's membership dated 12 May 1991, 46 per cent were working class and 28 per cent white-collar; only 24 per cent had higher education. At the 1990 congress, 57 per cent of delegates were 'workers', 'technical-engineering operatives' or 'teachers': *Ustanovchyi z"izd URP,* p. 52.

79 Nearly two-thirds (65 per cent) of delegates to the inaugural DPU congress and 80 per cent of those to the April 1992 party conference had at least higher education: *Volia,* no. 5, December 1990, and *Analiz anketnych danykh uchasnykiv 1-i' vseukrains'koi' partiinoi' konferentsii' DemPU.* Party leader Badz'o admitted that the party was often characterised as a 'party of philologists' whose 'so-called party cell number one' was to be found in the building of the Kiev Writers' Union; author's notes from the meeting of the Kiev oblast DPU, 1 February 1992.

80 *Literaturna Ukraina,* 27 June 1991.

81 *Literaturna Ukraina,* 31 May 1990. An English translation of the manifesto and a full list of the eighty-six signatories can be found in *Journal of Ukrainian Studies,* vol. 15, no. 2 (Winter) 1990, pp. 85–111.

82 Dmytro Pavlychko, 'Za nezalezhnu demokratychnu Ukrainu vstupne slovo', in *Ideini zasady Demokratychnoi' partii' Ukrainy: z materialiv ustanovchoho z"izdu* (Kiev: Prosvita, 1991), p. 15; Yurii Badz'o, 'Chomu nam potribna bahatopartiinist'?', *Volia,* no. 15–16 (September), 1991.

83 Yurii Badz'o, 'Politychna sytuatsiia v Ukraini i rol' u suspil'nomu protsesi Demokratychnoi' partii Ukrainy', in *Ideini zasady DPU,* p. 23.

84 Author's interview with Badz'o, 29 April 1992; *Protokoly DemPU*, 27 December 1990, April and May 1991, passim; *Volia*, nos. 9–10 (June), 1991.

85 Yurii Badz'o, *Pro suspil'no-politychnu situatsiiu v kraïni, pro proekt prohramy, orhanizatsiinyi stan i cherhovi zavdannia DemPU*. *Dopovid' na pershii vseukraïns'kii konferentsiï DemPU*, 11–12 April 1992; *Visnyk: informatsiinyi b'iuleten' natsional'noï rady DemPU*, nos. 1–3, 1991–2.

86 Oleksandr Burakovs'kyi, 'Zvitna dopovid' na tretikh zborakh Rukh', *Narodna hazeta*, no. 9 (March), 1992.

87 On early proposals for such a union, see *Holos Ukraïny*, 16 May 1992, and *Narodna hazeta*, no. 18 (May), 1992. On the DPU's second congress, see *Demokrat: No. 1. Informatsiino-metodychnyi biuleten' Natsional'noï Rady Demokratychnoï partiï Ukraïny*, February 1993; and *Literaturna Ukraïna*, 22 October and 17 December 1992. On the 1994 congress, see *Rozbudova derzhavy*, no. 1 (January), 1995.

88 *Za vil'nu Ukraïnu*, 8 December 1990; V. Lytvyn, 'Ukraïns'ka Khrystyians'ko-demokratychna Partiia', *Polityka i chas*, no. 5 (April), 1991, pp. 62–5; V. Mikhailiv, 'Ukrainskaia natsional'naia partiia', *Politika i vremia*, no. 2 (February), 1992, pp. 64–8; *Visnyk UNP*, 1990–1, passim; V. Lytvyn, 'Ukraïns'ka narodna-demokratychna partiia', *Polityka i chas*, no. 15 (November), 1991, pp. 54–9; *Nezalezhnist'*, 1990–1, passim; *Moloda Halychyna*, 10 April 1990; and V. Mikhailiv, 'Politicheskoe ob"edinenie "Gosudarstvennaia samostoiatel'nost' Ukrainy" (GSU)', *Politika i vremia*, no. 3 (March), 1991, pp. 72–5.

89 Oleh Vitovych, 'Bo my – natsionalisty', *Visti prestsentru UMA*, no. 8 (July), 1991; and 'Zaiava vykonavchoï rady UMA', *Vil'ne slovo*, 19 March 1991.

90 'Politychna rezolutsiia VI sesiï Ukraïns'koï natsional'noï asambleï', *Zamkova hora*, no. 19, 1991.

91 *Zoloti vorota*, no. 5, 1990; *Visnyk Kyïvs'koho komitetu UMA*, no. 1 (June), 1991.

92 Oleksa Haran', 'Do voli – cherez natsional'nyi kongres', *Moloda hvardiia*, 12 October 1990; Riina Kionka, 'The Congress Convenes', *Report on the USSR*, vol. 2, no. 12, 23 March 1990, p. 33.

93 See the remarks by Luk"ianenko in *Moloda hvardiia*, 12 October 1990; and *Protokoly zasidannia sekretariatu URP*, 18 and 20 March 1991.

94 Joseph Rothschild, *Ethnopolitics: A Conceptual Framework* (New York: Columbia University Press, 1981), pp. 72–3; Giovanni Sartori, *Parties and Party Systems: A Framework for Analysis* (Cambridge: Cambridge University Press, 1976), vol. I, pp. 342–9.

95 The National Party and People's Democratic Party left the UIA in 1991 and merged to form the Ukrainian National-Conservative Party in summer 1992: *Post-postup*, no. 19, 1992, and no. 1, 1993.

96 Dmytro Korchyns'kyi, 'Vse i nehaino', *Biblioteka Ukraïns'koï natsionalistychnoï spilky* (Kiev: party material, 1991); Stanislav Ishenko, 'Natsionalizm spravzhnii i "demokratychnyi"', *Napriam*, no. 5 (May), 1991.

97 Oleh Vitovych, 'Bo my – natsionalisty', *Visti prestsentru UMA*, no. 8 (July), 1991.

98 *Moloda Halychyna*, 23 April 1992; *Post-postup*, no. 23, 1992; *Vechirnii Kyïv*, 16 April 1992.

99 *Moloda hvardiia*, 26 September 1990; *Zemlia i volia*, no. 1 (August), 1990.

100 *Holos Ukraïny*, 13 March 1993; author's interview with Serhii Plachynda, 11 February 1992.
101 P. M. Serhin, 'Partiia chy spilka?', *Zemlia i volia*, no. 2 (October), 1990.
102 That is before President Kuchma finally issued a decree authorising the 'deetatisation' (*rozderzhavlennia*), if not the privatisation, of land: Serhii Ter'okhin and Oleksandr Moshonets', 'Zemlia!!! I volia"? ...', *Post-postup*, no. 41, 1994.
103 *Sil's'ki visti*, 8 June and 2 October 1990.
104 Roman Koval', *Pidstavy natsiokratii* (Kiev: DSU, 1994), p. 10.
105 Ibid., p. 9; Roman Koval', 'Chy povynni Ukraïntsi dbaty pro dobrobut Rosiian?', *Rivne*, 27 July 1991; Anatol' Shcherbatiuk, 'Dukh krovi', *Slovo*, no. 4 (March), 1992. See also Roman Koval', *Chy mozhlyve Ukraïno-Rosiis'ke zamyrennia?*; Koval', *Z kym i proty koho* (Kiev: DSU, 1992); and Koval', *Pro vorohiv, soiuznykiv i poputnykiv* (Kiev: DSU, 1993).
106 For material on Dontsov, see the journals *Napriam*, *Derzhavnist'* and *Natsionalist* (the last published by the Club of Supporters of Dmytro Dontsov in L'viv), 1990–4, passim; and *Ukraïns'ki problemy*, no. 1, 1991. For the OUN-UPA, see *Neskorena Natsiia*, no. 14 (August), 1992; *Derzhavnist'*, no. 3 (August), 1992; along with more mainstream publications such as the URP's *Sobornist'*, nos. 5–10, 1990; and *Nezalezhnist'*, nos. 1–11, 1991; or the DPU's *Volia*, no. 13–14 (August), 1991. See also Sviatoslav Pakholkiv, 'OUN i ïï chas', *Slovo*, 1991, passim.
107 The DSU refused to admit non-Ukrainians or former communists as members: author's interviews with Ivan Kandyba and Roman Koval', 2 and 5 May 1992.
108 *Visti prestsentru UMA*, no. 8 (July), 1991.
109 For example, *Pravda Ukrainy*, 18 February and 19 March 1989; *Radians'ka Ukraïna*, 16 and 29 August 1990.
110 *URP-inform*, no. 19, 3 September 1991; and letter by DPU leader Yurii Badz'o to all local party heads dated 9 August 1991.
111 Mykola Porovs'kyi, 'Rukh zaimet'sia ideolohiieiu derzhavy', and 'Rukh i perspektyva', *Holos Ukraïny*, 25 January and 12 February 1992. See also Yurii Badz'o, *Vlada – opozytsiia – derzhava v Ukraïni s'ohodni. Dumky proty techii* (Kiev: Smoloskyp, 1994).
112 V"iacheslav Chornovil, 'Rukh mozhe staty masovishoiu i vplyvovishoiu politychnoiu syloiu', *Narodna hazeta*, no. 19 (December), 1991; and 'Shcho dali?', *Za vil'nu Ukraïnu*, 24 January 1992; Oleksandr Lavrynovych, 'Musymo vyznachytysia', *Narodna hazeta*, no. 1 (January), 1992.
113 *Narodna hazeta*, nos. 9 and 10 (March), 1992; *Vechirnii Kyïv*, 4 March 1992; *Holos Ukraïny*, 3 March 1992; *Za vil'nu Ukraïnu*, 3 and 7 March 1992; *Literaturna Ukraïna*, 5 March 1992; and *Nezavisimaia gazeta*, 3 March 1992.
114 On the CNDF, see *Samostiina Ukraïna*, no. 31 (August), 1992; *Holos Ukraïny*, 4 August 1992; *Literaturna Ukraïna*, 6 August 1992; and *Vechirnii Kyïv*, 3 August 1992. On the fourth Rukh congress, see *IV Velyki Zbory Narodnoho Rukhu Ukraïny. Stenohrafichnyi zvit* (Kiev: Rukh, 1993); *Holos Ukraïny*, 4 and 8 December 1992; *Literaturna Ukraïna*, 17 December 1992; and *Nezavisimost'*, 9 December 1992.

115 *Holos Ukraïny*, 23 February 1993; *Literaturna Ukraïna*, 25 February 1993.
116 *IV Velyki Zbory Narodnoho Rukhu Ukraïny*, pp. 17 and 86; author's interview with V"iacheslav Chornovil, 22 March 1993.
117 The DPU claimed a membership of 3,000. None of the other member parties of the congress were a significant force, although Prosvita claimed 105,000 members on 1 January 1993 (see pp. 132–3 in this volume): *Pozacherhovyi z"izd URP*, p. 11; plus information supplied by DPU and Prosvita secretariats.
118 Roman Solchanyk and Taras Kuzio, 'Democratic Political Blocs in Ukraine', *RFE/RL Research Report*, vol. 2, no. 16, 16 April 1993; and Yevhen Boltarovych, 'Pohliad na Kongres natsional'no-demokratychnykh syl cherez pryzmu formuvannia politychnoï struktury suspil'stva', *Rozbudova derzhavy*, no. 1 (January), 1993.
119 *Narodna hazeta*, no. 27 (July), 1992.
120 *Samostiina Ukraïna*, no. 31 (August), 1992.
121 V. Lytvyn, *Politychna arena Ukraïny*, p. 388; *Samostiina Ukraïna*, nos. 27 and 31 (July and August), 1992.
122 *Demokratychna Ukraïna*, 18 January 1994.
123 *Post-postup*, no. 19, 1992.
124 *Nezavisimost'*, 17 January 1992; *Pershyi z"izd ob"iednannia 'Nova Ukraïna'. Prohramni dokumenty i statut* (Kiev: party material, 1992).
125 *Post-postup*, no. 35, 29 September–5 October 1993.
126 *Nezavisimost'*, 10 December 1993; *Holos Ukraïny*, 25 and 27 January 1994.
127 *Zamkova hora*, no. 19, 1991; *Natsionalist*, no. 2, 1991. The UNA's Viktor Mel'nyk mocked the OUN in his 'OUN: sproba povernennia', *Ukraïns'ki obriï*, no. 6, 1992.
128 Andrii Shkil', interviewed in *Za vil'nu Ukraïnu*, 16 February 1993.
129 Author's interview with Dmytro Korchyns'kyi, 12 May 1992.
130 'Prohrama Ukraïns'koï natsional'noï asambleï', *Ukraïns'ki obriï*, no. 1, 1994.
131 'Politychna prohrama UNA', *Natsionalist*, no. 2, 1992; 'Ideol'ohichna pliatforma Ukraïns'koï natsionalistychnoï spilky', *Ukraïns'ki obriï*, no. 6, 1992; and Viktor Mel'nyk, 'Orientyr – zmina svitohliadu', *Ukraïns'ki obriï*, no. 8, 1992.
132 Oles' Babii, 'UNSO i natsional'na perspektyva', *Ukraïns'ki obriï*, no. 5, 1992.
133 Author's interview with UNSO leader Dmytro Korchyns'kyi, 12 May 1992. UNSO's programme is in *Zamkova hora*, no. 9, 1992. See also Taras Kuzio, 'Paramilitary Groups in Ukraine', *Jane's Intelligence Review*, March 1994, pp. 123–5; and Bohdan Nahaylo, 'Ukraine' in the special *RFE/RL Research Report* issue on extremism, vol. 3, no. 16, 22 April 1994.
134 *Vechirnii Kyïv*, 14 May 1992; *Za vil'nu Ukraïnu*, 16 February 1993. The figure of 14,000 seems to have represented the nominal total membership of all the component parts of the old UIA.
135 *Neskorena Natsiia*, no. 1 (January), 1993.
136 *Ukraïns'ke slovo*, 4 June 1993; Serhii Taran (ed.), *OUN: mynule i maibuttia* (Kiev: O. Ol'zhycha, 1993).
137 Slava Stets'ko, 'Ukraïns'kyi natsionalizm i ioho rolia v zakriplenni ta

rozbudovi Ukraïns'koï Samostiinoï Sobornoï Derzhavy', *Konferentsiia Uk-raïns'kykh Natsionalistiv: vybrani materiialy* (Kiev: KUN, 1992).

138 *Protokoly zasidannia sekretariatu URP*, 20 March 1991 and April 1991 passim; author's interview with Serhii Zhyzhko, 5 May 1992.

139 Roman Zvarych, interviewed by the author and Dominique Arel, 21 June 1994; *Holos Ukraïny*, 31 March 1992; *Vyzvol'nyi shliakh*, no. 1 (January), 1993; and *Na novomu etapi: vybrani materiialy pershoho zboru KUN* (Kiev: KUN, 1993).

140 *Neskorena Natsiia*, no. 17 (December), 1993.

141 *Shliakh peremohy*, 16 April 1994; *Zerkalo nedeli*, no. 8, 1995.

142 *Materialy nadzvychainoï konferentsiï UKRP* (Kiev: party material, 1992); *Vechirnii Kyïv*, 19 June 1992; 'II z"ïzd UKRP', *Klych*, no. 19, 1994.

143 *Zerkalo nedeli*, no. 8, 1995; 'Stepan Khmara – yakyi vin naspravdi?', *Klych*, no. 14, 1994.

144 *Holos Ukraïny*, 31 October 1992; *Za vil'nu Ukraïnu*, 13 June, 27 October, 7 November, and 3 December 1992; and *Ukraïns'ki visti*, 29 November 1992. For Moroz's modern-day views, see his 'Adieu, meine Herren', *Derzhavnist'*, no. 1 (January–March), 1992, pp. 22–9.

145 Omar Uzarashvili, 'Sotsial-natsionalisti: peretvoryty halychynu na prusiiu', *Demoz*, no. 3, 1994; *Vidozva SNPU*, party brochure dated summer 1992. See also the party's journal *Sotsial natsionalist*, 1994–5, passim.

146 *Post-postup*, no. 49, 1992; *Ukrainian Weekly*, 14 March 1993; *Narodnaia armiia*, 18 March 1993.

147 Grzegorz Ekiert, 'Democratic Processes in East Central Europe: A Theoretical Reconsideration', *British Journal of Political Science*, vol. 21, part 3 (July 1991), pp. 285–313.

148 *Prosvita*, no. 31 (October), 1991; *Slovo*, no. 19 (December), 1991. See also *Holos Ukraïny*, 14 December 1993.

149 D. O. Svidnyk, 'Vidrodzhennia "Prosvita"', in Ivanychuk *et al.*, *Narys istoriï Prosvity*, pp. 86–117, at pp. 113–15; *Holos Ukraïny*, 14 April 1992; and *Narodna hazeta*, no. 13 (May), 1992.

150 List provided by Prosvita secretariat (down from 140,000 in 1991).

151 On the founding congress of the UOU, see *Za vil'nu Ukraïnu*, 24 and 27 July 1991; and *Literaturna Ukraïna*, 25 July 1991. On the November congress, see *Za vil'nu Ukraïnu*, 6 and 7 November 1991; and *Literaturna Ukraïna*, 31 October and 7 November 1991.

152 Oleksandr Sliusarev, 'Nam potribna nova spilka', and 'Nabahato vazhche zrobyty real'nu spravu', *Ukraïns'ki obriï*, nos. 4 and 5 (March), 1993.

153 The relatively moderate General Skypyl's'kyi defeated the radicals' standard-bearer Colonel Sliusarev by 346 votes to 194: *Ukraïns'ki obriï*, nos. 7 and 11, 1993.

154 Taras Kuzio, 'Ukraine's Young Turks – The Union of Ukrainian Officers [sic]', *Jane's Intelligence Review*, vol. 5, no. 1 (January 1993); *Holos Ukraïny*, 7 April 1992; *Visti z Ukraïny*, 24 February–2 March 1994; *Vechirnii Kyïv*, 4 September 1992.

155 *Ukraïns'ki obriï*, no. 10, 1992.

156 *L'vivs'ki novyny*, no. 12, 1988. The one exception was the UNA-UNSO, whose rough-house tactics against 'speculators' and 'Mafiosi' won it some

support even in unpromising areas like Luhans'k: Yurii Korzhykov, 'Skhidni motyvy UNA-UNSO', *Demoz*, no. 5, 1995.
157 *URP-inform*, no. 12, 18 July 1991.
158 *Holos Ukraïny*, 23 February 1995.
159 *Moloda Halychyna*, 25 June 1991; *Za vil'nu Ukraïnu*, 27 June 1991; Volodymyr Lytvyn, 'Novi politychni partiï i robitnychnyi rukh', *Polityka i chas*, no. 13 (September), 1991, pp. 41–6; and *Mist: hazeta vil'nykh profspilok*, no. 11, September 1993.
160 *Novosti i sobytiia* (Donets'k), nos. 20–1, 1993.
161 *Za vil'nu Ukraïnu*, 12 June 1993.
162 *Zakon i biznes*, no. 16 (April), 1992; *Holos Ukraïny*, 21 April 1992 and 10 March 1993. Kuchma resigned from his UUIM post after his election as president.
163 *Post-postup*, no. 43, 1992; *Donetskii kriazh*, 17–23 September 1993.
164 *Holos Ukraïny*, 3 February and 30 March 1993; *Robitnycha hazeta*, 2 April 1993; and *Molod' Ukraïny*, 2 March 1993.
165 V. A. Holovenko and M. Yu. Pashkov, *Zbirnyk materialiv pro molodizhni ob"iednannia Ukraïny* (Kiev: Ukrainian Scientific-Research Institute on the Problems of Youth, 1991); Taras Karpalo, *The Ukrainian Student Movement: A Brief Account* (London: Ukrainian Central Information Service, 1991, bulletin no. 120).
166 Nataliia Chernysh *et al.*, *Natsional'na svidomist' students'koï molodi: sotsiolohichnyi analiz* (Edmonton, Ont.: CIUS, 1993); Oleksandr Bulavin and Oleksandr Korniievs'kyi, 'Molod' i maibutnie suchasnykh polityzovanykh hromads'kykh ob"iednan", *Politolohichni chytannia*, no. 4, 1992, pp. 128–39.
167 *Molod' Ukraïny*, 18 April 1991.
168 S. Yanovs'kyi, 'SNUM: z kym i proty koho?', *Radians'ka osvita*, 24 April 1990; *Biblioteka Ukraïns'koï natsionalistychnoï spilky: zbirka stattei, chastyna 1* (Kiev: Samizdat, 1991); *Moloda halychyna*, 21 January 1992.
169 See the L'viv journal *Napriam*, 1991–2, passim.
170 *Politychne ob"iednannia 'Tretia Respublika': informatsiinyi visnyk*, no. 1 (March), 1992.
171 Ann Lencyk Pawliczko (ed.), *Ukraine and Ukrainians Throughout the World: A Demographic and Sociological Guide to the Homeland and Its Diaspora* (Toronto: University of Toronto Press, 1994); V. B. Yevtukh *et al.* (eds.), *Zberihaiuchy ukraïns'ku samobutnist'* (Kiev: Intel, 1992); V. I. Patrushev *et al.*, *Ukraïns'ka diaspora u sviti* (Kiev: Znannia, 1993); and the journal *Ukraïns'ka diaspora*, 1993–5 passim.
172 *Holos Ukraïny*, 13 November 1991, 23 January and 10 June 1992; *Za vil'nu Ukraïnu*, 18 and 21 January 1992; *Vechirnii Kyïv*, 30 July 1992; *Literaturna Ukraïna*, 22 July 1993; and Zastavnyi, 'Ukraïns'ke natsional'no-kul'turne vidrodzhennia', in his *Skhidna ukraïns'ka diaspora*, pp. 131–7.
173 *Literaturna Ukraïna*, 23 September 1993.
174 *Ukrainian Weekly*, 31 October 1993; and *My – grazhdane Rosii: Materialy 1 Kongressa ukraintsev v Rossii* (Moscow: Slavianskii dialog, 1994).
175 *Narodna armiia*, 6 March 1992.
176 *Informatsiinyi biuleten' ukraïns'koho komitetu 'Helsinki-90'*, no. 1 (August),

1990; *Robitnycha hazeta*, 13 August 1992. In June 1991 the society organised the first All-World Congress of Ukrainian Political Prisoners in Kiev: *Samostiina Ukraïna*, no. 7 (June), 1991.

177 *Za vil'nu Ukraïnu*, 1 May 1991.

178 *Moloda hvardiia*, 11 March 1991.

179 Vasyl Markus, *Religion and Nationalism in Soviet Ukraine After 1945* (Cambridge, Mass.: Ukrainian Studies Fund, 1985); and Markus, 'Religion and Nationalism in Ukraine', in Petro Ramet (ed.), *Religion and Nationalism in Soviet and Eastern European Politics* (Durham, N.C.: Duke University Press, 1984), pp. 59–81. See also the collection of Church samizdat documents, O. Zinkevych, O. Voronyn, and T. R. Lonchyna (eds.), *Martyrolohiia ukraïns'kykh tserkov: dokumenty, materialy Khrystians'kii samvydav Ukraïny* (Baltimore: Smoloskyp, 1985–7).

180 Bociurkiw, 'Ukrainian Catholic Church'.

181 CSACOU, f. 1, op. 11, delo 2051, p. 6; and delo 1853, pp. 117–22.

182 Leila Prelec, 'Where Orthodox and Catholic Meet', and Leila Tsakarissianou, 'Dysfunctional Family or Bridge to Unity?', *Catholic World Report*, February 1994, pp. 24–36. See also the interview with Frank E. Sysyn in *Ukrainian Weekly*, 29 August 1993.

183 *Postup*, no. 5 (21 May), 1991, quoting an official report to the Ukrainian Parliament. *Ukrainian Weekly*, 26 December 1993 claimed that the Uniates had 2,200 churches and 'more than 4 million faithful'.

184 *Ukrainian Weekly*, 18 and 25 July 1993.

185 Serhii Plokhy, 'Between Moscow and Rome: The Struggle for the Greek-Catholic Patriarchate', *Ukrainian Weekly*, 6 February 1994.

186 David Marples and Ostap Skrypnyk, 'Patriarch Mstyslav and the Revival of the Ukrainian Autocephalous Orthodox Church', *Report on the USSR*, 11 January 1991.

187 As n. 183. The UAOC was also making some progress in Volhynia, a strongly nationalist area with no real Uniate tradition since 1839.

188 Bohdan Bociurkiw, 'Politics and Religion in Ukraine: The Orthodox and the Greek Catholics', in Michael Bordeaux (ed.), *The Politics of Religion in Russia and the New States of Eurasia* (Armonk, N. Y.: M. E. Sharpe, 1995), pp. 131–62; John Anderson, *Religion, State and Politics in the Soviet Union and Successor States* (Cambridge: Cambridge University Press, 1994), pp. 188–91; and Andrii Tkachuk, *Mytropolyt Mstyslav* (Kiev: Biblioteka Ukraïntsia, no. 3–6, 1993), pp. 35–59.

189 *Holos Ukraïny*, 29 May 1992.

190 Filaret's biography can be found in *Moscow News*, no. 29, 1992.

191 *Holos Ukraïny*, 27 June 1992.

192 Ibid., 2 June 1992.

193 Information supplied by the UOC (KP) chancellery in Kiev.

194 *Holos Ukraïny*, 7 September 1993.

195 Ibid., 22 and 23 October 1993. See also the interview with Romaniuk in *Literaturna Ukraïna*, 23 December 1993. Romaniuk won eighty-five votes to Filaret's thirty-four: Bociurkiw, 'Politics and Religion in Ukraine', p. 161.

196 *Nezavisimost'*, 5 January 1994.

197 The first poll was only undertaken in urban areas: Jaroslaw Martyniuk, 'Religious Preferences in Five Urban Areas of Ukraine', *RFE/RL Research Report*, vol. 2, no. 15, 9 April 1993. The second was broader and more representative: Martyniuk, 'The State of the Orthodox Church in Ukraine', *RFE/RL Research Report*, vol. 3, no. 7, 18 February 1994.

198 Wilson and Bilous, 'Political Parties in Ukraine'; Andrew Wilson and Valentin Yakushik, 'Politychni orhanizatsii v Ukraïni (deiaki problemy stanovlennia i rozvytku)', *Suchasnist'*, May 1992, pp. 160–5.

199 Maurizio Cotta, 'Building Party Systems After the Dictatorship: The East European Case in Comparative Perspective', in Geoffrey Pridham and Tatu Vanhanen (eds.), *Democratisation in Eastern Europe: Domestic and International Perspectives* (London: Routledge, 1994), pp. 99–127.

4 NATIONAL COMMUNISM

1 Levko Luk''ianenko, *De dobryi shliakh?* (Kiev: URP, 1994), p. 18. Cf. Luk''ianenko's comment that 'the glittering victory [in the December 1991 referendum] only became possible because both nationalists and communists agitated for independence': *Samostiina Ukraïna*, no. 20 (May), 1992.

2 James E. Mace, *Communism and the Dilemmas of National Liberation: National Communism in Soviet Ukraine, 1918–1933* (Cambridge, Mass.: Harvard University Press, 1983); Liber, *Soviet Nationality Policy*.

3 Ivan Lysiak-Rudnytsky, 'Volodymyr Vynnychenko's Ideas in the Light of His Political Writing', in his *Essays in Modern Ukrainian History*, pp. 417–46; Natalia Kychyhina, 'Politychna kontseptsiia V. K. Vynnychenka', *Politolohichni chytannia*, no. 2, 1994, pp. 83–95; Holota, *Symon Petliura*.

4 Ivan Maistrenko, *Istoriia Komunistychnoï partiï Ukraïny* (Munich: Suchasnist', 1979), pp. 32–80; Heorhii Kas'ianov, 'Vlada ta inteligentsiia na Ukraïni v roky NEPu', *Journal of Ukrainian Studies*, vol. 15, no. 2 (Winter 1990), pp. 19–32.

5 Maistrenko, *Istoriia Komunistychnoï partiï Ukraïny*, pp. 45–8; S. O. Vasyl'chenko, V. K. Vasylenko, P. L. Varhatiuk and L. M. Hordiienko, *Storinky istoriï Kompartiï Ukraïny: zapytannia i vidpovidi* (Kiev: Lybid', 1990), pp. 85–7 and 90–2. The Ukrainian communists were known as the Communist Party (Bolshevik) of Ukraine until 1951.

6 Reprinted in *Politolohichni chytannia*, no. 3, 1993, pp. 179–268. See also Ivan Lysiak-Rudnyts'kyi, 'Ukraïns'kyi komunistychnyi manifest', in his *Istorychni ese* (Kiev: Osnovy, 1994), vol. II, pp. 113–20.

7 M. O. Skrypnyk, *Vybrani tvory* (Kiev: Ukraïna, 1991).

8 Yu. I. Shapoval, *Ukraïna 20–50-kh rokiv: storinky nenapysanoï istoriï* (Kiev: Naukova dumka, 1993), chapters 1 to 3; Shkandrij, *Modernists, Marxists and the Nation*, chapter 2; and V. A. Hrechenko, 'Do istoriï vnutripartiinoï borot'by v Ukraïni u 20-ti roky', *Ukraïns'kyi istorychnyi zhurnal*, no. 9, 1993, pp. 114–21. In the Soviet 1920s there were of course no west Ukrainians in the party, although there were some links between the CP(b)U and the CPWU.

9 Danylenko *et al.*, *Stalinizm na Ukraïni*, p. 252.

10 Hrushevs′kyi returned to work in the Academy of Sciences in 1924, fell out of favour again in the 1930s and died in Russia in 1934.

11 Mykhailo Volobuiev, *Do problemy ukraïns′koï ekonomiky: dokumenty ukraïns′ koho komunizmu* (New York: Prolog, 1962).

12 Mykola Khvyl′ovyi, *Tvory u dvokh tomakh* (Kiev: Dnipro, 1990), 2 vols.; Shkandrij, *Modernists, Marxists and the Nation*, chapter 4; and George S. N. Luckyi, *Literary Politics in the Soviet Ukraine, 1917–1934* (Durham, N.C.: Duke University Press, 2nd edn, 1990). Khvyl′ovyi and VAPLITE were always more radical than Skrypnyk and Shums′kyi, but enjoyed a degree of official protection.

13 Cf. George G. Grabowicz, 'Province to Nation: Nineteenth-Century Ukrainian Literature as a Paradigm of the National Revival', *Canadian Review of Studies in Nationalism*, vol. 16, no. 1–2 (1989), pp. 117–32.

14 Khvyl′ovyi, 'Ukraïna chy Malorosiia?', in *Tvory*, vol. II, pp. 576–621.

15 Anthony D. Smith, *The Ethnic Revival* (Cambridge: Cambridge University Press, 1981), chapter 5; Smith, *Theories of Nationalism* (London: Holmes and Meier, 1983), chapters 6 and 10.

16 As the Soviet state was formally an ethno-territorial state it could not really be described as Austro-Marxist. The quote is from Motyl, *Sovietology, Rationality, Nationality*, chapter 6, at p. 88. See also Motyl, 'From Imperial Decay to Imperial Collapse: The Fall of the Soviet Empire in Comparative Perspective', in Rudolph and Good, *Nationalism and Empire*, pp. 15–43; and Philip G. Roeder, 'Soviet Federalism and Ethnic Mobilisation', *World Politics*, vol. 43, 1991, pp. 196–232.

17 Motyl, *Sovietology, Rationality, Nationality*, pp. 96 and 93. See also S. N. Eisenstadt, 'Centre–Periphery Relations in the Soviet Empire: Some Interpretative Observations', in Motyl, *Thinking Theoretically About Soviet Nationalities*, pp. 203–23.

18 Motyl, *Sovietology, Rationality, Nationality*, pp. 87–8 and 96–7.

19 Vasyl′chenko *et al.*, *Storinky istoriï Kompartiï Ukraïny*, pp. 484–5; and Bohdan Krawchenko, 'Changes in the National and Social Composition of the Communist Party of Ukraine from the Revolution to 1976', *Journal of Ukrainian Studies*, vol. 9, no. 1 (Summer 1984), pp. 33–54.

20 V. L. Savel′iev, 'Storinky politychnoï biohrafiï M. V. Pidhornoho', *Ukraïns′kyi istorychnyi zhurnal*, no. 1 (January), 1991, pp. 78–86. See also Borys Lewytzkyj, *Politics and Society in Soviet Ukraine, 1953–1980* (Edmonton, Ont.: CIUS, 1984); Yaroslav Bilinsky, *The Second Soviet Republic: The Ukraine After World War II* (New Brunswick, N.J.: Rutgers University Press, 1964); and V. K. Baran, *Ukraïna pislia Stalina: narys istoriï 1953–1985 rr.* (L′viv: Svoboda, 1992).

21 Dmytro Pavlychko, 'Chomu ya holosuvav za Leonida Kravchuka', *Literaturna Ukraïna*, 30 June 1994.

22 V. L. Savel′iev, 'Chy buv P. Yu. Shelest vyraznykom "ukraïns′koho avtonomizmu"?', *Ukraïns′kyi istorychnyi zhurnal*, no. 4, 1991, pp. 94–105, refutes this view. See especially the remarks by Drach and Chornovil quoted on p. 102.

23 Kas′ianov, *Nezhodni*, p. 96.

24 Vitalii Koval′, 'Protokol odnoho Plenumu. Khto "znimav" Olesia Honchara

z posady holovy pravlinnia Spilky pys'mennykiv Ukraïny', *Literaturna Ukraïna*, 14 October 1993; Savel'iev, 'Chy buv P. Yu. Shelest vyraznykom "ukraïns'koho avtonomizmu"?', p. 102; Kas'ianov, *Nezhodni*, p. 78–9.

25 See the reprint of a 1968 CPU Central Committee document in *Holos Ukraïny*, 27 August 1994.

26 On Shelest, see Kuzio and Wilson, *Ukraine: Perestroika to Independence*, pp. 44–7; Grey Hodnett, 'The Views of Petro Shelest', *Annals of the Ukrainian Academy of Arts and Sciences in the United States*, vol. 14, nos. 37–8 (1978–80), pp. 209–43; Jaroslaw Pelenski, 'Shelest and His Period in Soviet Ukraine (1963–1972): A Revival of Controlled Ukrainian Autonomism', in Potichnyj, *Ukraine in the 1970s*, pp. 283–305; and Yaroslav Bilinsky, 'Mykola Skrypnyk and Petro Shelest: An Essay in the Persistence and Limits of Ukrainian National Communism', in J. R. Azrael (ed.), *Soviet Nationality Politics and Practices* (New York: Praeger, 1978).

27 On Shcherbyts'kyi, see Kuzio and Wilson, *Ukraine: Perestroika to Independence*, pp. 47–50; Bohdan Krawchenko (ed.), *Ukraine After Shelest* (Edmonton, Ont.: CIUS, 1983); Potichnyj, *Ukraine in the 1970s*; Yaroslav Bilinsky, 'Shcherbytsky, Ukraine and Kremlin Politics', *Problems of Communism*, vol. 32, no. 4 (July–August 1983), pp. 1–26; and Lytvyn and Sliusarenko, 'Na politychnii areni Ukraïny'. One of Shcherbyts'kyi's aides produced an apologia in 1993: Vrublevskii, *Vladimir Shcherbitskii*. See also Oleh Bazhan, ' "Mene nazyvaiut' suchasnym Kochubeiem . . ." Notatky na poliakh politychnoï biohrafiï V. Yu. Malanchuka', *Literaturna Ukraïna*, 2 December 1993.

28 Roman Solchanyk, 'Language Politics in the Ukraine'; Arel, *Language and the Politics of Ethnicity*, chapter 4; and Oleksa Myshanych, 'Ukraïns'ka literatura pid zaboronoiu: 1937–1990', *Literaturna Ukraïna*, 18 August 1994.

29 Alexander J. Motyl, *Will the Non-Russians Rebel? State, Ethnicity and Stability in the USSR* (Ithaca: Cornell University Press, 1987) deals mainly with Ukraine and remains interesting despite its unfortunate timing (Motyl's answer was 'no'). The political conditions that Motyl describes as preventing rebellion in the mid-1980s were about to be undermined by Gorbachev's reforms.

30 CSACOU, f. 1, op. 11, delo 2023, p. 1, dated 27 February 1989.

31 CSACOU, f. 1, op. 11, delo 2051, p. 1; f. 1, op. 11, delo 2033, p. 10; and f. 1, op. 1, delo 1737. During 1989 there were 28 criminal and 1,125 'administrative' cases against 'extremists': f. 1, op. 2, delo 1093, p. 267.

32 CSACOU, f. 1, op. 2, delo 1002, pp. 13 and 15.

33 Volodymyr Lytvyn, *Politychna arena Ukraïny*, p. 99.

34 CSACOU, f. 1, op. 11, delo 2051; f. 1, op. 11, delo 1775.

35 Apart from one isolated statement as late as August 1989, namely 'I will not sit round a table with Chornovil, but it's necessary to talk with others': CSACOU, f. 1, op. 2, delo 1005, p. 115 (a Central Committee document dated 7 August 1989).

36 CSACOU, f. 1, op. 11, delo 2061 and delo 1881.

37 CSACOU, f. 1, op. 2, delo 976, pp. 46 and 42; f. 1, op. 2, delo 1005, pp. 60 and 115–8, at p. 118.

38 CSACOU, f. 1, op. 11, delo 2032; interview with Leonid Kravchuk, *Ukraïns'ka hazeta*, no. 5, 1994; Valentyn Chemerys, *Prezydent: Roman-ese* (Kiev: Svenas, 1994), p. 40.

39 At the Ukrainian Central Committee plenum on 28 September 1989, Ivashko won 136 votes as against 43 for his more conservative rival Stanislav Hurenko: CSACOU, f. 1, op. 2, delo 992, p. 75.

40 Roman Solchanyk, 'Shcherbitsky Leaves the Political Arena: The End of an Era?', *Report on the USSR*, RL 457/89, 6 October 1989.

41 This chapter does not describe events at the all-Union level in detail as it is assumed readers will already be familiar with them.

42 CSACOU, f. 1, op. 2, delo 996, pp. 14 and 16; delo 11021, pp. 100–1.

43 CSACOU, f. 1, op. 11, delo 1892; and delo 2181, pp. 19–83.

44 CSACOU, f. 1, op. 2, delo 11021, pp. 96–8.

45 CSACOU, f. 1, op. 2, delo 1093, pp. 160 and 166.

46 CSACOU, f. 1, op. 2, delo 1093. See also the 'programmatic principles' of the CPU published in *Radians'ka Ukraïna*, 5 April 1990.

47 *Holos Ukraïny*, 15 August 1991.

48 CSACOU, f. 1, op. 2, delo 1021, p. 99.

49 Ibid., pp. 99–102. On the congress, see *Radians'ka Ukraïna*, 27–9 June 1990.

50 At the February 1990 plenum Ivashko stressed that 'the fate of the party itself' was at stake: CSACOU, f. 1, op. 2, delo 1093, pp. 5–16, at p. 7.

51 Speech of the leading nationalist deputy Larysa Skoryk at the founding conference of the Congress of National-Democratic Forces in Kiev in August 1992: *Samostiina Ukraïna*, no. 31 (August), 1992.

52 'Hei, vy ... otamany!', *Zakarpats'ka pravda*, 30 April 1991. National-democrats were even more explicit in private: *Protokoly prezidiï DemPU*, nos. 10 and 15, 5 March and 23 April 1991; Bohdan Horyn', *Stratehiia i taktyka URP*, speech delivered at L'viv conference of URP, 2 February 1991.

53 H. P. Kharchenko, CPU first secretary in Zaporizhzhia, at the Twenty-Eighth Ukrainian Party Congress: CSACOU, f. 1, op. 2, delo 1022, p. 31.

54 Leonid Kravchuk and Serhii Kychyhin, *Leonid Kravchuk: ostanni dni imperiï ... Pershi roky nadiï* (Kiev: Dovira, 1994), p. 41.

55 See CSACOU, f. 1, op. 11, delo 2093; and f. 1, op. 2, delo 1026; and the discussion on the new party programme in November 1989: CSACOU, f. 1, op. 2, delo 1000.

56 CSACOU, f. 1, op. 11, delo 2051, pp. 35–9, 55–6 and 77–9; f. 1, op. 11, delo 2089, pp. 21, 37 and 45.

57 CSACOU, f. 1, op. 2, delo 1105, pp. 20–3.

58 CSACOU, f. 1, op. 11, delo 2268, p. 19.

59 CSACOU, f. 1, op. 2, delo 996, p. 33; delo 1021, p. 116.

60 Kravchuk and Kychyhin, *Leonid Kravchuk*, p. 203.

61 CSACOU, f. 1, op. 2, delo 1024, p. 58; delo 996, p. 9.

62 CSACOU, f. 1, op. 11, delo 2185, p. 111; f. 1, op. 2, delo 1117, p. 34. See also the letter in *Ternopil' Vechirnii*, 15 June 1991.

63 Interview with communist deputy Mykola Shkarban, *Holos Ukraïny*, 26 June 1991. See also 'Ugrozhaet li KPU raskol?', *Vechernii Kiev*, 19 June 1991.

64 CSACOU, f. 1, op. 2, delo 1105, p. 53; delo 1117, pp. 9–10.
65 CSACOU, f. 1, op. 2, delo 1021, pp. 15 and 166; f. 1, op. 2, delo 1054, p. 36.
66 Ivan Salii, *Ya povertaius'*, p. 154.
67 *Materialy XXVIII z"izdu Komunistychnoi'partii' Ukraïny, 13–14 hrudnia 1990 roku (druhyi etap)* (Kiev: Ukraïna, 1991).
68 CSACOU, f. 1, op. 2, delo 1117, p. 10; delo 1035, p. 2. See also 'Zauvazhennia i propozytsiï partiinykh i radians'kykh orhaniv do Statutu Kompartiï Ukraïny': CSACOU, f. 1, op. 11, delo 2185, dated 23 August to 5 October 1990.
69 Oleksandr Moroz, *Kudy idemo?* (Kiev: Postup, 1993), pp. 115 and 111. See also Moroz, 'Parlaments'ka bil'shist'', *Polityka i chas*, no. 9 (June), 1991; his comments in *Pravda*, 16 July 1991; and Borys Oliinyk, *Dva roky v Kremli* (Kiev: Sil's'ki visti, 1992), p. 37.
70 CSACOU, f. 1, op. 2, delo 1117, p. 33; delo 1021, p. 144.
71 CSACOU, f. 1, op. 11, delo 2280, p. 18.
72 'Protokol zasedaniia plenuma TsK Kompartii Ukrainy 26 avgusta 1991 g.', in S. I. Hurenko, A. P. Savchenko and V. G. Matveev (eds.), *Kommunisticheskaia partiia Ukrainy: khronika zapreta* (Donets'k: Interbuk, 1992), pp. 38–50, at pp. 39 and 41; this volume is a collection of documents on the last days of the CPU.
73 *Pozacherhova sesiia Verkhovnoi' Rady ukraïns'koï RSR dvanadtsiatoho sklykannia: biuleten' no. 1* (Kiev: Vydannia Verkhovnoï Rady UkRSR, session of 24 August 1991), p. 84. Moroz claims to have proposed a more resolute and independent line during the coup: Moroz, *Kudy idemo?*, pp. 125–6.
74 The group's programme was published in *Radians'ka Ukraïna*, 3 June 1990. See also *Vechirnii Kyïv*, 30 March 1990.
75 'Pro konsolidatsiiu Kompartiï Ukraïny ta protydiiu stvorenno v nii fraktsiinykh uhrupuvan'': CSACOU, f. 1, op. 11, delo 2165, pp. 69–72, document dated 13 April 1990.
76 Author's conversation with Valerii Khmel'ko, co-leader of first the Democratic Platform and then the PDRU, 29 February 1995.
77 *Vechirnii Kyïv*, 3 July 1990.
78 CSACOU, f. 1, op. 11, delo 2279, p. 158; f. 1, op. 2, delo 996, p. 6; f. 1, op. 11, delo 2253, p. 40.
79 On Kravchuk, see Leonid Kravchuk, *Ye taka derzhava – Ukraïna* (Kiev: Globus, 1992; a collection of speeches and interviews); Chemerys, *Prezydent: Roman-ese*; and Kravchuk and Kychyhin, *Leonid Kravchuk*. On the rise of the national communists, see Kuzio and Wilson, *Ukraine: Perestroika to Independence*, chapter 8; and Haran', *Ubyty drakona*, pp. 157–69.
80 Kravchuk interviewed in *Holos Ukraïny*, 3 September 1994.
81 CSACOU, f. 1, op. 11, delo 2093, p. 39.
82 'Propozytsiï z deiakykh aktual'nykh pytan' kul'turnoï polityky': CSACOU, f. 1, op. 11, delo 2165, pp. 102–9 and 84.
83 *Holos Ukraïny*, 15 August 1991.
84 It is fascinating to speculate what might have happened if Ivashko had remained at the helm. A more united CPU would probably have put up greater resistance to the national communist temptation.

85 At the Twenty-Eighth CPU Congress, Hurenko defeated the token opposition of Ivan Salii, party first secretary in Podil', Kiev, by 1,383 votes to 194: CSACOU, f. 1, op. 2, delo 1024, pp. 207–8; Salii, *Ya povertaius'*, p. 155. In the parliamentary voting, Kravchuk won 224 votes in the first round as against 140 for Yukhnovs'kyi, the opposition's candidate. Yukhnovs'kyi then withdrew from the second round, allowing Kravchuk to win with 239 votes: V. Lytvyn, *Politychna arena Ukraïny*, p. 241.

86 Thomas F. Remington, 'Introduction', in his *Parliaments in Transition*, pp. 1–27.

87 Kravchuk and Kychyhin, *Leonid Kravchuk*, p. 95.

88 Either in Moscow or on party business in Ukraine. Moreover, because many CPU deputies were local bigwigs (factory directors, collective farm chairmen), they had their own affairs to attend to.

89 CSACOU, f. 1, op. 11, delo 2202, p. 1.

90 'Pro posylennia roli Komunistiv – narodnykh deputativ v stabilizatsiï suspil'no-politychnoï obstanovky v respublitsi': CSACOU, f. 1, op. 11, delo 2202, pp. 9–15; and f. 1, op. 2, delo 1130, p. 166.

91 Once again Gorbachev's policies were having unforeseen effects. The attempt to transfer power from the party to the (local) state simply deprived him of compliant negotiating partners.

92 Taniuk, *Khto z"ïv moie m"iaso?*, p. 323; and Taniuk, 'Komentar do tr'okh zasidan' Prezydiï Verkhovnoï Rady Ukraïny', in Taniuk and Krymchuk, *Khronika oporu*, pp. 114–22; Serhii Bilokin' *et al.*, *Khto ye khto v ukraïns'kii politytsi* (Kiev: Tov. Petra Mohyly, 1993), p. 208 and passim.

93 Dominique Arel, 'Voting Behaviour in the Ukrainian Parliament: The Language Factor', in Remington, *Parliaments in Transition*, pp. 125–58, at pp. 146–7.

94 CSACOU, f. 1, op. 11, delo 2202, p. 14; f. 1, op. 2, delo 1130, p. 168.

95 CSACOU, f. 1, op. 11, delo 2198, p. 6.

96 CSACOU, f. 1, op. 2, delo 1064, p. 110; f. 1, op. 11, delo 2198, pp. 32 and 31.

97 CSACOU, f. 1, op. 2, delo 1063, p. 26; f. 1, op. 11, delo 2165, pp. 94–8. See also Hurenko's comments in *Radians'ka Ukraïna*, 15 March 1991 and *Pravda Ukrainy*, 6 March 1991. Vitalii Masol, prime minister/head of the cabinet of ministers from 1987 to October 1990, attacked 'Galician ideological aggression' in the same fashion: Vitalii Masol, '"Parad suverenitetov"': raspad soiuza SSR', in his *Upushchennyi shans* (Kiev: Molod', 1993), pp. 53–81, at p. 64.

98 Ivan Pliushch, *Khto my i kudy idemo* (Kiev: Ukraïna, 1993), pp. 54–5, 62, 70–4 and 83.

99 *Holos Ukraïny*, 22 November and 15 August 1991; *Vechirnii Kyïv*, 10 January 1992. On the use of Cossack mythology, see Frank E. Sysyn, 'The Reemergence of the Ukrainian Nation and Cossack Mythology', *Social Research*, vol. 58, no. 4 (Winter 1991), pp. 845–64; Motyl, *Dilemmas of Independence*, pp. 85–7; and Serhii M. Plokhy, 'Historical Debates and Territorial Claims: Cossack Mythology in the Russian–Ukrainian Border Dispute', in Starr, *Legacy of History*, pp. 147–70.

100 *Komsomol'skoe znamia*, 4 September 1991.

101 *News from Ukraine*, no. 25 (June), 1991.
102 CSACOU, f. 1, op. 2, delo 1130, pp. 19–23, 50 and 89–93; *Pravda*, 4 February 1991.
103 CSACOU, f. 1, op. 2, delo 1135, p. 14; f. 1, op. 2, delo 1130, pp. 8–29; and f. 1, op. 11, delo 2256, p. 43; Kravchuk and Kychyhin, *Leonid Kravchuk*, pp. 16 and 101.
104 CSACOU, f. 1, op. 2, delo 1147; f. 11, op. 11, delo 2256 and delo 2257.
105 CSACOU, f. 1, op. 2, delo 1130, p. 89.
106 Ibid., p. 184.
107 Kravchuk's supporters seem to have influenced the more radical draft for a new Ukrainian constitution presented to the Central Committee in July 1991: CSACOU, f. 1, op. 11, delo 2279. See also Roman Solchanyk, 'Ukraine Considers a New Constitution', *Report on the USSR*, vol. 3, no. 23, RL 215/91, 7 June 1991.
108 CSACOU, f. 1, op. 2, delo 1130.
109 CSACOU, f. 1, op. 2, delo 1140, p. 112. According to information supplied to the author by Dominique Arel, 75 per cent (181 members) of the original 'Group of 239' voted in favour of the hardline resolution to place only Gorbachev's question on the ballot.
110 For the views of some of Kravchuk's supporters, see 'Prezydent hotovyi. A my?' and 'Soiuz neporushnyi? . . .', *Holos Ukraïny*, 26 June and 19 July 1991.
111 See for example the contrasting speeches of Levko Luk''ianenko and Stepan Khmara at the second URP congress in June 1991: *II z"izd URP*, pp. 7–44.
112 *Zakon URSR pro prezydenta ukraïns'koï RSR* (Kiev: Ukraïna, 1991); Andrew Wilson, 'Ukraine: Two Presidents, But No Settled Powers', in Ray Taras (ed.), *Presidential Systems in Post-Communist States: A Comparative Analysis* (forthcoming).
113 'Stenohrama narady v TsK KPU z pershymy sekretariamy obkomiv partiï': CSACOU, f. 1, op. 2, delo 1145, dated 17 June 1991; Roman Solchanyk, 'Ukraine and the Union Treaty', *Report on the USSR*, vol. 3, no. 30, 26 July 1991.
114 On Kravchuk's role during the coup, see Kuzio and Wilson, *Ukraine: Perestroika to Independence*, pp. 171–3; Roman Solchanyk, 'Ukraine: Kravchuk's Role', *Report on the USSR*, vol. 3, no. 36, 6 September 1991; Valentyn Chemerys, 'Serpnevi podiï 91-ho. U zv''iazku z tym, shcho zdiisneno antykonstytutsiini zakhody . . .', *Holos Ukraïny*, 29 April 1994; and Taniuk and Krymchuk, *Khronika oporu*, pp. 102–23 and 170.
115 Alexander J. Motyl, 'The Conceptual President: Leonid Kravchuk and the Politics of Surrealism', in Timothy J. Colton and Robert C. Tucker (eds.), *Patterns in Post-Soviet Leadership* (Boulder: Westview, 1995), pp. 103–21.
116 *Za vil'nu Ukraïnu*, 12 January 1992; *Holos Ukraïny*, 24 January 1992 and 7 December 1991.
117 Kravchuk and Kychyhin, *Leonid Kravchuk*, pp. 129 and 99.
118 *Za vil'nu Ukraïnu*, 9 June 1992; an interview with Kravchuk in the leading nationalist newspaper in western Ukraine.
119 Leonid Kravchuk, 'Vystup na kongresi Ukraïntsiv', *Holos Ukraïny*,

24 January 1992. See also Kravchuk, 'My ne imeem prava prenebrech' urokami proshlogo!', *Golos Ukrainy*, 11 September 1993.

120 Kravchuk, *Ye taka derzhava – Ukraïna*, pp. 39, 51, 53, 62 and 44; Ivan Pliushch, *Khto my i kudy idemo*, p. 121.

121 Kravchuk and Kychyhin, *Leonid Kravchuk*, p. 120.

122 *Vechirnii Kyïv*, 10 January 1992; Kravchuk, *Ye taka derzhava – Ukraïna*, pp. 59 and 61; Ivan Pliushch, *Khto my i kudy idemo*, pp. 217–20.

123 Kravchuk, *Ye taka derzhava – Ukraïna*, pp. 44; Ivan Pliushch, *Khto my i kudy idemo*, pp. 285–7 and 300–4; Anatolii Zlenko, 'Vazhlyvyi krok u Yevropu', and 'Yevropeiskii vybor', *Holos Ukraïny*, 17 June and 12 August 1994.

124 *Holos Ukraïny*, 15 August 1991.

125 *Literaturna Ukraïna*, 16 September 1993; *Holos Ukraïny*, 10, 11 and 14 September 1993. See also Motyl, 'Conceptual President', pp. 115–6 and 120.

126 Leonid Kravchuk, 'Vil'na tserkva – u vil'nii derzhavi', *Holos Ukraïny*, 21 November 1991.

127 Kravchuk's speech to Parliament, *Holos Ukraïny*, 7 December 1991.

128 Kravchuk and Kychyhin, *Leonid Kravchuk*, pp. 117, 118 and 119.

129 Kravchuk, *Ye taka derzhava – Ukraïna*, p. 71; Ivan Pliushch, 'Liudy chekaiut' na zminy, i pov"iazuiut' ïkh z novymy demokratychnymy sylamy', *Holos Ukraïny*, 20 April 1994.

130 Andrew Wilson and Ihor Burakovs'kyi, *Economic Reform in Ukraine* (London: Royal Institute of International Affairs, 1996). See also *Post-postup*, nos. 12a and 14, 1992; *Vechirnii Kyïv*, 27 March 1992; and the interview with Yemel'ianov in *Holos Ukraïny*, 7 July 1992.

131 See for example comments such as 'the cold reception given by electors in the east and south to Kravchuk shows that his orientation to the nationalist west is leading society up a blind-alley': Nikolai Morkishchev, 'Opasnost' raskola', *Donetskii kriazh*, no. 27, 8–14 July 1994. See also the argument of Dominique Arel, 'Ukraine: The Temptation of the Nationalizing State', in Vladimir Tismaneanu (ed.), *Political Culture and Civil Society in Russia and the New States of Eurasia* (Armonk, N. Y.: M. E. Sharpe, 1995), pp. 157–88.

132 Speech of communist leader Petro Symonenko at the First (Twenty-Ninth) Congress of the revived CPU in *Partiia Kommunistov vozrozhdaetsia. Dokumenty i materialy vtorogo etapa Vseukrainskoi konferentsii kommunistov i s'ezd Kommunisticheskoi partii Ukrainy* (Kherson: party material, 1993), p. 21.

133 Rogers Brubaker, 'Nationhood and the National Question in the Soviet Union and Post-Soviet Eurasia: An Institutionalist Account', *Theory and Society*, vol. 23, no. 1 (1994), pp. 47–78, at p. 66. See also Brubaker's article, 'National Minorities, Nationalizing States and External National Homelands in the New Europe', *Daedalus*, vol. 124, no. 2 (Spring 1995), pp. 107–32. On the importance of elites and institutional resources, see Valerii Tishkov, 'Inventions and Manifestations of Ethno-Nationalism in and After the Soviet Union', in Kumar Rupesinghe *et al.* (eds.), *Ethnicity and Conflict in a Post-Communist World: The Soviet Union, Eastern Europe and China* (London: Macmillan, 1992), pp. 41–65.

134 For example, Bilous, *Politychni ob"iednannia Ukraïny*, pp. 61–2 and 92–5. Cf. Mykola Riabchuk, 'Democracy and the So-Called "Party of Power" in Ukraine', *Political Thought*, no. 3, 1994, pp. 154–9.

135 Ivan Pliushch toyed with the Labour Congress of Ukraine in 1993 (which was also backed by the official trade unions), but it never became a strong political force. While still in office, Kravchuk flirted first with Rukh and then with the CNDF, but was always wary of their relatively narrow political base. Once out of office, he couldn't afford to be so choosy.

136 *Literaturna Ukraïna*, 19 January 1995. Porozuminnia claimed the support of 12,000 members and eighteen deputies in Parliament: *Holos Ukraïny*, 7 March 1995.

137 Andrew Wilson, 'The Growing Challenge to Kiev from the Donbas', *RFE/RL Research Report*, vol. 2, no. 33, 20 August 1993.

138 *Holos Ukraïny*, 30 October 1991; *Materialy ustanovchoho z"ïzdy Sotsialistychnoï partiï Ukraïny* (Kiev, party material, 1991); *Polityka i chas*, no. 17–18 (December), 1991, pp. 80–92; and Rostyslav Khotyn, 'Reanimatsiia natsional-komunizmu', *Slovo*, no. 21, 1991.

139 Yevhen Boltarovych, 'Sotsialistychna partiia Ukraïny: ideolohiia, polityka, perspektyva', *Rozbudova derzhavy*, no. 4 (September), 1992; Bilokin' *et al.*, *Khto ye khto v ukraïns'kii politytsi*, p. 221.

140 *Holos Ukraïny*, 29 January and 14 February 1992.

141 Bilokin' *et al.*, *Khto ye khto v ukraïns'kii politytsi*; *Uriadovyi kur"ier*, no. 31 (July), 1992.

142 Author's interview with Yevhenii Marmazov, 9 March 1995. See also Hurenko *et al.*, *Kommunisticheskaia partiia Ukrainy*, pp. 37 and 50; and Pliushch's estimate in March 1992 that 'of the [original] group of "239" only around 100 remain': Ivan Pliushch, *Khto my i kudy idemo*, p. 115.

143 *Vechirnii Kyïv*, 14 July 1992; *Tovarysh*, no. 4 (June), 1992.

144 *Partiia Kommunistov vozrozhdaetsia*; *Donetskii kriazh*, no. 23, 25 June–1 July 1993; *Holos Ukraïny*, 22 June 1993. The CPU claimed a membership of 128,000 when officially registered in October 1993, but other sources suggested the total was nearer 46,000: *Holos Ukraïny*, 15 October 1993. Yevhenii Marmazov complained to the author of the party's narrow membership base.

145 'Prohrama Komunistychnoï partiï Ukraïny', *Komunist*, no. 12 (March), 1995, pp. 4–5.

146 Speech of CPU leader Petro Symonenko at the Second (Thirtieth) Congress of the CPU in March 1995, *Komunist*, no. 11 (March), 1995, pp. 4 and 6.

147 'Prohrama Komunistychnoï partiï Ukraïny', as no. 145.

5 A MINORITY FAITH: THE LIMITS TO NATIONALIST SUPPORT

1 See, for an example, Kathleen Mihalisko, 'Alla Yaroshyns'ka: Crusading Journalist from Zhitomir Becomes People's Deputy', *Report on the USSR*, RL 247/89, 24 May 1989.

2 Kamins'kyi, *Na perekhidnomu etapi*, p. 583.

3 Ibid., p. 584.

4 Yurii Kyrychuk, 'Narys istoriï UHS-URP', *Respublikanets'*, no. 2 (November–December), 1991, p. 88.

5 Ibid., p. 89–90. In both constituencies the official candidates ran unopposed, but the then current Soviet election rules required a candidate to receive an absolute majority of votes cast in order to be elected. Ukraine has also retained the Soviet practice of negative voting. Electors must cross off the names of all but the candidate they wish to support. It is therefore perfectly possible to cross out all names.

6 Kamins'kyi, *Na perekhidnomu etapi*, p. 585. Confirmed to the author in an interview with Volodymyr Cherniak, leading Rukh economist and former USSR deputy from Kiev, 2 August 1992. See also Kathleen Mihalisko, 'Ukrainian Party Takes Stock after Election Defeats', *Report on the USSR*, RL 278/89, 23 June 1989.

7 On the March 1990 election results, see Dominique Arel, 'The Parliamentary Blocs in the Ukrainian Supreme Soviet: Who and What Do They Represent?', *Journal of Soviet Nationalities*, vol. 1, no. 4 (Winter 1990–1), pp. 108–54; Peter J. Potichnyj, 'Elections in Ukraine', in *Berichte des Bundesinstituts für ostwissenschaftliche und internationale Studien*, no. 36, 1990; Potichnyj, 'Elections in Ukraine, 1990' in Gitelman, *Politics of Nationality*, pp. 176–214; and J. V. Koshiw, 'The March 1990 Elections in Ukraine', *Ukraine Today*, August 1990, pp. 5–8. For a comparison with the referenda of 1991, see Oleksii Redchenko, 'Hotuimo sany vlitku', *Narodna hazeta*, no. 12 (April), 1992.

8 Ivashko's more conciliatory approach to the opposition was one key reason, but other reasons were pressure from Moscow and a certain lack of confidence in the CPU: CSACOU, f. 1, op. 2, delo 996; op. 11, delo 1884 and delo 1940.

9 CSACOU, f. 1, 'Postanova Politburo TsK Kompartiï Ukraïny, no. 93/3, 16/1' (no opys) discusses the measures to be taken after Rukh's first congress.

10 CSACOU, f. 1, op. 11, delo 2067, p. 17.

11 Potichnyj, 'Elections in Ukraine, 1990', p. 179.

12 Arel, 'Parliamentary Blocs in the Ukrainian Supreme Soviet', pp. 126–7; Arel, *Language and the Politics of Ethnicity*, pp. 312–13.

13 *Vil'ne slovo*, no. 8, 1989.

14 *Slovo*, no. 3 (November–December), 1989; and *Vil'ne slovo*, no. 7, 1990.

15 For a list, see Potichnyj, 'Elections in Ukraine, 1990', pp. 210–11, n. 81.

16 V"iacheslav Chornovil, 'Do vykonavchoho komitetu UHS – zaiava', *Moloda Ukraïna*, no. 8, 1990.

17 Programmes in author's files. Luk"ianenko's programme can be found in his *Viruiu v Boha i v Ukraïnu*, pp. 274–7.

18 *Suchasni politychni partiï ta rukhy na Ukraïni*, eds. I. F. Kuras, F. M. Rudych, O. P. Smoliannykov and O. A. Spirin (Kiev: Instytut politychnykh doslidzhen', 1991), pp. 8–55, at p. 15.

19 Ibid., pp. 26, 13 and 39. The CPU election programme was published in *Radians'ka Ukraïna*, 3 December 1989.

20 See the roundtable discussion on the election results, 'Uroky vyborov', *Filosofskaia i sotsiologicheskaia mysl'*, no. 8 (August), 1990, pp. 3–41.

21 *Literaturna Ukraïna*, 12 April 1990.
22 Jonathan Aves, 'The Evolution of Independent Political Movements After 1988' and Geoffrey A. Hosking, 'Popular Movements in Estonia' in Hosking, Aves and Duncan, *Road to Post-Communism*, pp. 29–66, at pp. 48–9 and pp. 180–201, at p. 195, respectively. For Russia, see Gregory J. Embree, 'RSFSR Election Results and Roll Call Votes', *Soviet Studies*, vol. 43 (1991), pp. 1065–84.
23 On defections from the CPU in Parliament, see CSACOU, f. 1, op. 2, delo 1125, pp. 3–7.
24 Dominique Arel, 'Voting Behaviour in the Ukrainian Parliament', pp. 125–58, at p. 138.
25 Szporluk, 'Strange Politics of Lviv', pp. 215–31.
26 Arel, 'Parliamentary Blocs in the Ukrainian Supreme Soviet', p. 112. The Narodna rada gained one deputy from Kherson.
27 *Orhanizatsiini pryntsypy parlaments'koï fraktsiï 'Narodna rada'*, in author's possession, as is the *Statut klub deputativ Rukhu*.
28 'Narodna rada: 4 fraktsiï', *Holos*, no. 10 (May), 1991; Rostyslav Hotyn, 'Verkhovna rada Ukraïny: p''iatyrichku za pivroku?', *Nezalezhnyi ohliadach*, no. 1 (November), 1990; and 'Dovidka Demokratychnoï bloku', *Demokratychnyi vybir* (a PDRU paper from 1990), no. 11, 1990.
29 The seven were the two Horyn' brothers, Chornovil, Khmara, Luk''ianenko, Bohdan Rebryk and Levko Horokhivs'kyi.
30 The platform was drawn up by Luk''ianenko and Larysa Skoryk: *Ternystyi shliakh* (journal of the Ternopil' UHU-URP), no. 6 (June), 1990.
31 From a list supplied by the DPU secretariat, and information provided by DPU deputy Yevhen Hriniv, 10 May 1992.
32 Author's interview with Yurii Badz'o, 29 April 1992. Emphasis in original.
33 *Demokratychnyi vybir*, no. 11, 1991, p. 1.
34 Arel, 'Voting Behaviour in the Ukrainian Parliament', pp. 150–3.
35 *Moloda Halychyna*, 3 April 1992; author's interview with Volodymyr Filenko, 10 February 1992.
36 The CNDF faction first appeared in February 1992 as part of the campaign by its leader, Mykhailo Horyn', to take over Rukh: *Narodna hazeta*, no. 7 (February), 1992. In an interview with the author on 1 May 1992, Mykola Porovs'kyi claimed that the faction had grown to seventy members.
37 *Holos Ukraïny*, 30 September 1992. 'Fraktsiia Rukhu', *Vechirnii Kyïv*, 1 October, 1993 lists the same faction a year later. The difference between the two groups was largely political. Thirteen DPU deputies joined the CNDF group and three from the URP, but the Rukh faction consisted mainly of previously 'non-party' members of the Narodna rada. Both groups were dominated by west Ukrainians (twenty-six of the CNDF deputies and thirty-two for Rukh). On the other hand, deputies were allowed to be members of two factions, so there was always considerable overlap between the various groups.
38 CSACOU, f. 1, op. 11, delo 2005, pp. 45–7.
39 CSACOU, f. 1, op. 2, delo 1124, p. 2, and delo 1101, p. 3.
40 Information provided by URP mandate commission at the June 1991 party congress.

41 Information supplied by Yevhen Boltarovych in May 1992, theoretical secretary in the L'viv URP until 1992.

42 *Informatsiinyi zvit pro politychne stanovyshche na Zakarpatti* (from URP files), dated April–May 1991.

43 This impression is derived from the series of regional reports delivered by local URP heads to the party leadership in Kiev in 1991 (from the URP party archive).

44 See, for example, Badz'o's speech to the second DPU congress in December 1992, *Na shliakhu stanovlennia ta samousvidomlennia: zvitna dopovid' holovy natsional'noï rady DemPU druhomu z"ïzdovi partiï 12–13 hrudnia 1992 r.*, p. 4.

45 Author's interview with DPU secretary Hryhorii Kutsenko, 28 April 1992.

46 See also V. V. Popovych, 'Referendum SRSR i politychni oriientatsiï naselennia Ukraïny', *Filosofs'ka i sotsiolohichna dumka*, no. 9, 1991.

47 *Za vil'nu Ukraïnu*, 19 March 1991.

48 *Protokol sekretariatu URP*, nos. 7 and 8, 21 and 23 January 1991; 'Rozkol v URP?', *Holos*, nos. 8 and 9 (and 11), 1991; Hryhorii Hrebeniuk, 'Rozdumy nad mynulym i maibutnim', and Roman Koval', 'Try pohliady na nashi zavdannia', *Napriam*, no. 7 (August), 1991, pp. 2–7, and 7–12.

49 *Protokol no. 7. Zasidannia politychnoï rady Narodnoho Rukhu Ukraïny*, 4 February 1991; Mykola Porovs'kyi, 'Zvitna dopovid' na tretikh zborakh Rukhu', *Narodna hazeta*, no. 9 (March), 1992.

50 *Protokoly DemPU*, no. 10, 5 March 1991; *Holos Ukraïny*, 19 February 1991; *Volia*, no. 4 (February), 1991.

51 *URP-inform*, no. 3, 28 February 1991. An earlier meeting in January had decided on a boycott: *Protokol sekretariatu URP*, no. 11, 30 January 1991.

52 'Tiazhelye rody suvereniteta', *Vechernii Kiev*, 7 February and 13 March 1991; *Holos*, no. 2, 1991; and *Molod' Ukraïny*, 15 March 1991.

53 Doubts were expressed at a public *viche* ('assembly') in Khmel'nyts'kyi square in Kiev on 16 September: *Ukraïns'ki novyny*, nos. 9 and 10, 1991.

54 Interview with Oleksandr Moroz, *Kyïvs'kyi visnyk*, 28 November 1991.

55 Author's interviews with DMD leader Dmitrii Kornilov and RMC leader Yurii Meshkov, 14 July and 30 September 1993.

56 See the content analysis of the Ukrainian press in autumn 1991 in S. I. Suhlobin, 'Pytannia etnopolityky v suchasnii presi Ukraïny: identifikatsiia etnopolitychnoï informatsiï (za pidsumkamy kontent-analizu vseukraïns'koï presy', Yevtukh *et al.*, *Etnopolitychna sytuatsiia v Ukraïni*, pp. 52–74.

57 The polls were recorded in *Holos Ukraïny*, 1, 13 and 23 November 1991.

58 Valerii Khmel'ko, 'Referendum: khto buv "za" i khto "proty" ', *Politolohichni chytannia*, no. 1, 1992, pp. 40–52.

59 See for example the predominance of economic themes in Kravchuk's speeches before December 1991: Kravchuk, *Ye taka derzhava – Ukraïna*, pp. 130–63 and 185–6.

60 Kravchuk's programme was in *Holos Ukraïny*, 31 October 1991. See also ibid., 15 and 19 October and 1, 12, 19, 21, 26, 28 and 29 November 1991.

61 Tkachenko's programme, and an interview entitled 'Ya spoviduiu Marksyzm' ('I believe in Marxism') appeared in *Holos Ukraïny*, 6 November 1991.

62 From an election poster for Griniov. See also *Rabochaia gazeta*, 11 October and 6 November 1991; and *Holos Ukraïny*, 4 November 1991.
63 Taburians'kyi's campaign was covered in *Holos Ukraïny*, 23 November 1991.
64 *URP-inform*, no. 19, 3 September 1991.
65 On Chornovil's campaign, see *Holos Ukraïny*, 23 October and 23 November 1991; *Za vil'nu Ukraïnu*, 26 September 1991; *Vil'ne slovo*, 2 November 1991; and *Pravda Ukrainy*, 4 September 1991. A collection of his interviews and articles from the campaign was published in *Holos*, no. 21, 17–23 October 1991. Chornovil's official programme, 'Ukraïna: shliakh do svobodu: osnovni pryntsypy prohramy', can be found in *Holos Ukraïny*, 23 October 1991.
66 *URP-inform*, nos. 21 and 29, 17 September and 13 November 1991. The Christian Democratic and Peasant-Democratic Parties were split between Chornovil and Luk"ianenko. On Luk"ianenko's campaign, see *Trybuna*, no. 11, 1991; *Kul'tura i zhyttia*, no. 41, 1991; *Komsomol'skaia pravda*, 1 November 1991; *Holos hromadianyna*, no. 44–5, 1991; and *Holos Ukraïny*, 30 October, 24 and 27 November 1991. Luk"ianenko's election programme, 'P"iat' rokiv dostatno, shchob Ukraïna stala rozvynenoiu Yevropeis'koiu derzhavoiu. Ya znaiu, yak tsoho dosiahty!', is in *Za vil'nu Ukraïnu*, 13 November 1991.
67 *L'vivs'ki novyny*, no. 39, 1991.
68 For Yukhnovs'kyi's campaign, see his programme and interview in *Trybuna*, no. 11, 1991; plus his interviews in *Holos Ukraïny*, 16 October 1991, and *Moloda hazeta*, no. 1 (October), 1991.
69 The DPU's failure – they only collected 79,710 signatures – was particularly striking: *Holos Ukraïny*, 2 November 1991.
70 The author obtained the results by raion for half a dozen oblasts.
71 *Obshchestvennoe mnenie naseleniia Ukrainy o predstoiashchikh vyborakh Prezidenta Ukrainy i respublikanskom referendume o podtverzhdenii akta provozglasheniia nezavisimosti Ukrainy* (Kiev: Institut sotsiologii AN Ukrainy, September 1991), p. 6; *Holos Ukraïny*, 1 November 1991; and Khmel'ko, 'Referendum'.
72 For a more detailed analysis, see Wilson, 'Ukraine: Two Presidents, But No Settled Powers'.
73 *Za vil'nu Ukraïnu*, 17 October 1992 gave a figure of 20,000 for Rukh's membership in L'viv oblast; *Molod' Ukraïny*, 13 November 1992, gave 30,000.
74 Yurii Badz'o, *Pro suspil'no-polituchnu sytuatsiiu v kraïni, pro proekt prohramy, orhanizatsiinyi stan i cherhovi zavdannia Demokratychnoï Partiï: dopovid' na pershii vseukraïns'kii konferentsiï DemPU*, 11–12 April 1992, p. 5; author's interview with Badz'o, 29 April 1992.
75 Letter from Badz'o to local DPU organisations from DPU files, *Z peremohoiu, dorohi druzi!*, 4 July 1991, p. 5.
76 *L'vivs'ki novyny*, nos. 27 and 40, 2 July and 2 October 1991.
77 *URP-inform*, no. 1, 25 January 1991.
78 Author's interviews at the third URP congress on 1–2 May 1992. The author has no quantifiable information on this topic.

79 *Za vil'nu Ukraïnu*, 16 February 1993; *Vechirnii Kyïv*, 14 May 1992; V. Lytvyn, 'Pro suchasni ukraïns'ki partiï', pp. 62–101, at p. 82; V. Mikhailiv, 'Politicheskoe ob"edinenie "Gosudarstvennaia samostoiatel'nost Ukrainy" (GSU)', *Politika i vremia*, no. 3 (March), 1991, pp. 72–5, at p. 72; and *Moloda Halychyna*, 10 April 1990.

80 Dominique Arel and Andrew Wilson, 'The Ukrainian Parliamentary Elections', *RFE/RL Research Report*, vol. 3, no. 26, 1 July 1994; Marco Bojcun, 'The Ukrainian Parliamentary Elections of March–April 1994', *Europe–Asia Studies*, vol. 47, no. 2 (1995), pp. 229–49.

81 *Holos Ukraïny*, 19 and 25 February 1992.

82 People's deputy Al'bert Kornieiev, interviewed by the author and Dominique Arel, 8 July 1993.

83 Oleksandr Moroz, 'Oriientyr – trudovi kolektyvy', *Holos Ukraïny*, 2 April 1992; and 'Pro zahrozu natsionalistychnoho ekstremizmu ta natsional-fashyzmu v Ukraïni', *Tovarysh*, no. 7 (July), 1992.

84 Dmitrii Kornilov, interviewed by the author and Dominique Arel in Donets'k, 14 July 1993; Dmitrii Kornilov, 'Tak kto zhe bol'she liubit Ukrainu?', *Donetskii kriazh*, no. 3, 21–7 January 1994.

85 *Grazhdanskii kongress*, nos. 1 and 2, 1993; *Programmnye printsipy partii truda i ustav partii* (Donets'k: party material, 1993); *Tovarysh*, no. 7 (July), 1992; and *Partiia Kommunistov vozrozhdaetsia*.

86 Calculated from the Ukraïna list *Do vybortsiv Ukraïny*. Levko Luk"ianenko, the chairman of the Ukraïna group, describes the difficult process of reaching agreement in his *De dobryi shliakh?*, pp. 30–6.

87 *Zakhidnyi kur"ier*, 12 February to 2 April 1994; *Rivne*, 19 February–14 March 1994; *Halyts'ke slovo*, 2–30 March 1994; *Narodna sprava*, 5–26 March 1994; *Vil'ne zhyttia*, 26 February–27 March 1994; and *Berezhans'ke viche*, nos. 7–14, 1994.

88 Author's calculations from *Kreshchatyk*, 13 April 1994; and the list of UNA-UNSO candidates in *Ukraïns'ki obrii*, no. 7, 1994.

89 Four supporters of the PDRU, by then a declining force, were elected in 1994: three in Zaporizhzhia and one in Dnipropetrovs'k. However, the Zaporizhzhia group, also known as My ('We'), acted as independent liberals.

90 *Holos Ukraïny*, 12 July 1994.

91 *Holos Ukraïny*, 16 and 30 August 1994; *Nezavisimost'*, 17 August 1994; and *Ukrainian Weekly*, 27 November 1994. Luk"ianenko was prevented from taking his seat for several months while the left accused him of electoral malpractice.

92 *Vseukrainskie vedomosti*, 22 October 1994.

93 *Ukrainian Weekly*, 11 December 1994.

94 Author's calculations from the list of factions published in *Holos Ukraïny*, 12 July 1994, and from biographical information provided by the Slavonic Centre, Kiev.

95 Dominique Arel and Andrew Wilson, 'Ukraine Under Kuchma: Back to "Eurasia"?', *RFE/RL Research Report*, vol. 3, no. 32, 19 August 1994; Wilson, 'Ukraine: Two Presidents, But No Settled Powers'.

96 See the debate at the fifth Rukh congress and at the special congress of the

Ukrainian Republican Party in April 1994: *Rada*, 21 April 1994; *Pozacher-hovyi z"izd URP*, pp. 19–58.

97 *Ukraïns'ka hazeta*, no. 13, 1994.

98 For Kravchuk, see the mammoth interviews serialised in *Kievskie vedomosti* from 23 April 1994 onward and in *Ukraïns'ka hazeta*, nos. 1–5, 1994. For Kuchma see Oleksii Mustafin, 'Lytsar sumnoho imidzhu', *Visti z Ukraïny*, no. 22, 1994; and Mar"iana Chorna, 'Leonid Kuchma. Vchore, s'ohodni, i . . .', *Post-postup*, 29 April–6 May 1994.

99 Valerii Khmel'ko, 'KMIS znaie . . .', *Demokratychna Ukraïna*, 9 July 1994. According to Khmel'ko's poll, 41 per cent of Moroz voters intended to back Kuchma and only 16 per cent Kravchuk. Lanovyi voters split 26 per cent to 20 per cent in favour of Kravchuk.

100 Author's interviews with Levko Luk"ianenko and Pavlo Movchan, 23 and 26 October 1994.

101 In terms of levels of industrialisation and the number of Russophones, Kirovohrad is the Right Bank oblast that has most in common with neighbouring eastern Ukraine. Moreover, Kirovohrad was historically a transition zone between the densely populated regions of central Ukraine and New Serbia, *Novorossiia* and the open steppe.

102 The vote in Kiev was especially disappointing as the nationalist bloc Stolytsia ('Capital') won a convincing victory in the simultaneous municipal elections: *Khreshchatyk*, 2 July 1994.

103 In the first round, when Moroz was still in the race, Kravchuk's rural vote was estimated at only 28 per cent. Information kindly supplied by Valerii Khmel'ko of the Kiev Mohyla Academy (the survey size was 591; Khmel'ko placed Khmel'nyts'kyi in western Ukraine rather than in the centre).

104 *Molod' Ukraïny*, 12 July 1994.

105 Valerii Khmel'ko, 'Politychni oriientatsiï vybortsiv ta rezul'taty vyboriv do Verkhovnoï Rady', and 'Koho oberemo prezydentom? Za dva tyzhni do vyboriv prodovzhuvav lidyruvaty Kravchuk', May–June 1994; unpublished papers kindly supplied by Khmel'ko. In the first, Khmel'ko states that 'the political polarisation of the regions of Ukraine which became apparent at the parliamentary elections is connected more with the national-political orientation of elections than with a difference in socio-economic orienta-tion'.

106 See Iryna Bekeshkina, 'Sotsial'no-ekonomichni oriientatsiï naselennia Skhodu i Pivdnia Ukraïny', *Demoz*, no. 3, 1994.

6 THE NATIONALIST AGENDA: DOMESTIC POLITICS, UKRAINIANISATION AND THE STATE

1 Many of the points made in this section can also be found in the excellent analysis by Dominique Arel, 'Ukraine: The Temptation of the Nationalising State', pp. 157–88.

2 The first draft of the new post-Soviet Ukrainian constitution published in July 1992 referred throughout to *narod Ukraïny*, but in the face of nationalist criticism two subsequent drafts in January and October 1993 switched to *ukraïns'kyi narod*: *Holos Ukraïny*, 17 July 1992, *Konstytutsiia Ukraïny*

(proekt), 28 January 1993, and *Holos Ukraïny*, 30 October 1993. For nationalist criticism of the first draft, see *Rozbudova derzhavy*, no. 5 (October), 1992, especially pp. 47–8.

3 The concept of 'Russification' assumes a previous loyalty to Ukrainian language and culture which may not have existed. Many Russophone Ukrainians have indeed been deprived of access to their native language and culture; others have always existed in a Russophone environment.

4 *Kontseptsiia derzhavotvorennia v Ukraïni* (Kiev: Rukh, 1992), pp. 4–5.

5 Yevhen Boltarovych, 'URP: aspekty ideolohiï i polityky', *Nezalezhnist'*, no. 2 (December), 1990.

6 Szporluk, 'National Question', p. 102.

7 Ibid., pp. 100–6; and Szporluk, 'Reflections on Ukraine After 1994: The Dilemmas of Nationhood', *Harriman Review*, vol. 7, nos. 7–9 (March–May 1994). See also Motyl, *Dilemmas of Independence*, chapter 3; and Lowell Barrington, 'The Domestic and International Consequences of Citizenship in the Soviet Successor States', *Europe–Asia Studies*, vol. 47, no. 5 (1995), pp. 731–63.

8 V. S. Koval's'kyi (ed.), *Pravovi dzherela Ukraïny*, no. 1, 1994 (Kiev: Biuleten' zakonodavstva i yurydychnoï praktyky Ukraïny, 1994), pp. 39–41.

9 'Zaiava URP shchodo vvedennia pasportiv hromadianyna Ukraïny', *Samostiina Ukraïna*, no. 25 (June), 1992.

10 *Neskorena Natsiia*, no. 16, 1993.

11 *Literaturna Ukraïna*, 7 November 1991; *Holos Ukraïny*, 16 July 1992.

12 Yu. K. Kachurenko (ed.), *Prava liudyny. Mizhnarodni dohovory Ukraïny, deklaratsiï, dokumenty* (Kiev: Yurinform, 2nd edn, 1992), pp. 13–15.

13 See, for example, *Grazhdanskii kongress* (Kiev and Donets'k), no. 1, 1993; 'Programa deistvii i predvybornaia platforma Mezhregional'nogo Bloka reform', *Vybor* (Kharkiv), no. 1, 1994; 'Platforma Kommunisticheskoi partii Ukrainy na vyborakh v Verkhovnyi Sovet Ukrainy', *Komunist*, no. 1 (February), 1994; and Valentyna Ermolova, ' "Russkii vopros" v Ukraine', *Vseukrainskie vedomosti*, 6 December 1994.

14 'Platforma Kommunisticheskoi partii Ukrainy na vyborakh v Verkhovnyi Sovet Ukrainy', *Komunist*, no. 1 (February), 1994, p. 5.

15 'Pro zahrozu natsionalistychnoho ekstremizmu ta natsional-fashyzmu v Ukraïni', *Tovarysh*, no. 7 (July), 1992. See also 'Prohramna zaiava – u haluzi natsional'nykh vidnosyn', *Materialy ustanovchoho z"ïzdu SPU*.

16 *Partiia demokratychnoho vidrodzhennia Ukraïny: III-i z"ïzd* (Kiev: party material, May 1992), p. 8.

17 'Programma interdvizheniia Donbassa (proekt)', *Nash Donbass*, January 1993.

18 *Tovarysh*, no. 1 (April), 1992.

19 On Baltic nationalism, see Graham Smith, 'The Resurgence of Nationalism', and Smith, Aadne Aasland and Richard Mole, 'Statehood, Ethnic Relations and Citizenship', both in Smith (ed.), *The Baltic States: The National Self-Determination of Estonia, Latvia and Lithuania* (London: Macmillan, 1994), pp. 121–43 and 181–205; and Anatol Lieven, *The Baltic Revolution: Estonia, Latvia and Lithuania and the Politics of Independence* (London: Yale University Press, 1993), pp. 255–301.

20 On Ukrainian conceptions of 'homeland', see Trubenko and Horbyk, *Istorychno-heohrafichni doslidzhennia v Ukraïni*; and Zastavnyi, *Heohrafiia Ukraïny*, pp. 318–49.

21 Anthony D. Smith, *National Identity* (London: Penguin, 1991), pp. 21 and 16. See also Donald L. Horowitz, *Ethnic Groups in Conflict* (Berkeley: University of California Press, 1985), p. 68; and Colin Williams and Anthony D. Smith, 'The National Construction of Social Space', *Progress in Human Geography*, vol. 7, no. 4 (1983), pp. 502–18. Arel, *Language and the Politics of Ethnicity*, chapter 5 first made the point about the Ukrainian 'claim to indigenousness'.

22 'Zaiava tsentral'noho pravlinnia vseukraïns'koho tovarystva "Prosvita" im. T. Shevchenka', *Literaturna Ukraïna*, 28 July 1994. Cf. Yaroslav Dashkevych, 'Ukraïna i natsional'ni menshosti', *Derzhavnist'*, no. 3, 1991.

23 V. F. Soldatenko and Yu. V. Syvolov, 'Vytoky i peredvisnyky ukraïns'koï ideï', in Soldatenko, *Ukraïns'ka ideia*, pp. 5–25, at p. 8. An updated version of this article was published in *Ukraïns'kyi istorychnyi zhurnal*, no. 2–3, 1994, pp. 14–28.

24 Ivan Drach, 'Neznyshchenna voviky vikiv', *Literaturna Ukraïna*, 10 February 1994.

25 Mykhailo Horyn', 'Zbudui Ukraïnu u vlasnii dushi', in his *Zapalyty svichu u pit'mi* (Kiev: URP, 1994), p. 19.

26 Mykhailo Horyn', 'National'na yednist' – garant ukraïns'koï derzhavnosti', speech to the founding congress of the CNDF: *Samostiina Ukraïna*, no. 31 (August), 1992.

27 Anthony D. Smith, 'The Formation of Nationalist Movements', in Smith (ed.), *Nationalist Movements* (London: Macmillan, 1976), p. 5. Cf. John Hutchinson, *The Dynamics of Cultural Nationalism* (London: Allen and Unwin, 1987).

28 'Prohramovi zasady Kongresy natsional'no-demokratychnykh syl', *Samostiina Ukraïna*, no. 31 (August), 1992.

29 Levko Luk"ianenko, 'Dopovid' na III z"ïzdi Rukhu', in his *Viruiu v Boha i v Ukraïnu*, p. 299.

30 Mykhailo Horyn', 'Zbudui Ukraïnu u vlasnii dushi', p. 17.

31 Quoted in Mykola Riabchuk, 'Vid "Malorosiï" do "indoievropu": stereotyp "narodu" v ukraïns'kii suspil'nii svidomosti ta hromads'kii dumtsi', *Politolohichni chytannia*, no. 2, 1994, pp. 120–44, at p. 134, n 2.

32 Hryhorii Stoliarchuk, 'Novitni varvary. Do 60-richchia komunistychnoho holodomoru v Ukraïni', *Klych*, no. 4, 1993; Ivan Drach, 'Neznyshchenna voviky vikiv', *Literaturna Ukraïna*, 10 February 1994.

33 Anatolii Holiryi, 'Nasha yedyna i taka rizna natsiia', *Holos Ukraïny*, 24 July 1993.

34 'Zaiava URP do 75-i richnytsi utvorennia Tsentral'noï Rady', *Samostiina Ukraïna*, no. 14 (March), 1992. Cf. Mykola Lytvyn, 'Tut vyrishuiet'sia dolia derzhavy', *Samostiina Ukraïna*, no. 29, 1994.

35 Levko Luk"ianenko, 'Zvitna dopovid' holovy URP III z"ïzdovi', *Materiialy tret'oho z"ïzdu URP*, p. 15.

36 Oles' Honchar et al., 'Ukraïna – pravonastupnytsia UNR', *Rozbudova derzhavy*, no. 5 (October), 1992.

37 In the 1960s Ivan Dziuba and others tended to refer to a legitimate 'early Leninist' period (i.e. the Ukrainianisation of the 1920s), after which subsequent 'errors' and 'distortions' led to Russification.

38 Chapter 3, n. 106 in this volume lists material in the nationalist press eulogising the OUN-UPA. See also M. Bar and A. Zalens'kyi, 'Viina vtrachennykh natsii: Ukraïns'kyi samostiinyts'kyi rukh u 1939–1949 rr.', *Ukraïns'kyi istorychnyi zhurnal*, no. 6 (June), 1992, pp. 116–22; M. V. Koval', 'OUN-UPA: mizh "tretim reikhom" i stalins'kym totalitaryzmom', ibid., no. 2–3, 1994, pp. 94–102; Oleh Bahan, *Natsionalizm i natsionalis-tychnyi rukh: istoriia ta ideï* (Drohobych: Vidrodzhennia, 1994); Stepan Mechnyk, *U vyri voiennoho lykholittia: OUN i UPA u borot'bi z hitlerivs'kymy okupantamy* (L'viv: Krai, 1992); and Bohdan Zalizniak (ed.), *Zdaleka pro blyz'ke: zbirnyk statei* (L'viv: Memorial, 1992).

Attacks on the OUN-UPA in the left-wing and eastern and southern Ukrainian press were equally common, for example, P. Neprych, 'Ober-ezhno: fashyzm!', *Tovarysh*, no. 4 (June), 1992; and Nikolai Spiridov, 'Grozit li nam fashizm?', *Nash Donbass*, January 1993.

39 Oleh Orach, 'Shoven by ïm aploduvav. Khto i navishcho zchyniaie halas pro "nasyl'nyts'ku Ukraïnizatsiiu" ', *Literaturna Ukraïna*, 7 July 1994. See also the appeal signed by over 170 deputies in *Holos Ukraïny*, 4 February 1995.

40 'Zaiava tsentral'noho pravlinnia vseukraïns'koho tovarystva "Prosvita" im. Tarasa Shevchenka', *Literaturna Ukraïna*, 21 April 1994.

41 Vasyl' Pliushch, 'Ukraïns'ka derzhavnist' – nasampered', *Literaturna Ukraïna*, 14 July 1994; Vasyl' Zakharchenko, 'Zbuduiemo "yuzhnoros-siiskoe gosudarstvo Ukraina"?', *Literaturna Ukraïna*, 4 August 1994; Sviatoslav Karavans'kyi, 'Pro prava bil'shosti', *Klych*, no. 2 (April), 1993.

42 Declaration of the September 1994 conference, 'Mova derzhavna – mova ofitsiina', *Visnyk Prosvity*, special edn, no. 1, 1994.

43 Pavlo Movchan, *Mova – yavyshche kosmichne* (Kiev: Prosvita, 1994), pp. 149 and 138–9.

44 Orach, 'Shoven by ïm aploduvav'. The original version refers to the 'wheel of history', but makes poor English.

45 Kachurenko, *Prava liudyny*, p. 14. Cf. 'Zakon URSR pro movy v ukraïns'kii RSR', *Materialy pro rozvytok mov v ukraïns'kii RSR* (Kiev: Prosvita, 1991), pp. 3–12, at p. 4.

46 Deputy education minister Anatolii Pohribnyi, interviewed in *Literaturna Ukraïna*, 29 July 1993.

47 Larysa Masenko, 'Ofitsiina = derzhavna', *Literaturna Ukraïna*, 28 July 1994.

48 Valentin Mamutov, 'Dikoe pole – ne terra-inkognita' and Dmitrii Kornilov, 'Federatsiia – de-fakto. A de-yure?', *Donetskii kriazh*, 8–14 October and 25 June–1 July 1993. See also Dmytro Vydrin, 'Rosiiany v Ukraïni: pid chas referendumu, do i pislia', *Politolohichni chytannia*, no. 1, 1992, pp. 237–49. For the many Russians who continue to think of Kievan Rus' as the cradle of their civilisation, central Ukraine is also 'indigenous' Russian territory.

49 Anatolii Zheleznyi, 'Ukraina: kak vozniklo dvuiazychnie', *Donetskii kriazh*, 18–24 June 1993.

50 'Svobodnoe padenie. Gde prizemlimsia?', *Donetskii kriazh*, 24–30 Sep-

tember 1993; and Elena Lavrent'eva, 'V roli Parizha snimaetsia L'vov', *Donetskii kriazh*, 25 February–3 March 1994.

51 Dmitrii Kornilov, interviewed by the author and Dominique Arel, 14 July 1993.

52 See, for example, the rational choice model used to assess the likelihood of assimilation in David D. Laitin, Roger Peterson and John W. Slocum, 'Language and the State: Russia and the Soviet Union in Comparative Perspective', in Motyl, *Thinking Theoretically About Soviet Nationalities*, pp. 129–68.

53 *Language Versus Nationality in the Politics of Ukraine* (Glasgow: Glasgow University Press Release no. 4, 1994).

54 Anatolii Zubchevs'kyi, 'Leonid Kuchma – Prezydent', *Ukraïns'ka hazeta*, no. 15, 1994; Yevhen Repet'ko, 'Narid i natsiia', *Holos Natsii*, no. 24, 1993; Levko Luk''ianenko, 'Zvitna dopovid' holovy URP III z''izdovi', *Materiialy tret'oho z''izdu URP*, p. 13; *Sil's'ki visti*, 14 July 1994; and Mar''iana Chorna, 'Solom''ianyi bychok znaishov sobi hospodaria', *Post-postup*, 14–20 July 1994; and *Vechirnii Kyïv*, 15 July 1994.

55 Dominique Arel, *Language and the Politics of Ethnicity*, chapter 6; and Arel, 'Language Politics in Independent Ukraine: Towards One or Two State Languages?', *Nationalities Papers*, vol. 23, no. 3 (1995), pp. 597–622.

56 Author's interview with Levko Luk''ianenko, 23 October 1994.

57 Arel, *Language and the Politics of Ethnicity*, pp. 160 and 169; *Yug*, 20 January 1993; Mykhailo Horyn' at the first congress of the CNDF, *Samostiina Ukraïna*, no. 31 (August), 1992.

58 Les' Taniuk, 'Prezydentovi Ukraïny L. M. Kravchuku', *Literaturna Ukraïna*, 18 November 1993; Nataliia Kostenko et al., 'Ukrainian Mass Media and Freedom of Information', *Political Thought*, no. 4, 1994, pp. 148–55, at p. 154.

59 Only 63 per cent and 43 per cent watch UT-1 and UT-2, but 91 per cent of Ukrainian viewers watch Ostankino: *Final Report: The 1994 Parliamentary and Presidential Elections in Ukraine* (Brussels: European Institute for the Media, 1994), p. 26.

60 The author interviewed leading bureaucrats in Kiev and Donets'k with Dominique Arel in summer 1993. The first congress of Ukrainian pedagogues in December 1992 split over the Ukrainianisation issue: *Samostiina Ukraïna*, nos. 2 and 3 (January), 1993.

61 According to Alexander Baziliuk, leader of the Civic Congress of Ukraine, nationalists were 'using knowledge of the Ukrainian language and membership of the Ukrainian ethnos to occupy state posts ... without proper professional qualification': *Nash Donbass*, January 1993, p. 7.

62 *Visnyk Prosvity. Spetsial'nyi vypusk, no. 1, 1994. Mova derzhavna – mova ofitsiina* (Kiev: Prosvita, 1994).

63 'Zaiava tsentral'noho pravlinnia vseukraïns'koho tovarystva "Prosvita" im. Tarasa Shevchenka', *Literaturna Ukraïna*, 21 April 1994.

64 Author's interview with Pavlo Movchan, 26 October 1994. Cf. Ihor Yukhnovs'kyi, 'Ne treba nyshchyty ukraïns'ku movu', *Ukraïns'ka hazeta*, no. 17, 1994.

65 *Samostiina Ukraïna*, nos. 2 and 3 (January), 1993.

66 'Ukhvala rady URP pro reformy osvity', *Samostiina Ukraïna*, no. 4 (February), 1993. Cf. V. Miochyns'kyi, 'Shkola i natsiia', *Zamkova hora*, no. 10, 1993.

67 For example, *Istoriia Ukraïny dlia ditei shkil'noho viku* (Kiev: Znannia, 1992); V. A. Potul'nytskyi, *Teoriia ukraïns'koï politolohiï: Kurs lektsii* (Kiev: Lybid', 1993); O. I. Semkiv *et al.* (eds.), *Politolohiia* (L'viv: Svit, 2nd edn, 1994); Yu. M. Aleksieiev, A. H. Verterhel and V. M. Danylenko, *Istoriia Ukraïny. Pidhotovka do ispytu* (Kiev: Teal, 1993); and L. H. Mel'nyk *et al.*, *Istoriia Ukraïny: kurs lektsii u dvokh knyhakh* (Kiev: Lybid', 1992).

68 The nationalist schema is largely taken from the work of Hrushevs'kyi and his disciples (who drew on the fragmentary work of earlier historians), as further developed by historians in interwar Galicia and in the Ukrainian diaspora, although much of their work has been bowdlerised and some important elements have to be constructed ex nihilo. The first step toward reclaiming national history in 1988–91 therefore involved the large-scale reprinting of traditional and diaspora works, such as the pre-revolutionary historians Mykhailo Hrushevs'kyi, *Ocherk istorii Ukrainskogo naroda* (Kiev: Lybid', 1991); Mykola Arkas, *Istoriia Ukraïny-Rusi* (Kiev: Vyshcha shkola, 1991); and the Galician historian Ivan Kryp"iakevych's *Istoriia Ukraïny*.

69 CSACOU, f. 1, op. 11, delo 2032 and 2181, pp. 19–83.

70 See, for example, Partha Chaterjee, *The Nation and Its Fragments* (Princeton: Princeton University Press, 1993) on India, or Terence Ranger and Eric Hobsbawm (eds.), *The Invention of Tradition* (Cambridge: Cambridge University Press, 1983).

71 John Hutchinson, 'Cultural Nationalism and Moral Regeneration', in Hutchinson and Anthony D. Smith (eds.), *Nationalism* (Oxford: Oxford University Press, 1994), pp. 122–31, at p. 123. The use of the term 'myth' does not imply that the nationalist narrative is entirely fantastical. Much of it conforms with the outline of Ukrainian history given in chapter 1. In this sense, the Little Russian or Russian nationalist version of Ukrainian history is of course equally mythical.

72 For example, Valentin Mamutov, 'Dikoe pole – ne terra-inkognita', *Donetskii kriazh*, 8–14 October 1993; Zheleznyi, 'Ukraina: kak vozniklo dvuiazychnie'; Dmitrii Kornilov, 'Pro obgorelyi pen' i srednego brata', *Donbas*, no. 6, 1990, pp. 165–76; Analysis Department of the Party of Slavic Unity of Ukraine (Analiticheskii otdel Partii Slavianskogo Edinstva Ukrainy), 'Rusichi – novaia Slavianskaia natsiia?', *Slavianskoe edinstvo*, no. 2 (March), 1995; and A. A. Slin'ko (ed.), *Novye stranitsy v istorii Donbassa*.

73 Interview with V. Babkin, 'Vid naukovoho komunizmu – do naukovoho natsionalizmu?', *Holos Ukraïny*, 2 February 1994; Oleksandr Moroz, ' "Naukovyi natsionalizm" na derzhavnomu rivni?', *Viche*, March 1994, pp. 25–33; Yevgenii Bystritskii, 'Pochemu natsionalizm ne mozhet byt' naukoi', *Politicheskaia mysl'*, no. 2, 1994, pp. 33–9.

74 Some nationalists accept the alternative theory of Ukrainian ethnogenesis, namely their Asian/Iranian origin, but others dismiss this as a deliberate 'political' attempt 'to distance Ukraine from Europe': Anatolii Ponomar'ov, 'Pokhodzhennia ta etnichna istoriia ukraïntsiv', *Ukraïns'ka etnohrafiia* (Kiev: Lybid', 1994), pp. 96–111, at p. 97. See also V. I. Naulko, 'Formuvannia

ukraïns'koï narodnosti i natsiï', in Naulko *et al.* (eds.), *Kul'tura i pobut naselennia Ukraïny* (Kiev: Lybid', 1991), pp. 13–21, at p. 14.

75 Yu. V. Pavlenko, *Peredistoriia davnikh rusiv u svitovomu konteksti* (Kiev: Feniks, 1994); V. Bokan' *et al.*, *Istoriia kul'tury Ukraïny* (Kiev: Biblioteka Ukraïntsia, 1993), pp. 1–28; B. P. Chepurko, *Ukraïntsi: voskresinnia* (L'viv: Slovo, 1991); and V. A. Smolii and O. I. Hurzhii, *Yak i koly pochala formuvatysia ukraïns'ka natsiia* (Kiev: 1991). See also Serhii Plachynda, *Slovnyk davn'oukraïns'koï mifolohiï* (Kiev: Ukraïns'kyi pys'mennyk, 1993).

76 Chemerys, *Prezydent: Roman-ese*, p. 10.

77 H. K. Vasylenko, *Velyka Skifiia* (Kiev: Znannia, 1991), p. 3.

78 The text can be found *inter alia* in Orest Subtelny (Subtel'nyi), *Ukraïna: istoriia* (Kiev: Lybid', 1991), p. 495.

79 Yaroslav Dashkevych, 'Natsiia i utvorennia Kyïvs'koï Rusi', *Ratusha*, 9 September 1993; 'Osnovi etnichnoï istoriï ukraïns'koï natsiï. Mifolohizatsiia ta demifolohizatsiia', *Ratusha*, 4–5 September 1991; Oleksa Novak, 'Derzhava ukraïntsiv – Kyïvs'ka Rus'', *Klych*, nos. 6 and 7, 1993.

80 Vasyl' Levchenko, 'Razom z imperiieiu vmyraiut' fal'shyvi teoriï ta mify', *Klych*, nos. 2 and 3 (April), 1993.

81 'Ukraïna mizh skhodom i zakhodom', M. F. Tarasenko *et al.*, *Istoriia filosofiï Ukraïny* (Kiev: Lybid', 1993), pp. 511–20, at p. 519.

82 V. S. Hors'kyi, *Narysy z istoriï filosofs'koï kul'tury Kyïvs'koï Rusi* (Kiev: Naukova dumka, 1993).

83 Soldatenko and Syvolov, 'Vytoky i peredvisnyky ukraïns'koï ideï', p. 10.

84 Leonid Zalizniak, 'Ukraïna i Rosiia: rizni istorychni doli', *Starozhytnosti*, no. 19, 1991. For a discussion of this issue by Western historians, see Tibor Szamuely, *The Russian Tradition* (London: Secker and Warburg, 1974), who broadly supports the Ukrainian position, and Charles Halperin, *Russia and the Golden Horde: The Mongol Impact on Russian History* (London: I. B. Tauris, 1987), who disagrees.

85 Soldatenko and Syvolov, 'Vytoky i peredvisnyky ukraïns'koï ideï', p. 11.

86 'Ukraïna mizh skhodom i zakhodom', p. 517.

87 According to one typical analysis, 'the Grand Principality of Lithuania was a polyethnic state', which preserved 'a form of Ukrainian statehood which was [only] lost as a consequence of the Union of Lublin in 1569': Naulko, 'Formuvannia ukraïns'koï narodnosti i natsiï', p. 16.

88 Leonid Zalizniak, 'Ukraïna i "osoblyvyi shliakh Rosiï"', *Huta*, no. 1 (October), 1991.

89 Zalizniak, 'Ukraïna i Rosiia'; and Zalizniak, *Narysy starodavnoï istoriï Ukraïny* (Kiev: Abrys, 1994), pp. 163–88.

90 The concept of a *mythomateur*, the 'constitutive myth of a polity' or national group, is derived from John A. Armstrong, *Nations Before Nationalism* (Chapel Hill: University of North Carolina Press, 1982), pp. 8–9, as is the idea of 'Antemurale' or Christian frontier nations, p. 91.

91 Dziuba, 'Ukraïna i Rosiia', in Ostash, *Quo vadis Ukraïno?*, pp. 37–54, at p. 42. The Ukrainians would claim that they are restoring rather than revising the original meaning.

92 'Ukraïna mizh skhodom i zakhodom', p. 512.

93 V. A. Smolii *et al.* (eds.), *Ukraïns'ka kozats'ka derzhava: vytoky ta shliakhy*

istorychnoho rozvytku (Kiev and Cherkasy: Institute of History, 1994); and 'Ukraïns'ke kozatstvo: suchasnyi stan ta perspektyvy doslidzhennia problemy. (Materialy "kruhloho stolu")', *Ukraïns'kyi istorychnyi zhurnal*, no. 12, 1990, pp. 12–29.

94 Bohdan Korchmaryk, *Dukhovi vplyvy Kyieva na Moskovshchynu v dobu het'mans'koï Ukraïny* (L'viv: Samopomich, 1993).

95 Oleksa Myshanych (ed.), *Ukraïns'ke barokko* (Kiev: Academy of Sciences, 1993). The 1710 Cossack constitution of Hetman Pylyp Orlyk has been described as 'the first European constitution in the modern sense of the term', which provided a model blueprint for popular democracy well before the American and French revolutions: Sliusarenko and Tomenko, *Istoriia ukraïns'koï konstytutsiï*, p. 9. See also Iryna Kresina and Oleksii Kresin, *Het'man Pylyp Orlyk i ioho konstytutsiia* (Kiev: Biblioteka Ukraïntsia, no. 3–9, 1993).

96 'Khronolohiia dukhovnoho ta fizychnoho nyshchennia ukraïns'koï natsiï', *Visnyk Prosvity. Spetsial'nyi vypusk, no. 1, 1994*; or *Moloď Ukraïny*, 4 October 1994. Cf. '22 zaborony ukraïns'koï movy', *Klych*, no. 3 (April), 1993.

97 Pavlo Movchan, 'Bula, ye i bude!', *Visnyk Prosvity. Spetsial'nyi vypusk, no. 1, 1994.*

98 Yurii Badz'o and Ivan Yushchyk (eds.), *Naibil'shyi zlochyn imperiï: Materialy naukovo-praktychnoï konferentsiï 'Slobozhanshchyna. Holodomor 1932–1933 rokiv'* (Kiev: Prosvita, 1993). See also Oleksa Musiienko, *Ukraïns'kyi etnotsyd* (Kiev: Biblioteka Ukraïntsia/Rada, 1994).

99 See the surveys by Oleksandr Boldyrev (ed.), *Istorychni postati Ukraïny* (Odesa: Maiak, 1993); and Soldaterko, *Ukraïns'ka ideia*. On Mazepa, see Yu. O. Ivanchenko (ed.), *Mazepa* (Kiev: Mystetstvo, 1993); on Polubotok, see Valerii Shevchuk, 'Borot'ba Pavla Polubotoka za zberezhennia reshtok ukraïns'koï avtonomiï', *Rozbudova derzhavy*, no. 9 (September), 1994.

100 Luk"ianenko, *De dobryi shliakh?*, p. 57.

101 Volodymyr Serhiichuk, *Symvolika suverennosti – syn'o-zhovta* (Kiev: Biblioteka Ukraïntsia, no. 3–2, 1993), pp. 15 and 11. See also O. Pasternak, *Poiasnennia tryzuba* (Kiev: Veselka, 1991; a reprint of a 1934 edn); Volodymyr Panchenko, *Sobornyi herb Ukraïny* (Kiev: Biblioteka Ukraïntsia, no. 3–1, 1993); K. Yu. Hlomozda, 'Ukraïns'kyi prapor v konteksti tradytsii natsional'no-derzhavnoï symvoliky', in Khmil' *et al.*, *Ukraïna XX st*, pp. 164–76; and Bohdan Krawchenko, 'National Memory in Ukraine: The Role of the Blue and Yellow Flag', *Journal of Ukrainian Studies*, vol. 15, no. 1 (Summer 1990), pp. 1–21.

102 Volodymyr Serhiichuk, *Natsional'na symvolika Ukraïny* (Kiev: Veselka, 1992), p. 34.

103 Luk"ianenko, *De dobryi shliakh?*, p. 57.

104 *Iz istoriï flagov*, Intermovement of the Donbass poster, dated autumn 1991. 'Donbass' is here written with two *s*es to indicate use of the Russian language.

105 Andrii Hrechylo, 'Do pytannia pro natsional'nu symvoliku', *Samostiina Ukraïna*, no. 17 (November), 1991.

106 *Samostiina Ukraïna*, nos. 7 and 10 (February and March), 1992. Fifty-three

out of the seventy who voted against the adoption of the blue and yellow flag or abstained were from eastern and southern Ukraine.

107 Ivan Pliushch, 'Nastav chas pohlybliuvaty politychni ta ekonomichni reformy', *Holos Ukraïny*, 22 February 1994; Ivan Pliushch, *Khto my i kudy idemo*, p. 112.

108 Volodymyr Balenok, 'Prapor pravdy i dobra v Ukraïni', *Tovarysh*, no. 9, March 1994. The campaign has not proved as strong as that in neighbouring Belarus, where a referendum in spring 1995 endorsed the return of Soviet-era symbols.

109 P. T. Tron'ko and V. A. Voinalovych, *Uvichnena istoriia Ukraïny* (Kiev: Naukova dumka, 1992) provide an interesting study of monument construction in the Ukrainian SSR.

110 In one of his first decrees as president, Kuchma abolished the Council for Religious Affairs, which was widely seen as favouring the UOC (KP).

111 On the July 1995 events, see *Ukrainian Weekly*, 23 and 30 July 1995; *Nezavisimost'* and *Holos Ukraïny*, both for 21 July 1995.

112 Serhii Zdioruk, 'Natsional'na tserkva u konteksti derzhavotvorennia v Ukraïni', *Rozbudova derzhavy*, no. 1, 1994; and Serhii Bilokin', 'Dukhovnist' – nadbannia natsiï. Derzhavnyts'ka ideolohiia Kyïvs'koho patriarkhatu', *Samostiina Ukraïna*, no. 7 (March), 1994. See also Viktor Yelens'kyi, 'Tserkva i vybory', and 'Khrestonostsi: ukraïns'ki tserkvy i velyka polityka', *Post-postup*, no. 34, 22–9 September 1993 and no. 15, 11–16 April 1994 respectively.

113 'Khto i chomu shturmuvav Lavru?', *Holos Ukraïny*, 3 July 1992; Serhii Hrynchuk, 'I nekhai nam dopomozhe Boh ...', *Ukraïns'ki obriï,* no. 11, 1993; and M. Breus, 'Ukraïns'kyi natsionalizm ta khrystyianstvo', *Holos natsiï,* no. 40–1, 1993.

114 See for example *Nezavisimost'*, 17 February 1995 on events in Rivne.

115 Author's interview with Yevhen Sverstiuk, 4 September 1995.

116 Viktor Vovk and Oleksii Mustafin, 'Bogataia mnogoobraziem, sil'naia edinstvom', *Kyïvs'kyi sotsial-demokrat*, no. 1 (October), 1991.

117 A federalised Ukraine would most likely be a territorial federation like modern Germany, rather than an ethno-territorial federation like Yugoslavia or the USSR, but any boundaries which followed historical divisions would also coincide to an extent with ethnic and linguistic divides.

118 Mykhailo Horyn', 'National'na yednist' – garant ukraïns'koï derzhavnosti', speech at the first congress of the CNDF, *Samostiina Ukraïna*, no. 31 (August), 1992.

119 Author's interview with V"iacheslav Chornovil, 22 March 1993.

120 *Samostiina Ukraïna*, no. 13 (March), 1992.

121 'Vyborcha prohrama Ukraïns'koï respublikans'koï partiï', *Ternystyi shliakh*, 19 March 1994. See also *Samostiina Ukraïna*, nos. 7, 19, 22–4 and 28, 1992.

122 Vasyl' Osviienko, 'Chomu my proty federalizatsiï?', *Samostiina Ukraïna*, no. 15 (October), 1991; Yevhen Boltarovych, 'Federatyvna Ukraïna nikoly ne poduduie odes'kyi terminal', *Demoz*, no. 4, 1994; *Ukhvala pershoï konferentsiï DemPU: pro zahrozu suverenitetovi i terytorial'nii tsilisnosti Ukraïny* (Kiev, party material, 12 April 1992).

123 'Zaiava demokratychnoho ob"iednannia *Ukraïna* u *zv"iazku* z nastupom antyderzhavnyts'kykh, antyukraïns'kykh syl na Kharkivshchyni', *Literaturna Ukraïna*, 7 July 1994; Anatolii Horilyi, 'Nasha yedyna i taka rizna natsiia', *Holos Ukraïny*, 24 July 1994.

124 Mykhailo Horyn', 'National'na yednist' – garant ukraïns'koï derzhavnosti', speech at the first congress of the CNDF, *Samostiina Ukraïna*, no. 31 (August), 1992.

125 As early as April 1990, the CPU Politburo called for the Institute of History and others to 'prepare scientific and well-founded materials for the use of ruling organs to [reject] illegitimate territorial claims against the Ukrainian SSR': CSACOU, f. 1, op. 11, delo 2165, p. 83.

126 See, for example, *Samostiina Ukraïna*, no. 15 (October), 1991 on Bukovyna in 1918; or Stepan Rosokha, *Soim Karpats'koï Ukraïny* (L'viv: Memorial, 1991) on Transcarpathia in 1938–9. Cf. Petro Lavriv, 'Kubans'ka narodna respublika', *Visti z Ukraïny*, no. 27, 1994 on the Kuban' after 1917.

127 D. M. Fedaka (ed.), *Ukraïns'ki karpaty* (Uzhhorod: Karpaty, 1993), pp. 406–12 and 471–82; V. Markus' and V. Khudanych, *Za ukraïns'ke zakarpattia* (Uzhhorod: Grazhdan, 1994).

128 Andrew Wilson, 'The Donbas Between Ukraine and Russia: The Use of History in Political Disputes', *Journal of Contemporary History*, vol. 30, no. 2 (April 1995), pp. 265–89. See also Petro Lavriv, *Istoriia pivdenno-skhidnoï Ukraïny*, and Lavriv, 'Kolonizatsiia ukraïns'kykh i sumizhnikh stepiv', *Vyzvol'nyi shliakh*, nos. 4–7, 1994; T. A. Balabushevych, 'Terytoriia ta kordony zaporoz'kykh zemel' (1667–1775 rr.)', in Trubenko and Horbyk, *Istorychno-heohrafichni doslidzhennia v Ukraïni*, pp. 73–88; and Yaroslav Dashkevych, 'Dyskusiini pytannia natsional'noho budivnytstva Pivdnia Ukraïny', *Ukraïna: vchora i nyni* (Kiev: Academy of Sciences, 1993), pp. 89–99. Oleksandr Danyl'chenko, 'Pivden' Ukraïny: povernennia v maibutnie', *Viche*, no. 1, 1995, pp. 143–52 argues that until the end of the nineteenth century 'the clear majority of settlers [in the south] were Ukrainians ... from the neighbouring guberniias of Left Bank and Right Bank Ukraine', at pp. 149 and 150. For a commentary, see Plokhy, 'Historical Debates and Territorial Claims'.

129 Plokhy, 'Historical Debates and Territorial Claims', n. 44.

130 Levko Luk"ianenko, 'Zvitna dopovid' holovy URP III z"ïzdovi', *Materiialy tret'oho z"ïzdu URP*, p. 14.

131 Yaroslav Dashkevych, 'Ukraïntsi v Krimu (XV–pochatok XX st.)', *Suchasnist'*, April 1992, pp. 96–104; Vasyl' Chumak, *Ukraïna i Krym: spil'nist' istorychnoï doli* (Kiev: Biblioteka Ukraïntsia, no. 2–3, 1993), especially pp. 3–41. Cf. Andrew Wilson, *Crimean Tatars*.

132 On the early development of regional problems see Kuzio and Wilson, *Ukraine: Perestroika to Independence*, pp. 191–202; plus Roman Solchanyk, 'Centrifugal Movements in Ukraine and Independence', *Ukrainian Weekly*, 24 November 1991; and Solchanyk, 'The Politics of State-Building: Centre–Periphery Relations in Post-Soviet Ukraine', *Europe–Asia Studies*, vol. 46, no. 1, 1994, pp. 47–68.

133 M. P. Makara and I. I. Myhovych, 'Karpats'ki rusyny v konteksti

suchasnoho etnopolitychnoho zhyttia', *Ukraïns'kyi istorychnyi zhurnal*, no. 1, 1994, pp. 117–28, at p. 123.

134 *Moloda Halychyna*, 28 March 1992; *Post-postup*, 4–10 November and 11–17 November 1993.

135 Oleksa Myshanych, *Politychne rusynstvo i shcho za nym* (Uzhhorod: Hrazhda, 1993); Fedir Myshanych, 'Zakhystyty zakarpattia', *Respublikanets'*, no. 2, 1991. See also Yaroslav Dashkevych, 'Etnichni psevdomenshyny v Ukraïni', in Volodymyr Yevtukh and Arnold Suppan (eds.), *Etnichni menshyny Skhidnoï ta Tsentral'noï Yevropy* (Kiev: Intel, 1994), pp. 65–79.

136 *Pravda Ukrainy*, 3 December 1991. A draft autonomy law, 'Pro spetsial'nu samovriadnu administratyvnu terytoriiu Zakarpattia (proekt)', was published in early 1992 and approved by the oblast council (*Novyny Zakarpattia*, 1 February and 10 March 1992), but had still to be implemented in early 1995.

137 A loosely structured elite party, the Movement for Democratic Reforms, was formed in late 1993: *Holos Ukraïny*, 17 December 1993. See also Alfred A. Reisch, 'Transcarpathia and Its Neighbours', *RFE/RL Research Report*, vol. 1, no. 7, 14 February 1992.

138 Alfred A. Reisch, 'Transcarpathia's Hungarian Minority and the Autonomy Issue', *RFE/RL Research Report*, vol. 1, no. 6, 7 February 1992; D. Doroshenko, *Uhors'ka Ukraïna* (Uzhhorod: Hazeta srïbna zemlia, 1992).

139 *Post-postup*, 30 December 1993–5 January 1994.

140 'Bukovyna', *Zamkova hora*, no. 20, 1992; *Ukraïns'ki obriï*, no. 10, 1992; SWB, SU 1820 D/2.

141 Bohdan Nahaylo, 'Ukraine and Moldova: The View from Kiev', and 'Moldovan Conflict Creates New Dilemmas for Ukraine', *RFE/RL Research Report*, vol. 1, nos. 18 and 20, 1 and 15 May 1992; Vladimir Socor, 'Five Countries Look at Ethnic Problems in Southern Moldova', *RFE/RL Research Report*, vol. 3, no. 32, 19 August 1994; *Vechirnii Kyïv*, 21–2 May and 24 July 1992; *Za vil'nu Ukraïnu*, 19 March 1992; and *Post-postup*, no. 11, 1992.

142 Andrew Wilson, 'The Growing Challenge to Kiev from the Donbas', *RFE/RL Research Report*, vol. 2, no. 33, 20 August 1993; Ian Bremmer, 'The Politics of Ethnicity: Russians in the New Ukraine', *Europe–Asia Studies*, vol. 46, no. 2 (1994), pp. 261–83.

143 *Aktsent*, 1 April 1994; *Luganskaia pravda*, 2 April 1994.

144 The local soviet now has legislative powers, but Simferopil' and Kiev dispute whether it is a sovereign body: Kathleen Mihalisko, 'The Other Side of Separatism: Crimea Votes for Autonomy', *Report on the USSR*, vol. 3, no. 5, 1 February 1991; Andrew Wilson, 'The Elections in Crimea' and 'Crimea's Political Cauldron', *RFE/RL Research Report*, vol. 3, no. 25, 24 June 1994 and vol. 2, no. 45, 12 November 1993.

145 'Zaiava URP z pryvodu podii u Krymu', *Obizhnyk sekretariatu URP*, 31 May 1994; *Klych*, no. 6, 1993.

146 *Ukraïns'ki obriï*, no. 8, 1992. Cf. no. 2, 1994.

147 Chrystyna Lapychak, 'Crackdown on Crimean Separatism', *Transition*, vol. 1, no. 8, 26 May 1995. The Crimean presidency was abolished and

appointments to the Crimean government made subject to Kuchma's approval. Kiev also imposed its own choice of prime minister (Anatolii Franchuk) and chairman of Parliament (Yevhen Supruniuk). By autumn the Crimean constitution had largely been rewritten to Kiev's liking.

148 Charles Tarlton, 'Symmetry and Asymmetry as Elements of Federalism: A Theoretical Speculation', *Journal of Politics*, vol. 27 (1965), pp. 861–74. See also Graham Smith, 'Mapping the Federal Condition: Ideology, Political Practice and Social Justice', in Smith (ed.), *Federalism: The Multiethnic Challenge* (London: Longman, 1995), pp. 1–28.

149 Levko Luk″ianenko, *Hromadians′ke suspil′stvo: shcho tse i koly zbuduiemo?* (Kiev: URP, 1994); Yurii Badz′o, 'Chomu nam potribna bahatopartiinist′?', *Volia*, no. 15–16 (September), 1991; Rukh, *A Concept of State-Building in Ukraine* (Kiev: Taki spravy, 1993), pp. 16–20.

150 *Klych*, no. 1 (February), 1993.

151 *Samostiina Ukraïna*, no. 31 (August), 1992. The preference for presidential government was stronger amongst members of the CNDF than Rukh.

152 Wilson, 'Ukraine: Two Presidents, But No Settled Powers'.

153 Luk″ianenko, 'Ukraïntsi i ïkh konstytutsiia', *Samostiina Ukraïna*, no. 11 (August), 1991.

154 I. S. Koropeckyj (ed.), *The Ukrainian Economy: Achievements, Problems, Challenges* (Cambridge, Mass.: Harvard University Press, 1992); Koropeckyj (ed.), *The Ukraine Within the USSR: An Economic Balance Sheet* (New York: Praeger, 1977); and Koropeckyj, 'A Century of Moscow–Ukraine Economic Relations: An Interpretation', *Harvard Ukrainian Studies*, vol. 5, no. 4 (December 1981), pp. 467–96. See also the author's interview with Veniamin Sikora, published in *Central European*, May 1992.

155 For example, Ivan Pozputenko, 'Ekonomichnyi neokolonializm na marshi', *Vyzvolennia '91*; 'Ekonomika i derzhavna nezalezhnist′', *Samostiina Ukraïna*, no. 9 (July), 1991; Oleksa Didyk, 'Dlia nas hotuiut′ nove yarmo', *Ternystyi shliakh*, nos. 17 and 18 (June), 1991; *Vechirnii Kyïv*, 5 August 1991; and 'Potentsial Ukraïny', *Uriadovyi kur″ier*, no. 35–6 (November), 1991.

156 CSACOU, f. 1, op. 11, delo 2198, pp. 32–3.

157 Leonid Zalizniak, *Narysy starodavnoï istoriï Ukraïny*, pp. 209–11. Cf. Anton Filipenko, 'Nas vyshtovkhnut′ na peryferiiu', *Holos Ukraïny*, 6 May 1994.

158 Oleh Havrylyshyn, Marcus Miller and William Perraudin, 'Deficits, Inflation and the Political Economy of Ukraine', *Economic Policy*, no. 19 (October 1994), pp. 354–401, at p. 355. See also *IMF Economic Review: Ukraine* (London: IMF, 1992–4); *Economist Intelligence Unit: Quarterly Report for Ukraine, Belarus and Moldova* (London: EIU, 1993–5, passim); *The EBRD Annual Economic Review* (London: EBRD, 1992–4); and Helen Boss, 'Ukraine's First Year of Economic Statehood', in Gábor Hunya (ed.), *Economic Transformation in East-Central Europe and in the Newly Independent States* (Boulder: Westview, 1994), pp. 243–75.

159 Luk″ianenko, *De dobryi shliakh?*, p. 17; and Luk″ianenko, 'Ukraïna musyt′ zibratysia na sylakh. Dlia rishuchoho ryvka vpered', *Samostiina Ukraïna*, no. 10, 1994. Mykhailo Horyn′ talked of Russia's economic 'war' against Ukraine: *IV z″izd Ukraïns′koï respublikans′koï partiï* (Kiev: URP, 1993), p. 24.

160 *Ukraïns'ka hazeta*, no. 19, 1994. Cf. Oles M. Smolensky, 'Ukraine's Quest for Independence: The Fuel Factor', *Europe–Asia Studies*, vol. 47, no. 1 (1995), pp. 67–90.

161 Oleh Havrylyshyn, 'Ukraine's Economic Crisis, Its Causes and Prospects for Resolution', *Ukrainian Weekly*, nos. 47 and 48, 21 and 28 November 1993; and Marek Dabrowski, 'The Ukrainian Way to Hyperinflation', *Communist Economies and Economic Transformation*, vol. 6, no. 2 (1994), pp. 115–37.

162 Greater effort was made to contain monetary growth after December 1993 under new National Bank chairman Viktor Yushchenko, but the subsequent imbalance between monetary and fiscal policies only introduced a new source of instability.

163 The massive underpricing of Russian energy rather undermines the idea that Ukraine was an 'internal colony'.

164 F. Desmond McCarthy *et al.*, 'External Shocks and Performance Responses During Systemic Transition: The Case of Ukraine', *Ukrainian Economic Review*, vol. 1, no. 1–2, 1995, pp. 27–48; Helen Boss and Peter Hovlik, 'Slavic (Dis)Union: Consequences for Russia, Belarus and Ukraine', *Economics of Transition*, no. 2, 1994, pp. 233–54.

165 Author's interview with Levko Luk"ianenko, 23 October 1994. See also the attacks on the proposed CIS 'Economic Union' in *Literaturna Ukraïna*, 5 and 26 August, and 2 September 1993; and Bohdan Konvai, 'Ekonomichnyi soiuz ta interesy Ukraïny', *Rozbudova derzhavy*, no. 19 (October), 1994.

166 *Protokoly prezydiï DemPU*, nos. 10 and 22 (5 March and 2 July 1991).

167 'Aktual'ni aspekty potochnoï ekonomichnoï polityky URP', *URP-inform*, 13 September 1994. See also the speech of Stepan Khmara at the second congress of the UCRP; *Klych*, no. 19, 1994. For an attack on the national-democrats' tendency toward economic isolationism and 'national-soci-alism', and prejudice against trading links with Russia, see Yurii Boldyrev *et al.*, 'Sontse vstaie na Skhodi, abo chomy Ukraïna stala kraïnoiu zakhodu sontsia', *Holos Ukraïny*, 21 February 1995.

168 Daniel Kaufman, 'Market Liberalisation in Ukraine', *Transition*, vol. 5, no. 7 (September 1994).

169 Oleksandr Savchenko, 'Vid pryvatyzatsiï – do konvertovanoï hryvni. Rukhivs'ka prohrama ekonomichnoho rozvytku Ukraïny v umovakh neza-lezhnosti', *Za vil'nu Ukraïnu*, 14 January 1992; Volodymyr Pylypchuk, 'Peredvyborna ekonomichna platforma Demokratychnykh syl Ukraïny', *Literaturna Ukraïna*, 10 February 1994.

170 Oleksandr Shmorhun, *Ukraïna: shliakh vidrodzhennia (ekonomika, polityka, kul'tura)* (Kiev: Fundatsiia im. O. Ol'zhycha, 1994), p. 140.

171 *Nezalezhnii Ukraïni – nezalezhnu ekonomiku, hromadianam – vlasnist' i svobodu hospodariuvannia. Pohliad DemPU na nynishniu ekonomichnu sytuat-siiu*, document dated 24 January 1992; 'Zaiava KNDS shchodo ekono-michnoï polityky', *Samostiina Ukraïna*, no. 31 (August), 1992; Oleksandr Lavrynovych and Mykola Porovs'kyi, 'Liumpen nikoly ne stane hospo-darem', *Holos Ukraïny*, 16 May 1992.

172 Author's interviews with Oleh Pavlyshyn and Yurii Badz'o, 27 January and 29 April 1992.

7 THE NATIONALIST AGENDA: EXTERNAL AFFAIRS – UNTYING THE RUSSIAN KNOT

1 On Ukrainian foreign policy in general, see Charles J. Furtado Jr, 'Nationalism and Foreign Policy in Ukraine', *Political Science Quarterly*, vol. 109, no. 1 (Spring 1994), pp. 81–104; Ilya Prizel, 'The Influence of Ethnicity on Foreign Policy: The Case of Ukraine', in Roman Szporluk (ed.), *National Identity and Ethnicity in Russia and the New States of Eurasia* (London: M. E. Sharpe, 1994), pp. 103–28; James Gow, 'Independent Ukraine: The Politics of Security', *International Relations*, vol. 11, no. 3 (December 1992), pp. 253–67; and John Morrison, 'Pereyaslav and After: The Russian–Ukrainian Relationship', *International Affairs*, vol. 69, no. 4 (1993), pp. 677–703.

2 Dmitrii Kornilov, 'Tak kto zhe bol'she liubit Ukrainu?', *Donetskii kriazh*, no. 3, 21–7 January 1994.

3 See also Roman Solchanyk, 'Russia, Ukraine and the Imperial Legacy', *Post-Soviet Affairs*, vol. 9, no. 4 (1993), pp. 337–65; Roman Szporluk, 'The Ukraine and Russia', in Robert Conquest (ed.), *The Last Empire: Nationality and the Soviet Future* (Stanford: Hoover Institution Press, 1986); Zbigniew Brzezinski, 'The Premature Partnership', *Foreign Affairs*, March–April 1994, pp. 67–82.

4 'Ukraïns'ka, rosiis'ka ta pol's'ka natsional'ni ideï: totozhnist' chy protylezhnist'?', in Shmorhun, *Ukraïna: shliakh vidrodzhennia*, pp. 140–66; Petro Holubenko, *Ukraïna i Rosiia u svitli kul'turnykh vzaiemyn* (Kiev: Dnipro, 1993; first published in Toronto in 1987).

5 Author's interview with Levko Luk"ianenko, 23 October 1994.

6 'Vystup p. Dmytra Korchyns'koho na konferentsii ABN OT', *Visti prestsentru UMA*, no. 6 (June), 1991.

7 Roman Koval', *Pro vorohiv, soiuznykiv i poputnykiv*, p. 22.

8 'Zaiava provodu URP', *Samostiina Ukraïna*, no. 18 (April), 1992. Cf. Yu. O. Kurnosov, 'Nasyllia – holovnyi argument bil'shovyzmu', *Ukraïns'kyi istorychnyi zhurnal*, no. 12, 1991 and no. 1, 1992, pp. 16–28 and 3–17.

9 For the views of Russian politicians concerning Ukraine, see Jeremy Lester, 'Russian Political Attitudes to Ukrainian Independence', *Journal of Communist Studies and Transition Politics*, vol. 10, no. 2 (June 1994), pp. 193–233.

10 *Holos Ukraïny*, 3 March 1992. See also Ivan Drach, 'Politychna sytuatsiia na Ukraïni i zavdannia Rukhu', *Visnyk Rukhu*, no. 7 (November), 1990, pp. 8–9; and Dziuba, 'Ukraïna i Rosiia', pp. 37–54.

11 For attacks on Russia's Chechen policy, see Oleksandr Skipal's'kyi, 'Viis'kovyi dyktat yak forma rosiis'koï demokratiï', *Holos Ukraïny*, 24 December 1994; and the book published by KUN, Said-Khasan Abumuslimov, *Genatsid pradalzhaetsia; k voprosu o rossiiskoi ekspansii v Chechne* (Kiev: KUN, 1995).

12 *Natsionalist*, no. 2, 1991, p. 21; Roman Koval', 'Ukraïns'ki demokraty i demokraty Ukraïny', p. 61 and Koval', 'Rosiis'ki demokraty i problemy imperiï'.

13 Author's interview with Yurii Badz'o, 29 April 1992.

14 *Visnyk Prosvity. Spetsial'nyi vypusk, no. 1, 1994*, p. 2.

15 See Mykhailo Horyn', *Zapalyty svichu u pit'mi*, most of the articles in which are on this theme; Les' Taniuk, 'Ukraïna ta Yevropa', in *Khto z"iv moie m"iaso?*, pp. 337–43; and Vadym Levanovs'kyi, 'Povernennia do Yevropu', *Samostiina Ukraïna*, nos. 37–40 (October), 1994.

16 Mykhailo Horyn', 'Ukraïns'kyi shliakh do Yevropy', in *Zapalyty svichu u pit'mi*, p. 61.

17 *Protokoly DemPU*, no. 15, 1991; *Protokol nos. 7 & 9. Zasidannia Politychnoï Rady Narodnoho Rukhu Ukraïny*, 4 February and 10 March 1991.

18 Yurii Badz'o, *Nova pastka* (DPU document dated 16 December 1991), 16 December 1991; speech of V"iacheslav Chornovil, *IV Velyki Zbory Narodnoho Rukhu Ukraïny*, p. 12; *Ne spivdruzhnist', a spivrobitnytstvo!* (Declaration of the DPU, 12 December 1991).

19 V"iacheslav Chornovil in *Za vil'nu Ukraïnu*, 12 December 1991.

20 *Demokratychna Ukraïna*, 25 December 1991.

21 *Vechirnii Kyïv*, 15 January 1992; *Zvil'nytysia vid zahrozy novoho HKChP!* (Declaration of the DPU, 18 January 1992); *Ukhvala III Vseukraïns'kykh zboriv Narodnoho Rukhu Ukraïny* (Rukh documents, dated 1 March 1992).

22 Mykhailo Horyn', 'Ukraïns'kyi shliakh do Yevropy', p. 59.

23 Oleksandr Kyrychenko, ' "Rosiis'ka" polityka Vashingtonu', *Klych*, no. 4 (May), 1993.

24 See also Taras Kuzio, 'Ukraine and the Expansion of NATO', *Jane's Intelligence Review*, vol. 7, no. 9 (September 1995), pp. 389–91.

25 'Zaiava pro mozhlyvist' stvorennia Baltiis'ko-Chornomors'koï zony intensyvnoï ekonomichnoï spivpratsi', *Samostiina Ukraïna*, no. 13 (March), 1992; *Samostiina Ukraïna*, no. 4 (February), 1993; and *Prohamova deklaratsiia druhoho z"izdu DemPU (proekt)* (Kiev: Document supplied by DPU secretariat, 1992), p. 3.

26 'Zvitna dopovid' holovy URP Mykhaila Horynia', *IV z"izd URP*, pp. 24–5.

27 Zoia Yukhymchuk, 'Chy svidoma natsiia svoieï istorychnoï suti?', *Klych*, no. 3 (April), 1993; Horyn' in *IV z"izd URP*, p. 18.

28 Serhii Pyrozhkov, 'Geopolityka i voienna doktryna', *Holos Ukraïny*, 16 September 1993.

29 For an exchange of views over whether Ukraine should play the role of a buffer state, see Viktor Nebozhenko, 'Staty buferom? Nikoly!', and the interview with V"iacheslav Chornovil, 'Staty buferom? Chomu b ni . . .', *Holos Ukraïny*, 18 January and 21 February 1995.

30 Volodymyr Serhiichuk, 'Do istoriï stvorennia Chornomors'ko-Baltiis'koho soiuzu', *Rozbudova derzhavy*, no. 9 (September), 1994.

31 *Visti prestsentru UMA*, nos. 6 (June), and 8 (July), 1991; *Za vil'nu Ukraïnu*, 19 December 1992.

32 Speeches of Stepan Khmara at the second and first congresses of the UCRP; *Klych*, no. 19, 1994; *Vechirnii Kyïv*, 19 June 1992.

33 *Mizhmor"ia biuleten' ligy partiï kraïn Balto-Chornomors'ko-Adriiatychnoho regionu*, no. 1, August 1994; and *Samostiina Ukraïna*, nos. 29 and 31 (August), 1994. As well as the URP, DPU, KUN, Social Democrats and Ukrainian Greens, the inaugural meeting was attended by, amongst others, the Popular Front of Belarus, the Confederation for an Independent

Poland, Estonia's Pro Patria party, the Conservative Party of Lithuania and Latvia's 'For Motherland and Freedom' group.

34 Ian J. Brzezinski, 'Polish–Ukrainian Relations: Europe's Neglected Strategic Axis', *Survival*, no. 3, 1993, pp. 26–37.

35 For example, Oleksandr Skipal's'kyi, 'Faktor politychnoï stabilizatsiï', *Viis'ko Ukraïny*, no. 1–2, 1995.

36 *Klych*, no. 3 (April), 1993.

37 *Ukraïns'ka hazeta*, no. 19, 1994.

38 'Bezpeka dlia sebe – cherez bezpeku dlia vsikh', *Holos Ukraïny*, 1 December 1993.

39 Daniel Connelly, 'Black Sea Economic Cooperation', *RFE/RL Research Report*, vol. 3, no. 26, 1 July 1994.

40 See also Bohdan Chervak, 'Ukraïns'kyi natsionalizm i kontseptsiia "vlasnykh syl"', *Rozbudova derzhavy*, no. 9 (September), 1994.

41 Author's interview with Viktor Mel'nyk, 7 May 1992.

42 *Za vil'nu Ukraïnu*, 16 February 1993; *Zamkova hora*, no. 12, 1993; *Ukraïns'ki obriï*, no. 22, 1993.

43 *Ukraïns'ki obriï*, no. 6, 1993 and no. 1, 1994.

44 Author's interview with UNSO leader Dmytro Korchyns'kyi, 12 May 1992. See also *Post-postup*, no. 17, 1992.

45 'Viis'kova doktryna Ukraïns'koï natsional'noï asambleï', *Zamkova hora*, no. 1, 1992.

46 'Prohrama Ukraïns'koï natsional'noï asambleï', *Ukraïns'ki obriï*, no. 1, 1994.

47 Sossa, *Ukraïntsi: skhidna diaspora*; Zastavnyi, *Skhidna ukraïns'ka diaspora*; and Volodymyr Serhiichuk, *Ukraïntsi v imperiï* (Kiev: Biblioteka Ukraïntsia, no. 3, 1992).

48 I. Mel'nychuk, 'Sybirs'ki ukraïntsi', *Holos Ukraïny*, 12 February 1992; Ch. Mishchuk, 'Ukraïntsi v Sybiru', *Vil'na dumka*, no. 12, 1992.

49 Ivan Drach, 'Ukraïntsi v Rosiï: obiideni doleiu chy zabuti Ukraïnoiu?', *Literaturna Ukraïna*, 22 July 1993. Cf. Liliia Heorhiieva, 'Khto vony, Rosiis'ki Ukraïntsi?', *Holos Ukraïny*, 26 October 1993.

50 Author's interview with Levko Luk"ianenko, 23 October 1994; 'Zvernennia prezydentovi Ukraïny', *Literaturna Ukraïna*, 28 July 1994.

51 Ivan Drach, 'Neznyshchennia voviky vikiv', *Literaturna Ukraïna*, 10 February 1994.

52 'Pro vnesennia zmin i dopovnen' do konstytutsiï (osnovnoho zakonu) Ukraïny', *Holos Ukraïny*, 7 April 1992.

53 Author's interviews with Viktor Mel'nyk and Dmytro Korchyns'kyi of the UNA, 7 and 12 May 1992.

54 'Zaiava Ukraïns'kykh pys'mennykiv z pryvodu proektu dohovoru mizh Ukraïnoiu i Rosiieiu', *Literaturna Ukraïna*, 1 September 1994.

55 Ukrainians in neighbouring states to the west were more strongly influenced by the nineteenth-century national revival, but most Ukrainians in 'Lemko' Poland were dispersed in 1947, and Ukrainians in Slovakia are divided between Ukrainophile and Rusynophile orientations. See Chris Hann, 'Ethnicity in the New Civil Society: Lemko-Ukrainians in Poland', in L. Kürti and J. Fox (eds.), *Beyond Borders: Remaking Eastern European Identities in the 1990s* (New York: Columbia University Press, 1996); and

Hann, 'Intellectuals, Ethnic Groups and Nations', in Sukumar Periwal (ed.), *Notions of Nationalism* (Budapest: Central European University Press, 1995), pp. 106–28. On Ukrainians in (Czecho)Slovakia, see Yurii Bacha *et al.*, *Chomu, koly i yak? Zapytannia i vidpovidi z istoriï i kul'tury rusyniv-ukraïntsiv Chekho-Slovachchyny* (Presov-Kiev: Intel, 1992).

56 Serge Cipko, in 'The Second Revival: Russia's Ukrainian Minority as an Emerging Factor in Eurasian Politics', paper presented at the conference 'Peoples, Nations and Identities: The Russian–Ukrainian Encounter', Columbia University, New York, 21–3 September 1995, points out that Ukrainians in Zelenyi Klyn held a *fifth* congress in March 1993 to emphasise continuity with the Ukrainian movement in the Far East in 1917–21, but elsewhere the sense of *Ukrainian*, as opposed to localist or Russophone, consciousness is weak. See also his *Ukrainians in Russia: A Bibliographic and Statistical Guide* (Edmonton, Ont.: CIUS, 1994).

57 Despite the foundation of a Union of Ukrainians in Transdnistria in May 1992: *Za vil'nu Ukraïnu*, 1 February 1992; *Holos Ukraïny*, 13 May 1992; *Holos*, no. 19, 9 October 1991. See also Bohdan Nahaylo, 'Ukraine and Moldova: The View From Kiev', *RFE/RL Research Report*, vol. 1, no. 18, 1 May 1992.

58 Ustina Markus, 'Immigrants in Ukraine', *RFE/RL Research Report*, vol. 3, no. 26, 1 July 1994, p. 50.

59 V. D. Boiechko, O. I. Hanzha and B. I. Zakharchuk, 'Kordony Ukraïny: istoriia ta problemy formuvannia (1917–1940 rr.)', *Ukraïns'kyi istorychnyi zhurnal*, no. 1, 1992, pp. 56–77. In most of western Ukraine the ethnographic balance has improved in Ukraine's favour in the twentieth century, so the argument is less important.

60 *Sobornist'* implies cultural and social unity as well as geographical ingathering: Petro Serhiienko, *Sobornist' Ukraïny: poniattia, ideia i real'nist'* (Kiev: Biblioteka Ukraïntsia, 1993).

61 Zastavnyi, *Ukraïns'ki etnichni zemli*, pp. 164–7, 144–5 and 156–7.

62 I. I. Vynnychenko, 'Ukraïntsi na Kubani ta Stavropol'shchyni (kinets' XVIII–pochatok XX st.)', in Trubenko and Horbyk, *Istorychno-heohrafichni doslidzhennia v Ukraïni*, pp. 64–73; Petro Lavriv, 'Kubans'ki kozaky', *Narodna hazeta*, no. 8, 1993; 'Kuban'', *Vechirnii Kyïv*, 30 July 1992; and Sossa, *Ukraïntsi: skhidna diaspora*, pp. 8–9 and 12–13.

63 Vasyl' Boiechko, 'Kordony Ukraïny: Moldova', *Vechirnii Kyïv*, 24 July 1992; Ihor Nediukha, 'Prydnistrov''ia: doroha do myru chy stezhyna viiny?', *Vechirnii Kyïv*, 21 April 1992.

64 Anna-halia Horbach, 'Z Rumuns'kykh vrazhen'', *Samostiina Ukraïna*, no. 19, 1994; Yaroslav Dashkevych, 'Etnichni psevdomenshyny v Ukraïni', in Yevtukh and Suppan, *Etnichni menshyny Skhidnoï ta Tsentral'noï Yevropy*, pp. 65–79, at p. 69; V. I. Patrushev *et al.*, *Ukraïns'ka diaspora u sviti* (Kiev: Znannia, 1993), p. 12.

65 Sossa, *Ukraïntsi: skhidna diaspora*, pp. 9 and 13.

66 *Vechirnii Kyïv*, 30 July 1992; *Literaturna Ukraïna*, 26 May 1994. A Ukrainian paper, *Kozats'kyi krai*, was printed in Donets'k for export to the Kuban' after 1994.

67 Author's interview with Pavlo Movchan, 26 November 1994.

68 Oleksa Haran', *Ukraïna bahatopartiina*, pp. 29 and 37; *Visnyk UNP*, no. 1 (June), 1990; author's interviews with DSU leaders Ivan Kandyba and Roman Koval', 2 and 5 May 1992.
69 'Prohrama Ukraïns'koï natsional'noï asambleï', *Ukraïns'ki obrii*, no. 1, 1994.
70 *Vechirnii Kyïv*, 19 June 1992; *Ukraïns'ki obrii*, no. 8, 1992.
71 Author's interviews with Viktor Mel'nyk and Dmytro Korchyns'kyi of the UNA, 7 and 12 May 1992.
72 Ustina Markus, 'No Longer As Mighty', *Transition*, vol. 1, no. 13, 28 July 1995.
73 Levko Luk"ianenko, 'Ukraïns'ka armiia: yak ïï stvoryty?', *Samostiina Ukraïna*, no. 5 (June), 1991. Cf. V. F. Soldatenko, 'Zbroini syly v Ukraïni (hruden' 1917 r.–kviten' 1918 r.)', *Ukraïns'kyi istorychnyi zhurnal*, no. 12, 1992, pp. 42–58.
74 Kravchuk and Kychyhin, *Leonid Kravchuk*, p. 27.
75 Kuzio, *Dissent in Ukraine Under Gorbachev*, article 17. See also Kuzio and Wilson, *Ukraine: Perestroika to Independence*, pp. 179–81; Anatolii Rusnachenko, *Na shliakhu do natsional'noï armiï (1989–1991)* (Kiev: 1992); and Colonel Stephen D. Olynyk, 'Emerging Post-Soviet Armies: The Case of Ukraine', *Military Review*, vol. 74, no. 3 (March 1994).
76 The Declaration is in *Argumenty i fakty*, 21–7 July 1990. See also Kathleen Mihalisko, 'Ukraine's Declaration of Sovereignty', *Report on the USSR*, RL 329/90, 27 July 1990.
77 *Kontseptsiia ukraïns'koï armiï* (document prepared by the Rukh council on military affairs, 1991); *Za vil'nu Ukraïnu*, 7 February 1991; and *Holos*, no. 3, 1991.
78 'Zaiava provodu URP', *Samostiina Ukraïna*, no. 31 (August), 1992.
79 *Samostiina Ukraïna*, no. 3 (January), 1992.
80 Stephen Foye, 'The Ukrainian Armed Forces: Prospects and Problems', *RFE/RL Research Report*, vol. 1, no. 26, 26 June 1992. Cf. the slightly higher estimates made by the Republican Party in *Molod' Ukraïny*, 21 August 1992.
81 For a review of the Black Sea fleet dispute, see Ustina Markus, 'The Ukrainian Navy and the Black Sea Fleet', *RFE/RL Research Report*, vol. 3, no. 18, 6 May 1994.
82 *Za vil'nu Ukraïnu*, 14 December 1991; *Holos Ukraïny*, 10 December 1991.
83 Levko Luk"ianenko, 'Zvitna dopovid' holovy URP III z"ïzdovi', *Materiialy tret'oho z"ïzdu URP*, p. 14. Luk"ianenko gave no indication whether these were Russians born in Ukraine or in the RSFSR. See also *Samostiina Ukraïna*, no. 6 (February), 1992.
84 *Samostiina Ukraïna*, no. 31 (August), 1992.
85 *Vechirnii Kyïv*, 8 June 1992.
86 *Holos Ukraïny*, 8 April 1993. On the campaign against Morozov, see *Holos Ukraïny*, 27 April 1993, and Morozov's memoir of his time in office in *Ukraïns'ka hazeta*, nos. 1–4, 1994.
87 Interview with Morozov, *Moloda Halychyna*, 9 June 1992. Only 10,000 refused to take the oath; Taras Kuzio, *Ukrainian Security Policy* (Washington, D.C.: Praeger/Centre for Strategic and International Studies, 1995), p. 100; while a mere 6,800 ethnic Ukrainians had

returned to Ukraine by September 1992: *Narodna armiia*, 15 September 1992.

88 *Nezavisimost'*, 8 April 1994. See the attack by former UOU head Vilen Martyrosian on the organisation in *Narodna armiia*, 17 April 1993.

89 'Posytsiia URP shchodo rozbudovy Zbroinykh Syl Ukraïny', *Samostiina Ukraïna*, no. 25 (June), 1992.

90 The 'concept' for the service was published in *Narodna armiia*, 22 January, 18 and 24 March 1993.

91 *Holos Ukraïny*, 17 November 1993.

92 See, for example, the pedagogic guide for educating national guardsmen 'Tematychni plany humanitarnoï pidhotovky osobovoho skladu NGU na 1995 rik', published in *Surma*, no. 1, 1995, pp. 56–68. *Surma* was a more overtly nationalist journal founded after the influence of the Social-Psychological Service in the main army journal *Viis'ko Ukraïny* was scaled down in 1994.

93 Ivanchenko, *Mazepa*; Volodymyr Kravtsevych, 'Voïny, polityky i ... rozvidnyky', *Holos Ukraïny*, 26 February 1994.

94 Volodymyr Serhiichuk, 'V UPA – vsia Ukraïna', *Viis'ko Ukraïny*, no. 6, 1993, pp. 74–84.

95 For example, *Holos Ukraïny*, 22 June and 8 October 1994; Volodymyr Mukhin, 'Pam"iat', zvernuta do nashadkiv', *Viche*, no. 1 (January), 1995; and for the celebrations of the fiftieth anniversary of the war's end, *Holos Ukraïny*, January–June 1995 passim.

96 Volodymyr Serhiichuk, *Mors'ki pokhody zaporozhtsiv* (Kiev: Biblioteka Ukraïntsia, no. 5, 1992); Andrii Panibud'laska and Borys Kantseliaruk, *Istoriia ukraïns'koï zbroï* (Kiev: Biblioteka Ukraïntsia, no. 3-7, 1993); Vladimir Kravtsevych, *Ukrainskii derzhavnyi flot* (Kiev: Krai, 1992); and Plokhy, 'Historical Debates and Territorial Claims', pp. 160–1. Cf. Douglas L. Clarke, 'The Saga of the Black Sea Fleet', *RFE/RL Research Report*, vol. 1, no. 4, 24 January 1992.

97 *Argumenty i fakty*, 21–7 July 1990. The 'Conception of National Defence and Building the Armed Forces of Ukraine', in *Holos Ukraïny*, 19 December 1991, was also short on specific details.

98 'Pro "Osnovni napriamy zovnishn'oï polityky Ukraïny"', *Holos Ukraïny*, 24 July 1993.

99 'Zaiava Ukraïns'koï konservatyvnoï respublikans'koï partiï z pytannia yadernoho statusu Ukraïny', *Klych*, no. 2 (April), 1993. See also Vasyl' Tarasenko, 'Viis'kova kontseptsiia Ukraïny: natsional'ni interesy ponad use!', *Samostiina Ukraïna*, no. 16 (May), 1993.

100 'Viis'kova doktryna Ukraïns'koï natsional'noï assambleï', *Zamkova hora*, no. 1, 1992.

101 O. M. Honcharenko (ed.), *Natsional'na bezpeka Ukraïny: istoriia i suchasnist'* (Kiev: Institute of World Economy and International Relations, 1993); Serhii Pyrozhkov *et al.*, 'Do pytannia pro rozrobku voiennoï doktryny Ukraïny', *Politolohichni chytannia*, no. 4, 1993, pp. 30–56; Kuzio, *Ukrainian Security Policy*, pp. 64–81, also available as Kuzio, *Natsional'na bezpeka Ukraïny* (Kiev: Viis'ko Ukraïny, nos. 4–5, 1994); Olga Alexandrova, 'Russia as a Factor in Ukrainian Security Concepts', *Aussenpolitik*,

vol. 45, no. 1 (1994), pp. 68–78; Stephen Blank, 'Russia, Ukraine and European Security, 1992–1993', *European Security*, vol. 3, no. 1 (Spring 1994), pp. 182–207.

102 'Posytsiia URP shchodo rozbudovy Zbroinykh Syl Ukraïny', *Samostiina Ukraïna*, no. 25 (June), 1992.

103 Mykhailo Horyn', 'Zvitna dopovid' holovy URP IV z"ïzdovi', *IV z"ïzd URP*, p. 25; 'Zaiava provodu URP', *URP-inform*, 13 January and 14 April 1992; and *Ukraïns'ki obriï*, no. 1, 1993.

104 For the final version see *Holos Ukraïny*, 29 October 1993; *Narodna armiia*, 26 October 1993; and Charles J. Dick, 'The Military Doctrine of Ukraine', *Journal of Slavic Military Studies*, vol. 7, no. 3 (September 1994), pp. 507–20.

105 John F. Mearsheimer, 'The Case for a Ukrainian Nuclear Deterrent', and Steven E. Miller, 'The Case Against a Ukrainian Nuclear Deterrent', *Foreign Affairs*, vol. 72, no. 3 (Summer 1993), pp. 50–80; Taras Kuzio, 'Nuclear Weapons and Military Policy in Independent Ukraine', *Harriman Institute Forum*, vol. 6, no. 9 (May 1993); Sherman Garnett, 'The Sources and Conduct of Ukrainian Nuclear Policy: November 1992 to January 1994', in George Quester (ed.), *The Nuclear Challenge in Russia and the New States of Eurasia* (New York: M. E. Sharpe, 1995), pp. 125–51; and Garnett, *Yadernaia politika Ukrainy: istoki, obraz deistvii, perspektivy* (Moscow: Carnegie Centre, 1994).

106 *Natsionalist*, no. 2, 1991, p. 24; *Neskorena Natsiia*, no. 3 (October), 1991.

107 Bohdan Nahaylo, 'The Shaping of Ukrainian Attitudes Toward Nuclear Arms', *RFE/RL Research Report*, vol. 2, no. 8, 19 February 1993.

108 *Holos Ukraïny*, 26 October 1991.

109 Serhii Plachynda, 'Yak zupynyty rozval derzhavy: peredvyborna prohrama USDP', *Literaturna Ukraïna*, 24 February 1994.

110 'Ukhvala provodu URP', *Samostiina Ukraïna*, no. 2 (January), 1993; *Prohrama DemPU (korotka redaktsiia)*, p. 4. These conditions were confirmed in author's interviews with Yurii Badz'o, 29 April 1992, V"iacheslav Chornovil, 22 March 1993, and Levko Luk"ianenko, 23 October 1994.

111 Ivan Kandyba, 'Prypynyty vyvezennia yadernoï zbroï z Ukraïny', *Neskorena Natsiia*, no. 4 (March), 1992; Volodymyr Shlemko (then head of the DSU), 'Ukraïni – status yadernoï derzhavy', *Holos Ukraïny*, 23 July 1993; *Klych*, no. 2 (May), 1993; *Holos natsiï*, no. 24, 1993; *Zamkova hora*, no. 7, 1993; author's interviews with Roman Koval', Viktor Mel'nyk and Dmytro Korchyns'kyi, 5, 7 and 12 May 1992 respectively.

112 'Zaiava Ukraïns'koï konservatyvnoï respublikans'koï partiï z pytannia yadernoho statusu Ukraïny', *Klych*, no. 2 (April), 1993; 'Vertaiuchys' do yadrovoho statusu Ukraïny', *Holos natsiï*, no. 24 (July), 1993.

113 Borys Oliinyk, 'Svitlo i tini stanovlennia', *Holos Ukraïny*, 3, 5 and 6 February 1993.

114 Valerii Pylypenko, 'Bez'iadernyi status. Chto dumaiut ob etom nashi grazhdane', *Golos Ukrainy*, 6 August 1993. Valerii Khmel'ko, 'Tretii rik nezalezhnosti: shcho vyiavyly druhi prezydents'ki vybory', *Ukraina segodnia*, no. 6, 1994 cites 36 per cent in favour of a nuclear Ukraine in the west and Right Bank, and 25 per cent elsewhere.

115 John W. R. Lepingwell, 'The Trilateral Agreement on Nuclear Weapons', *RFE/RL Research Report*, vol. 3, no. 4, 28 January 1994.
116 *Holos Ukraïny*, 9 December 1994.
117 Michael Mihalka, 'Ukraine: Salvaging Nuclear Arms Control', *Transition*, vol. 1, no. 7, 12 May 1995. Ukraine had provisionally ratified START-1 in November 1993, but with so many conditions that the vote was unacceptable to the West. The conditions were removed the following February.
118 The Massandra summit had revealed the extent of Ukrainian isolation and vulnerability to Russian pressure. US brokerage encouraged Russia to adopt a more concrete form of words on Ukrainian security and the inviolability of Ukrainian borders than it had ever offered in the past, when it had insisted on only recognising Ukrainian borders 'within the USSR' or 'within the CIS'.
119 *Uriadovyi kur"ier*, 22 November 1994.
120 Oliinyk, *Dva roky v Kremli*, pp. 104–5.
121 *Holos Ukraïny*, 21 July 1994. Cf. 'Yevraziiskii soiuz. Kontesptsiia (proekt)', *Grazhdanskii kongress*, no. 1, 1993; Vadym Levandovs'kyi, 'Ukraine in Geopolitical Concepts in the First Third of the Twentieth Century', *Politychna dumka*, no. 3, 1994, pp. 174–84; and Levandovs'kyi, 'Yevraziistvo', *Politolohichni chytannia*, no. 2, 1992, pp. 287–92.
122 Nicholas V. Riasanovsky, *The Emergence of Eurasianism* (Berkeley: University of California Press, 1967); and his article by the same name in *Californian Slavic Studies*, no. 4 (1967), pp. 39–72.
123 Dmitrii Kornilov, 'Federatsiia – de-fakto. A de-yure?', *Donetskii kriazh*, 25 June–1 July 1993.
124 Alexander Solzhenitsyn, *The Russian Question at the End of the Twentieth Century* (London: Harvill Press, 1995), pp. 90–6.
125 The term is used in its proper nineteenth-century sense, implying the belief that Ukraine and Russia are coexistent rather than antagonistic cultures.
126 Dmitrii Vydrin, 'Naidem ly obshchii yazyk? Obiazany!', *Viche*, August and September 1994, pp. 68–79 and 60–73.
127 Borys Oliinyk, 'Svitlo i tini stanovlennia', *Holos Ukraïny*, 3, 5 and 6 February 1993.
128 *Holos Ukraïny*, 9 December 1994.
129 At a roundtable of political parties and organisations organised by President Kravchuk in January 1993 to discuss Ukrainian attitudes to the CIS, all the nationalist groups demanded that Ukraine should immediately 'withdraw from the CIS', centrists and liberals argued that 'Ukraine should use certain advantages from its participation in the CIS', while left-wing groups supported membership unequivocally: *Holos Ukraïny*, 6 January 1993.
130 *Pershyi z"izd ob"iednannia 'Nova Ukraïna'*, p. 24.

8 CONCLUSIONS: NATIONALISM AND NATIONAL CONSOLIDATION

1 Archie Brown (ed.), *Political Culture and Communist Studies* (London: Macmillan, 1984); Smith, 'Formation of Nationalist Movements', pp. 8

and 17; Walker Connor, 'The Nation and Its Myth', in Smith, *Ethnicity and Nationalism*, pp. 48–57.

2 Farmer, *Ukrainian Nationalism in the Post-Stalin Era*.

3 Many leaders of the national movement in the late 1980s and 1990s had such a background. Yurii Shukhevych, first leader of the UNA, was the son of the wartime commander of the UPA, and suffered thirty years of imprisonment and exile (during which he went blind) because of his paternity alone. The father of the Horyn' brothers was a prominent nationalist activist in interwar Poland, arrested by both the Poles and the Soviets.

4 Sysyn, 'Reemergence of the Ukrainian Nation and Cossack Mythology'; Plokhy, 'Historical Debates and Territorial Claims'; Wilson, 'Donbas Between Ukraine and Russia'.

5 Mykola Riabchuk, 'Vid "Malorosiï" do "indoievropu"', at pp. 130–1 and 133.

6 Oksana Khomchuk, 'Na dohovori mizh Ukraïnoiu ta Rosiieiu ye pliamy, yaki ne vyvodiat'sia navit' Rosiis'koiu naftoiu', *Post-postup*, no. 37, 1994.

7 Viktor Mel'nyk, 'Het' usikh, a todi het' tykh, khto zalyshyt'sia', *Natsionalist*, no. 1, 1992; Roman Koval', 'Ukraïns'ki demokraty i demokraty Ukraïny'.

8 See the following commentaries: V. O. Shved, 'Kontseptual'ni pidkhody politychnykh partii ta ob"iednan' do problem etnopolitychnoho rozvytku Ukraïny', in Yevtukh *et al.*, *Etnopolitychna sytuatsiia v Ukraïni*, pp. 36–52; and O. M. Maiboroda, 'Pro pidkhody do rozv"iazannia natsional'noho pytannia v Ukraïni za umov bahatopartiinosti', in Khmil' *et al.*, *Ukraïna XX st*, pp. 146–63.

9 'Post-nationalist' is their own term. Both groups were founded on opposition to ultra-nationalism and support for more decisive economic reform, but include both liberal nationalists and centrists.

10 Horowitz, *Ethnic Groups in Conflict*, p. 68; James G. Kellas, *The Politics of Nationalism and Ethnicity* (London: Macmillan, 1991), pp. 51–71; Rothschild, *Ethnopolitics*.

11 'Bez rozbudovy natsiï ne bude i derzhavy', *Literaturna Ukraïna*, 10 June 1993.

12 Stanislav Kul'chyts'kyi, 'Derzhava – bez svoieï nazvy', *Holos Ukraïny*, 22 July 1993. See also the post-election comment in *Sil's'ki visti*, 14 July 1994; and *Vechirnii Kyïv*, 15 July 1994.

13 V. A. Tishkov, 'O novykh podkhodakh v teorii i praktike mezhnatsional' nykh otnoshenii', *Sovietskaia etnografiia*, no. 5 (September–October), 1989, pp. 3–14; Tishkov, 'Inventions and Manifestations of Ethno-Nationalism'.

14 See Morozov's memoir in *Ukraïns'ka hazeta*, nos. 1–4, 1994.

15 Reuters, AP, 17 March 1995; Andrew Wilson, 'Presidential and Parliamentary Elections in Ukraine: The Issue of Crimea', in Maria Drohobycky, *Crimea: Dynamics, Challenges and Prospects* (Washington, D.C.: American Association for the Advancement of Science/Rowman and Littlefield, 1995), pp. 107–31.

16 Wilson, 'Ukraine: Two Presidents, But No Settled Powers'.

17 It is worth noting that the Czech and Slovak Republics were forced to part company during the economic liberalisation period.

18 See the complaints against regional economic discrimination made by M. Chumachenko (from Donets'k), 'Problemy rehional'noho samovriaduvannia v Ukraïni', *Ekonomika Ukraïny*, no. 6, 1993, pp. 3–13.

19 Oleh Vitovych, interviewed in *Respublika*, no. 5 (August), 1992. Cf. V. Lytvyn, *Politychna arena Ukraïny*, pp. 435–7.

20 'Ideol'ohichna pliatforma Ukraïns'koï natsionalistychnoï spilky', *Ukraïns'ki obrii,* no. 6, 1992.

21 Interview with Valentyn Moroz, *Za vil'nu Ukraïnu*, 26 September 1992.

22 Roger Griffin, 'The Socio-Political Determinants of Fascism's Success', chapter 8 in his *The Nature of Fascism* (London: Routledge, 1991).

Select bibliography

PRIMARY SOURCES

ARCHIVAL

Central State Archive of Civic Organisations of Ukraine (CSACOU), formerly the archive of the Communist Party in Ukraine
Protokoly politychnoï rady Narodnoho Rukhu Ukraïny, Spring 1991
Protokoly prezydiï DemPU, 1990–1

Protokoly URP, 1990–1

LITERATURE

II z"ïzd Ukraïns'koï respublikans'koï partiï, ed. B. Proniuk (Kiev: URP, 1991)
IV Velyki Zbory Narodnoho Rukhu Ukraïny. Stenohrafichnyi zvit (Kiev: Rukh, 1993)
IV z"ïzd Ukraïns'koï respublikans'koï partiï (Kiev: URP, 1993)
Badz'o, Yurii, *Nova pastka* (DPU document dated 16 December 1991)
Vlada – opozystiia – derzhava v Ukraïni s'ohodni. Dumky proty techiï (Kiev: Smoloskyp, 1994)
Chornovil, V"iacheslav, 'Do vykonavchoho komitetu UHS – zaiava', *Moloda Ukraïna*, no. 8, 1990
Komentar do proiektu 'decliaratsiï pryntsypiv' (UHU document dated 21 October 1989)
Druhi vseukraïns'ki zbory Narodnoho Rukhu Ukraïny – dokumenty (Kiev: Rukh, 1991)
Grazhdanskii kongress, nos. 1 and 2, 1993
Horyn', Bohdan, *Stratehiia i taktyka URP* (URP document dated 2 February 1991)
Horyn', Mykhailo, *Zapalyty svichu u pit'mi* (Kiev: URP, 1994)
Hurenko, S. I., A. P. Savchenko and V. G. Matveev (eds.), *Kommunisticheskaia partiia Ukrainy: khronika zapreta* (Donets'k: Interbuk, 1992)
Ideini zasady Demokratychnoï partiï Ukraïny: z materialiv ustanovchoho z"ïzdu (Kiev: Prosvita, 1992)
Ideolohiia i taktyka URP: materiialy teoretychnoï konferentsiï (Kiev: URP, 1991)
Konferentsiia Ukraïns'kykh Natsionalistiv: vybrani materiialy (Kiev: KUN, 1992)
Kontseptsiia derzhavotvorennia v Ukraïni (Kiev: Rukh, 1992)
Kontseptsiia ukraïns'koï armiï (Kiev: Rukh, 1991)

Kravchuk, Leonid, *Ye taka derzhava – Ukraïna* (Kiev: Globus, 1992)
Kravchuk, Leonid and Serhii Kychyhin, *Leonid Kravchuk: ostanni dni imperii*...
   Pershi roky nadii (Kiev: Dovira, 1994)
Luk"ianenko, Levko, *De dobryi shliakh?* (Kiev: URP, 1994)
'Do istorii ukraïns'koho pravozakhysnoho rukhu', *Vyzvolennia '91*, nos.
   1–3 (February–March), 1991
Ne dam zahynut' Ukraïni! (Kiev: Sofiia, 1994)
Shcho dali? (London: Ukrainian Central Information Service, 1989)
Spovid' u kameri smertnykiv (Kiev: Vitchyzna, 1991)
Viruiu v Boha i v Ukraïnu (Kiev: Pam"iatky Ukraïny, 1991)
Masol, Vitalii, *Upushchennyi shans* (Kiev: Molod', 1993)
*Materialy XXVIII z"izdu Komunistychnoï partii Ukraïny, 13–14 hrudnia 1990 roku
   (druhyi etap)* (Kiev: Ukraïna, 1991)
Materialy pro rozvytok mov v ukraïns'kii RSR (Kiev: Prosvita, 1991)
Materiialy tret'oho z"izdu Ukraïns'koï respublikans'koï partii (Kiev: URP, 1992)
Materialy ustanovchoho z"izdu Sotsialistychnoï partii Ukraïny (Kiev: party material,
   October 1991)
Mizhmor"ia biuleten' ligy partii kraïn Balto-Chornomors'ko-Adriiatychnoho regionu,
   no. 1, August 1994
Moroz, Oleksandr, *Kudy idemo?* (Kiev: Postup, 1993)
   Vybir (Kiev: Postup, 1994)
Movchan, Pavlo, *Mova – yavyshche kosmichne* (Kiev: Prosvita, 1994)
Narodni deputaty Ukraïny – predstavnyky Demokratychnoho bloku (Rukh docu-
   ment, spring 1990)
Oliinyk, Borys, *Dva roky v Kremli* (Kiev: Sil's'ki visti, 1992)
Orhanizatsiini pryntsypy parlaments'koï fraktsii 'Narodna rada' (Kiev: Document
   supplied by Rukh secretariat)
Partiia demokraticheskogo vozrozhdeniia Ukrainy – materialy uchreditel'nogo s"ezda
   (Kiev: UkrNIINTI, 1991)
Partiia demokratychnoho vidrodzhennia Ukraïny: III-i z"izd (Kiev: party material,
   May 1992)
*Partiia Komunistov vozrozhdaetsia. Dokumenty i materialy vtorogo etapa Vseuk-
   rainskoi konferentsii kommunistov i s'ezd Kommunisticheskoi partii Ukrainy*
   (Kherson: party material, 1993)
Pershyi z"izd ob"iednannia 'Nova Ukraïna'. Prohramni dokumenty i statut (Kiev:
   conference documents, June 1992)
Pliushch, Ivan, *Khto my i kudy idemo* (Kiev: Ukraïna, 1993)
*Pozacherhova sesiia Verkhovnoï Rady ukraïns'koï RSR dvanadtsiatoho sklykannia:
   biuleten' no. 1* (Kiev: Vydannia Verkhovnoï Rady UkRSR, session of
   24 August 1991)
Pozacherhovyi z"izd Ukraïns'koï respublikans'koï partii (Kiev: URP, 1994)
Programmnye printsipy partii truda i ustav partii (Donets'k: party material, 1993)
'Prohrama Komunistychnoï partii Ukraïny', *Komunist*, no. 12 (March), 1995
Prohramova deklaratsiia druhoho z"izdu DemPU (proekt) (Kiev: Document
   supplied by DPU secretariat, 1992)
Sajewych, George and Andrew Sorokowski (eds.), *The Popular Movement of
   Ukraine for Restructuring – Rukh: Programme and Charter* (Ellicott City, USA:
   Smoloskyp, 1989)

Salii, Ivan, *Ya povertaius'* (Kiev: Dovira, 1993)
Shmorhun, Oleksandr, *Ukraïna: shliakh vidrodzhennia (ekonomika, polityka, kul'tura)* (Kiev: Fundatsiia im. O. Ol'zhycha, 1994)
Statut klub deputativ Rukhu (Kiev: Document supplied by Rukh secretariat, 1991)
Taniuk, Les', *Khto z"ïv moie m"iaso?* (Drohobych: Vidrodzhennia, 1994)
Taniuk, Les' and G. P. Krymchuk (eds.), *Khronika oporu* (Kiev: Dnipro, 1991)
Ukhvaly III Vseukraïns'kykh zboriv Narodnoho Rukhu Ukraïny (Rukh documents, dated 1 March 1992)
Ukhvaly pershoï konferentsiï DemPU: pro zahrozu suverenitetovi i terytorial'nii tsilisnosti Ukraïny (Kiev: Documents supplied by DPU secretariat, April 1992)
Ustanovchyi z"ïzd Ukraïns'koï respublikans'koï partiï (Kiev: RUKHinform, 1990)
Visnyk Prosvity. Spetsial'nyi vypusk, no. 1, 1994. Mova derzhavna – mova ofitsiina (Kiev: Prosvita, 1994)
Zakon URSR pro prezydenta ukraïns'koï RSR (Kiev: Ukraïna, 1991)
Zlenko, Anatolii, 'Vazhlyvyi krok u Yevropu', *Holos Ukraïny*, 17 June 1994
'Yevropeiskii vybor', *Holos Ukraïny*, 12 August 1994

PAPERS AND JOURNALS

The following were used extensively for 1990–5 (party allegiance is indicated in brackets where appropriate).

Demokratychnyi vybir (PDRU)
Demoz
Filosofs'ka i sotsiolohichna dumka
Holos (Republican Club)
Holos natsiï (UNA)
Holos Ukraïny/Golos Ukrainy
Kievskie vedomosti
Klych (UCRP)
Komsomol'skaia pravda
Komunist (CPU)
Kreshchatyk
Kyïvs'kyi visnyk
Literaturna Ukraïna
L'vivs'ki novyny (URP)
Molod' Ukraïny
Moloda Halychyna
Napriam (independent/DSU)
Narodna hazeta (Rukh)
Neskorena Natsiia (DSU/independent)
Nezavisimost'
Politika i vremia / Polityka i chas
Politolohichni chytannia
Politychna dumka / Political Thought
Post-postup (earlier known as *Postup*)
Pravda Ukrainy

Rabochaia gazeta/Robitnycha hazeta
Rivne
Rozbudova derzhavy (URP)
Samostiina Ukraïna (URP)
Shliakh peremohy (KUN)
Sotsial natsionalist (SNPU)
Suchasnist'
Tovarysh (SPU)
Ukraïns'ka hazeta
Ukraïns'ki novyny
Ukraïns'ki obriï (UNA)
Ukraïns'kyi istorychnyi zhurnal
Uriadovyi kur''ier
URP-inform (URP)
Vechirnii Kiev
Viche
Vil'ne slovo (Rukh)
Volia (DPU)
Za vil'nu Ukraïnu
Zakhidnyi kur''ier
Zamkova hora (UNU-UNA)

INTERVIEWS CONDUCTED BY THE AUTHOR

Badz'o, Yurii, leader of the DPU from 1990 to 1992, 29 April 1992
Cherniak, Volodymyr, economist and prominent member of Rukh, 2 August
    1992
Chornovil, V''iacheslav, leader of Rukh, 22 March 1993
Filenko, Volodymyr, co-leader of the PDRU, 10 February 1992
Hryniv, Yevhen, DPU deputy, 10 May 1992
Kandyba, Ivan, leader of DSU from 1990 to 1993, 2 May 1992
Khmel'ko, Valerii, co-leader of first the Democratic Platform and then the
    PDRU, 29 February 1995
Korchyns'kyi, Dmytro, UNA-UNSO leader, 12 May 1992
Kornieiev, Al'bert, leading east Ukrainian deputy, 8 July 1993 (with Dominique
    Arel)
Kornilov, Dmitrii, head of the Democratic Movement of the Donbass, 14 July
    1993 (with Dominique Arel)
Koval', Roman, leader of the DSU after 1993, 5 May 1992
Kutsenko, Hryhorii, secretary of the DPU, 28 April 1992
Luk''ianenko, Levko, leader of the UHU and URP from 1988 to 1992,
    23 October 1994
Marmazov, Yevhenii, member of secretariat of Communist Party of Ukraine,
    9 March 1995
Mel'nyk, Viktor, UNA-UNSO leader, 7 May 1992
Meshkov, Yurii, president of Crimea from January 1994, 30 September 1993
Movchan, Pavlo, head of *Prosvita*, 26 October 1994
Pavlyshyn, Oleh, deputy leader of URP from 1991 to 1993, 27 January 1992

Plachynda, Serhii, leader of UPDP, 11 February 1992
Popovych, Myroslav, Rukh spokesman in 1989, 23 January 1992
Sverstiuk, Yevhen, former dissident and editor of *Nasha vira*, 4 September 1995
Zvarych, Roman, former KUN leader, 21 June 1994 (with Dominique Arel)

SECONDARY SOURCES

ENGLISH-LANGUAGE

Arel, Dominique, *Language and the Politics of Ethnicity: The Case of Ukraine* (Ph.D, University of Illinois at Urbana-Champaign, 1993)
  'The Parliamentary Blocs in the Ukrainian Supreme Soviet: Who and What Do They Represent?', *Journal of Soviet Nationalities*, vol. 1, no. 4 (Winter 1990–1), pp. 108–54
  'Ukraine: The Temptation of the Nationalizing State', in Vladimir Tismaneanu (ed.), *Political Culture and Civil Society in Russia and the New States of Eurasia* (Armonk, N.Y.: M. E. Sharpe, 1995), pp. 157–88
  'Voting Behaviour in the Ukrainian Parliament: The Language Factor', in Remington, *Parliaments in Transition*, pp. 125–58
Arel, Dominique and Andrew Wilson, 'Ukraine Under Kuchma: Back to "Eurasia"?', *RFE/RL Research Report*, vol. 3, no. 32, 19 August 1994
  'The Ukrainian Parliamentary Elections', *RFE/RL Research Report*, vol. 3, no. 26, 1 July 1994
Armstrong, John A., *Ukrainian Nationalism* (Englewood, Colo.: Ukrainian Academic Press, 2nd edn, 1990)
Bilinsky, Yaroslav, *The Second Soviet Republic: The Ukraine After World War II* (New Brunswick, N. J.: Rutgers University Press, 1964)
Bociurkiw, Bohdan, 'Politics and Religion in Ukraine: The Orthodox and the Greek Catholics', in Michael Bordeaux (ed.), *The Politics of Religion in Russia and the New States of Eurasia* (Armonk, N.Y.: M. E. Sharpe, 1995), pp. 131–62
Bojcun, Marco, 'The Ukrainian Parliamentary Elections of March–April 1994', *Europe–Asia Studies*, vol. 47, no. 2 (1995), pp. 229–49
Bremmer, Ian, 'The Politics of Ethnicity: Russians in the New Ukraine', *Europe–Asia Studies*, vol. 46, no. 2 (1994), pp. 261–83
Brown, Archie (ed.), *Political Culture and Communist Studies* (London: Macmillan, 1984)
Brubaker, Rogers, 'Nationhood and the National Question in the Soviet Union and Post-Soviet Eurasia: An Institutionalist Account', *Theory and Society*, vol. 23, no. 1 (1994), pp. 47–78
Farmer, Kenneth, *Ukrainian Nationalism in the Post-Stalin Era: Myths, Symbols and Ideology in Soviet Nationality Policy* (The Hague: Martinus Nijhoff, 1980)
Friedgut, Theodore H., *Iuzovka and Revolution* (Princeton: Princeton University Press, 1989 and 1994), 2 vols.
  'Pluralism and Politics in an Urban Soviet: Donetsk, 1990–1991', in Carl R. Saivetz and Anthony Jones (eds.), *In Search of Pluralism: Soviet and Post-Soviet Politics* (Boulder: Westview, 1994), pp. 45–61

Furtado, Charles J. Jr, 'Nationalism and Foreign Policy in Ukraine', *Political Science Quarterly*, vol. 109, no. 1 (Spring 1994), pp. 81–104

Gow, James, 'Independent Ukraine: The Politics of Security', *International Relations*, vol. 11, no. 3 (December 1992), pp. 253–67

Grabowicz, George G., 'Province to Nation: Nineteenth-Century Ukrainian Literature as a Paradigm of the National Revival', *Canadian Review of Studies in Nationalism*, vol. 16, no. 1–2 (1989), pp. 117–32

Griffin, Roger, *The Nature of Fascism* (London: Routledge, 1991)

Guthier, Steven L., 'The Popular Basis of Ukrainian Nationalism in 1917', *Slavic Review*, vol. 38, no. 1 (March 1979), pp. 30–47

Hamm, Michael F., *Kiev: A Portrait, 1800–1917* (Princeton: Princeton University Press, 1993)

Herlihy, Patricia, *Odessa: A History, 1794–1914* (Cambridge, Mass.: Harvard University Press, 1986)

Horowitz, Donald L., *Ethnic Groups in Conflict* (Berkeley: University of California Press, 1985)

Hosking, Geoffrey A. (ed.), *Church, Nation and State in Russia and Ukraine* (London: Macmillan, 1991)

Hroch, Miroslav, *Social Preconditions of a National Revival in Europe* (Cambridge: Cambridge University Press, 1985)

Hunchak (Hunczak), Taras (ed.), *The Ukraine, 1917–1921: A Study in Revolution* (Cambridge, Mass.: Harvard Ukrainian Research Institute, 1977)

Hutchinson, John, *The Dynamics of Cultural Nationalism* (London: Allen and Unwin, 1987)

International Foundation for Election Systems, *Ukraine's New Parliament* (Kiev: April 1994)

Kaiser, Robert J., *The Geography of Nationalism in Russia and the USSR* (Princeton: Princeton University Press, 1994)

Kappeler, Andreas, *Kleine Geschichte der Ukraine* (Munich: C. H. Beck, 1994)

Kellas, James G., *The Politics of Nationalism and Ethnicity* (London: Macmillan, 1991)

Khmel'ko, Valerii, with assistance from Andrew Wilson, 'The Political Orientations of Different Regions and Ethno-Linguistic Groups in Ukraine Since Independence' (forthcoming)

Krawchenko, Bohdan, 'Changes in the National and Social Composition of the Communist Party of Ukraine from the Revolution to 1976', *Journal of Ukrainian Studies*, vol. 9, no. 1 (Summer 1984), pp. 33–54

Social Change and National Consciousness in Twentieth-Century Ukraine (Oxford: St Antony's/Macmillan, 1985)

Krawchenko, Bohdan (ed.), *Ukraine After Shelest* (Edmonton, Ont.: CIUS, 1983)

Ukrainian Past, Ukrainian Present (London: Macmillan, 1993)

Kubijovyc, Volodymyr and Danylo Husar Struk (eds.), *Encyclopaedia of Ukraine* (Toronto: University of Toronto Press, 1984–93)

Kuzio, Taras (ed.), *Dissent in Ukraine Under Gorbachev: A Collection of Samizdat Documents* (London: Ukrainian Press Agency, 1989)

Kuzio, Taras and Andrew Wilson, *Ukraine: Perestroika to Independence* (London: Macmillan, 1994)

Lewytzkyj, Borys, *Politics and Society in Soviet Ukraine, 1953–1980* (Edmonton, Ont.: CIUS, 1984)

Liber, George O., *Soviet Nationality Policy, Urban Growth and Identity Change in the Ukrainian SSR, 1923–1934* (Cambridge: Cambridge University Press, 1992)

Mace, James E., *Communism and the Dilemmas of National Liberation: National Communism in Soviet Ukraine, 1918–1933* (Cambridge, Mass.: Harvard University Press, 1983)

Magocsi, Paul Robert, *The Shaping of a National Identity: Subcarpathian Rus', 1848–1948* (London: Harvard University Press, 1978)

Ukraine: A Historical Atlas (Toronto: University of Toronto Press, 1985)

'The Ukrainian National Revival: A New Analytical Framework', *Canadian Review of Studies in Nationalism*, vol. 16, nos. 1–2 (1989), pp. 45–62

Markus, Ustina, *Soviet Counterinsurgency: The Guerrilla Wars in the Western Republics* (Ph.D, London School of Economics and Political Science, University of London, 1992)

Marples, David R., *Stalinism in Ukraine in the 1940s* (London: Macmillan, 1992)

Morrison, John, 'Pereyaslav and After: The Russian–Ukrainian Relationship', *International Affairs*, vol. 69, no. 4 (1993), pp. 677–703

Motyl, Alexander J., 'The Conceptual President: Leonid Kravchuk and the Politics of Surrealism', in Timothy J. Colton and Robert C. Tucker (eds.), *Patterns in Post-Soviet Leadership* (Boulder: Westview, 1995), pp. 103–21

Dilemmas of Independence: Ukraine After Totalitarianism (New York: Council of Foreign Relations Press, 1993)

Sovietology, Rationality, Nationality: Coming to Grips with Nationalism in the USSR (New York: Columbia University Press, 1990)

The Turn to the Right: The Ideological Origins and Development of Ukrainian Nationalism, 1919–1929 (Boulder: East European Monographs, 1980)

Will the Non-Russians Rebel? State, Ethnicity and Stability in the USSR (Ithaca: Cornell University Press, 1987)

Motyl, Alexander J. (ed.), *Thinking Theoretically About Soviet Nationalities: History and Comparison in the Study of the USSR* (New York: Columbia University Press, 1992)

Pelenski, Jaroslaw, 'Shelest and His Period in Soviet Ukraine (1963–1972): A Revival of Controlled Ukrainian Autonomism', in Potichnyj, *Ukraine in the 1970s*, pp. 283–305

Plokhy, Serhii M., 'Historical Debates and Territorial Claims: Cossack Mythology in the Russian–Ukrainian Border Dispute', in S. Frederick Starr (ed.), *The Legacy of History in Russia and the New States of Eurasia* (London: M. E. Sharpe, 1994), pp. 147–70

Potichnyj, Peter J., 'Elections in Ukraine, 1990', in Zvi Gitelman (ed.), *The Politics of Nationality and the Erosion of the USSR* (London: Macmillan, 1992), pp. 176–214

Potichnyj, Peter J. (ed.), *Ukraine in the 1970s* (Oakville, Ont.: Mosaic Press, 1975)

Potichnyj, Peter J. and Howard Aster (eds.), *Ukrainian–Jewish Relations in Historical Perspective* (Edmonton, Ont.: CIUS, 1988)

Prizel, Ilya, 'The Influence of Ethnicity on Foreign Policy: The Case of Ukraine', in Roman Szporluk (ed.), *National Identity and Ethnicity in Russia and the New States of Eurasia* (London: M. E. Sharpe, 1994), pp. 103–28

Radziejowski, Janusz, *The Communist Party of Western Ukraine* (Edmonton, Ont.: CIUS, 1983)

Remington, Thomas F. (ed.), *Parliaments in Transition: The New Legislative Politics in the Former USSR and Eastern Europe* (Boulder: Westview, 1994)

Riabchuk, Mykola, 'Democracy and the So-Called "Party of Power" in Ukraine', *Politychna dumka*, no. 3, 1994, pp. 154–9

Riasanovsky, Nicholas V., *The Emergence of Eurasianism* (Berkeley: University of California Press, 1967)

Roeder, Philip G., 'Soviet Federalism and Ethnic Mobilisation', *World Politics*, vol. 43, 1991, pp. 196–232

Rothschild, Joseph, *Ethnopolitics: A Conceptual Framework* (New York: Columbia University Press, 1981)

Rudnytsky, Ivan Lysiak-, *Essays in Modern Ukrainian History* (Edmonton, Ont.: CIUS, 1987)

Rudnytsky, Ivan Lysiak- (ed.) *Rethinking Ukrainian History* (Edmonton, Ont.: CIUS, 1981)

Shkandrij, Myroslav, *Modernists, Marxists and the Nation: The Ukrainian Literary Discussion of the 1920s* (Edmonton, Ont.: CIUS, 1992)

Smith, Anthony D., *The Ethnic Revival* (Cambridge: Cambridge University Press, 1981)

National Identity (London: Penguin, 1991)

Theories of Nationalism (London: Holmes and Meier, 1983)

Smith, Anthony D. (ed.), *Nationalist Movements* (London: Macmillan, 1976)

Solchanyk, Roman, 'Centrifugal Movements in Ukraine and Independence', *Ukrainian Weekly*, 24 November 1991

'Language Politics in the Ukraine', in Isabelle T. Kreindler (ed.), *Sociolinguistic Perspectives on Soviet National Languages* (Berlin: Mouton de Gruyter, 1985), pp. 57–105

'The Politics of State-Building: Centre–Periphery Relations in Post-Soviet Ukraine', *Europe–Asia Studies*, vol. 46, no. 1 (1994), pp. 47–68

'Russia, Ukraine and the Imperial Legacy', *Post-Soviet Affairs*, vol. 9, no. 4 (1993), pp. 337–65

Solchanyk, Roman (ed.), *Ukraine: Chernobyl' to Sovereignty* (London: Macmillan, 1992)

Subtelny, Orest, *Ukraine: A History* (Toronto: University of Toronto Press, 1988, 2nd edn 1994)

Sysyn, Frank E., 'The Reemergence of the Ukrainian Nation and Cossack Mythology', *Social Research*, vol. 58, no. 4 (Winter 1991), pp. 845–64

Szporluk, Roman, 'The National Question', in Timothy J. Colton and Robert Levgold (eds.), *After the Soviet Union: From Empire to Nations* (New York: W. W. Norton, 1992), pp. 84–112

'Reflections on Ukraine After 1994: The Dilemmas of Nationhood', *Harriman Review*, vol. 7, nos. 7–9 (March–May 1994)

'The Strange Politics of Lviv: An Essay in Search of an Explanation', in Zvi Gitelman (ed.), *The Politics of Nationality and the Erosion of the USSR* (London: Macmillan, 1992), pp. 215–31

Tishkov, Valerii, 'Inventions and Manifestations of Ethno-Nationalism in and After the Soviet Union', in Kumar Rupesinghe *et al.* (eds.), *Ethnicity and*

286   Select bibliography

Conflict in a Post-Communist World: The Soviet Union, Eastern Europe and China (London: Macmillan, 1992), pp. 41–65

Torke, Hans-Joachim and John-Paul Himka (eds.), *German–Ukrainian Relations in Historical Perspective* (Edmonton, Ont.: CIUS, 1994)

Wilson, Andrew, *The Crimean Tatars* (London: International Alert, 1994)

'Crimea's Political Cauldron', *RFE/RL Research Report*, vol. 2, no. 45, 12 November 1993

'The Donbas Between Ukraine and Russia: The Use of History in Political Disputes', *Journal of Contemporary History*, vol. 30, no. 2 (April 1995), pp. 265–89

'The Elections in Crimea', *RFE/RL Research Report*, vol. 3, no. 25, 24 June 1994

'The Growing Challenge to Kiev from the Donbas', *RFE/RL Research Report*, vol. 2, no. 33, 20 August 1993

'Ukraine', in Bogdan Skajkowski (ed.), *Political Parties of Eastern Europe, Russia and the Successor States* (London: Longman, 1994), pp. 577–604

'Ukraine: Two Presidents, But No Settled Powers', in Ray Taras (ed.), *Presidential Systems in Post-Communist States: A Comparative Analysis* (forthcoming)

'Ukrainian Nationalism: A Minority Faith', *Slavonic and East European Review*, vol. 73, no. 2 (April 1995), pp. 282–8

Wilson, Andrew and Artur Bilous, 'Political Parties in Ukraine', *Europe–Asia Studies*, vol. 45, no. 4 (1993), pp. 693–703

Wilson, Andrew and Ihor Burakovs'kyi, *Economic Reform in Ukraine* (London: Royal Institute of International Affairs, 1996)

UKRAINIAN- AND RUSSIAN-LANGUAGE

Badz'o, Yurii and Ivan Yushchyk (eds.), *Naibil'shyi zlochyn imperii: Materialy naukovo-praktychnoi konferentsii 'Slobozhanshchyna. Holodomor 1932–1933 rokiv'* (Kiev: Prosvita, 1993)

Bahan, Oleh, *Natsionalizm i natsionalistychnyi rukh: istoriia ta idei* (Drohobych: Vidrodzhennia, 1994)

Baran, V. K., *Ukraïna pislia Stalina: narys istorii 1953–1985 rr.* (L'viv: Svoboda, 1992)

Bekeshkina, Iryna, 'Sotsial'no-ekonomichni oriientatsiï naselennia Skhodu i Pivdnia Ukraïny', *Demoz*, no. 3, 1994

Bilokin', Serhii *et al.*, *Khto ye khto v ukraïns'kii polytytsi* (Kiev: Tov. Petra Mohyly, 1993)

Bilous, Artur, *Politychni ob"iednannia Ukraïny* (Kiev: Ukraïna, 1993)

Boltarovych, Yevhen, 'L'vivshchyna: politychni syly i politychnyi spektr', *Respublikanets'*, no. 2, 1991

Chemerys, Valentyn, *Prezydent: Roman-ese* (Kiev: Svenas, 1994)

Chepurko, B. P., *Ukraïntsi: voskresinnia* (L'viv: Slovo, 1991)

Chumak, Vasyl', *Ukraïna i Krym: spil'nist' istorychnoi doli* (Kiev: Biblioteka Ukraïntsia, no. 2–3, 1993)

Dashkévych, Yaroslav, *Ukraïna: vchora i nyni* (Kiev: Academy of Sciences, 1993)

Ermolova, Valentyna, '"Russkii vopros" v Ukraine', *Vseukrainskie vedomosti*, 6 December 1994

Haran', Oleksa, *Ubyty drakona. Z istorii Rukhu ta novykh partii Ukrainy* (Kiev: Lybid', 1993)

Ukraina bahatopartiina (Kiev: Pam"iatky Ukraïny, 1991)

Vid stvorennia Rukhu do bahatopartiinosti (Kiev: Znannia, 1992)

Holubenko, Petro, *Ukraïna i Rosiia u svitli kul'turnykh vzaiemyn* (Kiev: Dnipro, 1993; first published in Toronto in 1987)

Hrechenko, V. A., 'Do istorii vnutripartiinoï borot'by v Ukraïni u 20-ti roky', *Ukraïns'kyi istorychnyi zhurnal*, no. 9, 1993, pp. 114–21

Hunchak, Taras, *Ukraïna persha polovyna XX stolittia* (Kiev: Lybid', 1993)

Hunchak (Hunczak), Taras and Roman Solchanyk (Sol'chanyk) (eds.), *Ukraïns'ka suspil'no-politychna dumka v 20 stolitti: dokumenty i materialy* (Munich: Suchasnist', 1983), 3 vols.

Ivanychuk, Roman, Teofil' Komarynets', Ihor Mel'nyk and Alla Serediak (eds.), *Narys istorii Prosvity* (L'viv: Prosvita, 1993)

Kamins'kyi, Anatol', *Na perekhidnomu etapi: 'hlasnist'', 'perebudova' i 'demokraty-zatsiia' na Ukraïni* (Munich: Ukrainian Free University, 1990)

Kas'ianov, Heorhii, *Nezhodni: ukraïns'ka inteligentsiia v rusi oporu 1960–80-kh rokiv* (Kiev: Lybid', 1995)

Ukraïns'ka inteligentsiia 1920-kh–1930-kh rokiv: sotsial'nyi portret ta istorychna dolia (Kiev: Globus, 1992)

Ukraïns'ka inteligentsiia na rubezhi XIX–XX stolit' (Kiev: Lybid', 1993)

Khmel'ko, Valerii, 'Koho oberemo prezydentom? Za dva tyzhni do vyboriv prodovzhuvav lidyruvaty Kravchuk' (unpublished paper supplied by Dr Khmel'ko, dated May–June 1994)

'Politychni oriientatsii vybortsiv ta rezul'taty vyboriv do Verkhovnoï Rady' (unpublished paper supplied by Dr Khmel'ko, dated May–June 1994)

'Referendum: khto buv "za" i khto "proty"', *Politolohichni chytannia*, no. 1, 1992, pp. 40–52

Khmil', I. S. with V. S. Horak, O. M. Maiboroda and V. M. Tkachenko (eds.), *Ukraïna XX st. Problemy natsional'noho vidrodzhennia* (Kiev: Naukova dumka, 1993)

Khvyl'ovyi, Mykola, *Tvory u dvokh tomakh* (Kiev: Dnipro, 1990), 2 vols.

Kornilov, Dmitrii, 'Tak kto zhe bol'she liubit Ukrainu?', *Donetskii kriazh*, no. 3, 21–7 January 1994

Koval', Roman, *Chy mozhlyve Ukraïno-Rosiis'ke zamyrennia?* (Stryi: Myron Tarnavs'kyi, 1991)

Pidstavy natsiokratii (Kiev: DSU, 1994)

Pro vorohiv, soiuznykiv i poputnykiv (Kiev: DSU, 1993)

Z kym i proty koho (Kiev: DSU, 1992)

Kurnosov, Yu. O., *Inakomyslennia v Ukraïni (60-ti–persha polovyna 80-kh rr. XX st.)* (Kiev: Institute of History, 1994)

Kychyhina, Natalia, 'Politychna kontseptsiia V. K. Vynnychenka', *Politolohichni chytannia*, no. 2, 1994, pp. 83–95

Kyrychuk, Yurii, 'Narys istorii UHS-URP', *Respublikanets'*, nos. 2 and 3, 1991–2

Lavriv, Petro, *Istoriia pivdenno-skhidnoï Ukraïny* (L'viv: Slovo, 1992)

Lytvyn, Volodymyr, *Politychna arena Ukraïny: diiovi osoby ta vykonavtsi* (Kiev: Abrys, 1994)

Lytvyn, Volodymyr and A. H. Sliusarenko, 'Na politychnii areni Ukraïny (90-ti rr.). Rozdumy istorykiv', *Ukraïns'kyi istorychnyi zhurnal*, nos. 1 and 2–3, 1994, pp. 9–30 and 28–51

Maistrenko, Ivan, *Istoriia Komunistychnoï partiï Ukraïny* (Munich: Suchasnist', 1979)

Musiienko, Oleksa, *Ukraïns'kyi etnotsyd* (Kiev: Biblioteka Ukraïntsia/Rada, 1994)

Myshanych, Oleksa, *Politychne rusynstvo i shcho za nym* (Uzhhorod: Hrazhda, 1993)

'Ukraïns'ka literatura pid zaboronoiu: 1937–1990', *Literaturna Ukraïna*, 18 August 1994

Naulko, V. I. *et al.* (eds.), *Kul'tura i pobut naselennia Ukraïny* (Kiev: Lybid', 1991)

Ostash, Ihor (ed.), *Quo vadis, Ukraïno?* (Kiev: Maiak, 1992)

Panchenko, Volodymyr, *Sobornyi herb Ukraïny* (Kiev: Biblioteka Ukraïntsia, no. 3–1, 1993)

Pavlychko, Dmytro, 'Chomu ya holosuvav za Leonida Kravchuka', *Literaturna Ukraïna*, 30 June 1994

Popovych, V. V., 'Referendum SRSR i politychni oriientatsiï naselennia Ukraïny', *Filosofs'ka i sotsiolohichna dumka*, no. 9, 1991

Potul'nytskyi, V. A., *Teoriia ukraïns'koï politolohiï: Kurs lektsii* (Kiev: Lybid', 1993)

Pryliuk, Yu. D. (ed.), *Konstytutsiini akty Ukraïny. 1917–1920. Nevidomi konstytutsiï Ukraïny* (Kiev: Filosofs'ka i sotsiolohichna dumka, 1992)

Redchenko, Oleksii, 'Hotuimo sany vlitku', *Narodna hazeta*, no. 12 (April), 1992

Riabchuk, Mykola, 'Vid "Malorosii" do "indoievropy": stereotyp "narodu" v ukraïns'kii suspil'nii svidomosti ta hromads'kii dumtsi', *Politolohichni chytannia*, no. 2, 1994, pp. 120–44

Rudnyts'kyi, Ivan Lysiak-, *Istorychni ese* (Kiev: Osnovy, 1994), 2 vols.

Rusnachenko, Anatolii, *Na shliakhu do natsional'noï armii (1989–1991)* (Kiev: 1992)

Savel'iev, V. L., 'Chy buv P. Yu. Shelest vyraznykom "ukraïns'koho avtonomizmu"?', *Ukraïns'kyi istorychnyi zhurnal*, no. 4, 1991, pp. 94–105

Semkiv, O. I. *et al.* (eds.), *Politolohiia* (L'viv: Svit, 2nd edn, 1994)

Serhiichuk, Volodymyr, *Natsional'na symvolika Ukraïny* (Kiev: Veselka, 1992)

Symvolika suverennosti – syn'o-zhovta (Kiev: Biblioteka Ukraïntsia, no. 3-2, 1993)

Ukraïntsi v imperiï (Kiev: Biblioteka Ukraïntsia, no. 3, 1992)

Serhiienko, Petro, *Sobornist' Ukraïny: poniattia, ideia i real'nist'* (Kiev: Biblioteka Ukraïntsia, 1993)

Shapoval, Yurii, *Ukraïna 20–50-kh rokiv: storinky nenapysanoï istoriï* (Kiev: Naukova dumka, 1993)

Slin'ko, A. A. (ed.), *Novye stranitsy v istorii Donbassa* (Donets'k: Donets'k University Press, 1992)

Soldatenko, V. F. (ed.), *Ukraïns'ka ideia. Pershi rechnyky* (Kiev: Znannia, 1994)

Sosnovs'kyi, M., *Dmytro Dontsov: politychnyi portret* (New York: Trident International, 1974)

Sossa, Rostyslav, *Ukraïntsi: skhidna diaspora* (Kiev: Mapa, 1993)

Suchasni politychni partiï ta rukhy na Ukraïni, eds. I. F. Kuras, F. M. Rudych, O. P. Smoliannykov and O. A. Spirin (Kiev: Institut politychnykh doslidzhen', 1991)

Tarasenko, M. F. *et al.*, *Istoriia filosofiï Ukraïny* (Kiev: Lybid', 1993)

Trubenko, V. S. and V. I. Horbyk (eds.), *Istorychno-heohrafichni doslidzhennia v Ukraïni* (Kiev: Naukova dumka, 1994)

Vasyl'chenko, S. O., V. K. Vasylenko, P. L. Varhatiuk and L. M. Hordiienko, *Storinky istorii' Kompartii' Ukraïny: zapytannia i vidpovidi* (Kiev: Lybid', 1990)

Volobuiev, Mykhailo, *Do problemy ukraïns'koï ekonomiky: dokumenty ukraïns'koho komunizmu* (New York: Prolog, 1962)

Vovk, Viktor and Oleksii Mustafin, 'Bogataia mnogoobraziem, sil'naia edinstvom', *Kyïvs'kyi sotsial-demokrat*, no. 1 (October), 1991

Vrublevskii, Vitalii, *Vladimir Shcherbitskii: pravda i vymysly* (Kiev: Dovira, 1993)

Vydrin, Dmytro, 'Rosiiany v Ukraïni: pid chas referendumu, do i pisliia', *Politolohichni chytannia*, no. 1, 1992, pp. 237–49

Yevselevs'kyi, L. I., and S. Ya. Faryna, *Prosvita v Naddniprians'kii Ukraïni* (Kiev: Prosvita, 1993)

Yevtukh, Volodymyr *et al.* (eds.), *Etnopolitychna sytuatsiia v Ukraïni* (Kiev: Intel, 1993)

Zaitsev, Oleksandr, 'Predstavnyky ukraïns'kykh politychnykh partii zakhidnoï Ukraïny v parlamenti Pol'shchi (1922–1939 rr.)', *Ukraïns'kyi istorychnyi zhurnal*, no. 1, 1993, pp. 72–84

Zalizniak, Leonid, *Narysy starodavnoï istorii' Ukraïny* (Kiev: Abrys, 1994)

'Ukraïna i "osoblyvyi shliakh Rosii"', *Huta*, no. 1 (October), 1991

'Ukraïna i Rosiia: rizni historychni doli', *Starozhytnosti*, no. 19, 1991

Zastavnyi, F. D., *Heohrafiia Ukraïny* (L'viv: Svit, 1994)

Skhidna ukraïns'ka diaspora (L'viv: Svit, 1992)

Ukraïns'ki etnichni zemli (L'viv: Svit, 1993)

Zheleznyi, Anatolii, 'Ukraina: kak vozniklo dvuiazychnie', *Donetskii kriazh*, 18–24 June 1993

Zhmyr, V. F., D. B. Yanevs'kyi, D. Tabachnyk and V. Rybchuk, 'Problema bahatopartiinosti', *Filosofs'ka i sotsiolohichna dumka*, nos. 9 and 10, 1990, pp. 3–17 and 17–36

Index

6815